Barron's Regents Exams and Answers

Global History and Geography

MICHAEL J. ROMANO, Ph.D.
Former District Chairperson, Northport School District, Northport, New York

WILLIAM STREITWIESER, B.A., M.A.
Former Social Studies Teacher, Northport High School, Northport, New York

Glossary by
MARY MARTIN
Social Studies Teacher, Greene Central School, Greene, New York

BARRON'S

Barron's Educational Series, Inc.

All inquiries should be addressed to:
Barron's Educational Series, Inc.
250 Wireless Boulevard
Hauppauge, New York 11788
www.barronseduc.com

ISBN-13: 978-0-8120-4344-0
ISBN-10: 0-8120-4344-8
ISSN 1069-2932

PRINTED IN THE UNITED STATES OF AMERICA
9 8 7 6 5 4 3 2 1

Contents

Introduction

THE TWO-YEAR GLOBAL HISTORY AND GEOGRAPHY COURSE

After the two-year Global History and Geography course in New York State, there is a Regents examination. All 10th-grade students are required to take the Regents examination if they want to receive a Regents diploma. The focus of social studies is to help students understand how history, geography, economics, government, and civics have influenced the past, present, and future. The Global History and Geography courses that are given in the 9th and 10th grades are part of a required K-12 social studies program in New York. On the elementary and middle school level, students learn about their community, state, and nation. Global History is built on the premise that we live in an interdependent world and that no nation can isolate itself from the world. What happenes in other nations impacts our lives and the way we live. Thus, to have a better understanding of our country's history and growth, it is important to understand the events that are occurring in the world today. In September 1998 the Global History and Geography course replaced the Global Studies course. The old Global Studies approach divided the world into eight regions, such as Africa and the Middle East. Students studied the particular areas from ancient times to the present. After seven or eights weeks, students moved on to a different area of the world. *The new Global History approach is chronological and highlights major themes and concepts by studying what is happening in different world regions during the same time period.*

The two-year Global History course is divided as follows:

Unit 1: Ancient World (400 B.C. to 500 A.D.)—A study of the Ancient Civilizations of Asia, Africa, and Europe
Unit 2: Expanding Zones of Exchange and Encounter (500 to 1200)—A study of how different regions of the world encountered and exchanged ideas with each other from the Gupta Empire to the Crusades
Unit 3: Global Interaction (1200 to 1650)—A study of how the interaction of Japanese, Mongol, and African Civilizations and the spirit of the Renaissance led to the exchange of ideas, trade, and changes in society
Unit 4: The First Global Age (1450 to 1750)—A study of how the encounter among the Ming, Ottoman, Spanish, Portuguese, and Mesoamerican empires led to changes in the world
Unit 5: Age of Revolution (1750 to 1914)—A study of how the Scientific Revolution, the Enlightenment, political revolution, nationalism, industrialism, and imperialism influenced the world
Unit 6: A Half Century of Crisis and Achievement—A study of how World War I, the Russian Revolution, rise of dictatorship in Europe, the rise of nationalism in Asia and the Middle East, and World War II affected the world
Unit 7: The 20th Century Since 1845—A study of the political, economic, and social changes that influenced Europe, Asia, Latin America, the United States, and the Middle East
Unit 8: Global Connections and Interactions—A study of how overpopulation, urbanization, globalization, ethnic rivalry, and other economic and political issues are influencing the world

The underlying theme of Global History and Geography is the importance of geography in studying a society as well as the fact that the world has been coming closer together since the 13th century. The Global History and Geography Regents examination is also designed to reflect the five social studies standards that are: U.S. History, World History, Geography, Economics, Civics, Citizenship, and Government.

WHAT IS THE FORMAT OF THE GLOBAL HISTORY AND GEOGRAPHY REGENTS?

The Global History and Geography Regents is a three-hour test that contains questions on topics, concepts, skills and themes from each historical era that is covered in the two-year Global History and Geography course. Be sure to review information from units in Grades 9 and 10.

Each examination will include:

Part I:	**Multiple-Choice Questions:**	**50 items**	**55% of the test**
Part II:	**Thematic Essay**	**1**	**15% of the test**
Part III:	**Document-Based Question**	**1**	**15% scaffolding**
			15% analytical essay
			100% of the test

Unlike the former Global Studies Regents, there will be no choices for the essay question. The Thematic Essay, the Scaffolding question of the Document-Based Question and the Analytical Document-Based Essay will be scored holistically, using a specific standard that is outlined in the scoring rubric. The passing score will be based on the student's average on the entire test.

How to Use This Book to Study

This book contains various features that will enable you to get the most out of your review and help you score well on the Regents. The book is divided into the following sections: **Test-Taking Tips; Glossary of Important Terms, International Organizations and Agreements, and Important People; and Previous Regents Examinations, Answers, and Self-Analysis Charts.** Read each of these sections carefully and you will be on the road to success.

TEST-TAKING TIPS

These hints, suggestions, and practice questions will help you become a better test taker and enable you to develop the skills that will lead to success on the Regents. The sample Multiple-Choice Questions, the Thematic Essay, and the Document-Based Question will provide you with specific strategies on how to answer these questions. Review this section after you have taken two or three practice Regents. This step will help you realize how these hints have improved your score.

GLOSSARY

The Glossary contains important terms, people, and international agreements and organizations that are part of the Global History and Geography course of study. The Glossary should be used as a study guide to help you focus on the key turning points, terms, and people in Global History.

PREVIOUS REGENTS EXAMINATIONS AND ANSWERS

This third section contains previous Global Studies and History Regents with an analysis of the right and wrong answers. These Regents are an excellent study guide because they focus on the key content areas of the course. Answer the multiple-choice questions first. This step will provide you with an overview of your strengths and weaknesses. Review the answers because they will provide you with additional information about a particular question.

Carefully read the model answers for the Thematic Essay and the DBQ. This step will help you understand how the scoring rubric is used to determine the essay score on a scale of 1–5.

SELF-ANALYSIS CHART

The self-analysis chart following the Answers Explained for each Regents has been designed to help you note the number of questions and the frequency of the questions in each of the five social studies standards. You should use the chart to analyze your strengths and deficiencies in each of the historical periods.

STEPS FOR SUCCESS

1. Read your notes, review packets, and material on the topics in the course.
2. Read the Test-Taking Tips.
3. Check the Glossary to make sure that you are familiar with the information that it contains.
4. Look over past examinations to become familiar with the format and types of tests.
5. Take the most recent Regents examination and try to complete it within the specified time period.
6. Check all your answers in Part I and carefully read all explanations for the correct and incorrect answers as well as questions you were unable to answer.
7. Complete the Self-Analysis Chart; this will help you focus on the areas in which you need more review.

8. Read your essay answer for each question and compare your response with the one given in the book; check the rubric to determine how you have scored on this part of the examination.
9. Recheck your notes, review Test-Taking Tips, and continue to take more practice regents
10. Always think positive—you will succeed!

Test-Taking Tips

HELPFUL HINTS FOR ALL TESTS

TIP 1

Be prepared and have an optimistic approach.

- Organize/review your notes.
- Don't cram; develop good study habits throughout the year.
- Complete all your written and reading assignments on time.
- Be familiar with the format of the test.
- Review past examinations under test conditions (no headphones, CD players, etc.).
- Visit *www.barronseduc.com* for the latest information on the Regents.
- Come prepared for the test; bring pens and pencils.
- Focus on the test.
- Relax and be positive.

TIP 2

Carefully read the directions and questions.

- Be familiar with the test directions before you take the exam.
- Know how much time is allocated for each part of the exam.
- Become familiar with the grading of the test and which questions are worth more points.
- Circle or highlight important terms or phrases.
- Know how many questions you must answer from each part of the test.
- Ask for assistance from the proctor when the directions are unclear.

TIP 3

Budget your time.

- Make a note of when the test began and when it will end.
- Wear a watch or make sure that the clock in the room is working so that you can keep track of the time.
- Quickly look over the entire examination first before you begin to answer any questions.
- Outline a time frame. It makes sense to spend more time on the parts that are worth more points; a good guide would be to spend one hour on the short answers and two hours on the Thematic and DBQ essays.
- Answer the easy questions first. Don't get stuck on one question. Move on to the next questions; you might find a clue or hint in other sections of the test.
- Don't leave early if you finish before the three-hour limit. Recheck your answers; you may want to add information or you may have omitted something asked for in the question.

TIP 4

Don't give up on your reasoning abilities.

- Don't leave out any questions.
- Restate the question in your own words so that you understand it.
- Try to connect the question with some ideas or topic that you have covered in class or on your test.
- Check the whole test to determine if you can use any information from one part to help you answer a question on another part.
- Make a list of the Global History Connections: cultural diffusion, migration, regional empire, belief systems, trade/conflict. See if any of these topics can help you answer a question.

TIP 5
When in doubt, guess.

- Answer all questions. Remember that an unanswered question receives no credit; there is no penalty for guessing.
- Go with your first choice.
- Eliminate the least obvious choices; try to use a 50–50 lifeline, then make an educated guess.

Let's review the **Helpful Hints** for all tests:

1. Be confident and optimistic.
2. Carefully read the directions and questions.
3. Budget your time.
4. Don't give up on your reasoning abilities.
5. When in doubt—guess.

SPECIFIC HELPFUL HINTS FOR ANSWERING MULTIPLE-CHOICE QUESTIONS

The Global History and Geography Regents has many kinds of multiple-choice questions. They require knowledge of some basic facts and analysis or application of the facts.

TIP 1

Read the questions carefully and underline the key words.

WHY WILL THIS TIP HELP YOU?

- It helps you avoid making careless mistakes.
- It focuses on the key ideas.
- It directs your answer to what is being tested.

WHEN SHOULD YOU UTILIZE THIS TIP?

- When taking any multiple-choice test.

The example below shows the importance of key words. The key words provide the specific meaning of the question and point you to the correct response.

EXAMPLE

The Silk Road was important to China because it provided
1 contact with other cultures through trade
2 a means of administering civil service examinations
3 a military route for the defense of the northern border
4 a means for the country to expand its borders

(taken from a Test Sampler Draft)

By underlining *Silk Road* and *China*, you are focusing on the key points of the question. You are being asked to show the connection between the Silk Road and its importance to China. The correct answer is Choice 1. It contains the only statement that has a direct connection with Silk Road and trade route. The other choices deal with topics concerning military or political issues.

PRACTICE

Underline the key words in the following question:

Which term is used to describe the spread of Buddhism from India through Southeast Asia?

1 ethnocentrism
2 isolationism
3 imperialism
4 cultural diffusion

(from an actual Regents exam)

You should have underlined *spread*, *Buddhism*, *India*, and *Southeast Asia* because they are the important terms in the question. The correct choice is 4 because cultural diffusion is a term used to describe the spread of ideas to different societies. The other terms are not related to religion.

TIP 2

Answer the easy questions first and leave the difficult questions for later.

WHY USE THIS TIP?

- It instills confidence.
- It enables you to use your time more efficiently.
- It provides an opportunity to find clues/ideas in other answers that can be useful in answering the ones left blank.

WHEN DO YOU USE THIS TIP?

- This tip is helpful whenever you take a test that contains difficult or unfamiliar questions

Easy questions are those that contain limited vocabulary, short statements, and are readily answered from the given information.

EXAMPLE

Which aspect of a nation's culture is most directly influenced by the physical geography of that nation?
1 form of government
2 religious belief
3 population distribution
4 social class system

(from an actual Regents exam)

Choice 3 is the obvious answer; it is the only choice that is connected to physical geography. The other choices are not related to the main idea of the question and have little to do with a nation's geography.

PRACTICE

An aspect of society that an economist would study in depth would be the
1 development of self-image and causes of mental illness
2 problem of scarcity of resources
3 origins of religion, legends, and festivals
4 migratory patterns of animals

(taken from a Test Sampler Draft)

The correct answer is 2. Economics is the only social science that deals with scarcity and resources. The other choices relate to different types of social sciences.

TIP 3

Read all choices. Look out for decoys.

WHY USE THIS TIP?

- It encourages you to read all possible answers before making a selection.
- It makes you aware that initial choices may seem correct but sometimes are not.

WHEN DO YOU USE THIS TIP?

- When taking a multiple-choice test.

Be a patient test taker. Very often, the decoy precedes the correct choice and the careless student will choose the incorrect answer.

EXAMPLE

Which slogan expressed the ideals of the Bolshevik Revolution of 1917?
1 Liberty, Equality, and Fraternity
2 Bread, Land, and Peace
3 Land and Liberty
4 Nationalism, Democracy, and the People's Livelihood
(from an actual Regents exam)

The correct choice is 2. It is the only choice that applies specifically to the Bolshevik Revolution. However, all three choices are historical slogans and represent other revolutions that occurred in history.

PRACTICE

One reason for both the French Revolution (1789) and the Cuban Revolution (1959) was that
1 people often rebel when they are governed by a foreign power
2 the monarchs did not meet the needs of culturally diverse populations
3 the writings of Karl Marx encouraged workers and the industrialists to unite
4 existing governments failed to address the major economic differences between social classes
(from an actual Regents exam)

Did you select number 3? It is an attractive choice, but the French Revolution took place *before* Karl Marx wrote, and indicated that the workers would revolt against the industrialists. However, Choice 4 is correct because revolutions take place when governments ignore the needs of the people.

TIP 4

Check for clues found in other questions and among the choices in the actual question.

WHY USE THIS TIP?

- It helps you to make connections and associations among various questions.
- It helps you to utilize the test as an educational tool.
- It enables you to find information that can help in answering other questions in the test.

WHEN DO YOU USE THIS TIP?

- Whenever necessary; all tests should be an assessment of your knowledge as well as an educational tool.

Sometimes you can find clues to the correct answer in other questions on the same test. The two questions below demonstrate how connections and associations can be made between different questions on the same Regents.

EXAMPLE (CLUE IN ANOTHER QUESTION)

In many Latin American nations, the leadership roles assumed by the military and by the Roman Catholic Church evolved from
1 Native American beliefs
2 the development of the triangular trade
3 the effects of matriarchal societies
4 Spanish colonial rule

(from an actual Regents exam)

The correct response is 4. You can get a clue to the right answer from the question below, which appeared on the same exam.

Which statement best illustrates the contradictory actions of the Catholic Church in colonial Latin America?

1 The Jesuits destroyed the temples of the Native Americans, but allowed them to continue their religious rituals.
2 The Church expressed concern over the mistreatment of Native Americans, but supported the encomienda system
3 The Church moved many Native Americans from Spanish territory to Portuguese territory, but encouraged the importation of African slaves.
4 The Pope endorsed the Treaty of Tordesillas, but outlawed further exploration

(from an actual Regents exam)

The correct choice is 2. Most students will remember that the Spanish controlled Latin America and that the Church converted the Native Americans, but also resented their being mistreated by the Spaniards. The role of the Spanish would provide a clear hint to the correct answer for the first question.

Practice (Clue found among choices)

What would most likely be included in a description of an area's physical geography?
1 customs and traditions
2 distribution of goods and services
3 systems of government
4 landforms of continents and currents of oceans

(taken from a Test Sampler Draft)

The correct choice is number 4. Landforms of continents and currents of oceans are the only terms that deal with physical geography. Choice 1 is cultural, choice 2 is economic, and choice 3 deals with an area's government.

TIP 5
Use the process of elimination.

WHY USE THIS TIP?

- It helps you discard the wrong choices.
- It narrows down the possible correct choices and increases the possibility of getting the right answer.

WHEN DO YOU USE THIS TIP?

- Whenever you face a tough question and are unsure about the correct response.

Always use the process of elimination to arrive at a conclusion when you are uncertain about the answer. Look at the example below and begin using this process.

EXAMPLE

"Archduke Franz Ferdinand Assassinated!"
"Germany declares war on Russia and France!"
"Peace Treaty signed at Versailles!"

Which event is referred to in these headlines?
1 Franco-Prussian War
2 Crimean War
3 World War I
4 Cold War

(from an actual Regents exam)

You may not be familiar with all the headlines, but you can eliminate Choice 4 because Russia and the United States opposed each other in the Cold War. If you know that Archduke Ferdinand was from Austria, you can rule out the Franco-Prussian War. You can eliminate Choice 2 if you remember that England and Russia fought in the Crimean War. Thus, you have arrived at your answer—Choice 3.

PRACTICE

One similarity in the Mesopotamian, Egyptian, Ancient Indian (Harappan), and Ancient Chinese civilizations was that they each developed
1 democratic governments
2 monotheistic religions
3 irrigation systems
4 industrialized economies

(taken from a Test Sampler Draft)

Congratulations if you selected Choice 3! Questions that ask for similarities between groups are good because if you know a fact about one, you know that it is the same for all. You remember that none of the ancient civilizations was democratic or monotheistic (with the exception of the Hebrews) and all developed an agricultural society. Thus, the only similarity is that all of these civilizations developed irrigation systems.

TIP 6

Identify differences among the choices.

WHY USE THIS TIP?

- It helps you decide between general and specific answers.
- It helps you identify decoys.

WHEN DO YOU USE THIS TIP?

- When several choices seem correct.
- When you have reduced the answer to two choices.

How do you answer a question when several choices seem to be correct? Tip 6 provides you with a way to recognize the difference among these choices. Try the following examples.

Example

The Native American population of Mexico in 1492 has been estimated at 25 million; the population in 1608 has been estimated at 1.7 million. This decrease in population was mainly a result of

1 crop failures brought on by poor weather conditions
2 emigration of Native Americans to Europe and Africa
3 wars between various native groups
4 diseases introduced by the Spanish

(from an actual Regents exam)

This is a difficult question because it mainly implies that to some extent more than one of these choices are correct. Choice 2 does not fit since there was no emigration of Native Americans to Europe and Africa. Crop failures, Choice 1, and wars between Native Americans,

Choice 3, did result in the death of some Native Americans; however, diseases, such as smallpox and measles, introduced by the Spanish, were the main factor that led to the decimation of the Native American population. Choice 4 is the best answer.

PRACTICE

> The strong showing by the Communist Party in the Russian Presidential election of 1996 suggests that large numbers of Russian people
>
> 1 favored a return to Stalin's policy of imprisoning dissidents
> 2 feared continuing economic instability and high inflation
> 3 wanted the Russian Orthodox Church to play a larger role in government
> 4 supported a return to isolationist policies
>
> (from an actual Regents exam)

This again is a difficult question because two of the wrong choices have elements of truth. While some people did want a return to stability, as stated in Choice 1, they rejected Stalin's strict policies. Choice 3 is a possible option because the Russian people have resumed worshiping in the Russian Orthodox Church; however, there is no evidence to suggest an end to separation of church and state. Choice 4 is incorrect because Russian leaders wanted to reject isolationism and play a greater role in world politics. Therefore, this leaves Choice 2 as the correct answer because many Russian people do indeed fear inflation and instability.

TIP 7

Don't select an answer that is correct in itself but is wrong as it relates to the question.

WHY USE THIS TIP?

- It assists you in relating answer choices to the question.
- It guides you in focusing on the question and its connection to the answer.

WHEN DO YOU USE THIS TIP?

- Whenever answering a multiple-choice question.

Quite often one or more of the options are accurate, but are the wrong answer for that question. Always keep in mind which choices best relate to the specific question. Try the following.

EXAMPLE

Which economic policy of the Soviet Union in the 1980s was the most different from the economic policies of Stalin?
1 government ownership of the means of production
2 the development of heavy industry
3 central planning of basic economic decisions
4 private management

(from an actual Regents exam)

All of the choices describe the Soviet economy in the 1980s; however, Choice 4 is the one that best answers the question. Gorbachev's policy of perestroika was a direct rejection of Stalin's command economy.

PRACTICE

The amount of carbon dioxide in the atmosphere has increased in recent years. Environmentalists suggest this change is a direct result of the

1 improper storage of solid and nuclear wastes
2 overcutting of forests and the increased use of fossil fuels
3 dumping of inorganic material into lakes and rivers
4 use of herbicides and toxic substances such as asbestos and DDT

(from an actual Regents exam)

Choices 1, 3, and 4 are all regarded as environmental hazards that reduce the quality of life and may cause death. However, they do not contribute to the increase in the level of carbon dioxide. Choice 2 is the correct statement for this question because overcutting of forests leads to global warming.

TIP 8
Always pick the broader encompassing option.

WHY USE THIS TIP?

- It is helpful when two choices are accurate but one choice more fully answers the question.

WHEN DO YOU USE THIS TIP?

- When two or more choices are correct but one of the choices includes the other.

This is a valuable tool when answering questions that call for inclusive answers. Below is a sample of this type of question.

EXAMPLE

People in both Japan and India eat very little meat. A study of these cultures would show that

1 although these cultures have similar practices, the reasons for these practices differ
2 the raising of cattle in both nations is very different due to the extreme climate
3 neither culture is concerned with health issues
4 the governments of both nations enforce strict dietary laws

(from an actual Regents exam)

Use the process of elimination in answering the question (Tip 5). You could have eliminated Choice 2 because you know that Indians do not eat meat because of religious reasons. You can cross out Choices 3 and 4 because both of these governments are secular democratic governments. They would not ignore health issues nor impose dietary laws. The most general answer is Choice 1 and is likely to be true of both countries.

Practice

Which factor is the best indicator of the wealth of a nation?
1 Gross National Product (GNP)
2 Prime Interest Rate
3 Number of millionaires
4 Defense spending

(from an actual Regents exam)

Choices 2, 3, and 4 have some validity since they indicate certain characteristics of an economy. However, Choice 1 is a broader statement and a more accurate way to measure the total economic activity during a set time period.

TIP 9

Have an idea about the answer before looking at the answer choices.

WHY USE THIS TIP?

- It helps you to recall an idea or term associated with the question.
- It helps you to stimulate your memory.

WHEN DO YOU USE THIS TIP?

- Whenever you answer a multiple-choice question.
- When interpreting cartoons.

When you read a question you should put it in the context of the time period and associate the important events in that era. Try the following example.

Example

As a result of the Glorious Revolution and the English Bill of Rights of 1689, the government in Great Britain gradually became a
1 theocracy
2 limited monarchy
3 direct democracy
4 socialist republic

(from an actual Regents exam)

As you read this question, you should have thought how the Glorious Revolution and the Bill of Rights brought about an end to absolute power and established a limited monarchy. There was little interest in Great Britain in a theocracy or a direct democracy. Therefore, Choice 2 is correct.

Try this tip when you look at a cartoon. Interpret the meaning of the cartoon before looking at the choices.

PRACTICE

Base your answer to this question on the cartoon below and on your knowledge of social studies.

Gorrell, Richmond Times-Dispatch

What is the main idea of this 1994 cartoon?

1 Haiti's lack of industrialization has led to economic stagnation
2 Haiti's limited experience with democracy has made it difficult to establish this form of government
3 The desire for democracy has led Haiti to neglect its development of modern technology
4 The presence of American industry has failed to improve Haiti's economy

(from an actual Regents exam)

The cartoon suggests that Haiti has to put many parts together to develop a democracy. The words "Some assembly required" provides the focus of the cartoon. Focusing on these words will enable you to select Choice 2 as the correct answer.

TIP 10
Make educated guesses.

WHY USE THIS TIP?

- Because there is no penalty for guessing.
- Because any answer is better than no answer.
- Because using the process of elimination helps you to arrive at the right answer.

WHEN DO YOU USE THIS TIP?

- When there is no penalty for guessing.
- When there is nothing to lose; a blank answer is wrong anyway.

Remember, you should use guessing as a last resort! The question below will give you an opportunity to use the technique of intelligent guessing to arrive at the correct answer.

EXAMPLE

The contributions of the Golden Age of Islamic civilization include

1 advances in mathematics
2 irrigation systems
3 polytheistic beliefs
4 gunpowder and guns

(from an actual Regents exam)

Even if you are not certain of the choices, you can make an informed guess that Choice 1 is the correct answer. You probably realize that Arabic numbers are used worldwide and that we borrowed them from the Muslims.

PRACTICE

Which practice was similar under the rule of the Bolsheviks in Russia and of the Nazi Party in Germany?
1 establishing communism in their respective nations
2 permitting a series of multiparty elections
3 increasing the power of the middle class
4 limiting government opposition through intimidation and fear

(from an actual Regents exam)

Choice 4 is the correct answer. It contains the key words—*limiting*, *intimidation*, and *fear*—all essential features of the two ideologies. Communism and Fascism are opposed to each other and thus Choice 1 is eliminated. A series of multiparty elections would not exist in a dictatorship so you can rule out Choice 3.

CHECKLIST FOR ANSWERING THE MULTIPLE-CHOICE QUESTIONS

1. Read the questions carefully and underline key words.
2. Answer the easy questions first.
3. Read all the choices. Look out for decoys.
4. Check for clues found in other questions and among the choices in the question.
5. Use the process of elimination.
6. Identify differences among the choices.
7. Don't select an answer that is correct in itself but is wrong as it relates to the question.
8. Always pick the broader encompassing option.
9. Have an idea about the answer before looking at the answer choices.
10. Make educated guesses.

STRATEGIES FOR ANSWERING THE THEMATIC ESSAY QUESTION

There will be one Thematic Essay on the Regents. It will count for 15 percent of the examination. The Thematic Essay requires you to **interpret, understand, and explain key concepts that link several events in Global History**.

THEMES	EXAMPLES
Major Belief Systems	Judaism; Confucianism
Turning Points in History	Fall of Rome; French Revolution; Birth of Islam
Forms of Government (Political System)	Monarchy; Democracy
Economic Systems	Communism; Capitalism
Geography and the Environment	Early River Civilization; Global Economy
Justice/Human Rights	Code of Hammurabi; Justinian Code; Violations (i.e., Holocaust, Apartheid)
Science/Technology	Invention of Printing Press; Neolithic Revolution
Movement of People/Goods (Cultural Diffusion)	Crusades; Silk Road
Nationalism	Italian/German Unification; Zionism
Imperialism	British in India; European Partition of Africa
Conflicts	Political (World War I, World War II) Religious (Northern Ireland, Middle East, India)
Culture/Intellectual Life	Roman, Gupta Civilizations; Renaissance

Most Thematic Essays will have the following parts:

THE THEME: Identifies the broad concept that will be the topic of the essay. Usually, there is a general explanation statement that provides more focus to the question.

THE TASK: Provides the instruction for what you will need to write about your topic or concept.

SUGGESTIONS: Provide you with a specific area that you might choose to discuss in your essay. **Note:** These are only suggestions and you are not limited to these examples. **Beware:** Pay attention if the suggestions caution you not to choose the United States as your topic. Students will lose credit if they do not follow the directions.

Thematic Essay

Directions: Write a well-organized essay that includes an introduction, several paragraphs addressing the task below, and a conclusion.

Theme: Justice and Human Rights

Throughout history, the human rights of certain groups of people have been violated. Efforts have been made to address these violations.

Task:

- Define the term "human rights"
- Identify *two* examples of human rights violations that have occurred in a specific time and place
- Describe the causes of these human rights violations
- For *one* of the violations identified, discuss *one* specific effort that was made or is being made to deal with the violation

You may use any example from your study of global history. Do *not* use the United States in your answer. Some suggestions you might wish to consider include: Christians in the early Roman Empire, native peoples in Spain's American colonies, untouchables in India, blacks in South Africa, Jews in Nazi Germany, Muslims in Bosnia, Kurds in Iraq or Turkey, or Tibetans in China.

You are *not* limited to these suggestions.

STEP 1

Read the entire question first.

This will help you focus on what is expected of you in the essay.

STEP 2

Analyze the task.

Review key phrases and words in the task directions that you must include in your essay. In the sample Thematic Essay on page 26, taken from an actual Regents exam, you should underline the key words in the directions:

- *Define* human rights.
- *Identify* two examples of violations in different time periods.
- *Describe* the causes of these violations.
- *Discuss* one specific effort to deal with the violations.

By listing these items, you can begin to organize your outline.

STEP 3

Check the suggestions.

This will help you recall the importance of themes in different places and time periods.

STEP 4
Organize the information.

Begin to outline the information you could include in your essay. In the sample Thematic Essay on page 26, you might include:

- Definition of human rights: rights and liberties guaranteed by birth; freedom of religion; right to vote
- Identify two human rights violations: Apartheid (South Africa); Holocaust (Germany)
- Causes: White minority control; black majority; separation of races; Hitler's extermination of Jews; Nuremberg Laws; Kristallnacht
- Effort to deal with violations: Role of Nelson Mandela and Bishop Tutu; economic boycott in South Africa

STEP 5
Identify the main ideas of the essay.

Use the theme or the task of the Thematic Essay to create your topic or thesis statement. An example of a thesis statement might be as follows:

> Throughout history, the human rights of certain groups such as the blacks in South Africa and the Jews in Germany have been violated.

STEP 6

Write the introductory paragraph.

The introductory paragraph should connect the thesis or topic to the main idea of the essay. You might include in your paragraph a definition of human rights and two examples, such as the blacks in South Africa and the Jews in Germany. Below is an example of an introductory paragraph:

> Human rights are those rights and liberties that are guaranteed to everyone from birth by virtue of belonging to a civil society. These rights include freedom of religion, the right to vote, and freedom of expression without fear of abuse by government officials. In 1948 the United Nations adopted a Universal Declaration of Human Rights, which set forth those basic liberties and freedoms to which all people are entitled. Throughout history, the human rights of people such as the blacks in South Africa and the Jews in Nazi Germany have been violated. (**Note:** the introductory paragraph concludes with the thesis statement.)

STEP 7

Write the supporting paragraphs.

Each of these paragraphs should deal with one aspect or part of the task. These paragraphs should explain your answer with facts, details, and examples. Check the facts from the outline as you are writing. Remember the following:

1. Develop your essay logically.
2. Do not list facts. Analyze, evaluate, compare, or contrast various aspects.
3. Do not use meaningless facts unrelated to the theme.
4. Use concrete examples to support your ideas.
5. Make sure that you have completed all the assigned tasks listed in the question.

STEP 8

Write the concluding paragraph.

Restate or rewrite the thesis summarizing the essay. Make sure that your essay has both a strong introduction and a strong conclusion. You will not receive full credit if either of these pieces is missing or weak. A good concluding paragraph would be as follows:

> Human rights violations such as those in South Africa and Nazi Germany have existed throughout history. It is is important to be aware of these violations and for society to make an effort to ensure that they never happen again. History has shown that the global community does not benefit when any group of people becomes victims of intolerance or injustice.

STEP 9

Check the essay against the generic scoring rubric.

Depending on time, reread your essay to check for errors of facts, spelling, or grammar. Check to see if the essay is organized, reads clearly, and makes sense. The following scoring rubric will appear after the Thematic Essay Question in your Regents exam booklet. It shows exactly what an essay must contain to receive a particular score. For example, in order to abtain a score of 4, the rubric indicates your essay must contain relevant facts and examples. If, while checking your essay against the rubric, you discover you've neglected to include relevant facts, you can add them at this time.

THEMATIC ESSAY GENERIC SCORING RUBRIC

Score of 5:

- Shows a thorough understanding of the theme or problem
- Addresses all aspects of the task
- Shows an ability to analyze, evaluate, compare and/or contrast issues and events
- Richly supports the theme or problem with relevant facts, examples, and details
- Is a well-developed essay, consistently demonstrating a logical and clear plan of organization
- Introduces the theme or problem by establishing a framework that is beyond a simple restatement of the task and concludes with a summation of the theme or problem

Score of 4:

- Shows a good understanding of the theme or problem
- Addresses all aspects of the task
- Shows an ability to analyze, evaluate, compare and/or contrast issues and events
- Includes relevant facts, examples, and details, but may not support all aspects of the theme or problem evenly
- Is a well-developed essay, demonstrating a logical and clear plan of organization
- Introudces the theme or problem by establishing a framework that is beyond a simple restatement of the task and concludes with a summation of the theme or problem

Score of 3:

- Shows a satisfactory understanding of the theme or problem
- Addresses most aspects of the task or addresses all aspects in a limited way

- Shows an ability to analyze or evaluate issues and events, but not in any depth
- Includes some facts, examples, and details
- Is a satisfactorily developed essay, demonstrating a general plan of organization
- Introduces the theme or problem by repeating the task and concludes by repeating the theme or problem

Score of 2:
- Shows limited understanding of the theme or problem
- Attempts to address the task
- Develops a faulty analysis or evaluation of issues and events
- Includes few facts, examples, and details, and may include information that contains inaccuracies
- Is a poorly organized essay, lacking focus
- Fails to introduce or summarize the theme or problem

Score of 1:
- Shows very limited understanding of the theme or problem
- Lacks an analysis or evaluation of the issues and events
- Includes little or no accurate or relevant facts, examples, or details
- Attempts to complete the task, but demonstrates a major weakness in organization
- Fails to introduce or summarize the theme or problem

Score of 0: Fails to address the task, is illegible, or is a blank paper

CHECKLIST FOR WRITING THE THEMATIC ESSAY

1. Read the entire question first.
2. Analyze the task.
3. Check the suggestions.
4. Organize the information.
5. Identify the main ideas of the essay.
6. Write the introductory paragraph.
7. Write the supporting paragraphs.
8. Write the concluding paragraph.
9. Check the essay against the generic scoring rubric.

Here is your task: Use these steps to answer the following Thematic Essay question from a past Test Sampler Draft. Use the Thematic Essay Rubric (pages 31–32) to evaluate your answer.

Thematic Essay

Directions: Write a well-organized essay that includes an introduction, several paragrphs explaining your position, and a conclusion.

Theme: Belief Systems

> At various times in global history, members of different religions have acted to bring people together. Members of these same religions have also acted to divide people and have caused conflict.

Task:

> Choose *two* religions from your study of global history and geography.
> For *each* religion:
> - Describe *two* basic beliefs of the religion
> - Explain how members of the religion, at a specific time and place, acted either to unify society or to cause conflict in society

You may use any example from your study of global history and geography. Some suggestions you might wish to consider include: Judaism in the Middle East, Roman Catholicism in Latin America, Hinduism in India, Islam in Iran, Protestant Reformation and the Counter Reformation in Europe, animism in Africa, Shintoism in Japan, and Buddhism in Southeast Asia.

You are *not* limited to these suggestions.

STRATEGIES FOR ANSWERING THE DOCUMENT-BASED ESSAY QUESTION (DBQ)

There will be one Document-Based Essay question on the Regents. It will count for 30 percent of the examination. The Document-Based Essay question requires students to write an essay incorporating information from several documents. The documents may consist of both primary and secondary sources including maps, charts, political cartoons, graphs, or photographs. Remember, the documents may look different but they are all related to a single subject or theme. The DBQ tests a student's ability to **interpret and draw conclusions from historical documents**.

Most DBQ questions will have the following parts:
GENERAL DIRECTIONS: The directions tell you what to do for each part of the question.
HISTORICAL CONTEXT: This is the theme of the question. Read the historical context before you start to answer the question. Each document is related to or takes a position on that theme.
TASK: This statement defines what you must do as you examine the documents. The task is usually in the form of a question.
PART A—SHORT ANSWERS: In this part, you study between six and eight documents. Each document will be followed by one or more possible questions to which you will provide a short response. This portion of the test is worth 15 percent of the exam grade.
PART B—ESSAY: In this part, you will answer an essay question on the same topic as the documents. This portion of the test is worth 15 percent of the exam grade.

STEP 1
Read the question carefully.

Determine what you must do. Read the Historical Context and underline or box the main topic of the question.

Historical Context:

> Economic systems attempt to meet the needs of the people. Capitalism and communism represent two different ways to meet people's economic needs.

(from an actual Regents exam)

The key words to underline would be: *Economic systems; capitalism; communism; different ways; economic needs*.

STEP 2

Read the task.

As you read, circle key words and phrases and try to identify the theme or issue in the question.

Task:

> - Describe how these two economic systems attempt to meet the needs of the people.
> - Evaluate how successful each system has been at meeting the economic needs of the people.

(from an actual Regents exam)

You should have circled the following: *Describe*; *two economic systems*; *evaluate*; *successful*.

Write down any information that you know about the theme, task, or issue.

STEP 3

Read and analyze each document.

Highlight key words and phrases. Take note of the author, date of the document, and the place. When reviewing each document, assess "How is the document related to the theme?" How does Document 1 compare with or contrast to ideas in Document 4?"

Document 1

> Capitalists are rich people who own factories and have lots of money and workers. . . . A factory can belong to one person in Capitalism but in [Communism] it belongs to the government. . . . I am for the idea of [Communism]. It seems to me that you have more of an opportunity to live well. You won't lose your job in [Communism] . . . I've heard about the unemployment problem in America. People can't find any kind of job. . . . That's the way we heard about it—that [in] the West, unemployment, everything there is bad, a real mess.
>
> —"Katia," a 16-year-old ninth grader from Moscow, 1980s

(from an actual Regents exam)

Document 4

> Andrei, his wife, his father, and [his] elder son all have to work on the collective farmlands . . . He is not stupid and sees that almost all the produce ends up in the hands of the Government. The local Communist party boss is always coming back . . . for more and more. Andrei and his family know ahead of time that they are going to get [a] very small return for working on the collectivized fields. Naturally this condition [changes] their attitudes. They are constantly on a sort of slow-down strike . . .
>
> —T. P. Whitney, "The Russian Peasant Wars on the Kremlin," 1954

(from an actual Regents exam)

In Document 1, you should have noted that it was written by a 16-year-old ninth grader from Moscow in the 1980s. Compare the statement with Document 4 written in the 1950s. How are they different? What other outside information can be applied to them?

STEP 4
Begin to answer Part A.

Summarize the main viewpoints expressed in each document and answer the question following each document. These short-answer questions are called **Scaffolding** because Scaffolding provides the foundation for answering the essay portion (Part B).

NOTE: Answers to the Scaffolding questions should be *concise* and *straightforward*—one or two sentences are sufficient.

Document 3

> Above all, [the government] . . . will have to take the control of industry and of all branches of production out of the hands of . . . competing individuals, and instead institute a system as a whole, that is for the common account [good], according to a common plan, and with the participation of all members of society. It will . . . abolish [eliminate] competition. . . . Private property must therefore be abolished.
>
> —Friedrich Engels, *Principles of Communism*

(from an actual Regents exam)

3a) Who controls the means of production and all property in a Communist system?

You would receive a score of 1 if you stated the following: Government, not the individual, controls the means of production and all property.

3b) What happens to competition in a Communist system?

You would receive a score of 1 if you stated the following: Competition is abolished.

STEP 5

Begin to organize your essay for Part B.

Make an outline or chart of key ideas from each document, separating them to reflect both sides of the task. Below is a summary of the key ideas from the documents of the Regents exam the preceding documents were taken from.

Capitalism

Unemployment—Document 1
Success to industrious and hard-working—Document 2

Supply and demand—Document 2
Rewards talent—Document 2
Laissez-faire—Documents 2 and 5
Private ownership—Document 3
Economic class distinction—Document 6
Negative aspects of factory system—Document 6
Free enterprise—Document 7

Communism
Classless society—Documents 1 and 6
Concept of common good—Document 3
Government control of industry—Document 3
Elimination of private property—Document 3
Collectivization—Document 4
Exploitation by leadership—Document 4
Five-year plan—Document 7
Free social and medical services—Document 8
No unemployment—Document 8

STEP 6

Begin to write your essay for Part B

You can approach this part as you would a Thematic Essay, but you should try to incorporate outside information from your Global History and Geography course. Write an introductory paragraph in which you state your position (if necessary) and the varying issues that your essay will discuss. Below is an example of an introductory paragraph that you might use in answering a DBQ that contains these points:

Capitalism and communism are two types of economic systems that have attempted to meet the needs of the people. Each of these economic systems must address the following three questions: What goods and services should be produced? How should these goods and services be produced? Who should consume these goods and services?

STEP 7

Write the body of your essay.

Refer to the documents to provide the conflicting views and to support your position or thesis. Include specific historical examples and refer to the documents you analyzed in Part A. **Do not merely copy the documents or use long passages from them**. Try to summarize the documents in your own words in one or two sentences.

Document 5

> *The Wealth of Nations* carries the important message of *laissez faire*, which means that the government should intervene as little as possible in economic affairs and leave the market to its own devices. It advocates the liberation of economic production from all limiting regulation in order to benefit the people . . .
>
> —Adam Smith, *The Wealth of Nations*

A good way to summarize this document is to refer to Part A in which your response included the idea that government should leave business alone (laissez-faire).

STEP 8

Evaluate/analyze the different viewpoints expressed in the documents.

Note that the documents contain a variety of ideas on the topic, in this case, capitalism and communism. Some documents are contradictory. This is not done to confuse you but to assess how you will analyze different points of view. In your answer, you should know how the documents support/oppose your thesis or viewpoints.

Remember you must use at least **four** documents to receive full credit.

STEP 9

Write your conclusion.

Restate or rewrite the thesis summarizing the essay. Make sure that you have responded to all parts of the question, check for a strong introduction, and include a judgment in your conclusion if the question warrants it. Below is a conclusion that you might use in answering the DBQ.

Capitalism has become the dominant economic system in the world today because it has been successful in providing a stable economic environment that gives society basic needs as well as allowing freedom for each individual. However, there are concerns that capitalism has resulted in widening the gap between the rich and the poor in our industrial society and between the developed and underdeveloped nations of Africa and Latin America. Pope John Paul II has applauded the fall of communism and the freedom associated with capitalism. However, he has also reminded all capitalistic countries that we must insure that capitalism meets the social needs of the people.

STEP 10

Check the essay against the generic scoring rubric.

Proofread the essay to see if it is clear and logical and that the facts are accurate. The following scoring rubric will appear after the Document-Based Essay question in your Regents exam booklet. It will help you decide if your essay has enough detail, relevant outside information, and facts to receive a score with which you will be satisfied. Notice that to receive a score of 4 or 5 you must correctly analyze and interpret at least **four** documents. Comparing your essay to the rubric will make sure you have included four documents in your essay.

DOCUMENT-BASED QUESTION
GENERIC SCORING RUBRIC

Score of 5:

- Thoroughly addresses all aspects of the *Task* by accurately analyzing and interpreting at least **four** documents
- Incorporates information from the documents in the body of the essay
- Incorporates relevant outside information
- Richly supports the theme or problem with relevant facts, examples, and details
- Is a well-developed essay, consistently demonstrating a logical and clear plan of organization
- Introduces the theme or problem by establishing a framework that is beyond a simple restatement of the *Task* or *Historical Context* and concludes with a summation of the theme or problem

Score of 4:

- Addresses all aspects of the *Task* by accurately analyzing and interpreting at least **four** documents
- Incorporates informatioin from the documents in the body of the essay
- Incorporates relevant outside information
- Includes relevant facts, examples, and details, but discussion may be more descriptive than analytical
- Is a well-developed essay, demonstrating a logical and clear plan of organization
- Introduces the theme or problem by establishing a framework that is beyond a simple restatement of the *Task* or *Historical Context* and concludes with a summation of the theme or problem

Score of 3:

- Addresses most aspects of the *Task* or addresses all aspects of the *Task* in a limited way, using some of the documents
- Incorporates some information from the documents in the body of the essay
- Incorporates limited or no relevant outside information
- Includes some facts, examples, and details, but discussion is more descriptive than analytical
- Is a satisfactorily developed essay, demonstrating a general plan of organization

- Introduces the theme or problem by repeating the *Task* or *Historical Context* and concludes by simply repeating the theme or problem

Score of 2:
- Attempts to address some aspects of the *Task*, making limited use of the documents
- Presents no relevant outside information
- Includes few facts, examples, and details; discussion restates contents of the documents
- Is a poorly organized essay, lacking focus
- Fails to introduce or summarize the theme or problem

Score of 1:
- Shows limited understanding of the *Task* with vague, unclear references to the documents
- Presents no relevant outside information
- Includes little or no accurate or relevant facts, details, or examples
- Attempts to complete the *Task*, but demonstrates a major weakness in organization
- Fails to introduce or summarize the theme or problem

Score of 0: Fails to address the *Task*, is illegible, or is a blank paper

CHECKLIST FOR WRITING THE DBQ ESSAY

1. Read the question carefully.
2. Read the task.
3. Read and analyze each document.
4. Begin to answer Part A.
5. Begin to organize your essay for Part B.
6. Begin to write your essay for Part B.
7. Write the body of your essay.
8. Evaluate/analyze the different viewpoints expressed in the documents.
9. Write your conclusion.
10. Check the essay against the generic scoring rubric.

Here is your task. Use these steps to answer the following DBQ Essay question taken from a past Test Sampler. Use the Document-Based Specific Rubric (pages 53–54) to evaluate your answer.

Document-Based Essay

This task is based on the accompanying documents (1–6). Some of these documents have been edited for the purposes of this task. This task is designed to test your ability to work with historical documents. As you analyze the documents, take into account both the source of each document and the author's point of view.

Directions: Read the documents in Part A and answer the questions after each document. Then read the directions of Part B and write your essay.

Historical Context:

Throughout history, societies have held different viewpoints on governmental decision making and the roles of citizens in this decision-making process. The decision-making process can range from absolute control to democracy.

Task:

Using information from the documents and your knowledge of global history and geography, write an essay in which you

- Compare and contrast the different viewpoints societies have held about the process of governmental decision making and about the role of citizens in the political decision-making process.
- Discuss the advantages and disadvantages of a political system that is under absolute control or is a democracy.

NOTE: The scoring rubric for this essay appears on pages 53–54.

Part A: Short Answer

Directions:

- Analyze the documents and answer the questions that follow each document in the space provided.

Document 1

> The Wise Man's policy, accordingly,
> Will be to empty people's hearts and minds,
> To fill their bellies, weaken their ambition,
> Give them sturdy frames and always so,
> To keep them uninformed, without desire,
> And knowing ones not venturing to act.
>
> Be still while you work
> And keep full control
> Over all.
>
> —Lao Tzu (6th century B.C.)

1. What role does the citizen play in this political system?

____

____

Document 2

"We are a democracy because the power to make the laws is given to the many rather than the few. But while the law gives equal justice to everyone, it has not failed to reward excellence. While every citizen has an equal opportunity to serve the public, we reward our most distinguished [best] citizens by asking them to make our political decisions. Nor do we discriminate against the poor. A man may serve his country no matter how low his position on the social scale.

An Athenian citizen does not put his private affairs before the affairs of the state; even our merchants and businessmen know something about politics. We alone believe that a man who takes no interest in public affairs is more than harmless—he is useless."

—"Pericles' Funeral Oration"
Athens, 5th century B.C.

2. According to Pericles, what is a responsibility of a citizen in a democracy?

____

____

Document 3

> ". . . Whereas . . . King James II, . . . did attempt to undermine . . . the laws and liberties of this kingdom . . .
>
> Therefore, the Parliament declares:
>
> 1. That the King's supposed power of suspending laws without the consent of Parliament is illegal.
>
> 4. That the levying of taxes for the use of the king without the consent of Parliament is illegal.
>
> 8. That the king should not interfere with the election of members of Parliament.
>
> 13. And that to redress grievances and amend, strengthen, and preserve the laws, Parliament ought to be held [meet] frequently."
>
> —The English Bill of Rights, 1689

3. How did the English Bill of Rights change governmental decision making?

____

____

Document 4

"But what happens when the sun sets?"

4. Based on this cartoon, who controlled the government of France from the mid-1600s to the early 1700s?

____

____

Document 5

After Socialism, Fascism combats the whole complex system of democratic ideology [theory], and repudiates [denies] it, whether in its theoretical premises [basis] or in its practical application. Fascism denies that the majority, by the simple fact that it is a majority, can direct human society; it denies that numbers alone can govern by means of a periodical consultation [elections], and it affirms the . . . beneficial, and fruitful [useful] inequality of mankind, which can never be permanently leveled through . . . universal suffrage.

—Benito Mussolini, 1932

5. What was the basis of Mussolini's argument against democracy?

____

____

Document 6

> "We the Japanese people, acting through our duly elected representatives in the National Diet [legislature], resolve that never again shall we be visited with the horrors of war through the action of government, do proclaim that sovereign power resides with the people and do firmly establish this Constitution. Government is a sacred trust of the people, the authority for which is derived from the people, the powers of which are exercised by the representatives of the people, and the benefits of which are enjoyed by the people. This is a universal principle of mankind upon which this Constitution is founded. We reject and revoke all constitutions, laws, ordinances, and rescripts in conflict herewith."
>
> —The Japanese Constitution of 1947

6. Which universal principle is the basis for the Japanese Constitution?

____

____

Part B: Essay

Directions:

- Write a well-organized essay that includes an introduction, several paragraphs, and a conclusion.
- Use evidence from the documents to support your response.
- Do not simply repeat the contents of the documents.
- Include specific related outside information.

Historical Context:

Throughout history, societies have held different viewpoints on governmental decision making and the role of citizens in this decision-making process. The decision-making process can range from absolute control to democracy.

Task:

Using information from the documents and your knowledge of global history and geography, write an essay in which you

- Compare and contrast the different viewpoints societies have held about the process of governmental decision making and about the role of citizens in the political decision-making process.
- Discuss the advantages and disadvantages of a political system that is under the absolute control of a single individual or a few individuals, or a political system that is a democracy.

Be sure to include specific historical details. You must also include additional information from your knowledge of global history and geography.

DOCUMENT-BASED ESSAY SPECIFIC RUBRIC

5

- Uses at least half of the documents provided
- Places documents in historical context
- Incorporates relevant outside information related to document
- Uses the terms "absolute monarch," "democracy," and "fascism" correctly
- Either compares or contrasts societies' viewpoints on the process of governmental decision making
- Either compares or contrasts the citizen's role in the decision-making process
- Analyzes advantages and disadvantages of each political system
- Weaves documents into body of essay
- Writes a well-developed essay, consistently demonstrating a logical and clear plan of organization
- Includes a strong introduction and conclusion

4

- Uses at least half of the documents provided
- Places documents in historical context
- Incorporates relevant outside information related to documents
- Uses the terms "absolute monarch," "democracy," and "fascism" correctly
- Either compares or contrasts societies' viewpoints on the process of governmental decision making
- Either compares or contrasts the citizen's role in the decision-making process
- Discusses advantages and disadvantages of each political system
- Discussion of documents may be descriptive or analytical
- Writes a well-developed essay, demonstrating a logical and clear plan of organization
- Includes a good introduction and conclusion

3

- Uses at least two of the documents provided
- Use of documents within the historical context may be in error
- Incorporates limited outside information related to documents
- Has limited understanding of political terms

- Understands some aspect of the process of governmental decision making
- Understands some aspect of the citizen's role in the decision-making process
- Has limited understanding of different political systems
- Generally discusses advantages and disadvantages of a political system
- Reiterates information from documents
- Writes a satisfactorily developed essay, demonstrating a general plan of organization
- Restates the theme in the introduction and concludes with a restatement of the task

2

- Attempts to address task with at least one document
- No relevant outside information is apparent
- Knowledge of political terms and systems is vague, general, or incorrect
- Reiterates contents of document
- Does not understand process of governmental decision making or citizen's role
- Writes a poorly organized essay lacking focus
- Has vague or missing introduction or conclusion

1

- Demonstrates a very limited understanding of the task
- Cannot distinguish between aspects of the task
- Fails to use or vaguely refers to documents
- Contains factual errors
- Essay demonstrates a major weakness in organization
- Vague or missing introduction or conclusion

0

- Fails to address the question
- No response
- Blank paper

Glossary

The Glossary that follows contains a list of terms, international organizations, and important people that are an integral part of the Global History and Geography course of study. The Glossary should be used as a device to help you recall some significant terms, people, and concepts in Global History and Geography. It is not all-inclusive but is one study tool to prepare you for the Global History and Geography Regents.

IMPORTANT TERMS

absolute monarchy system in which a ruler (king or queen) has complete authority over the government without limits on his/her powers.

absolutism political system in which the monarch has supreme power and control over the lives of the people in the country.

acid rain toxic pollution that is produced by the burning of fossil fuels. It affects plants, animals, and people who have a respiratory illness.

African National Congress (ANC) group formed in 1912 to work for blacks' rights in South Africa. This group led the fight against apartheid and continues to encourage independence for the black majority.

Age of Exploration period from 1400 to 1600 during which European monarchs sent explorers to find new trade routes, resources, and land in Asia, Africa, and the Americas.

agrarian economy economic system that centers on agriculture as the chief source of wealth.

Agrarian Revolution change in the farming method in England during the 1600s that dramatically increased farm production.

alliance agreement between two or more countries that provides for their mutual defense or protection.

animism traditional African religion; a belief that the spirit dwells in all living and nonliving things.

anthropologist social scientist who studies the physical characteristics, origins, cultures, and artifacts of human beings.

anti-Semitism prejudice against the Jewish people.

apartheid (Afrikaans word—apartness) an official policy of strict segregation of the races; practiced in South Africa from 1945 until it was repealed in 1991.

appeasement policy of giving in to the demands of the aggressor to avoid war; policy used by England and France to satisfy Hitler's demands for land during the 1930s.

Arabic numerals numbers first developed by mathematicians in Gupta, India, and adapted by most of the Western world (counting 1, 2, 3, etc.).

archaeologist social scientist who studies past human life by examining the monuments and relics left by ancient people.

archipelago chain or group of islands.

aristocracy government ruled by nobles or the upper class.

armistice temporary agreement to stop fighting.

astrolabe instrument that determines latitude by measuring the position of the stars; one of the technological improvements that the Europeans borrowed from the Muslims that contributed to the Age of Exploration.

balance of power distribution of military and economic powers among rival nations so that one nation does not have more power than its neighbors or other nations.

balance of trade difference in value between a nation's imports and exports over a period of time.

Black Death bubonic plague or contagious disease during the 14th century whose death toll is estimated to have exceeded 100 million in Europe, Asia, and Africa.

Bolsheviks left-wing majority group of the Russian Socialist Democratic Party under the leadership of Nikolai Lenin, which seized control of the government by revolution in November 1917; the group was later called Communists.

bourgeoisie middle class between aristocrats and workers. This term was used by Marx and Engels in the *Communist Manifesto* to describe the capitalists, or factory owners, who exploit the worker, or the proletariat. In the Middle Ages, the bourgeoisie were members of the merchant class or the townspeople of the city.

Buddhism major religion of eastern and central Asia founded in 6th century B.C. and based on the teaching of Siddhartha Gautama, who believed people must reject the material world and follow a philosophy of self-denial and meditation.

Bushido traditional code of the Japanese warrior class (the samurai) during the feudal period; emphasizes loyalty and honor to the local warlord over allegiance to the Emperor.

Byzantine Empire eastern part of the Roman Empire; existed from 330 A.D. to 1453 A.D.; preserved the rich cultural heritage of the ancient Greeks; saved Roman texts from destruction after the fall of the western part of the Roman Empire in 476 A.D.

caliph title for the successor to Muhammad as the political and religious leader of Islam.

calligraphy elaborate handwriting that Chinese and Arab scholars turned into an art form; characters or symbols represent words or ideas.

capitalism economic system in which the means of production and the distribution of goods and wealth are controlled by individuals and operated for profit. Consumers have freedom of choice to buy or not buy goods.

caste system division of society into four major groups based on occupation or birth; a rigid social system that was characteristic of traditional Hindu Indian society.

Christianity belief system based on the teachings of Jesus Christ that began in the Middle East about 2,000 years ago and was rooted in the monotheistic religion of Judaism.

citizen member of a state or country.

city-state small independent state that consists of a city and the territory surrounding it; associated with Ancient Greece.

civil disobedience nonviolent or passive resistance; refusal to obey unjust laws that are morally wrong.

civilization advanced form of society characterized by a complex social system, some form of writing, and advances in science and technology.

clan extended family unit or groups of families that have a common ancestor or family ties.

Classical Period name for the period in history that pertains to the artistic style of ancient Greece and Rome; their civilization was at its highest and was considered the Golden Age.

class system social division of society based on wealth, birth, education, occupation, or race.

codified law organized and written set of rules or laws.

Cold War period of tension and hostility between the United States and the Soviet Union after 1945 because of their different political and economic systems; worldwide struggle without actual fighting between the two powers; ended in 1991 with the collapse of the Soviet Union.

collectivization system under communism in which many small farms were combined into large farms owned and operated by the government and worked by the peasants; started by Stalin in the late 1920s.

command economy economic system in which the central authority makes all the production decisions on what and how to produce goods.

Commercial Revolution changes in the economies of Europe in the Middle Ages in which there was a growth of towns, banking systems, and trade among nations; the economic changes that opened up Europe to a global economy based on worldwide trade.

communism form of socialism proposed by Karl Marx and Friedrich Engels; characterized by a classless society that supports a common ownership of the means of production and equal distribution of the products of society; no class struggle and the government will wither away.

Confucianism belief system based on the teaching of the Chinese philosopher Confucius, also known as Kung Fu Zi; emphasizes traditional values such as obedience, knowing each person's role in society, and respect for education, elders, and leaders.

conquistadors Spanish explorers who conquered land in the Americas for Spain during the 1500s and 1600s.

Constitutional Monarchy system of government in which the power of the king or queen is limited or defined by the legislature or parliamentary body.

consumer goods tangible economic products used to satisfy the wants and needs of a society.

containment policy of the United States toward the Soviet Union during the Cold War to prevent the spread of communism in the world.

coup d'état (French term) swift overthrow of the government by force or by a small group of people.

Crusades religious wars between Christian Europe and the Muslims for control of the Holy Lands lasting from 1096 A.D. until 1246 A.D.

cultural diffusion spread of ideas, customs, and technology from one group or region to another culture.

Cultural Revolution program organized by Mao-Zedong in China in the 1960s against those who opposed the Communist government. Mao used the Red Guards (Chinese Youths) to purge China of anyone who disagreed with his ideas or policies.

culture people's way of life, which includes language, customs, religion, traditions, and institutions.

cuneiform ancient Sumerian form of writing developed around 3000 B.C. The wedge-shaped characters were formed by pressing a stick into wet clay.

Czar title of the Russian Emperor; also spelled tsar.

decolonization process by which European colonies in Africa and Asia became independent countries after World War II ended.

deforestation destruction of a forest, especially the tropical rain forest, to clear the land to raise food or sell the lumber. The remaining soil is of poor quality because heavy rains wash away the nutrients; the land becomes barren.

democracy system of government in which the people rule.

demographic pattern population distribution.

depression period of drastic economic decline, characterized by a large increase in unemployment, falling prices, and wages.

desalination process of removing salt from sea water in order to make it drinkable.

desertification process by which fertile land becomes a desert due to natural causes or sometimes by man's destructive use of the land.

détente relaxation of tension between the United States and the Soviet Union during the 1970s. The policy was developed by U.S. President Richard Nixon and Soviet leader Leonid Brezhnev.

developed countries highly industrialized nations that have advanced technology.

developing countries countries that are in the process of industrializing, have limited resources, and poor educational and health systems; mainly located in Africa, Asia, and Latin America.

dharma religious duties and rights of each individual of each class within the Hindu belief system.

Diaspora forced scattering of the Jewish people from their homeland in Palestine by the Chaldeans in 586 B.C. and later by the Romans in

70 A.D., resulting in the establishment of Jewish communities throughout Europe and North Africa; scattering of African people because of the slave trade.

dictatorship system of government in which one person or one party rules the government with absolute control.

disarmament reduction or limiting weapons and military forces as outlined in a treaty.

dissident a person who openly disagrees with the policies or methods of a political party or government, such as those who disagree with the policies of the Communist Party in China or Cuba.

divine right belief that the king or queen was God's earthly representative and received all power directly from God.

domestic system system of manufacturing prior to the Industrial Revolution in which weavers and craftsmen produced goods at home.

dynasty series of rulers from the same family or line of descent.

economics study of how people make a living; how goods and services are produced and distributed to satisfy people's needs.

embargo government order restricting the selling of a particular product to or trading with another nation.

empire groups of territories controlled by one ruler or government.

encomienda system established by the Spanish government in the Americas that enabled the colonists to tax or get labor from the Native Americans.

enlightened despot absolute ruler who bases decisions on the Enlightenment ideas; uses absolute power to begin social changes.

Enlightenment period known as the Age of Reason in 18th-century Europe. Enlightenment thinkers believed that one could use reason to understand the universe; they rejected traditional ideas based on authority.

Estates-General legislative assembly of France composed of clergy, nobles, and commoners.

ethics standards or rules that guide human behavior.

ethnic cleansing term used to describe the forcible removal or murder of Muslims from former Yugoslav provinces of Bosnia and Herzegovina by the Serbian Christian majority during the years 1992–1995; similar policy used by Serbs in Kosovo against the Muslims in 1998.

ethnic group group of people sharing a common language, religion, history, and cultural heritage.

ethnocentrism prejudicial belief that one's culture or standards are superior to those of other societies.

Eurodollar uniform currency introduced in Europe in 1999.

expansionism policy of increasing a nation's territory at the expense of another nation.

exploitation term used to describe how the mother countries took advantage of their colonies to insure that their own economies grew.

extended family family made up of grandparents, parents, children, aunts, uncles, and cousins whose members may live in the same household or area; this type of family structure exists primarily in a traditional society.

extraterritorality special right of citizens of a foreign country to be tried for a crime by the laws and courts of their own nation; applied to Westerners in China during the 19th and 20th centuries.

factory system system that brought workers and machines together to produce goods in large quantities; began in the British textile industry during the Industrial Revolution.

famine drastic shortage of food that results in severe starvation and hunger.

fascism political philosophy that glorifies the nation over the individual. A dictator has complete control, suppresses all opposition, promotes a policy of extreme nationalism and racism, and has no regard for democracy.

Fertile Crescent large arc of land in the Middle Eastern area between the Tigris and Euphrates Rivers; mostly desert or semiarid land; called the Cradle of Civilization.

feudalism political, economic, and social system developed in Europe and Japan during the 1100s in which land is controlled by the local lord, who owed allegiance to a higher lord or monarch. The lord allowed serfs to work the land in exchange for protection.

Five Pillars of Wisdom basic beliefs of Islam that include: one God, Allah, praying five times a day, fasting during the month of Ramadan, making a pilgrimage to Mecca, and giving alms to the poor.

Five-Year Plan series of economic goals set by the government in either a Communist or Socialist system; instituted by Joseph Stalin in Russia in 1927 to build up industry and improve farm production.

fossil fuels fuel such as oil, coal, wood, and natural gas.

free enterprise economic system in which individuals and businesses have the freedom to operate for profit with little or no government interference.

free trade removal of trade restrictions among nations.

genocide deliberate effort to kill all members of an ethnic or religious group.

geography one of the social sciences that studies the people, the environment, and the resources of an area.

glasnost Russian term for "openness"; refers to Mikhail Gorbachev's effort in the 1980s to introduce political reform in the Soviet Union by providing freedom of speech and press.

globalization integration of capital, technology, and information across national borders, creating a single global market and, to some degree, a global village.

Great Depression worldwide economic decline that began in 1929 and ended in 1940; businesses and banks failed and there was widespread joblessness.

Great Leap Forward five-year economic program introduced by Mao Zedong in China in 1958; designed to improve China's agricultural and industrial production.

greenhouse effect rise in the global temperature due to excessive carbon dioxide and pollutants that create a layer in the atmosphere that traps the heat.

Green Revolution twentieth-century technological advances in agriculture that have led to increased food production on a limited parcel of land.

gross national product (GNP) total value of goods and services produced in one year; indicator of a country's standard of living.

heavy industry industries requiring complex machinery in the production of iron, steel, and coal.

heliocentric theory belief that the sun is the center of the universe and that earth and the planets revolve around it.

hierarchy group of people or things arranged or organized by rank or level of importance.

hieroglyphics ancient Egyptian writing system that uses pictures and symbols to represent sounds, words, or ideas.

Hinduism major religion of India based on a rigid caste system containing rules for proper behavior. Karma, or a person's behavior, influences his or her reincarnation after death into a higher or lower caste. An endless cycle of rebirth is created for each soul.

Holocaust Nazi genocide against Jews and other minorities during World War II, resulting in the death of millions of people.

Holy Land sacred Israel/Palestine area where Christian, Islamic, and Judaic shrines are located commemorating the birth of their religions.

humanism intellectual and cultural movement of the Renaissance stressing the significance of each individual; focused on the secular world and a return to a study of the classical works of Greece and Rome.

human rights freedom and rights that all people belonging to a society are entitled to, such as freedom of expression, life, religion, right to vote, and equal protection before the law.

ideology system of beliefs and ideas that guide a nation or group of people.

illiteracy inability to read or write; one measure of a country's industrial development and standard of living.

imperialism policy whereby one nation dominates by direct or indirect rule the political, economic, and social life of a foreign country, region, or area.

indemnity payment of damages or losses suffered in war.

Industrial Revolution historical event that began in the textile industry in England in the 18th century resulting in the shift from the manufacturing of goods by hand to the use of machinery, along with social and economic changes accompanying this change.

inflation economic cycle resulting in a general rise in prices and a decline in the purchasing power of money.

interdependence mutual way in which the economies of countries are dependent on the goods, resources, and knowledge from other parts of the world.

Internet global computer connection using telephone lines or modems providing online contact with people and information on most subjects.

intifada Palestinian uprising against the territory held by Israel that lasted from 1987 until 1988.

Iron Curtain term coined by Winston Churchill in 1946 to describe an imaginary line dividing Soviet Communist-dominated Eastern Europe and the democracies of Western Europe.

Islam name that means submission to the will of God; major religion of the Middle East founded in the seventh century A.D. by the prophet Muhammad whose teachings include belief in one God—Allah.

Islamic Fundamentalists Muslims who believe that public and private behavior should be guided by the principles and values in the Koran. They are against the materialism of Western society.

isolationism policy of avoiding or limiting involvement in the affairs or conflicts of other nations.

jihad Muslim holy war to spread the Muslim faith.

Judaism monotheistic religion of the Hebrews whose spiritual and ethical principles are rooted in the Old Testament of the Bible and in the Talmud.

junta group of military officers who rule a country after seizing power.

Justinian Code codification of Roman law by the Emperor Justinian in the 6th century that greatly influenced the Western legal system.

kaiser German word for emperor used in the 1870s and early 1900s.

karma belief in Hinduism, that people's lifelong deeds and actions affect their fate in their future life.

kibbutz collective farms established by Jewish settlers in Israel that are based on socialist principles of shared ownership and communal living.

Koran sacred book of Islam containing the revelations made by Allah to Muhammad.

kulak group of wealthy peasants in the Soviet Union who opposed the collectivization of agriculture in the 1920s and 1930s.

laissez-faire economic policy stating that there should be a "hands off" or limited government involvement with private business.

Law of Twelve Tablets basis of Roman law written on twelve tablets around 450 B.C. and displayed in the marketplace for all to see and know.

less-developed countries (LDC) countries with few industries and poor health and educational systems.

liberalism political philosophy supporting social changes, democracy, and personal freedom.

liberation theology movement in the Catholic Church in Latin America in the late 1970s and 1980s urging the clergy to take an active role in changing the social conditions of the poor.

limited monarchy system of government in which the king's powers are not absolute but specifically guided by a constitution or legislative body.

literacy rate percentage of people in a country with the ability to read and write; method used to measure the standard of living of a country.

mandate of heaven belief in ancient China that the Emperor received the authority to rule from heaven (God), and in return, the people owed compete obedience to the ruler; divine right theory.

manoralism economic and social system in Medieval Europe; a self-sufficient community in which the serfs were bound to the land and were required to work on the lord's manor or estate that consisted of farmland, a village, the lord's castle, and surrounding lands administered by the lord.

market economy economic system in which the laws of supply and demand and the price system influence the decisions of the consumer and the producers of goods.

Marshall Plan formally known as the European Recovery Act; American economic aid package proposed by Secretary of State George Marshall in 1947 to assist European countries in rebuilding after World War II as a way to strengthen democratic governments against communism. The United States gave $17 billion in aid from 1947 to 1951.

Marxism political and economic theory developed by Karl Marx and Friedrich Engels in support of an economic interpretation of history that contributed to a class struggle between the haves and have nots; belief that private ownership must be abolished in favor of collective ownership.

matriarchy system in which ancestry is traced through the mother and her descendants.

medieval historical period known as the Middle Ages lasting from about 500 A.D. until the beginning of the 1400s.

Meiji Restoration period lasting from 1868 to 1912 when Japan adopted Western ways in order to become a modern and industrialized nation.

mercantilism economic theory developed during the 17th and 18th centuries in which the colonies existed for the benefit of the mother country; wealth and power of a country based on exporting more than it imported through strict regulation of colonial trade.

mestizo people of mixed European and Native American ancestry in the Spanish colonies of Latin America.

militarism policy glorifying the armed forces; support of aggressive military preparedness.

mixed economy economic system combining government regulation of industries with private enterprise or capitalistic characteristics.

modernization change in a nation from a traditional economy or way of life to modern ideas, methods, and technology.

monopoly complete control by one person or group over a particular product or market resulting in the ability to set or fix market prices.

monotheism belief in one God.

monsoons seasonal winds from the Indian Ocean that bring heavy rain. They dominate the climate of South Asia, the Middle East, and East Africa.

Mosque Muslim house of worship.

multinational corporation large business enterprises such as Coca-Cola and McDonald's that have branches in many countries.

Muslim follower of the Islamic religion.

nationalism feeling of pride in and loyalty to one's nation or group and its traditions; belief that each group is entitled to its own nation or government.

nationalization government seizure of private businesses or industries.

nation-state political state that developed in Western Europe at the end of the Middle Ages with the decline of feudalism. At that time, the strong monarchs of England and France united people of a common nationality who began to transfer their loyalty from the local lord to the monarch who molded a unified national state. Today it refers to a country with a strong central government and a common history and culture.

natural laws rules of human behavior based on reason and an inborn sense of morality. Enlightenment philosophers thought these laws were universal.

Nazism policies associated with German dictator Adolf Hitler of the National Socialist Party stressing militarism, racism, and extreme nationalism.

Neolithic Revolution the New Stone Age (8000–300 B.C.) or the Agricultural Revolution; changes brought about when people began to settle in small communities, domesticated animals, and secured food by farming.

neutrality policy of not supporting any one side in a conflict.

New Economic Policy (NEP) policy introduced by Lenin in 1921 in the Soviet Union providing for some restoration of private enterprise and capitalism in order to ease the economic crisis created by the civil war in Russia (1918–1921).

nomad person who has no fixed home and travels from place to place in search of food and other necessities of life.

nonaggression pact agreement between two nations to not attack each other.

nonalignment policy that some Third World nations followed during the Cold War of not supporting either the United States or the Soviet Union.

nuclear family family structure usually found in industrial societies consisting of only parents and their children.

oligarchy form of government in which a small group or elite has power.

oral tradition the practice of passing on history and culture of a society through the spoken word.

overpopulation condition in many developing countries where the population is too large to be supported by the available resources of the region.

Palestine Liberation Organization (PLO) group formed in 1964 and led by Yasir Arafat whose goal was to establish a Palestinian homeland by the use of terrorist tactics in the lands occupied by Israel. The PLO later renounced terrorism and became the official organization to negotiate with Israel over the creation of a Palestinian state.

Pan-Africanism nationalist movement that began in the early 1900s encouraging unification and cooperation among all African nations.

Pan-Arabism mid-twentieth-century movement promoting the unification of all Arab countries based on cultural and political ties.

Pan-Slavism nationalist movement promoting the cultural and political unification of Slavic people.

parliamentary system type of government in which representatives to the legislative branch of government (Parliament) are democratically elected by the people and the majority party in Parliament selects a prime minister from their ranks. Parliament has supreme legislative powers.

passive resistance form of civil disobedience using nonviolent methods; technique used by Indian leader Mohandas Gandhi, included the boycott of British goods and refusal to pay taxes or serve in the army as a way to promote Indian independence. A similar approach was adopted by Dr. Martin Luther King, Jr., in the civil rights movement in the United States during the 1960s.

patriarchy family organization in which the father or eldest son heads the household.

patricians wealthy landowners or nobles of the ancient Roman Empire.

Pax Mongolia brief period of peace and prosperity in Eurasia during the Mongol rule of Kublai Khan.

Pax Romana time of Roman peace and relative prosperity in the Mediterranean world beginning in 27 B.C. and lasting over 200 years during the time of the Roman Empire.

peaceful coexistence Soviet policy adopted by Nikita Khrushchev in the 1950s, believing that communism and democracy could exist with each other peacefully and avoid hostility.

peasants small farmers or laborers who work the land.

peninsular person born in Spain or Portugal who was eligible for the highest position in the Latin American colonies.

per capita income average income per person of all the citizens in a country; one way to measure the standard of living of a country.

perestroika Russian term for reconstructing; Gobachev's economic policy of the 1980s promoting private enterprise and the free market system instead of a strict government-planned economy.

pharaoh title of rulers of ancient Egypt who had absolute power.

planned economy system in which the government determines what, how much, and who is allowed to receive the goods that are produced; used by the Soviet Union starting in 1927 and lasting until the 1980s.

pogroms organized attacks or persecutions against a minority group, particularly the Jews in czarist Russia.

polis independent city-state in ancient Greece.

polytheism worship or belief in many gods.

population distribution average number of people in a particular area or region.

population explosion large increase in the world's population due to the availability of better medical technology contributing to a longer life expectancy for children and adults.

prehistoric referring to a period of time prior to written history, around 3000 B.C.

primary source eyewitness account or firsthand information about people or events such as diaries or legal documents.

privatization returning or selling of government facilities to private individuals or investors.

proletariat term used by Marx and Engels to describe the industrial working class in capitalist countries.

propaganda spreading of ideas, information, and rumors to promote a cause or damage an opposing cause.

protectorate form of imperial control in which the foreign country allows the local ruler to remain in power but controls affairs behind the scenes.

Protestant Reformation period beginning in 1527 in Europe when Martin Luther challenged the authority of the Pope resulting in the formation of new Christian churches that opposed the rules and doctrines of the Roman Catholic Church.

racism prejudice and discrimination based on the premise that one group is superior to another because of race.

reactionary political leader who is opposed to change or wants to restore the old order such as those leaders at the Congress of Vienna in the 1800s.

recession decline in economic activities that lasts for a limited amount of time.

reform to try to make things better by change.

reincarnation Hindu belief that the soul is reborn in different forms that indicate whether a person led a good or bad life.

Renaissance French word meaning rebirth; period of reawakened interest in the classical works of art, literature, and architecture of Greece and Rome that originated in Italy and spread throughout all of Europe from the 1300s until the 1600s; challenged the ideas and structure of the Middle Ages.

reparation payment for war damages.

republic form of government in which the people choose their officials.

revolution sudden and drastic change resulting in the overthrow of the existing government or political system by force, as in the Russian Revolution; changes in cultural systems, as in the Industrial or Computer Revolution.

Russification policy adopted by Russian Tsar Alexander III in 1882. Its purpose was to unite the empire's many provinces. It became an official policy of intolerance and persecution of non-Russian people. Jews were singled out in particular for persecution.

samurai members of the Japanese warrior class during the medieval period.

sanctions penalties or actions imposed on a nation by other countries for breaking international laws in order to end its illegal activity.

satellite countries countries politically and economically controlled by a nearby country such as the Eastern European countries that were dominated by the Soviet Union after World War II.

savanna broad grassy plain with few trees in a tropical or subtropical region that has an irregular rain pattern.

scapegoats people who are made to bear the blame for the actions of others; technique used by the Nazi Party in Germany against the Jews for problems confronting the country in the 1920s and 1930s.

scarcity fundamental economic problem describing limited resources combined with unlimited wants and needs.

Scientific Revolution period in science during the 16th and 17th centuries in which scientists challenged traditional authority and used observations and reason to reach conclusions; contributed to advances in medicine and mathematics.

scramble for Africa time period from 1890 to 1914 when European imperialistic countries divided up the continent for markets and raw materials.

secondary source information about past historical events based on the knowledge collected from several sources.

secularism rejection of the importance of religion in favor of worldly matters.

self-determination right of the people to make their own decisions about their political and economic development.

serf peasant in feudal times who was legally bound to the land, owned by the lord and subject to the will of the lord.

Shintoism native Japanese religion stressing the connection between people and the forces of nature. In the 18th century it became the national religion of Japan extolling nationalism, ancestor worship, and divinity of the emperor.

shoguns military generals who ruled Japan from the 12th century to the 1800s.

Sikhs people who live primarily in the Punjab area of Northern India; followers of a religion formed in the early 1500s that blends elements of Islam and Hinduism, rejects the caste system, and is monotheistic.

Silk Road ancient Chinese commercial route that stretched for over 4,000 miles, allowing China to exchange its silk for Middle Eastern and European products.

social contract political theory of 17th- and 18th-century Europe stating that there is an agreement between the people and the government, with people giving up power to their leader in return for life, liberty, and property; governments that fail to fulfill their agreement can be changed.

socialism system in which the government owns and operates all the essential means of production, distribution, and exchange of goods; society as a whole, not the individuals, owns all the property.

social mobility ability to move from one social class to another through education or improvement in income or occupation.

Solidarity independent trade union movement led by Lech Walesa of Poland contributing to the demise of communism.

Soviet bloc countries in the Cold War that were allied with or supported the Soviet Union.

sphere of influence area or region of a country in which a foreign country had exclusive trading privileges such as the right to build railroads and factories; special regions along the coast of China in the 19th century controlled by European imperial countries.

standard of living measure of how well people are living based upon the availability of resources and wealth.

status quo describing a state of affairs existing as they are at the present time.

subsistence agriculture type of farming in which the farmer and his family can barely make a living.

suffrage the right to vote.

Superpowers the United States and the Soviet Union, which dominated world politics from the end of World War II until the late 1980s.

supply and demand economic theory of a market economy that prices reflect the demand for a product and its availability.

tariff tax on goods coming into the country usually to protect industries from foreign competition.

technology use of science and inventions to help society achieve its basic needs or improve a way of living.

Ten Commandments religious and moral laws of Judaism; also adopted by the Christians as part of their moral laws.

terrorism deliberate use of force or violence by an organized group to achieve its political goals.

theocracy nation ruled by religious leaders who base their power on the Divine Right.

Third World term used to describe the developing nations of Africa, Asia, and Latin America.

totalitarianism government in which one person or group controls all aspects of the political, economic, social, religious, educational, and cultural life of the nation with no regard for individual rights.

total war commitment of a nation's entire military and civilian resources to the war effort.

trade deficit excess of imports over exports.

traditional economy economic system that meets the basic needs of its people through fishing, hunting, and gathering; basic economic decisions are made according to customs or habits.

tyrant ruthless and unfair ruler in ancient Greece who gained power by force and established a one-man rule.

untouchable (harijan) name derived from the ideas that others would be made dirty and impure from touching them; social group belonging to the lowest caste in Hinduism who do all the undesirable work; outlawed by the Indian Constitution but still prevalent in some communities.

urbanization development of cities due to the movement of people from rural areas in search of jobs and better opportunities.

utopian 19th-century socialist who believed in the ideal society in which all members of society worked for the common good and shared equally in the economic success of the group.

vassal lord in medieval Europe who received land from a more powerful lord in exchange for loyalty and service.

vernacular language of the people in a country; language used by Renaissance writers to replace Latin, which was the language of the church or scholars.

war crimes atrocities committed by the military or the government against the civilian population during armed conflicts; they include mass murders, genocide, rape, or persecution of religious or racial groups. Since World War II, war crime tribunals such as Nuremburg and The Hague have been set up to deal with these crimes against humanity.

welfare state system under which the government assumes responsibility for the people's social and economic well-being.

Westernization process of adapting Western culture and technology; adapted by Peter the Great of Russia in the 18th century and during the Meiji Restoration of Japan in the 19th century.

zero population growth situation in which the birth rate of a country equals the death rate.

Zionism worldwide organized movement to build or gain support for a Jewish homeland in Palestine.

INTERNATIONAL ORGANIZATIONS AND AGREEMENTS

Antarctic Treaty treaty signed in 1959 by the United States, the Soviet Union, and ten other nations forbidding the building of military bases, testing of nuclear weapons, or disposing of radioactive wastes by these nations in the area near the Antarctic. It was meant to foster cooperation among scientists from all nations who conduct research on the continent; other nations later signed this treaty.

ANZUS Pact mutual defense agreement among Australia, New Zealand, and the United States, signed in 1951 to contain communism; considered an attack upon one of the others as dangerous to its own safety.

Arab League organization founded by Arab nationalists in 1945 to promote Arab unity during times of crisis; worked jointly for common economic, political, and social goals; presently, all sixteen nations in the Middle East are members along with four other African nations in which the majority of the population is Arab.

Asia Pacific Economic Cooperation Group (APEC) group formed by the nations of the Pacific Rim including countries in Southeast Asia, East Asia, and the Americas that border the Pacific Ocean; goal is to promote trade and investment across the Pacific region and the world.

Association of Southeast Asian Nations (ASEAN) organization consisting of seven members that are archipelago nations in Southeast Asia and nations on the Indochina peninsula; seeks to promote economic and cultural cooperation as well as solve regional disputes.

Camp David Accords agreement negotiated by President Jimmy Carter between Prime Minister Menachem Begin of Israel and President Anwar Sadat of Egypt; later became the basis of the peace treaty in 1979 calling for diplomatic recognition of Israel by Egypt and normalization of relations, the return of the Sinai Peninsula to Egypt in exchange for the opening of the Suez canal to Israel, and discussion on Palestinian self-rule in the West Bank and the Gaza Strip.

Caribbean Community and Common Market (CARICOM) formed in 1973 to promote cooperation in the areas of economics and foreign policy among the 13 Caribbean countries.

Commonwealth of Independent States (CIS) association created in December 1991 to replace the government when the Soviet Union collapsed; consisted of 12 of the 15 independent republics including Russia, Ukraine, and Belarus, whose city of Minsk became CIS headquarters; designed to promote economy and political cooperation among the former Communist republics.

Commonwealth of Nations (originally known as the British Commonwealth of Nations established by the Statute of Westminster enacted in 1931); voluntary association linking Great Britain and its former colonies on an equal basis; 47 members try to coordinate economic, political, social, and military matters.

Council of Europe old European organization established by the Treaty of London; an international organization in Strasbourg comprised of 41 democratic countries of Europe. Its purpose is to promote democratic stability and economic and social progress for Europe; composed of a committee of ministers, a secretariat, selected for five years, and an assembly of delegates; council advises on social, political, and economic matters but has no power of enforcement. It is an influential organization because all European nations are members and participate in activities.

Dayton Accord agreement negotiated to end the conflict in Bosnia-Herzegovina in November 1995 at Dayton, Ohio by three presidents: Slobodan Milosevic of Serbia, Aliza Izetbegovic of Bosnia-Herzegovina, and Franjo Tudjman of Croatia, with strong diplomatic assistance from U.S. President Bill Clinton; signed in December; provided for the partition of Bosnia and Herzegovina into two distinct areas—a Serb republic and a Muslim Croat federation; 60,000 multinational forces were provided to safeguard the peace.

European Economic Community (EEC) organization established in 1958 by Belgium, Luxembourg, France, Italy, the Netherlands, and West Germany, which agreed to form a Common Market to expand free trade by eliminating internal tariff barriers and allowing labor and capital to move freely among member nations. Now called the European Union, it includes Great Britain, Ireland, Spain, Portugal, Greece, and Denmark; by the 1990s, membership increased to 15 countries with the addition of Finland, Sweden, and Austria.

European Parliament legislative branch of the European Union founded in 1958; composed of 518 representatives elected by the votes of member nations for five years; powers are advisory with all final decisions requiring approval of the ministers of the Council of Europe.

European Union group that includes the countries that were members of the European Coal and Steel Community, European Atomic Energy Commission, and the European Economic Community (Common Market); official name since 1967 after the merger of these three organizations into one governing unit.

General Agreement on Tariffs and Trade (GATT) agreement signed in 1947 to provide for free trade among member nations and to settle trading disputes; consists of 110 members; Group of Seven (G7) representing the seven most productive economies—Britain, Canada, France, Germany, Italy, Japan, and the United States—meet annually to discuss common economic problems. In 1995, the World Trade Organization (WTO) was formed as the successor to GATT.

Helsinki Accords major diplomatic nonbinding agreement signed on August 1, 1975, at Helsinki, Finland, among the United States, Canada, the Soviet Union, and 32 European nations except Albania; agreed to legitimize the USSR's World War II territorial gains (status quo in Europe), agreed to respect human rights, and to promote scientific and cultural exchanges with each other.

International Court of Justice agency of the United Nations consisting of 15 judges; power to settle disputes among nations by majority vote; nations that submit disputes must agree in advance to accept all decisions.

International Monetary Fund (IMF) financial agency of the United Nations established after World War II to promote international trade, help developing nations with troubled economies, and provide balance for currencies of member nations.

Israeli-PLO Accord (The Oslo Accord) agreement negotiated by Israeli Prime Minister Yitzhak Rabin and Palestinian Yasir Arafat in September 1993; provided for Israel and PLO recognition of each other, eventual Palestinian self-government in the West Bank and Gaza Strip, and the gradual withdrawal of Israeli troops from these areas; implemented in May 1994 in the West Bank city of Jericho and the Gaza Strip. In 1995, following difficult negotiations with the PLO, Israel agreed to the removal of forces from other Palestinian areas and the establishment of a Palestinian police force to govern these regions.

League of Nations world peace organization with headquarters in Geneva, Switzerland, created by the Versailles Treaty at the end of World War I. Failure of the United States to join and the lack of power to enforce decisions contributed to its demise as a peacekeeping organization; precursor of the UN, which replaced the League at the end of World War II.

Montreal Protocol agreement signed in 1987 at Montreal, Canada, by 46 nations; urged that the world's nations reduce the use of chemicals that were damaging the earth's ozone layers.

North Atlantic Treaty Organization (NATO) defensive alliance formed in 1949 as a way to contain communism in Europe; members Britain, France, Belgium, the Netherlands, Luxembourg, Denmark, Iceland, Italy, Norway, Portugal, Canada, and the United States agreed that an attack on one was an attack on all and they would assist each other; Greece, Turkey, West Germany, and Spain later became members; extended membership to Poland, Hungary, and Czech Republic in 1997.

North American Free Trade Agreement (NAFTA) agreement signed by the United States, Canada, and Mexico in 1991 and implemented in 1993; designed to remove all tariffs, quotas, and trade barriers among the three nations over a 15-year period.

Northern Ireland Peace Accord agreement reached on April 10, 1998 (Good Friday) to bring peace to Northern Ireland; representatives of United Kingdom, Republic of Ireland, and leaders of Protestants and Catholics of Northern Ireland participated in the negotiations; agreed to a 108-member Northern Ireland Assembly in which Protestants and Catholics would share power, ending 26 years of direct rule from London; encouraged cooperation between Northern Ireland and the Republic of Ireland on issues of agriculture and tourism; renunciation of the Irish Republic to territorial claims in Northern Ireland; accord approved in May in a referendum by 71 percent of voters in Northern Ireland and 94 percent of voters in the Republic of Ireland.

Nuclear Test Ban Treaty signed in 1963 by Great Britain, the Soviet Union, and the United States prohibiting the testing of nuclear weapons in the atmosphere; underground testing was still permitted; nations could withdraw from the treaty if the test ban jeopardized national interest; the United Nations voted in 1996 to prohibit all future nuclear testing; only Pakistan and India failed to agree to it.

Organization of African Unity founded in 1963 by Kwame Nkrumah of Ghana to promote African unity, end colonialism, and foster cooperative approaches in foreign policies, economics, education, and defense; by 1994, with the end of white dominance in South Africa, there were 53 members with the admission of South Africa into the group.

Organization of American States (OAS) regional organization set up in 1948 to promote common defense of Western Hemisphere, democracy, economic cooperation, and human rights; headquarters in Washington, D.C.; members include the United States and 31 South American, Central American, and Caribbean countries; pressure by the United States led to the expulsion of Cuba, an original member, in 1962.

Organization of Petroleum Exporting Countries (OPEC) organization founded in 1960 by Iran, Iraq, Kuwait, Saudi Arabia, and Venezuela to control production and price of oil; membership expanded to include Algeria, Ecuador, Gabon, Indonesia, Iraq, Libya, Nigeria, Qatar, and United Arab Emirates.

SALT I and SALT II (Strategic Arms Limitations) agreements signed in 1972 and 1979; designed to limit the spread of nuclear weapons and reduction of specific types of new missile systems such as ICBM and SLBM; limits set on the number of heavy bombers carrying nuclear weapons and air-to-surface ballistic missiles with ranges of more than 375 miles.

START I (Strategic Arms Reduction Treaty) treaty signed by President George Bush and Soviet leader Mikhail Gorbachev on July 31, 1991, to reduce their strategic nuclear forces over a seven-year period by 25 to 35 percent; agreed to destroy their nuclear arsenals; ratified by the United States and Russia in 1992. Later, the former Republics of the Soviet Union Belarus, Kazakhstan, and Ukraine agreed to transfer their nuclear forces to Russia.

START II treaty signed by Presidents George Bush and Boris Yeltsin in January 1993; called for reduction of Russian nuclear warheads to 3,000 and those of the United States to 3,500 by the year 2003 or by the end of 2000, if the United States agreed to finance the dismantling of weapons in Russia; ratified by the United States in 1996; rejected by the Russian Parliament in 1997.

United Nations (UN) world peace organization established in 1945 with 185 members; included six major components: General Assembly, Secretariat, Economic and Social Council, International Court of Justice, Trusteeship Council (largely inactive with the end of colonialism), and Security Council. The Security Council keeps world peace and has five permanent members: China, France, former USSR, United Kingdom, and the United States, with ten rotating members. It has many specialized and autonomous agencies such as the World Bank, World Health Organization, and World Trade Organization.

Universal Declaration of Human Rights adopted by the United Nations General Assembly on December 10, 1948; outlined the basic rights of all individuals without regard to race, color, sex, or nationality.

Warsaw Pact mutual defense alliance formed in 1955 by Russia and its satellite nations of Eastern Europe; agreed to assist each other if attacked by Western powers; Cold War answer to NATO. The treaty is no longer operational since the collapse of communism in 1991.

World Bank specialized agency of the UN (International Bank for Reconstruction and Development) established in 1944; created to provide economic and technical help for developing nations to improve their condition; single most lending agency in international development.

World Health Organization (WHO) UN agency whose main activities include setting of international health standards. It provides information on fighting infectious diseases such as AIDS.

World Court (International Court of Justice) court consisting of 15 judges who meet in The Hague, Netherlands, and decide cases by majority votes; judges settle disputes between nations according to the principles of international law; nations submitting disputes to the court agree in advance to accept its decisions.

World Trade Organization (WTO) successor to GATT; organization with a membership of 117 countries; purpose is to make global trade free for all. The agency monitors trade agreements so that a trade benefit granted to one member must be extended to all other members; tries to settle disputes and foster the development of prospering economies by keeping tariffs low and promoting fair competition.

IMPORTANT PEOPLE

Akbar the Great (1542–1605) greatest Mogul Emperor of India; Muslim leader who promoted religious toleration with the Hindu majority; married a Hindu princess; established a strongly centralized rule and competent civil service.

Alexander the Great (356–323 B.C.) became king of Macedonia in 336 upon assassination of his father Philip; proceeded to control Greece and conquered the entire Persian Empire (Egypt, Asia Minor, the Fertile Crescent, and India); laid the foundation for the fusion of Greek and Middle Eastern cultures during the Hellenistic period; maintained peace and unity in the Middle East, which later influenced the Romans.

Annan, Kofi (1938–) elected UN secretary-general in 1997 for a five-year term of office; first secretary-general to rise through the ranks of the organization; first black African from sub-Saharan area (Ghana) to serve as head of the United Nations; educated in the United States; proposed UN reform such as consolidation of offices and revision of the UN charter to improve efficiency.

Arafat, Yasir (1929–2004) chief spokesman and leader of the Palestine Liberation Organization (PLO) since 1969; chief goal—destruction of the state of Israel. In 1974 he was the first representative of a nongovernmental agency to address the UN General Assembly; in 1988 he renounced terrorism; supported UN-sponsored resolution for a peaceful resolution of the Arab-Israeli crisis; formally recognized Israel's right to exist in 1993 and negotiated an accord with Israeli Prime Minister Rabin, providing for gradual implementation of Palestinian self-rule in the West Bank and Gaza Strip (over the next five years). In 1996 he was elected president of Palestinian-controlled areas of Gaza and the West Bank. The peace process has stalled over the issue of control of Jerusalem. Arafat promised to proclaim a Palestinian State in the West Bank by September 2000.

Aristotle (384–322 B.C.) Greek philosopher who wrote works on philosophy, science, government, and literature; served as personal tutor to Alexander the Great; his works influenced European thinking for over 200 years.

Assad, Hafez-al (1928–2000) president of Syria from 1971 to 2000; defense minister and leader of nationalist Ba'ath Party who led a successful coup after Syria's loss of the Golan Heights to Israel in the 1967 Six-Day War; domestic popularity rose after the 1973 Arab-

Israeli war in which Syria failed to gain the Golan Heights but the army performed creditably; authoritarian ruler who faced opposition at home from Muslim fundamentalists; supported the United States in the Gulf War of 1990; prior to his death expressed a willingness to negotiate with Israel over the Golan Heights.

Ataturk, Kemal (1881–1938) means Father of Turks; military officer who led the revolution in 1923 to overthrow the sultan; first president of Turkey from 1923 to 1938; introduced reform to create a secular state based on Western customs; Islamic law and Arabic script replaced by Western laws and alphabet; women were given the right to vote; separation of church/public schools; encouraged Western dress.

Augustus (63 B.C.–14 A.D.) first emperor of Rome; attained sole power after defeat of Mark Antony; Pax Romana, administrative reform that laid the foundation for growth of the Empire that lasted for centuries.

Begin, Menachem (1913–1992) Israeli prime minister from 1977 to 1983; signed Camp David Accords with Egypt calling for recognition of Israel, discussion of self-rule for Palestine, and withdrawal of Israeli troops from Sinai Peninsula; shared the Nobel Peace Prize in 1978 with Egyptian President Anwar Sadat.

Bismarck, Otto von (1815–1898) Prussian-born landowner known as the Iron Chancellor; responsible for unifying the German state into the German Empire in 1871 by a policy of Blood and Iron; unified Germany; dominated central Europe; upset the balance of power leading to an alliance between England and France in 1904.

Bolívar, Simón (1783–1830) Creole leader of the South American independence movement against Spanish rule; liberator of South America; led a series of campaigns resulting in independence for Venezuela, Colombia, Ecuador, Peru, and Bolivia.

Bonaparte, Napoleon (1769–1821) general and emperor of France; called "Son of Revolution"; gained control of France by a coup d'état in 1799; crowned emperor in 1801; very popular due to his reform of the French legal system (Napoleonic Code) and educational system (state-controlled education); improved finance system; conquered and dominated most of Europe except England; defeated by Allied Forces of Prussia, Russia, and England; exiled to Elba; returned and defeated at Waterloo; exiled to Saint Helena. He influenced the growth of nationalism in Europe.

Boutros Boutros-Ghali (1922–) first African and Arab to serve as secretary-general of United Nations; served from 1992 to 1997; member of Egyptian delegation that helped to negotiate Camp David Accords in 1978.

Brezhnev, Leonid (1906–1982) Soviet leader from 1964 to 1982 who succeeded Nikita Khrushchev; longest-ruling Communist leader after Stalin; followed the policy of détente; signed SALT, Helsinki Accords; harsh policy toward dissidents; invaded Czechoslovakia (1968) and Afghanistan (1980) to protect Soviet interests.

Castro, Fidel (1927–) Cuban revolutionary leader; premier since 1959 when he overthrew the Fulgencio Batista dictatorship; established Communist state; one of the last Communist leaders in the world; aided Communist movements in Africa and Latin America.

Catherine the Great (1729–1796) German-born empress of Russia who ruled from 1792 to 1796; extended Russia's border to the south against Ottoman Turks by securing a warm water port on Black Sea; in the West took part in the partition of Poland; efficient ruler who codified laws; began state-sponsored education for boys and girls; ruthless toward serfs; last of the great absolute monarchs of the 1700s.

Cavour, Camillo di (1810–1861) Italian political leader of Piedmont Sardinia from 1852 to 1859 and 1860 to 1861; considered the "Brains of Italian unification."

Charlemagne (742–814) king of the Franks; emperor of Holy Roman Empire from 800 to 814; founder of the first empire in the West after the fall of Rome; oversaw a cultural revival of arts and learning.

Chiang Kai-shek (1888–1975) also known as Jiang Jieshi; military leader of Chinese Nationalist Party (Kuomintang) after the death of Sun Yat-sen in 1925; involved in a civil war with Communist forces of Mao Zedong from 1927 to 1949; exiled to Taiwan after being defeated by Communists in 1949; strongly supported by the United States during his presidency of the Nationalist government of Taiwan from 1950 to 1975.

Churchill, Winston (1874–1965) prime minister of England during World War II; strongly condemned England's policy of appeasement toward Germany prior to World War II; coined the term "Iron Curtain" describing Eastern European countries under communism after 1945.

Columbus, Christopher (1451–1506) Italian explorer in the service of Spain who in 1492 attempted to reach Asia by sailing west and found the Western Hemisphere, thereby opening up continents to European exploration.

Confucius (551–479 B.C.) Chinese philosopher, teacher, and political advisor; founded Confucianism, a system of ethical conduct stressing the importance of tradition, respect for learning, obedience, reverence to family, and golden rule. His teaching's dominated China for over 2,000 years.

Copernicus, Nicolaus (1473–1543) Polish astronomer who advanced the heliocentric theory that earth and the other planets revolve around the sun; rejection of traditional view of earth as the center of the universe.

Darwin, Charles (1809–1882) British naturalist; wrote *The Origin of the Species*, stating the theory of evolution that human beings are evolved by natural selection or survival of the fittest; theory used by Europeans to justify Imperialism, "White Man's Burden," in the scramble for Africa.

Da Vinci, Leonardo (1452–1519) central figure of Italian Renaissance; artist, painter, engineer, scientist; most famous paintings are *Mona Lisa* and *The Last Supper*.

Deng Xiaoping (1904–1997) Chinese Communist political leader from 1976 to 1997; implemented economic reforms modernizing industry and allowing some privatizing of agriculture and consumer industries; allowed increased contact with the West; harsh treatment for the protest movement for political freedom at Tiananmen Square.

Descartes, René (1596–1650) French scientist, mathematician, and philosopher; considered the Father of Analytic Geometry; stressed power of reason: "I think, therefore I am."

Diaz, Porfirio (1830–1915) Mexican dictator, or *caudillo*, from 1876 to 1880 and from 1884 to 1911; brought foreign investments and economic stability to Mexico; prosperity for the rich and poverty for the lower classes.

Elizabeth I (1533–1603) absolute monarch of England from 1588 to 1603; restored the power of the Anglican Church; defeated the Spanish Armada in 1588; established England as a power in Europe; began colonization of the New World; brought peace and prosperity to the country.

Engels, Friedrich (1820–1895) German philosopher, socialist, and associate of Karl Marx; wrote the *Communist Manifesto*.

Frederick the Great (1712–1786) king of Prussia; ruled from 1740 to 1786; doubled the size of his kingdom through foreign wars and converted the country into an important European power; enlightened despot who supported educational and legal reforms and religious freedom.

Gama, Vasco da (1469–1524) Portuguese explorer who in 1498 sailed around southern Africa to India; first successful water journey from Europe to Asia; established Portuguese monopoly of Indian trade replacing Arab domination of the trade route.

Galilei, Galileo (1564–1642) Italian physicist and astronomer; discovered the law of falling bodies; used a telescope to confirm Copernicus' theory; Catholic Church condemned him as a heretic and forced him to recant.

Gandhi, Mohandas (1869–1948) Hindu nationalist leader of India's independence movement from Great Britain; revered as a prophet; called *Mahatma* (saintly one); advocated civil disobedience and passive resistance to achieve his goals; against mistreatment of women and Untouchables; assassinated in 1948 by a Hindu extremist.

Garibaldi, Giuseppe (1807–1882) Italian general and nationalist who led his volunteers (Red Shirts) in the capture of Naples and Sicily; the conquest led to the formation of a united Italy; known as "Sword of Italian Unification."

Genghis Khan (ca. 1167–1227) name means Universal Ruler; Mongol warrior; founded the largest land empire by unifying the Mongols; empire extended to Korea, Northern China, Central Asia, Middle East, and parts of European Russia; it had disintegrated by the late thirteenth century.

Gorbachev, Mikhail (1931–) Soviet leader of Communist Party who ruled from 1986 to 1991; introduced liberal policies of *glasnost*, or openness, for more democracy, and *perestroika,* economic reforms encouraging more free-market activities; was awarded Nobel Peace Prize in 1990 for permitting self-rule in Eastern Europe; resigned when Soviet Union collapsed in 1991.

Hammurabi (ca. 1792–1750 B.C.) king of Babylon who conquered city-states in the Tigris-Euphrates Valley forming the Babylonian Empire; responsible for the Code of Hammurabi, the oldest legal written code of laws that established rules for property, trade, slavery, and fair treatment of women.

Hitler, Adolf (1889–1945) German chancellor from 1933 to 1945; leader of the Nazi Party; brutal dictator whose policies led to the murder and persecution of Jews, and other minorities and dissidents; promoted extreme nationalism contributing to World War II; conquered Europe except for England; defeated by allied forces of United States, England, France, and Russia in 1945.

Ho Chi Minh (1890–1969) president of North Vietnam; founded Vietnamese Communist Party; Nationalist leader against French and United States in the Vietnam War.

Hussein, ibn Tala (King Hussein) (1935–1999) called Father of Modern Jordan, he ruled from 1955–1999; instrumental in drafting UN Resolution 242 in 1967 calling for Israel to withdraw from all occupied lands; resolution served as a benchmark for future negotiations; a shrewd political leader who survived the demands of Arab neighbors, Israel and Palestinian refugees, who are a majority in his country; in 1994 signed a peace treaty with Israel becoming the second Arab leader to end a state of war with Israel which had technically existed since 1945.

Hussein, Saddam (1937–2006) president and dictator of Iraq from 1979–2003; expansion policies led to war against Iran and the United States (Persian Gulf War 1990); despite disastrous defeat in both wars, maintained power by destroying all opposition, especially Kurd minority; development of chemical weapons led to problems with the United Nations and war with the United States starting in 2003.

Ivan IV (1533–1584) grandson of Ivan the Great; called Ivan the Terrible; created secret police to subdue *boyars* (aristocracy); extended Russian territories; attained absolute power and first to be crowned as tsar; ruled from 1547–1584; his death led to a civil war and foreign invasion of Russia.

Ivan the Great (1440–1505) ruled Russia from 1462–1505; ended Mongolian domination of his Moscow kingdom; first to assume title of tsar as a mandate from God.

Jefferson, Thomas (1743–1826) American statesman; third president of the United States (1801–1809); drafted Declaration of Independence borrowing from John Locke's idea of natural rights and the social contract; a child of the Enlightenment.

Jiang Zemin (1926–) Communist leader of China since 1997; introduced economic reforms to increase private ownership; little toleration for political dissenters.

Khomeini, Ayatollah (1900–1989) Islamic Fundamentalist who returned from exile in 1978 to lead a revolution resulting in the overthrow of the Shah of Iran; established an Islamic republic based on ideas contained in the Koran; rejected Westernization, particularly the United States, which he called "The Great Satan"; supported militants who held 52 American hostages for 444 days.

Khrushchev, Nikita (1894–1971) Stalin's successor, who became the first secretary of the Communist Party after Stalin's death in 1953; eliminated all opposition in a power struggle to become preeminent leader of the country; began the process of de-Stalinization in 1956; tried to increase agricultural production; supported peaceful coexistence but suppressed the Hungarian Revolution and constructed the Berlin Wall.

Klerk, Frederick Willem de (1936–) president of South Africa; released Nelson Mandela from prison in 1990; repealed the apartheid law; negotiated a plan to end white minority rule; shared the Nobel Peace Prize with Mandela in 1993; became a member of Mandela's government in 1994.

Lenin, Vladimir Ilyich (1870–1924) also known as Nikolai; founder of Bolshevik Party in Russia; set up Communist government in 1917; created Union of Soviet Socialist Republics in 1922 after defeating anticommunist forces of the Tsar and foreign nations; his death in 1924 led to a power struggle between Stalin and Trotsky.

Locke, John (1632–1704) seventeenth-century English philosopher; wrote *Two Treatises of Government* to justify the Glorious Revolution; asserted that people possessed the natural right to life, liberty, and property, that people enter a social contract with a government to achieve these goals, and if a government does not live up to these purposes, the people have the right to revolt. His ideas influenced Jefferson's Declaration of Independence and Rousseau's book, *Social Contract*.

Louis XIV (1638–1715) ruler of France known as "The Sun King"; reigned from 1643 to 1715; divine right ruler who exercised unlimited powers, put down nobles' revolts, established loyal middle-class civil servants, built an extravagant palace at Versailles, and developed commerce and industry. His lavish court and endless foreign wars left France almost bankrupt.

L'Ouverture, François (1743–1803) revolutionary leader of Haiti; led struggle for independence from Napoleon; ruled from 1798 to 1802; his success ended Napoleon's dream of an empire in the Americas.

Luther, Martin (1483–1546) German priest and leader of the Protestant

Reformation against the Catholic Church; challenged papal authority and questioned the selling of indulgences in *95 Theses* in 1517.

Machiavelli, Niccolò (1469–1527) Italian who served the Florentine Republic as secretary and diplomat; author of *The Prince*, which describes how rulers maintain and hold power: the ruler can ignore right or wrong and accept the idea that "the end justifies the means"; the successful ruler must be lion and fox (powerful and cunning).

Magellan, Ferdinand (ca. 1480–1521) Portuguese sea captain who led a Spanish-backed expedition sailing west around the southern tip of South America, crossed the Pacific, and was killed in the Philippines; his ship sailed around Africa and returned to Spain in 1522. He proved the world is round by being the first to circumnavigate the globe.

Mandela, Nelson (1918–) South African statesman; leader of the African National Congress; arrested in 1962 for his opposition to apartheid; spent 27 years in jail; became the international symbol for freedom against white minority rule in South Africa; released in 1990 and negotiated a plan with the white government to turn South Africa into a multiracial democracy; shared the Nobel Peace Prize with Frederick de Klerk in 1993; elected first black president in a free election in 1994; served from 1995 to 1999.

Mao Zedong (also known as Mao Tse-tung) (1893–1976) Chinese Communist leader who led the struggle against Nationalists from 1927 to 1949; established his regime in 1948 and ruled the People's Republic of China from 1949 to 1976; introduced Great Leap Forward to industrialize China and compelling people to join communes; initiated the Cultural Revolution to diminish all opposition and strengthen his power; his book *Quotations of Chairman Mao* promoted terrorist tactics; became a cult symbol (Maoism).

Marx, Karl (1818–1883) German philosopher and founder of modern socialism; wrote the *Communist Manifesto* with Friedrich Engels (1820–1895), proposing an economic interpretation of history; wrote *Das Kapital*, an analysis of economic and political aspects of capitalism.

Mazzini, Giuseppe (1805–1871) Italian patriot and founder of Young Italy, a secret society to promote Italian unity; headed short-lived Republic of Rome in 1849; continued his efforts for independence from Austria from abroad; "Soul of Italian Unification."

Muhammad (570–632) Arabian prophet; proclaimed himself messenger of Allah; founded Islam, the Muslim religion.

Mussolini, Benito (1883–1945) Fascist dictator of Italy (1924–1945); called *Il Duce* (leader); ally of Germany (Rome-Berlin Axis) in World War II; shot by Italian partisans in 1945.

Nassar, Gamal Abdel (1918–1970) president of Egypt from 1956 to 1970; seized power with other military officers by overthrowing King Farouk in 1953; nationalized the Suez Canal, resulting in war with Britain, France, and Israel; promoted economic businesses and irrigation projects such as the Aswan High Dam; supported Pan-Arabism to encourage unity in Arab world.

Nehru, Jawarhalal (also known as Pandit Nehru) (1889–1964) first prime minister of independent India in 1947, serving until his death in 1964; supported Gandhi's policy of civil disobedience; imprisoned during the 1930s for his activities; rejected Gandhi's proposal for hand production; urged industrialization; set up mixed economy; leader of nonaligned nations in the Cold War; father of Indira Gandhi, India's Prime Minister from 1966 to 1977.

Netanyahu, Benjamin (1949–) conservative prime minister of Israel from 1996 to 1999; his party opposed additional concessions to the Palestinians on the issue of the West Bank and Gaza Strip; replaced as prime minister in 1999 by moderate leader Ehud Barak.

Nkrumah, Kwame (1909–1972) African leader who became the first prime minister of Ghana; American-educated; promoted Pan-Africanism encouraging cooperation among African states; deposed in 1966 due to resentment created by his dictatorial policies.

Nicholas II (1868–1918) last Romanov Tsar of Russia; ruled from 1894 to 1917; abdicated in the Russian Revolution of March 1917; killed with his entire family by Bolsheviks (Communists) in 1918.

O'Higgins, Bernardo (1778–1842) Chilean general who led a revolt against Spain in 1816; ruled Chile from 1817 to 1823.

Owens, Robert (1771–1858) English industrialist and socialist; established utopian communities in New Lanark, Scotland, and New Harmony, Indiana, both of which failed.

Pahlevi, Shah Muhammed Reza (1919–1980) last shah of Iran who ruled from 1941 to 1978; autocratic ruler; employed secret police (Savak) and permitted no political opposition; encouraged economic and social modernization, including land reforms, literacy, and women's rights; pro-Western foreign policy; special relationship with the United States; overthrown by Ayatollah Ruhollah Khomeini in

1978; workers protested the poor economic conditions; religious leaders opposed his modernization policies.

Perón, Juan (1895–1974) elected president of Argentina in 1946 with the support of the military; established a dictatorial government; widely popular due to his wife, Eva; instituted economic nationalization of many industries (public works program) and political and social reforms; opposed by the Catholic Church; the poor economic conditions led to his exile to Spain in 1955; returned in 1973 and was reelected President; died in 1974.

Perry, Matthew (1794–1858) U.S. Navy Commodore; led the fleet that sailed into Tokyo harbor in 1854 and negotiated the reopening of Japan to American trade, which led to the resignation of the Shogun and modernization (Westernization) of Japan.

Peter the Great (1672–1725) Russian tsar from 1682 to 1725; wanted to model Russia after European culture instead of Byzantine or Asian culture; introduced Western ideas of science, education, and the military to make Russia strong; the need for windows (seaports) in the West led to war against Sweden, resulting in a port on the Baltic Sea; built St. Petersburg; absolute ruler who controlled the Nobles and the Russian Orthodox Church; his Westernization efforts had little impact on Russian masses.

Plato (427–347 B.C.) Greek philosopher; student of Socrates and teacher of Aristotle; wrote *The Republic* in which he rejected democracy for the ideal state ruled by philosophers.

Polo, Marco (1254–1324) Venetian merchant who visited China in 1275; lived at the court of the Mongol ruler Kublai Kahn until 1292; his book describing his visit to China aroused European interest in China's riches and led to European overseas exploration.

Rabin, Yitzhak (1922–1995) Israel's prime minister from 1974 to 1977 and 1992 to 1995; first prime minister to meet with Palestinian leader Yasir Arafat; agreed to set up Palestinian self-rule in the Gaza Strip, the city of Jericho, and the West Bank; negotiated a peace treaty with King Hussein of Jordan; awarded the Nobel Peace Prize in 1994; assassinated in 1995.

Rousseau, Jean-Jacques (1712–1778) French philosopher of the Enlightenment; wrote the *Social Contract*, claiming that "Man is born free and everywhere he is in chains," and that the people give power to the government (General Will) to act for the good of the people and also have the right to overthrow the government if it fails the people; his ideas were used to support democracy and justify dictatorship under the General Will.

Sadat, Anwar (1918–1981) Egyptian president from 1970 to 1981; directed nation's policy away from dependence on Soviet Union; promoted foreign investments, some privatization of businesses; first Arab leader to visit Israel; signed Camp David Accords with Israeli Prime Minister Menachem Begin in 1978; shared the Nobel Peace Prize with Begin; assassinated in 1981.

Siddhartha Gautama (566–486 B.C.) founder of Buddhism; Indian nobleman who left his comfortable life for one of self-denial and meditation; rejected Hindu caste system; as Buddha, the Enlightened One, he taught Four Noble Truths to achieve Nirvana.

Smith, Adam (1723–1790) social philosopher and economist; founder of modern economics; authored *The Wealth of Nations*; believed in the doctrine of laissez-faire—government should keep a "hands-off" approach to business.

Socrates (469–399 B.C.) Greek philosopher of ancient Athens; advocated the maxim, "Know thyself"; left no written works; refused to renounce his principles even in the face of death when accused of treason for corrupting the minds of youth.

Stalin, Joseph (Josef Dzhugashvili) (1879–1953) dictator of the Soviet Union from 1925 to 1953; used his position as general secretary of the Communist Party to gain absolute power; established a totalitarian state; crushed all opposition by terror and mass executions; introduced a five-year plan to transform Russia into an industrial giant; allied with the West during World War II.

Suleiman the Magnificent (1494–1566) Ottoman sultan who ruled from 1520 to 1566; strong military leader; extended Ottoman control in the Balkans as far as Vienna; conquered North Africa and Mesopotamia; introduced a fair system of justice and strict control of finances; supporter of the arts; made Istanbul into a city of imposing architecture.

Sun Yat-sen (also known as Sun Yixian) (1866–1925) leader of the Chinese revolt against the Manchu Dynasty in 1911; founded the Chinese Republic; briefly served as president; believed in three principles of democracy, nationalism, and people's livelihood to make China strong.

Teresa, Mother (1910–1997) Roman Catholic nun who founded a missionary order to provide food, shelter, and medical help for underprivileged people of India; won the Nobel Peace Prize in 1979 for her humanitarian efforts.

Trotsky, Leon (Lev Bronstein) (1879–1940) Russian revolutionary who worked with Lenin to overthrow the Tsar in November 1917; directed the Red Army in the civil war from 1917 to 1922; lost the power struggle with Stalin after Lenin's death; exiled and assassinated in Mexico by Stalin's order in 1940.

Tutu, Desmond (1931–) Anglican Archbishop in South Africa who won the Nobel Peace Prize in 1984 for his opposition to apartheid; his leadership created worldwide pressure on South Africa to end its repressive policies; appointed head of Truth and Reconciliation by Nelson Mandela to investigate the injustices of apartheid.

Voltaire (François Marie Arouet) (1694–1778) French philosopher; major figure of the Enlightenment; supported control by enlightened absolute rulers and despots; his satirical works mocked the Church and royal authority; exiled to England for three years; praised Britain's limited monarchy; credited with the statement, "I disapprove of what you say, but I will defend to the death your right to say it."

Walesa, Lech (1943–) first democratically elected president of Poland, from 1990 to 1995, in the post-Soviet era; electrician in a Gdansk shipyard who led a strike for better wages and living conditions against the Communist government; formed Solidarity, an independent labor union; arrested for his activities and released; became an international hero; awarded the Nobel Peace Prize in 1983. In 1989 he helped to make Solidarity a legal political party and end Communist rule in Poland.

Yelstin, Boris (1931–) rival of Gorbachev who opposed the slow pace of political and economic reform of the 1980s; elected president of the Russian Republic in 1991; led the resistance to the conservative coup to oust Gorbachev; resigned from the Communist Party and became the first popularly elected president of Russia with the end of communism in 1991; elected in 1996 to a five-year term as president of the Russian federation. Unable to solve Russia's economic problems and ethnic tensions, his poor personal health caused him to resign the presidency in 1999 in favor of Valdimir Putin, his protegé.

Zapata, Emiliano (1879 [?]–1919) Mexican revolutionary and Native Indian leader who helped overthrow the dictator Porfirio Diaz; supported by peasants whose battle cry was "Land and liberty!"; assassinated in 1919.

Regents Examinations, Answers, Self-Analysis Charts, and Regents Specification Grids

Examination August 2006

Global History and Geography

PART I: MULTIPLE CHOICE

Directions (1–50): For each statement or question, write in the space provided, the *number* of the word or expression that, of those given, best completes the statement or answers the question.

1 • Height above sea level
• Distance from the equator
• Amount of rainfall
• Average daily temperature

Which aspect of geography is most influenced by these factors?

1 natural boundaries
2 climate
3 topography
4 mineral resources 1____

2 Which activity would be most characteristic of people in a traditional society?

1 serving in government assemblies
2 working in an industrialized city
3 having the same occupation as their parents
4 establishing a mercantile system of trade 2____

3 • Large areas in the north and south received less than ten inches of rainfall annually.
- The presence of waterfalls and rapids slowed river travel.
- Highlands and steep cliffs limited exploration.

In which region did these geographic factors have an impact on European exploration and colonization?

1 South America
2 Southeast Asia
3 subcontinent of India
4 Africa 3____

4 What is the main reason the Neolithic Revolution is considered a turning point in world history?

1 Fire was used as a source of energy for the first time.
2 Spoken language was used to improve communication.
3 Domestication of animals and cultivation of crops led to settled communities.
4 Stone tools and weapons were first developed. 4____

5 Which heading best completes the partial outline below?

> I. ____________________
>
> A. Centralized governments
> B. Organized religions
> C. Social classes
> D. Specialization of labor

1 Economic Development in Ancient Egypt
2 Cultural Diffusion in Mohenjo-Daro
3 Features of the Old Stone Age
4 Characteristics of Civilizations 5____

6 The Pillars of Emperor Asoka of the Mauryan Empire and the Code of Hammurabi of Babylon are most similar to the

1 ziggurats of Sumeria
2 map projections of Mercator
3 Great Sphinx of the Egyptians
4 Twelve Tables of the Romans 6____

7 A similarity between Bantu migrations in Africa and migrations of the ancient Aryans into South Asia is that both moved

1 across the Atlantic Ocean
2 from rural lands to urban areas
3 in search of additional food sources
4 for religious freedom 7____

8 Which factor led to the development of civilizations in ancient Mesopotamia?

1 political harmony
2 favorable geography
3 religious differences
4 universal education 8____

9 Which statement most likely represents the view of a citizen of ancient Athens visiting Sparta?

1 "The government and society in Sparta are so strict. The people have little voice in government."
2 "I feel as though I have never left home. Everything here is the same as it is in Athens."
3 "This society allows for more freedom of expression than I have ever experienced in Athens."
4 "I have never heard of a society like Sparta that believes in only one God." 9____

10 One similarity between animism and Shinto is that people who follow these belief systems

1 practice filial piety
2 worship spirits in nature
3 are monotheistic
4 are required to make pilgrimages 10____

11 • Buddhist temples are found in Japan.
• Most Indonesians study the Koran.
• Catholicism is the dominant religion in Latin America.

These statements illustrate a result of

1 westernization
2 cultural diffusion
3 economic nationalism
4 fundamentalism 11____

12 Which group introduced the Cyrillic alphabet, Orthodox Christianity, and domed architecture to Russian culture?

1 Mongols
2 Vikings
3 Jews
4 Byzantines 12____

13 The topography and climate of Russia have caused Russia to

1 depend on rice as its main source of food
2 seek access to warm-water ports
3 adopt policies of neutrality and isolation
4 acquire mineral-rich colonies on other continents 13____

14 One of the major achievements of Byzantine Emperor Justinian was that he

1 established a direct trade route with Ghana
2 defended the empire against the spread of Islam
3 brought Roman Catholicism to his empire
4 preserved and transmitted Greek and Roman culture 14____

15 Both European medieval knights and Japanese samurai warriors pledged oaths of

1 loyalty to their military leader
2 devotion to their nation-state
3 service to their church
4 allegiance to their families 15____

16 What was a significant effect of Mansa Musa's pilgrimage to Mecca?

1 The African written language spread to southwest Asia.
2 Military leaders eventually controlled Mali.
3 Islamic learning and culture expanded in Mali.
4 The trading of gold for salt ended. 16____

17 A direct impact that the printing press had on 16th-century Europe was that it encouraged the

1 spread of ideas
2 beginnings of communism
3 establishment of democracy
4 development of industrialization 17____

18 Which technological advancement helped unify both the Roman and the Inca Empires?

1 astrolabe
2 road system
3 gunpowder
4 wheeled carts 18____

19 Cervantes' literary classic *Don Quixote*, the rule of Isabella and Ferdinand, and the art of El Greco are associated with the

1 Golden Age in Spain
2 Hanseatic League in Germany
3 Glorious Revolution in England
4 Renaissance in Italy

19____

Base your answer to question 20 on the diagram below and on your knowledge of social studies.

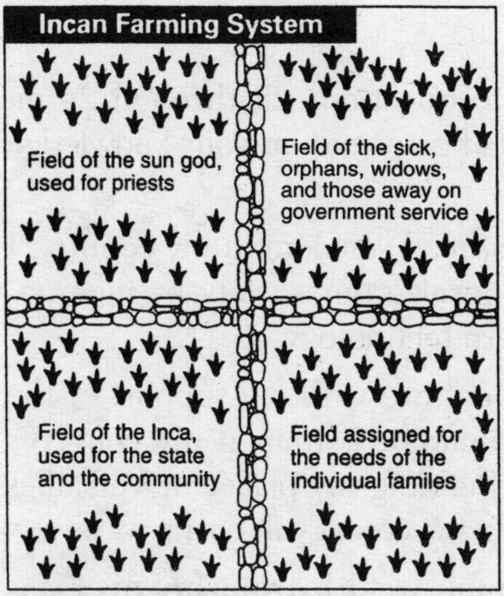

All land belonged to the community. Farmers grew crops in different fields.

Source: Ellis and Esler, *World History: Connections to Today*, Prentice Hall (adapted)

20 This diagram shows the Incas had a farming system that

1 provided crops for the entire society
2 left much of the land unfarmed
3 set aside fifty percent of the crops for those who farmed the fields
4 grew crops only for priests and government officials

20____

21 Which statement best describes a result of the encounter between Europeans and native populations of Latin America?

1 Native societies experienced rapid population growth.
2 European nations lost power and prestige in the New World.
3 Large numbers of natives migrated to Europe for a better life.
4 Plantations in the New World used enslaved Africans to replace native populations. 21____

Base your answers to questions 22 through 24 on the speakers' statements below and on your knowledge of social studies.

Speaker A: Although I spread serfdom in my country, I tried to modernize our society by incorporating western technology.

Speaker B: I promoted culture with my support of the arts. Unfortunately, I drained my country's treasury by building my palace at Versailles and involving my country in costly wars.

Speaker C: I gained much wealth from my overseas empire in the Americas. I waged war against the Protestants and lost.

Speaker D: I inherited the throne and imprisoned my foes without a trial. I dissolved Parliament because I did not want to consult with them when I increased taxes.

22 Which speaker represents the view of King Louis XIV of France?

1 *A*
2 *B*
3 *C*
4 *D* 22____

23 Which nation was most likely governed by *Speaker D*?

1 Russia
2 France
3 Spain
4 England

23____

24 Which type of government is most closely associated with all these speakers?

1 limited monarchy
2 absolute monarchy
3 direct democracy
4 constitutional democracy

24____

Base your answer to question 25 on the statements below and on your knowledge of social studies.

> . . . The Laws ought to be so framed, as to secure the Safety of every Citizen as much as possible.
>
> . . . The Equality of the Citizens consists in this; that they should all be subject to the same Laws . . .
>
> — *Documents of Catherine the Great*, W. E Reddaway, ed., Cambridge University Press (adapted)

25 These ideas of Catherine the Great of Russia originated during the

1 Age of Exploration
2 Age of Enlightenment
3 Protestant Reformation
4 French Revolution

25____

Base your answers to questions 26 and 27 on the speakers' statements below and on your knowledge of social studies.

Speaker A: Government should not interfere in relations between workers and business owners.

Speaker B: The workers will rise up and overthrow the privileged class.

Speaker C: Private property will cease to exist. The people will own the means of production.

Speaker D: A favorable balance of trade should be maintained by the use of tariffs.

26 Which two speakers represent Karl Marx's ideas of communism?

1 *A* and *B*
2 *B* and *C*
3 *B* and *D*
4 *C* and *D*

26 ____

27 Which speaker is referring to laissez-faire capitalism?

1 *A*
2 *B*
3 *C*
4 *D*

27 ____

Base your answers to questions 28 and 29 on the map below and on your knowledge of social studies.

Japanese Imperialism, 1875–1910

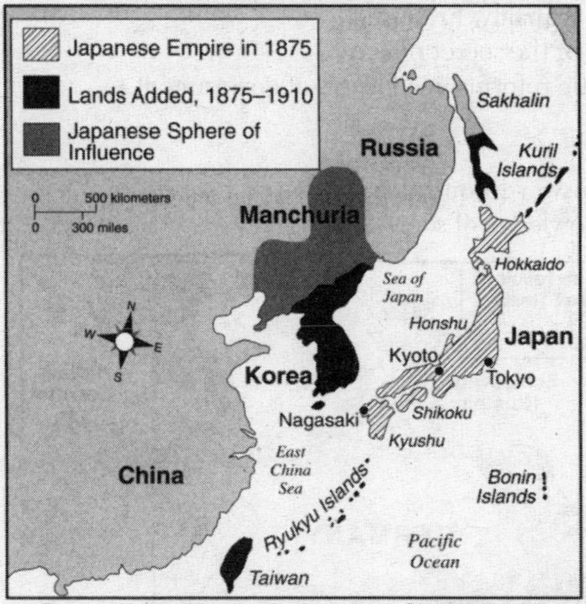

Source: Henry Brun et al., *Reviewing Global History and Geography*, AMSCO (adapted)

28 What was a basic cause of the political changes shown on this map?

1 Russia and Japan formed an alliance.
2 Korea defeated Japan in the Sino-Japanese War.
3 The Japanese people wanted to spread the beliefs of Shinto.
4 Japan needed raw materials for industrialization. 28____

29 Which event is associated with the changes shown on this map?

1 Opium War
2 Meiji Restoration
3 Chinese Nationalist Revolution
4 rise of the Soviet Union 29____

30 The Bolshevik Party in 1917 gained the support of the peasant class because they promised them

1 "Peace, Land, and Bread"
2 "Liberty, Equality, Fraternity"
3 abolition of the secret police
4 democratic reforms in all levels of government 30____

Base your answer to question 31 on the map below and on your knowledge of social studies.

Source: Geoffrey Barraclough, ed., *Hammond Concise Atlas of World History*, Hammond, 1998 (adapted)

31 Which time period in German history is most accurately represented in this map?

1 between World War I and World War II
2 just after the Berlin Conference
3 immediately after the Congress of Vienna
4 during unification under Bismarck 31____

32 Which statement describes one major aspect of a command economy?

1 Supply and demand determines what will be produced.
2 Most economic decisions are made by the government.
3 The means of production are controlled by labor unions.
4 The economy is mainly agricultural. 32____

33 Which area was once controlled by Britain, suffered a mass starvation in the 1840s, and became an independent Catholic nation in 1922?

1 Scotland
2 India
3 Ghana
4 Ireland 33____

34 Totalitarian countries are characterized by

1 free and open discussions of ideas
2 a multiparty system with several candidates for each office
3 government control of newspapers, radio, and television
4 government protection of people's civil liberties 34____

35 Which name would best complete this partial outline?

I. African Nationalists of the 20th Century
- A. Leopold Senghor
- B. Jomo Kenyatta
- C. Julius Nyerere
- D.________________

1 Atatürk [Mustafa Kemal]
2 Ho Chi Minh
3 José de San Martín
4 Kwame Nkrumah 35____

36 Since 1948, a major reason for the conflict between Arabs and Israelis is that each side

1 wants the huge oil reserves that lie under the disputed land
2 believes that the United States favors the other side in the conflict
3 claims sovereignty over the same land
4 seeks to control trade on the eastern end of the Mediterranean Sea 36____

37 In the 1980s, Mikhail Gorbachev's attempts to change the Soviet Union resulted in

1 an increase in tensions between India and the Soviet Union
2 a strengthening of the Communist Party
3 a shift from producing consumer goods to producing heavy machinery
4 a series of economic and political reforms 37____

Base your answer to question 38 on the diagram below and on your knowledge of social studies.

Cycle of the Ecological Environment

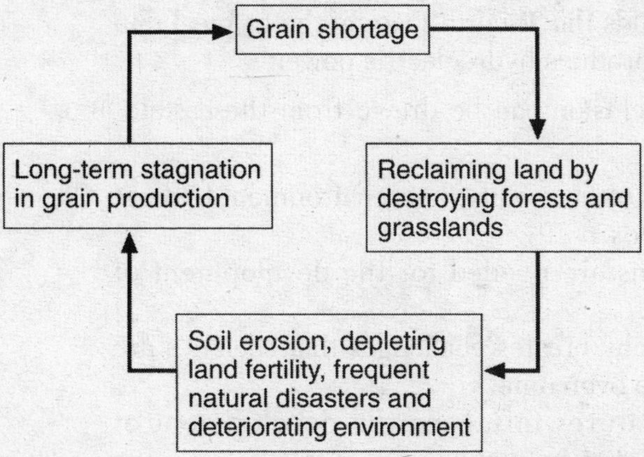

Source: Yan Ruizhen and Wang Yuan, *Poverty and Development*, New World Press, 1992 (adapted)

38 Which conclusion based on the ecological cycle shown in this diagram is most valid?

1 Grain yields increase as the amount of land reclaimed increases.
2 The destruction of forests leads to soil erosion.
3 Grain production has no impact on the environment.
4 Natural disasters have little effect on grain production. 38____

39 • Egypt builds the Aswan Dam to control flooding and produce hydroelectric power.
- China builds the Three Gorges Dam to control flooding and improve trade.
- Brazil builds the Tucuruí Dam in the tropical rain forest to produce hydroelectric power.

Which conclusion can be drawn from these statements?

1 Societies often modify their environment to meet their needs.
2 Monsoons are needed for the development of societies.
3 Topography creates challenges that societies are unable to overcome.
4 Land features influence the development of diverse belief systems. 39____

Base your answer to question 40 on the cartoon below and on your knowledge of social studies.

Ziraldo/Rio de Janeiro, Brazil
Cartoonists & Writers Syndicate
Source: Ziraldo Alves Pinto

40 What is the main idea of this Brazilian cartoon?

1 Relations between Latin America and the United States are mutually beneficial.
2 The United States wants to cut off political and economic relations with Latin America.
3 Latin American nations are self-sufficient and need not rely on the United States.
4 The United States wants to control its relationships with Latin America.

40 ____

41 **"Tensions Increase Over Kashmir"**

"Hindus and Muslims Clash in Calcutta Riots"

"Threat of Nuclear Conflict Worries World"

These headlines refer to events in which region?

1 Latin America
2 sub-Saharan Africa
3 subcontinent of India
4 East Asia 41_____

Base your answer to question 42 on the cartoon below and on your knowledge of social studies.

Source: Kim Song Heng, *Lianhe Zaobao*, 2002 (adapted)

42 The main idea of this 2002 cartoon is that East Timor is

1 experiencing massive floods that might destroy the nation
2 struggling with the arrival of large numbers of freedom-seeking refugees
3 facing several dangers that threaten its existence as a new nation
4 celebrating its success as an independent nation 42_____

43 One way in which the Tang dynasty, the Gupta Empire, and the European Renaissance are similar is that they all included periods of

1 religious unity
2 democratic reforms
3 economic isolation
4 cultural achievements 43____

44 What was one similar goal shared by Simón Bolívar and Mohandas Gandhi?

1 ending foreign control
2 promoting religious freedom
3 establishing a limited monarchy
4 creating collective farms 44____

45 The Armenian Massacre, the "killing fields" of the Khmer Rouge, and Saddam Hussein's attacks against the Kurds are examples of

1 apartheid
2 enslavement
3 human rights violations
4 forced collectivization 45____

46 In western Europe, the Middle Ages began after the collapse of which empire?

1 Mughal
2 Roman
3 Ottoman
4 Byzantine 46____

Base your answers to questions 47 and 48 on the chart below and on your knowledge of social studies.

Executions During the Reign of Terror

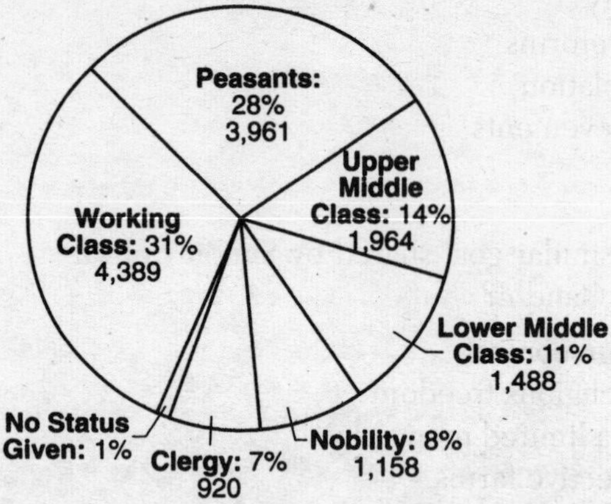

Source: Dennis Sherman et al., eds., *World Civilizations: Sources, Images, and Interpretations*, McGraw-Hill (adapted)

47 During which revolution did these executions occur?

1 French
2 Russian
3 Chinese
4 Cuban

47 ____

48 Which statement is best supported by information found in this chart?

1 Clergy were spared from the Reign of Terror.
2 The Reign of Terror affected all classes equally.
3 The Reign of Terror crossed social and economic boundaries.
4 Peasants were the most frequent victims of the Reign of Terror.

48 ____

Base your answer to question 49 on the passage below and on your knowledge of social studies.

> . . . Our foundation rests upon trade, because, as you see, we have a large part of our capital invested [in it]. And therefore we shall have little for exchange operations, and we are forced to exert our ingenuity elsewhere. This, however, in my opinion, does not involve greater risk than one incurs in exchanges today, especially when no risks at sea are run [That is, when shipments by sea are insured.]; nor does it bring smaller profits. And [trade operations] are more legal and more honorable. In them we shall so govern ourselves that every day you will have more reason to be content; may God grant us His grace.
>
> Source: Letter to the home office of the Medici from branch office at Bruges, May 14, 1464 (adapted)

49 This passage best illustrates circumstances that characterized the

1 Crusades
2 Age of Reason
3 Commercial Revolution
4 Scientific Revolution 49 ____

50 **"Germany, Austria-Hungary, and Italy Form Triple Alliance"**

"Serbian Nationalism Grows in Balkans"

"Archduke Franz Ferdinand Assassinated in Bosnia"

The events in these headlines contributed most directly to the

1 beginning of World War I
2 outbreak of the Cold War
3 development of communist rule in Europe
4 strengthening of European monarchies 50 ____

In developing your answer to Part II, be sure to keep this general definition in mind:

(a) explain means "to make plain or understandable; to give reasons for or causes of; to show the logical development or relationships of"

(b) discuss means "to make observations about something using facts, reasoning, and argument; to present in some detail"

PART II: THEMATIC ESSAY QUESTION

Directions: Write a well-organized essay that includes an introduction, several paragraphs addressing the task below, and a conclusion.

Theme: Movement of People and Goods: Trade

> Trade routes and trade organizations have had an impact on nations and regions. The effects have been both positive and negative.

Task:

> Identify ***two*** trade routes ***and/or*** trade organizations and for ***each***
> - Explain ***one*** reason for the establishment of the trade route or trade organization
> - Discuss ***one*** positive effect or ***one*** negative effect of the trade route or trade organization on a specific nation or region

You may use any example from your study of global history. Some suggestions you might wish to consider include the Silk Roads, the trans-Saharan trade routes of the African kingdoms, Mediterranean trade routes, the Hanseatic League, the British East India Company, the Organization of Petroleum Exporting Countries (OPEC), and the European Union (EU).

You are *not* limited to these suggestions.

Guidelines:

In your essay, be sure to:

- Develop all aspects of the task
- Support the theme with relevant facts, examples, and details
- Use a logical and clear plan of organization, including an introduction and a conclusion that are beyond a restatement of the theme

In developing your answers to Part III, be sure to keep this general definition in mind:

> **discuss means "to make observations about something using facts, reasoning, and argument; to present in some detail"**

PART III: DOCUMENT-BASED QUESTION

This question is based on the accompanying documents. It is designed to test your ability to work with historical documents. Some of these documents have been edited for the purposes of this question. As you analyze the documents, take into account the source of each document and any point of view that may be presented in the document.

Historical Context:

As World War II came to an end, a new conflict emerged between the United States and the Soviet Union. This conflict, known as the Cold War, affected many regions of the world, including **Europe**, **Asia**, and **Latin America**.

Task:

Using information from the documents and your knowledge of global history, answer the questions that follow each document in Part A. Your answers to the questions will help you write the Part B essay in which you will be asked to

- Discuss how the Cold War between the United States and the Soviet Union affected other nations ***and/or*** regions of the world

Part A: Short-Answer Questions

Directions: Analyze the documents and answer the short-answer questions that follow each document in the space provided.

Document 1

Europe After World War II

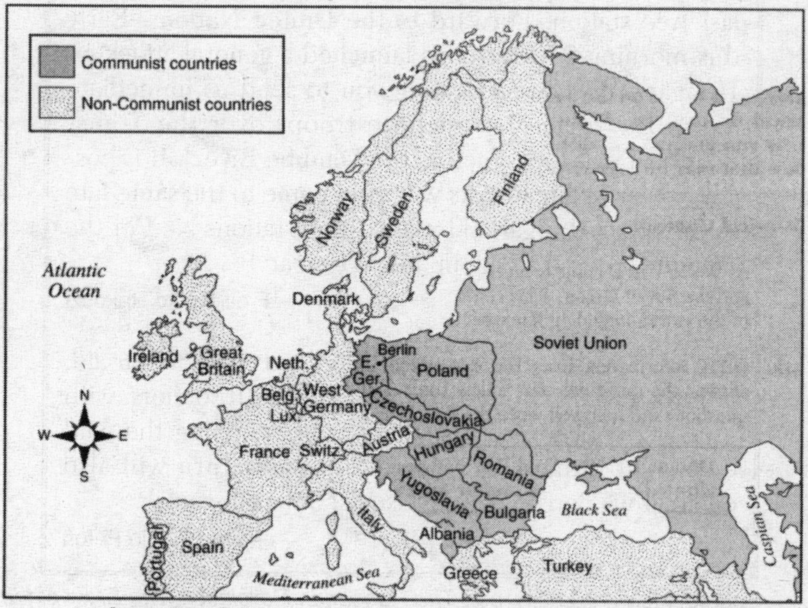

Source: Roger B. Beck et al., *World History: Patterns of Interaction*, McDougal Littell (adapted)

1 What does the information shown on this map indicate about the governments of Western Europe and Eastern Europe after World War II? [1]

____

____

Document 2a

Imre Nagy, the Hungarian leader, was forced out of office by the Soviet Communist government. The people of Hungary protested his removal from office.

> This is Hungary calling! This is Hungary calling! The last free station. Forward to the United Nations. Early this morning Soviet troops launched a general attack on Hungary. We are requesting you to send us immediate aid in the form of parachute troops over the Transdanubian provinces [across the Danube River]. It is possible that our broadcasts will soon come to the same fate as the other Hungarian broadcasting stations . . . For the sake of God and freedom, help Hungary! . . .
>
> — Free Radio Rakoczi
>
> Civilized people of the world, listen and come to our aid. Not with declarations, but with force, with soldiers, with arms. Do not forget that there is no stopping the wild onslaught [attack] of Bolshevism. Your turn will also come, if we perish. Save our souls! Save our souls! . . .
>
> — Free Radio Petofi

Source: Melvin J. Lasky, ed., *The Hungarian Revolution: The Story of the October Uprising as Recorded in Documents, Dispatches, Eye-Witness Accounts, and World-wide Reactions*, Frederick A. Praeger, 1957 (adapted)

2*a* Based on these broadcasts from Free Radio Rakoczi and Free Radio Petofi, state ***two*** reasons the Hungarian people were asking for help in 1956. [2]

(1) ____

____

(2) ____

____

Document 2b

> This morning the forces of the reactionary conspiracy [anti-Soviet plot] against the Hungarian people were crushed. A new Hungarian Revolutionary Worker-Peasant [Communist] Government, headed by the Prime Minister Janos Kadar, has been formed. . . .
>
> — Radio Moscow

Source: Melvin J. Lasky, ed., *The Hungarian Revolution: The Story of the October Uprising as Recorded in Documents, Dispatches, Eye-Witness Accounts, and World-wide Reactions*, Frederick A. Praeger, 1957

2*b* Based on this broadcast from Radio Moscow, state ***one*** result of the Hungarian Revolution. [1]

____

____

Document 3a

Berlin, Germany After World War II

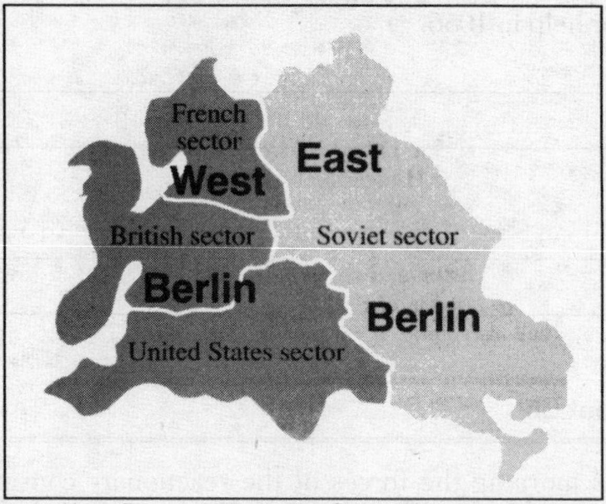

Source: Henry Brun et al., *Reviewing Global History and Geography*, AMSCO (adapted)

Berlin, 1961

Source: Heiko Burkhardt, dailysoft.com

Document 3b

3 Based on this map and the Burkhardt photograph, state ***one*** way the Cold War affected the city of Berlin. [1]

____

____

Document 4

. . . The preservation of peace forms the central aim of India's policy. It is in the pursuit of this policy that we have chosen the path of nonalinement [nonalignment] in any military or like pact or alliance. Nonalinement does not mean passivity of mind or action, lack of faith or conviction. It does not mean submission to what we consider evil. It is a positive and dynamic approach to such problems that confront us. We believe that each country has not only the right to freedom but also to decide its own policy and way of life. Only thus can true freedom flourish and a people grow according to their own genius.

We believe, therefore, in nonaggression and noninterference by one country in the affairs of another and the growth of tolerance between them and the capacity for peaceful coexistence. We think that by the free exchange of ideas and trade and other contacts between nations each will learn from the other and truth will prevail. We therefore endeavor to maintain friendly relations with all countries, even though we may disagree with them in their policies or structure of government. We think that by this approach we can serve not only our country but also the larger causes of peace and good fellowship in the world. . . .

Source: Prime Minister Jawaharlal Nehru, speech in Washington, D.C., December 18, 1956

4 According to Prime Minister Nehru, what was India's foreign policy in 1956? [1]

____

____

Document 5

Sook Nyul Choi was born in Pyongyang, Korea and immigrated to the United States during the 1950s. She integrates her autobiographical information into a work of historical fiction set in Korea between the end of World War II and 1950.

> . . . Our freedom and happiness did not last long. In June 1950, war broke out. North Korean and Communist soldiers filled the streets of Seoul, and were soon joined by Chinese Communist troops. Russian tanks came barreling through. In the chaos, many more North Korean refugees made their way to Seoul. Theresa and the other nuns finally escaped, and made their way to our house. They told us that the Russians and Town Reds had found out about Kisa's and Aunt Tiger's other activities. They died as all "traitors" did. They were shot with machine guns, and then hanged in the town square to serve as a lesson to others. We never heard any further news about the sock girls, or about my friend Unhi. I still wonder if they are alive in the North.

Source: Sook Nyul Choi, *Year of Impossible Goodbyes*, Houghton Mifflin Company

5 Based on Sook Nyul Choi's description, state ***two*** ways the beginning of the Korean War affected the people of Korea. [2]

(1) ______________________________

____

(2) ______________________________

____

Document 6a

War in Korea, 1950–1953

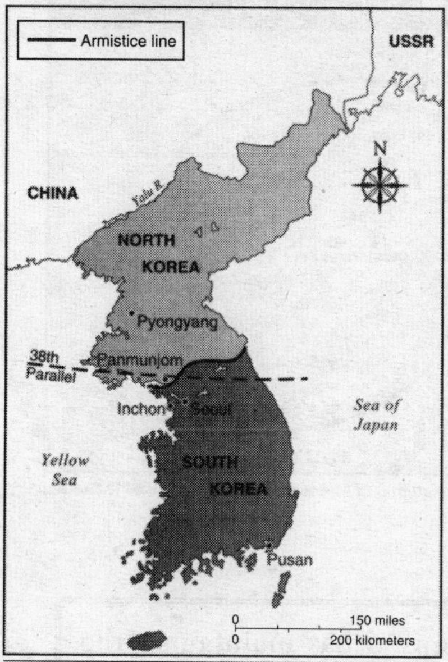

Document 6b

War in Vietnam, 1954–1973

Source: Burton F. Beers, *World History: Patterns of Civilization*, Prentice Hall (adapted)

6 Based on the information shown on these maps, state ***one*** similarity in the way the Cold War affected Korea and Vietnam. [1]

____

____

Document 7a

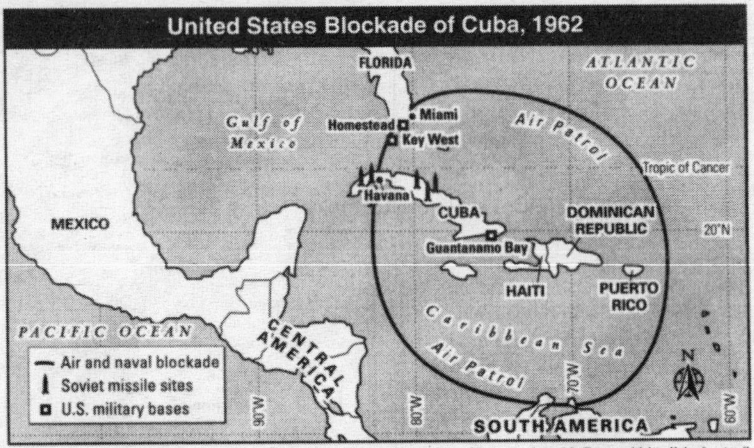

Source: *World History: Patterns of Interaction*, McDougal Littell (adapted)

Document 7b

This Government as promised has maintained the closest surveillance of the Soviet military build-up on the island of Cuba.

Within the past week unmistakable evidence has established the fact that a series of offensive missile sites is now in preparation on that imprisoned island.

The purpose of these bases can be none other than to provide a nuclear strike capability against the Western Hemisphere.

Upon receiving the first preliminary hard information of this nature last Tuesday morning at 9 A.M., I directed that our surveillance be stepped up. And having now confirmed and completed our evaluation of the evidence and our decision on a course of action, this Government feels obliged to report this new crisis to you in fullest detail.

The characteristics of these new missile sites indicate two distinct types of installations. Several of them include medium-range ballistic missiles capable of carrying a nuclear warhead for a distance of more than 1,000 nautical miles.

Each of these missiles, in short, is capable of striking Washington, D.C., the Panama Canal, Cape Canaveral, Mexico City or any other city in the southeastern part of the United States, in Central America or in the Caribbean area. . . .

Source: President John F. Kennedy, address to the nation on the Soviet arms buildup in Cuba, October 22, 1962

7 Based on this map and President John F. Kennedy's address, state ***one*** way the Cold War affected Cuba. [1]

____

____

Document 8a

> . . . Immediately after the revolution, the Sandinistas had the best organized and most experienced military force in the country. To replace the National Guard, the Sandinistas established a new national army, the Sandinista People's Army (Ejército Popular Sandinista—EPS), and a police force, the Sandinista Police (Policía Sandinista-PS). These two groups, contrary to the original Puntarenas Pact [agreement reached by Sandinista government when in exile] were controlled by the Sandinistas and trained by personnel from Cuba, Eastern Europe, and the Soviet Union. Opposition to the overwhelming FSLN [Sandinista National Liberation Front] influence in the security forces did not surface until 1980. Meanwhile, the EPS developed, with support from Cuba and the Soviet Union, into the largest and best equipped military force in Central America. Compulsory military service, introduced during 1983, brought the EPS forces to about 80,000 by the mid-1980s. . . .

Source: Library of Congress, Federal Research Division (adapted)

8*a* According to this document from the Library of Congress, what effect did the Cold War have on Nicaragua in the 1980s? [1]

___

___

Document 8b

Her [Violeta Chamorro] husband's murder sparked a revolution that brought the Sandinistas to power. Now Violeta Chamorro is challenging them in Nicaragua's presidential election.

> . . . "Violeta! Violeta! Throw them [Sandinistas] out! Throw them out!"
>
> Surrounded by outstretched hands, Mrs. Chamorro hugs everyone in reach. Then Nicaragua's most famous widow goes straight to her message. This is the town where my husband was born, she tells them. This is where he learned the values of freedom that cost him his life. This is where he would tell us to make a stand against the Sandinista regime.
>
> "I never thought that I would return to Granada as a candidate, raising the banner steeped in the blood of Pedro Joaquín Chamorro, to ask his people once again to put themselves in the front lines," she says. "But Nicaragua must win its freedom once again.
>
> "All across the world," she continues, her voice rising, "people like you are burying Communism and proclaiming democracy. So set your watches! Set them to the same hour as Poland, as Bulgaria, as Czechoslovakia, as Chile! Because this is the hour of democracy and freedom—this is the hour of the people!". . .

Source: Mark A. Uhlig, *New York Times*, February 11, 1990

8b According to Mark A. Uhlig, what political change did Violeta Chamorro hope to bring to Nicaragua? [1]

____

____

Part B: Essay

Directions: Write a well-organized essay that includes an introduction, several paragraphs, and a conclusion. Use evidence from *at least* ***five*** documents to support your response. Support your response with relevant facts, examples, and details. Include additional outside information.

Historical Context:

As World War II came to an end, a new conflict emerged between the United States and the Soviet Union. This conflict, known as the Cold War, affected many regions of the world, including **Europe**, **Asia**, and **Latin America**.

Task:

Using the information from the documents and your knowledge of global history, write an essay in which you

- Discuss how the Cold War between the United States and the Soviet Union affected other nations ***and/or*** regions of the world

Guidelines:

In your essay, be sure to:

- Develop all aspects of the task
- Incorporate information from *at least* ***five*** documents
- Incorporate relevant outside information
- Support the theme with relevant facts, examples, and details
- Use a logical and clear plan of organization, including an introduction and a conclusion that are beyond a restatement of the theme

Answers August 2006

Global History and Geography

Answer Key

PART I (1–50)

1. 2	**14.** 4	**27.** 1	**40.** 4
2. 3	**15.** 1	**28.** 4	**41.** 3
3. 4	**16.** 3	**29.** 2	**42.** 3
4. 3	**17.** 1	**30.** 1	**43.** 4
5. 4	**18.** 2	**31.** 1	**44.** 1
6. 4	**19.** 1	**32.** 2	**45.** 3
7. 3	**20.** 1	**33.** 4	**46.** 2
8. 2	**21.** 4	**34.** 3	**47.** 1
9. 1	**22.** 2	**35.** 4	**48.** 3
10. 2	**23.** 4	**36.** 3	**49.** 3
11. 2	**24.** 2	**37.** 4	**50.** 1
12. 4	**25.** 2	**38.** 2	
13. 2	**26.** 2	**39.** 1	

PART II: Thematic Essay See Answers Explained section.

PART III: Document-Based Essay See Answers Explained section.

Answers Explained

PART I

1. **2** Climate is the aspect of geography that is most influenced by these factors. Climate is the average weather a place has over a period of 20 to 30 years. Elevation or height above sea level influences climate. In general, high land areas are cooler than low land areas because air cools as it rises. Quito, the capital of Ecuador in South America, is located almost near the equator. Because the city sits high in the Andes Mountains, daytime temperatures do not rise above 90 degrees Fahrenheit. Nighttime temperatures can drop as low as 40 degrees Fahrenheit. Another factor that affects climate is latitude. Lands closest to the equator have a tropical climate. An example is the tropical rain forest. It has high temperatures and ample rainfall all year. Another tropical climate combines hot temperatures with a rainy season and a dry season. Areas farther north or south of the equator have temperate climates with a warm and cold season. Many areas of Central Asia and Europe have temperate climates. Located far from the equator, lands near the North and South Poles have arctic climates. They are cold all year and have about 8 inches of rain each year. Nearness to oceans also affects climate. Ocean currents carry warm or cool water in circular patterns around the world. These warm and cold currents are also factors that influence the climate of nearby coastal areas.

WRONG CHOICES EXPLAINED:

(1) Natural boundaries refer to mountains, rivers, and oceans that geographically define a country or continent.

(3) Topography describes the physical features of a place or region.

(4) Mineral resources are naturally occurring substances, such as coal, iron, zinc, gold, silver, and tin, that are usually obtained from the ground.

2. **3** The activity that would be most characteristic of people in a traditional society is having the same occupation as their parents. A traditional society is one in which the role of each individual and economic activity is determined by rituals and customs. In many countries, parents taught their children how to hunt, fish, and farm. In turn, their children taught their skills to the next generation. In a traditional society, everyone has a role and it tends to produce stability. However, traditional societies fail to meet the needs of changing economic times and fail to promote new ideas.

WRONG CHOICES EXPLAINED:

(1) Serving in government assemblies would not be characteristic of a traditional society. In a traditional society, the focus is the family and meeting the basic needs of the immediate family.

(2) and (4) Neither of these statements are characteristic of a traditional society. Working in an industrialized city and establishing a mercantile system

of trade destroyed the foundation of traditional society. A traditional society rejected industrialization and the mercantile system. A traditional society was primarily an agricultural society.

3. **4** Africa was the region in which these geographic factors had an impact on European exploration and colonization. Deserts cover about 40 percent of Africa. They include the Sahara in the north and the Kalahari and Namib Deserts in the south. The Sahara is a region that averages less than 10 inches of rain a year. Ten years can pass without rainfall. A few areas have grass that can support grazing animals. Parts of the Sahara are very harsh. Temperatures can reach as high as 130 degrees Fahrenheit. Africa has an enormous coastline but few good natural harbors. In addition, much of the interior is a high plateau. As rivers approach the coast, they cascade through a series of rapids and large waterfalls that hinder travel between the coast and the interior. Before the 1800s, Africa's coastline made it possible for Europe to build trading posts along the coastline. However, until the 19th century, its inhospitable interior, deserts, mountains, plateaus, and jungles discouraged exploration, and it remained unknown to the outside world. Thus, Europeans called Africa the Dark Continent. However, in the early 1800s, European explorers began pushing into the interior. The glowing reports of explorers reawakened Europe's interest in Africa and eventually led to the colonization of the continent.

WRONG CHOICES EXPLAINED:

(1), (2), and (3) None of these geographic factors had an impact on European exploration of South America, Southeast Asia, or the subcontinent of India.

4. **3** The main reason the Neolithic Revolution is considered a turning point in world history is that the domestication of animals and cultivation of crops led to settled communities. A turning point is a time when decisive changes occur. During the Neolithic Period, which lasted from 8000 B.C. to 4000 B.C., people came out of caves and settled near lakes, rivers, and seas. People settled in communities and secured food by farming. They learned to plow the soil, domesticate animals, and use the wheel and axle for transportation. People no longer had to search for food, and permanent settlements were established. The Neolithic Revolution or Agricultural Revolution led to the need for a government to establish order as people needed to work together to meet their basic needs. These developments were a turning point that created more complex societies.

WRONG CHOICES EXPLAINED:

(1) Fire was not used as a source of energy for the first time during the Neolithic Revolution. Fire was first used by hunters and gatherers during the Old Stone Age.

(2) Spoken language was previously used to improve communication during the Old Stone Age. The development of spoken language was an important

achievement, but it did not change the way the people lived. They still were hunters and gatherers.

(4) Stone tools and weapons were not first developed during the Neolithic Revolution. Early people first began to use stone tools over 2 million years ago. These people were nomads who moved from place to place to gather food.

5. **4** The heading that best completes the partial outline is "Characteristics of Civilizations." Although different from each other, civilizations everywhere have certain things in common. Cities were the birthplace of the first civilizations. The word *civilization* comes from the Latin word for "city." The first cities emerged after farmers began to cultivate land along river valleys and to produce surplus food, which in turn helped population growth. Villages swelled into cities. To produce these surpluses and oversee irrigation projects, a central government was needed. A city government was more powerful than a council of elders or the local chief of a farming village. A central government helped farmers build public works projects such as canals, dikes, and irrigation systems. The government also ensured that roads and bridges were built so that farmers and merchants could bring food to the markets in the cities. With the growth of cities, religion became a formal institution. Most cities had great temples where dozens of priests took charge of religious duties. They hoped that the gods would ensure plentiful crops and protect their cities. Works of art and architecture, such as temples and palaces, dominated the city scenery. These buildings demonstrated the power of the government. As civilizations grew, people needed to perform different jobs such as traders, government officials, artisans, or skilled craftsmen who made items by hand. Weavers turned plant fibers into cloth, and metalworkers made tools and weapons out of bronze. This created a specialization of labor, and people became ranked according to their jobs. Such ranking led to social classes. Priests and nobles were usually at the top followed by wealthy merchants and government officials. The majority of people were artisans and farmers. At the bottom were slaves.

WRONG CHOICES EXPLAINED:

(1), (2), and (3) None of these headings complete the partial outline. There are no statements about economic development in Ancient Egypt, cultural diffusion in Mohenjo-Daro, or features of the Old Stone Age.

6. **4** The Pillars of Emperor Asoka of the Mauryan Empire and the Code of Hammurabi of Babylon are most similar to the Twelve Tables of the Romans. Asoka was the grandson of King Chandragupta, who established the powerful Mauryan Empire in northern India. Asoka, who ruled from 232 B.C. to 209 B.C., expanded the Mauryan Empire to include all of India except its southern tip. Asoka had stone pillars set up across India, announcing laws and promising righteous government. On one pillar, he guaranteed righteous treatment for all Asoka's subjects. Others urged the people of his empire to

live righteously. The Code of Hammurabi is the oldest written legal system. This code, developed by King Hammurabi of Mesopotamia in 1705 B.C., consisted of 282 sections and set standards of justice. It specifically outlined which actions were considered violations and assigned a specific punishment for each violation. In 450 B.C., the plebeians (farmers, merchants, and traders) who made up the majority of the population of Ancient Rome, forced the patricians (the wealthy class) to have all the laws written down in what became known as the law of the Twelve Tables. These laws were displayed in the market and for the first time made it possible for plebeians to appeal a judgment handed down by a patrician judge.

WRONG CHOICES EXPLAINED:

(1) The ziggurats of Sumeria were pyramid temples dedicated to chief gods or goddesses of the city.

(2) Map projections of Mercator were some of the earliest projections developed. The projections accurately showed the directions north, south, east, and west. Mercator projections are useful for showing sailors' routes and ocean currents.

(3) The Great Sphinx of the Egyptians was commissioned by King Khafre (2558 B.C. to 2532 B.C.). The Sphinx was carved from the bedrock of the Giza Plateau. The Sphinx has the body of a lion with the head of a king or god. It is tremendous in size. The paws are estimated to be 50 feet long, while the entire length is 150 feet. The head is 30 feet long and 14 feet wide.

7. **3** A similarity between Bantu migrations in Africa and migrations of the ancient Aryans into South Asia is that both moved in search of additional food sources. The Bantu people originally lived in West Africa. As the Sahara regions began to dry out, these skilled farmers and herders migrated south and east in search of fertile land. The Bantus adopted their farming methods to suit their environment. However, anthropologists believe that as soon as Bantu farming methods began to exhaust the land, new fertile land had to be discovered. This constant moving caused the Bantus to displace many groups in central and southern Africa. The Bantu migration was between A.D. 500 to A.D. 1500. About 1500 B.C., nomadic warriors called Aryans conquered the Indus Valley. The Aryans, with their iron weapons and horse-drawn chariots, were excellent warriors. The Aryans were seeking water and pastureland for their horses and cattle. The Aryan migration into South Asia took hundreds of years. These nomadic herders valued cattle that provided them with food and clothing. Later when the Aryans became farmers, families continued to measure their wealth in livestock. By 500 B.C., the Aryan civilization began to decline.

WRONG CHOICES EXPLAINED:

(1) Neither the Bantu migrations in Africa nor the migrations of the ancient Aryans into South Asia moved across the Atlantic Ocean. Crossing the Atlantic Ocean led to the migration of Europeans to the Americas, not Africa or South Asia.

(2) The Bantus and ancient Aryans did not move from rural to urban areas. Both of these groups settled in farming or rural areas, not in major urban centers. They were looking for food that led to the creation of farming communities.

(4) Neither of these migrant groups was moving for religious freedom. The ancient Aryans brought Hinduism to India, and the Bantus practiced animism. They were forced to move because of the need for food, not religious reasons.

8. **2** Favorable geography led to the development of civilizations in ancient Mesopotamia. The geographic factor of fertile soil contributed to the development of the river valley civilization of ancient Mesopotamia along the Tigris and Euphrates Rivers. This river valley was called Mesopotamia from a Greek word meaning "land between the rivers." Although the area was hot and dry, people learned how to irrigate the land by diverting water from these rivers. The irrigation allowed settlements to grow and increase food supplies that supported a growing population and the development of civilizations. In the city-states of Sumeria along the Tigris-Euphrates Valley, villagers cooperated to meet the river's challenges. Royal officials provided leadership to help the people build the dikes and irrigation ditches to control the flooding. This development also promoted the growth of civilizations in ancient Mesopotamia. With few natural barriers, the area of Tigris-Euphrates became a crossroad where people mingled and shared customs and ideas.

WRONG CHOICES EXPLAINED:

(1) Political harmony did not contribute to the development of civilizations in ancient Mesopotamia. The leaders of Mesopotamia were hereditary rulers who were seen as the chief servant of the gods.

(3) Religious differences had little impact on the development of civilizations. In ancient Mesopotamia, people believed in polytheism, a belief in many powerful gods and goddesses. Each city-state had its own special god or goddess. This type of society did not promote cooperation among the different city-states.

(4) There was no universal education in ancient Mesopotamia. The priests and upper classes were the only two groups in society that were educated.

9. **1** The statement most likely representing the view of a citizen of ancient Athens visiting Sparta is "The government and society in Sparta are so strict. The people have little voice in government." Athens, in east-central Greece on the Attic Peninsula, was the leading Greek city-state. After 750 B.C., Athens slowly progressed from a monarchy or rule by one man to a democracy. Every citizen could directly participate in government by voting on issues to be decided by the city-state. Athens had a direct democracy, but only a minority of Athenians were actually citizens. Women, foreigners, and slaves were not considered citizens and could not participate in the government. Women were considered inferior to men, and slaves and had neither political

rights nor any personal freedoms. However, Athens gave a greater number of people a voice in the government than did any other society of its time. Sparta was situated in southern Greece on the Peloponnesian Peninsula. Sparta was a warrior society. The Spartans emphasized military might and made Sparta an armed camp. The government regulated all aspects of the people's lives. Spartan boys were taken from their homes at the age of seven and received a strict military education. Girls were also trained to exercise rigorously and strengthen their bodies in order to give birth to healthy boys for the army. Sparta was a military state but declined as a result of its rigid ways and inability to change.

WRONG CHOICES EXPLAINED:

(2), (3), and (4) None of these statements represents the view of a citizen of ancient Athens. Athens and Sparta did not have the same society. Athens promoted art, culture, and science. In contrast, and Sparta focused on militarism. Sparta did not allow for more freedom of expression than Athens. Sparta stressed conformity rather than individualism as in Athens. Neither of these societies promoted the belief in one god. Athens and Sparta shared a polytheistic religion, or the belief in many gods.

10. **2** One similarity between animism and Shinto is that people who follow these belief systems worship spirits in nature. Animism is the belief that the spirit of nature inhabits all living and nonliving objects. Many followers of traditional religions in Africa, Japan, Latin America, and Southeast Asia believe that every object on Earth is filled with a living spirit. They respect nature because they believe that the Supreme Being created all things. Some Pygmy tribes in Africa identify the forest with the Supreme Being. In the Amazon region of Brazil, some Indian tribes still pray to the various gods of nature. Shintoism is a traditional Japanese religion that stresses the link between people and the forces of nature. Shintoism has neither sacred writings nor an organized set of beliefs. For centuries, it did not even have a name. When the Buddhist missionaries reached Japan, they called the local Japanese beliefs Shinto, or "the ways of the gods." The Japanese believed that the spirit of kami lived in everything from plants and animals to rocks and mountains. Spirits also controlled natural forces such as earthquakes and typhoons. Through prayers and offerings, the Japanese tried to win the favor of the kami. For example, peasants appealed to the friendly spirits to send good harvests.

WRONG CHOICES EXPLAINED:

(1) Animism and Shintoism did not practice filial piety. Filial piety is a respect for parents. The respect for parents is one of the essential beliefs of Confucianism.

(3) Neither animism nor Shintoism is monotheistic. Monotheism is the belief in one god. These belief systems promote the idea of many gods.

(4) These belief systems do not require a person to make pilgrimages.

11. **2** These statements illustrate a result of cultural diffusion. Cultural diffusion is the spread of ideas and customs from one group of people to another. The religion of Buddhism began in India, around 600 B.C. Buddhism attracted many followers in India, and eventually missionaries spread the religion to China, Tibet, Korea, and Japan. In 552, Buddhist missionaries arrived in Japan. However, Buddhism in Japan was divided into many different sects. Commoners favored a sect that believed anyone could enter paradise through faith. The samurai followed Zen Buddhism that came from China during the 1100s and 1200s. As Buddhism spread throughout Japan, the Japanese built Buddhist monasteries to resemble Chinese architecture. Islam was founded in A.D. 622 by the prophet Muhammad. The sacred text of Islam is the Koran. The Koran is the final authority on all matters and provides a guide to life for Muslims. In the 150 years after the death of Muhammad in 632, Islam spread over three continents. Between the 1200s and 1400s, Muslim traders from Arabia and India brought their religion to Southeast Asia. Islam spread along the trade routes into islands of what is now Indonesia. Parts of the Malay Peninsula and also such islands as Sumatra and Java became the strongholds of Islam. Nearly 90 percent of the people of Indonesia are Muslim. Indonesia is the largest Muslim community in the world. In the 1500s, Spain controlled a vast empire in Latin America. To Spain, winning souls for Catholicism was as important as gaining land. The Catholic Church played a key role in the colonies working with the government to convert Native Americans to Christianity. Franciscans, Jesuits, and other missionaries baptized thousands of Native Americans. These missionaries built churches and worked to convert the natives into loyal subjects of the Catholic king of Spain. Catholicism is still the dominant religion in Latin America today.

WRONG CHOICES EXPLAINED:

(1) Westernization is the adoption of western ideas, technology, and culture.

(3) Economic nationalism is a policy that protects the interests of one's own nation above the interests of other countries. A nation that follows a policy of protectionism over free trade is an example of economic nationalism.

(4) Fundamentalism is the movement that stresses strict adherence to a set of basic principles or values. Many fundamentalists have sought to gain political power in order to resist change that they think undermines their beliefs. Evangelical Protestants and Muslim fundamentalists have rejected many values of the modern world because these values focus on the secular over the spiritual.

12. **4** The Byzantines introduced the Cyrillic alphabet, Orthodox Christianity, and domed architecture to Russian culture. The Byzantine Empire introduced the Eastern Orthodox Church to Russia. In A.D. 863, two Greek monks, Cyril and Methodius, were sent by the Byzantine emperor to convert the Slavic people. They adopted the Greek alphabet so that they could translate the Bible into the Slavic language. The Cyrillic alphabet became the written script for Russia and the Ukraine and is still being used.

In 988, Russian King Valdimir married the sister of the Byzantine emperor and converted to Eastern Orthodox Christianity. Byzantine Christianity brought many changes to Russia. The Russians acquired a written language, and a class of educated priests emerged. The Russians adopted Byzantine art, music, and architecture. Byzantine domes capped with colorful carved "helmets" became the onion domes of the Russian churches.

WRONG CHOICES EXPLAINED:

(1) The Mongols were nomadic herders of central Asia. They ruled the modern-day nations of Russia and Iraq. In the 13th century, the Mongols created the largest land empire in history. Their territories extended from China to the frontiers of western Europe.

(2) Vikings were Norsemen who raided the coast of Europe from the 8th to 10th centuries A.D. The Vikings invaded Russia in the 800s and established the first Russian state at the city of Kiev.

(3) Jews (Hebrews) were Semites who lived in the land currently called Israel, the ancient land of Canaan. By 1000 B.C., the Jews set up the kingdom of Israel with Jerusalem as its capital. They believed that God had promised them this land. Over time, Hebrew beliefs evolved into the religion called Judaism.

13. **2** The topography and climate of Russia have caused Russia to seek access to warm-water ports. Russian winters are long and bitterly cold, while summers are short and hot. Harsh winters create transportation problems. Russia's only seaport was Archangel on the White Sea, which is choked with ice much of the year. Since its northern ports freeze during the winter, Russia sought warm-water ports to the south. Russia focused especially on seaports on the Black Sea that have access to the Mediterranean Sea and eventually the Atlantic Ocean. Peter the Great, who ruled Russia from 1682 to 1725, created a strong army in Europe to expand Russia and gain ports on the Black Sea. In a long war with Sweden, he won territories adjoining the Baltic Sea. Here he built his new seaport and capital, St. Petersburg, his "window to the west." Peter failed in his goal to gain a port that would not be closed due to freezing in the winter. He fought the Ottoman Turks to gain warm-water ports on the Black Sea but did not succeed. However, in 1795, Catherine the Great, another absolute ruler, gained the right of Russian ships to sail from the Black Sea into the Mediterranean Sea by traveling through the Turkish-controlled Dardanelles.

WRONG CHOICES EXPLAINED:

(1) Russia does not depend upon rice as its main source of food. The cold Russian climate is not suited for growing rice.

(3) The topography and climate of Russia did not cause it to adopt policies of neutrality and isolation. During most of the Renaissance, Russia was under the rule of the Mongols and cut off from western Europe. Russia also looked to Constantinople, not Rome, for leadership. This isolated Russia because

western Europe was Roman Catholic or Protestant and Constantinople had adopted the Eastern Orthodox branch of Christianity. Russia never followed a policy of neutrality toward its neighbors. Russia sought to extend its boundaries through war with its neighboring countries.

(3) Russia did not acquire mineral-rich countries on other continents. Russia has an abundance of mineral resources. Russia has sought to expand its boundaries either for security or to obtain warm-water ports for transportation.

14. **4** One of the major achievements of Byzantine Emperor Justinian was that he preserved and transmitted Greek and Roman culture. The Byzantine Empire drew its name from the ancient Greek city of Byzantium. After the fall of Rome in A.D. 476, the Byzantine Empire was regarded as the heir to Roman power and traditions. The Byzantine Empire remained a political and cultural force for nearly 1,000 years after the fall of Rome. To Europe, it was a symbol of the power and glory of Rome long after the Roman Empire had faded. Emperor Justinian (527 to 565) preserved Roman law. He set up a team of scholars to gather and organize the ancient laws of Rome, a collection of laws that became known as the Justinian Code. The code served as the basis of law for the Catholic and Medieval rulers. Byzantine architecture combined the features of Greco-Roman and Persian architecture by devising a rectangular building topped by a round dome. Saint Sophia, the famous church erected in Constantinople in the 6th century by Emperor Justinian, is an example of Byzantine architecture. Byzantine culture represented a continuation of classical knowledge, especially its Greek and Hellenistic aspects. The Byzantine Empire preserved Greek science, philosophy, and literature. When the empire declined in the 1400s, some of the ancient texts of Greece were carried to the West and helped to stimulate the revival of learning during the later Middle Ages and the Renaissance.

WRONG CHOICES EXPLAINED:

(1) The kingdom of Ghana was founded around A.D. 750 and controlled trade routes in West Africa. The Emperor Justinian, who lived in the 6th century, could not have established a direct trade route with Ghana. Traders began to use a direct water route to West Africa during the 16th century.

(2) Emperor Justinian did not have to defend the empire against the spread of Islam. Islam threatened the Byzantine Empire in the years after Justinian's death.

(3) Emperor Justinian followed the Eastern Orthodox Christian Church, not Catholicism. During the reign of Justinian, a division grew between the Catholics in Rome and the Byzantine Church. The Orthodox Christian Church, also called the Eastern Orthodox Church, was the Christian Church of the Byzantine Empire.

15. **1** Both European medieval knights and Japanese samurai warriors pledged oaths of loyalty to their military leader. Medieval knights and

Japanese samurai warriors were part of a system known as feudalism. During the Middle Ages in Europe, the central government could not protect its subjects from local warfare or foreign invasion. Thus, small farmers surrendered their lands to powerful local nobles in exchange for protection. At the heart of the feudal system was the oath of loyalty between a vassal to a lord. Local nobles or lords were given land by their ruler or king in exchange for military service. These lords had small armies of their own made up of knights, armed warriors on horseback. Every local lord had a force of knights ready to defend the land against all invaders or neighboring lords. Knights were bound by a code of chivalry. This code charged them to be brave, loyal, and true to their word. During the 1100s in Japan, the central authority of the king was weakened, and local war lords fought each other. To provide military protection for their lands, noble landowners recruited samurai warriors. The samurais were knights on horseback who lived like the knights in Europe by a strict code of conduct known as gushido, the way of the warrior. The samurais promised loyalty and support to their lords during times of peace and war. In return for this loyalty, the daimyo (the noble landowners) provided the samurai with social status and economic support. If a warrior brought dishonor to his order or family, he was expected to take his own life. Like European knights, Japanese warriors were expected to pledge loyalty to their lords.

WRONG CHOICES EXPLAINED:

(2) Medieval knights and Japanese samurai did not pledge an oath of devotion to their nation-state. There were no nation-states uniting the countries in Europe and Japan. There were no central authorities.

(3) Knights in medieval Europe were expected to do service for the church, but they swore oaths of loyalty to their military leader, not to the church. Their obligation was to protect their lord. Samurai warriors did not pledge oaths of loyalty to serve their church. Most samurai warriors practiced Zen Buddhism or Shintoism, which stressed individual development over service.

(4) Both medieval knights and samurai warriors were expected not to dishonor their families. However, their first allegiance was to provide military support to their lord.

16. **3** A significant effect of Mansa Musa's pilgrimage to Mecca was Islamic learning and culture expanded in Mali. Mansa Musa was Mali's greatest ruler. He ruled for 25 years, from A.D. 1312 to 1337.He introduced Islam to Mali and enhanced the prestige of Mali through a famous pilgrimage to Mecca in 1324. Arab writers noted that he traveled in grand style. He took with him more than 1,200 slaves, each dressed in silk and carrying bars of gold. He gave away so much gold that the price of gold fell. At Mecca, he invited a skilled architect, As-Sahili, to return to Mali. He built mosques and other fine buildings in the capital of Timbuktu, which became the center of Muslim culture. The city had three universities and 50,000 residents at its height of power. Ibn Battuta, a medieval Arab traveler, wrote in his book *The*

Rihala that Mali was a kingdom based on justice and one in which there were security and peace.

WRONG CHOICES EXPLAINED:

(1) Mansa Musa's pilgrimage to Mecca did not contribute to the spread of the African written language to southwest Asia. Mali's empire extended to north and west Asia and never to southeast Asia.

(2) Military leaders did not gain control of Mali because of Mansa Musa's pilgrimage to Mecca. The Mali Empire declined in the 1400s when the people could not agree on who should rule the kingdom.

(4) The trading of gold for salt did not end because of Mansa Musa's pilgrimage to Mecca. During his rule, Mansa Musa used his large army to control the trading routes that exchanged gold for salt. When the Mali Empire declined in 1450, the kingdom of Songhai still controlled the trade in gold and silver. The kingdom of Songhai expanded the trading of gold for salt to Europe and Asia.

17. **1** A direct impact that the printing press had on 16th-century Europe was that it encouraged the spread of ideas. About 1450, Johannes Gutenberg, a German printer, invented printing from a movable metal-type press. The first European book printed by machine was the Gutenberg Bible. With the Gutenberg Bible, the European age of printing had begun. Printing presses sprang up in Italy, Germany, the Netherlands, and England. By 1500, they turned out more than 20 million volumes. The printing revolution brought immense changes. It enabled a printer to produce hundreds of copies of books with movable type on rag paper. Printed books were cheaper and easier to produce than hand-copied works. With books more readily available, more people learned to read and write. Readers gained access to a broad range of knowledge ranging from medicine and law to astrology and mining. Printed books exposed educated Europeans to new ideas, greatly expanding their horizons. The increased circulation of books helped to spread the ideas of the Renaissance as well as the ideas of Martin Luther, contributing to the religious turmoil that engulfed Europe in the 1500s.

WRONG CHOICES EXPLAINED:

(2) The printing press did not contribute to the beginnings of communism. Karl Marx, the Father of Communism, wrote in the *Communist Manifesto* that the evils of industrialization would lead to the rise of communism.

(3) The printing press did not encourage the establishment of democracy. The American Revolution of 1776 and the French Revolution of 1789 promoted the ideas of democracy.

(4) The printing press did not encourage the development of industrialization. The development of industrialization was encouraged by the economic and social changes in England during the 18th century.

18. **2** The road system was the technological advancement that helped unify both the Roman and the Inca Empires. The Roman Empire extended throughout the Mediterranean from Spain to parts of Asia Minor. To the north, the Roman Empire spread to what is now France as well as into parts of Britain. A complex network of roads linked the empire to distant places like Prussia and southern Russia. These roads were originally built by the Romans for military purposes. The Romans built a network of all-weather military roads to link distant territories to Rome. Roman roads were also technological marvels. The army built a vast network of roads constructed of stone, concrete, and sand connecting Rome to all parts of the empire. The Appian Way was the most important, helping to unify the empire and promoting trade. Roman roads were so solidly built that many of them were used long after the fall of the empire. In the 1400s, the Incas in Peru conquered a large area that extended over 2,500 miles from the Andes Mountains to the Pacific coast. Like the Romans, the Incas built a great road system to unite the empire. The roads wound more than 12,000 miles through mountains and deserts. Hundreds of bridges spanned rivers and deep gorges. Steps were cut into steep slopes and tunnels dug through hillsides. All roads led to Cuzco, the center of the Inca Empire. The roads allowed armies and navies to move rapidly through the empire. At regular stations, runners waited to carry messages. Relays of runners could carry news of a revolt swiftly from a distant province of the capital. The Incas kept soldiers at outposts throughout the empire. Within days of an uprising, the soldiers would be on the move to crush the rebels. This remarkable road systems enabled the Incas, like the Romans, to control and unify their empire.

WRONG CHOICES EXPLAINED:

(1) The astrolabe was an instrument used to determine latitude by measuring the position of the stars. The astrolabe was used by sailors in the 15th and 16th centuries and had no impact on the Roman and Inca Empires.

(3) Gunpowder was developed by the Chinese in the 600s, which was almost two hundred years after the fall of the Roman Empire. The use of gunpowder by the Spanish helped to defeat the Incas.

(4) Wheeled carts were developed by the Sumerians around 3200 B.C. The wheeled carts did not help to advance unity in either the Roman or Inca Empire.

19. **1** Cervantes' literary classic *Don Quixote,* the rule of Isabella and Ferdinand, and the art of El Greco are associated with the Golden Age in Spain. The century from 1550 to 1650 was known for the brilliance of its art and literature. In 1469, Isabella of Castille married Ferdinand of Aragon. This marriage between the rulers of two powerful kingdoms opened the way for a unified state. They helped to reorganize the army and encouraged agriculture and industry. Under their leadership, Spain became a leader in the exploration of Asia and the discovery of the New World in the Americas. The wealth gained from the New World enabled Spain to become a leading

power in Europe and laid the foundation for the rise of the Golden Age of Spanish power. Philip II, the great-grandson of Isabella, became a patron of the arts and also founded academies of science and mathematics. In the early 1600s, Miguel de Cervantes wrote *Don Quixote,* the first modern novel in Europe. It poked fun at medieval tales of chivalry and knighthood. Don Quixote, an old man who thinks he is a brave knight in battle with a giant, actually turns out to be attacking a windmill. El Greco (the Greek) was a famous painter of this period. Born on the Greek island of Crete, El Greco had studied in Renaissance Italy before settling in Spain. He painted religious scenes such as the *Assumption of the Virgin* and dramatic views of the city of Toledo. Cervantes and El Greco are considered to have had an important influence on the literary and artistic history of Europe.

WRONG CHOICES EXPLAINED:

(2) The Hanseatic League in Germany was formed in the 13th century to cooperate in defending their mutual trading interests. The league had complete control over the trading of such basic goods as fish, fur, wax, and salt.

(3) The Glorious Revolution in England ended the divine right of the monarchy in that country. The Glorious Revolution of 1689 also led to the supremacy of Parliament and a series of reforms that made the British government more democratic than the rest of Europe at that time.

(4) The Renaissance in Italy was a period of reawakened interest in the classical works of art, literature, and architecture of Greece and Rome. The Renaissance began in Italy in 1300 and by 1600 had spread to all parts of western and northern Europe.

20. **1** This diagram shows the Incas had a farming system that provided crops for the entire society. Farmers had to spend each year working land for the emperor and the temples as well as for their own communities. All land belonged to the Incas. However, cultivation and crops were allotted to specific groups of people or, as the diagram indicates, for a particular purpose, such as sun god, orphans, or state and community. The government also took possession of each harvest, dividing it among the people and storing parts of it in case of famine. The Incan farming system divided land ownership in three ways: state lands, religious lands, and community lands.

WRONG CHOICES EXPLAINED:

(2), (3), and (4) None of these statements are shown in the diagram. The diagram shows that most of the lands were farmed but does not provide information on whether 50 percent of the crops were set aside for the farmers who farmed the land. The diagram shows that the sick, orphans, widows, as well as priests and government officials received crops.

21. **4** The statement that best describes a result of the encounter between Europeans and native populations of Latin America is that plantations in the New World used enslaved Africans to replace native populations.

Sugar cane, which was introduced into West India and elsewhere in the 1500s, had to be grown on plantations, which were large estates run by an owner. The Spanish used the encomienda system, or forced labor, to get Native Americans to work on these plantations. Those who resisted were hunted down and killed. Disease, starvation, and cruel treatment caused a decline in the population. The native population also declined because they had no immunity to diseases brought by the conquerors like the measles and smallpox. The death of many Native Americans from these new diseases created a need for a workforce for the Spanish colonists. The Spanish began bringing Africans as slave laborers to the Americas by 1530. The Africans were immune to tropical diseases and began to fill the labor shortage. As the demand for sugar products skyrocketed, the Spanish and other European countries began buying large numbers of Africans. The slaves were forced to work as field hands or servants in the houses of wealthy landowners. The slave trade eventually grew into a huge and profitable business. The trade involving Europe, Africa, and the Americas was sometimes referred to as the "Triangular Trade" because the sea routes among these three continents formed a vast triangle.

WRONG CHOICES EXPLAINED:

(1) Native societies did not experience a rapid population growth as a result of the encounter. The native population of the Americas declined by as much as 90 percent in the 1500s.

(2) European nations did not lose power and prestige in the New World as a result of the encounter. The Spanish established a vast empire in Latin America that included Mexico, Peru, and parts of the West Indies. The British and French established empires in North America.

(3) Large numbers of natives did not migrate to Europe for a better life. Most Native Americans were enslaved and not allowed to travel anywhere. Some Europeans brought Native Americans back to their country to satisfy the curiosity that the rulers had about these people.

22. **2** *Speaker B* represents the view of King Louis XIV of France. Louis XIV, who ruled France from 1643 to 1715, believed in the divine right of kings. During his 72-year reign, France became the center of culture. Louis XIV's palace at Versailles influenced the architectural style of Europe. It cost over $100 million and was filled with 1,400 fountains. Louis XIV used the elaborate architecture to impress his subjects and foreign visitors. Versailles became a reflection of French genius. Peter the Great of Russia and Frederick the Great of Prussia modeled their palaces on Versailles. The reign of Louis XIV is considered the Golden Age of France. French became the language of polite society and replaced Latin as the language of diplomacy and scholarship. French writers like Molière and Racine pursued their talents at the Court of Versailles. France was the leading nation of the European continent. However, Louis kept France at war for much of the time that he ruled. He pursued an aggressive foreign policy and was at war from 1667 to

1712 with Holland, Great Britain, or Austria. These wars left France on the brink of bankruptcy. Under Louis XIV, France was a wealthy, powerful state with great cultural influence. However, his extravagant lifestyle and the costly wars emptied the treasury and drained the manpower of the country.

WRONG CHOICES EXPLAINED:

(1) *Speaker A* represents the views of Peter the Great, who ruled Russia from 1672 to 1725.

(3) *Speaker C* represents the ideas of Philip II, who ruled Spain from 1556 to 1598.

(4) *Speaker D* represents the views of James II of England, who wanted to rule as an absolute ruler.

23. **4** England was the nation most likely governed by *Speaker D*. In the 1600s, the Stuart kings tried to rule England by divine right and without consulting Parliament. In the Petition of Rights (1628), Parliament protested the despotism of Charles I and reaffirmed that the king, according to English law, could not levy taxes without Parliament's consent. The petition also stated that the king was prohibited from imprisoning persons without specific charges and without the provision of a jury trial. By withholding new tax laws, Parliament compelled Charles I to sign the Petition of Rights. From 1642 to 1649, a civil war broke out between the Puritans (supporters of Parliament) and the Cavaliers (supporters of the king). The Puritans, led by Oliver Cromwell, defeated the Cavaliers and put Charles I on trial for treason. He was beheaded. The Puritans ruled England until 1659. Parliament, tired of the dictatorial rule of the Puritans, voted to ask the exiled son of Charles I to return to England to rule in 1660. Charles II was determined to avoid antagonizing Parliament. In 1679, he yielded to Parliament's wishes and signed the Habeas Corpus Act, which limited the king's power by providing that a prisoner must be brought before a judge with a statement of charges. The Habeas Corpus Act protected individuals against arbitrary arrest and imprisonment. In 1685, Charles II died and James II, brother of Charles, became king. James II offended the people by violating English laws and dissolving Parliament when it objected. As part of the Glorious Revolution, or bloodless revolution, in 1688, Parliament passed the Bill of Rights, which finally ended rule by divine right in England.

WRONG CHOICES EXPLAINED:

(1) Russia was governed by *Speaker A*.

(2) France was governed by *Speaker B*.

(3) Spain was governed by *Speaker C*.

24. **2** The type of government most closely associated with all these speakers is absolute monarchy. Absolutism is a political system in which the king or monarch has complete authority over the government without limits on his or her power. The political philosophy of absolutism dominated Europe throughout the 16th and 17th centuries.

WRONG CHOICES EXPLAINED:

(1) Limited monarchy is a system of government in which the monarch's powers are not absolute but specifically guided by a constitution or legislative body.

(3) Direct democracy is a system of government in which citizens participate directly rather than through elected representatives.

(4) Constitutional democracy is a system of government in which the powers of the government are outlined in a written document or constitution. In a constitutional democracy, the people vote for their officials.

25. **2** These ideas of Catherine the Great of Russia originated during the Age of Enlightenment. The Age of Enlightenment, also known as the Age of Reason, was an intellectual and cultural movement of the 18th century tying together the ideas of the Scientific Revolution. The Enlightenment thinkers believed that just as one could use reason to explain why things happen in the physical universe, there must be natural laws to govern society. They claimed that through reason and logic one could explain the laws of society and also solve the problems of society. These philosophers criticized the abuse of government and proposed ways to correct it. The writers of the Enlightenment created a new way of looking at power and authority as well as what makes up good and lawful government. Catherine the Great, who ruled Russia from 1762 to 1796, was an enlightened despot who justified her rule by claiming to rule in the people's interests by making good laws, promoting human happiness, and improving society. Catherine the Great read the works of Enlightenment writers such as Montesquieu and Voltaire. She revised and codified laws, patronized the arts, and undertook other public welfare projects.

WRONG CHOICES EXPLAINED:

(1) The Age of Exploration was the period from 1400 to 1600 during which European monarchs sent explorers to find new trade routes, resources, and land in Asia, Africa, and the Americas.

(3) The Protestant Reformation began in Europe in 1517 when Martin Luther challenged papal authority. The Protestant Reformation led to the formation of new Christian churches and destroyed the religious unity of Europe.

(4) The French Revolution of 1789 was a political, economic, and social revolution that ended the absolutism of Louis XVI. The French Revolution also ended social and economic injustices in France. The French Revolution was the first democratic uprising in Europe.

26. **2** *Speakers B* and *C* represent Karl Marx's ideas of communism. Karl Marx wrote the *Communist Manifesto* in 1848 and argued that economic conditions determined the course of history. He wrote that history is a struggle between the "have's and the have not's." In ancient times, the conflict was between plebeians and patricians. During the Middle Ages, the struggle was

between lords and serfs. In industrial societies, the struggle is between the capitalists (factory owners) and the proletariat (the workers). Marx and Engels predicted that the workers of the world would rise up against the capitalists, seize the means of production, and create a classless society in which the people would work together for the common good. The state would wither away. Under communism, the availability of goods and services would be so great that the society would be organized "from each according to his ability, to each according to his needs." Private property would be abolished.

WRONG CHOICES EXPLAINED:

(1), (3), and (4) None of these speakers together represents the ideas of Karl Marx. *Speaker A* represents the ideas of laissez-faire capitalism and *Speaker D* represents the views of mercantilism. Laissez-faire endorses that government should have a hands-off policy. Mercantilism is an economic theory developed during the 17th and 18th centuries and promotes the belief in a favorable balance of trade to ensure prosperity.

27. **1** *Speaker A* is referring to laissez-faire capitalism. The economic theory of laissez-faire capitalism proposes that governments should not interfere with business. Laissez-faire stemmed from the economic philosophers of the 18th-century Enlightenment. They argued that government regulation only interfered with the production of wealth. The economic ideas of laissez-faire were skillfully presented by Adam Smith in his book *Wealth of Nations.* Smith argued that the free market—the natural forces of supply and demand—should be allowed to operate and regulate business. The free market would produce more goods at lower prices, making them affordable by everyone. A growing economy would also encourage capitalists to reinvest new profits in new ventures. Smith and other capitalists argued that the marketplace was better off without any government regulation. However, Smith believed that the government had a duty to protect society and administer justice. Adam Smith's ideas of laissez-faire capitalism would gain increasing influence as the Industrial Revolution spread across Europe and to other areas of the world.

WRONG CHOICES EXPLAINED:

(2), (3), and (4) None of these speakers represents the ideas of laissez-faire capitalism.

28. **4** The basic cause of the political changes shown on this map was that Japan needed raw materials for industrialization. As a small island-nation, Japan lacked many basic resources necessary to ensure its growth as an industrial nation. Japan's late-19th-century industrialization created the need for raw materials, especially cotton, iron ore, coal, and oil. It wanted to gain markets for its manufactured goods. Japanese nationalists also wanted to replace European imperialism with Asian imperialism. In 1895, Japan defeated China in the Sino-Japanese War and forced the Chinese to give up their

claims to Korea. Japan also gained Taiwan and won special trading privileges. In 1904 to 1905, Japan fought Russia in the Russo-Japanese War. The Japanese victory stunned Western nations. For the first time in modern European history, an Asian nation had defeated a major European power. The treaty ending the war forced Russia to leave Korea and gave Japan a foothold in Manchuria. In 1910, Japan annexed Korea and forced its people to build railroads and roads for Japan's benefit. The Japanese took half of Korea's yearly rice crop to support the people at home and to achieve its goal of territorial expansion in Asia. Japan's imperialism enabled her to gain scarce raw materials for the country's industries.

WRONG CHOICES EXPLAINED:

(1) and (3) Neither of these two statements is shown on the map. There is no information about a Russo-Japanese alliance and whether the Japanese wanted to spread the beliefs of Shinto.

(2) Korea did not defeat Japan in the Sino-Japanese War. Japan defeated China in the Sino-Japanese War.

29. **2** The event associated with the changes shown on this map is the Meiji Restoration. During the Meiji Restoration from 1862 to 1912, Japan reversed its policy of isolation, ended feudalism, and began to modernize by borrowing from the Western powers. The goal of the Meiji leader, or enlightened ruler, was to make Japan a strong military and industrial power. The Meiji emperor realized that the nation had to modernize to avoid becoming a victim of imperialism. Japanese leaders sent students abroad to western countries to learn about their form of government, economies, technology, and customs. The government also brought foreign experts to Japan to improve industry. The Japanese adopted a constitution based on the model of Prussia with the emperor as the head. The new government was not intended to bring democracy, but to unite Japan and to make it equal to Western powers. The Meiji government established a banking system, modern shipyards, as well as factories for producing cement, glass, and textiles. The leaders also built up a modern army based on a draft and constructed a fleet of steam-powered iron ships. By imitating the West, Japan remained independent but also became an imperial power.

WRONG CHOICES EXPLAINED:

(1) The Opium War (1839 to 1842) was between England and China. China was defeated and forced to open up more ports to the British for trading. The British also gained control of Hong Kong.

(3) The Chinese Nationalist Revolution took place in 1911 by Dr. Sun Yixian (Sun Yat-sen). He is considered the father of modern China.

(4) The rise of the Soviet Union began during World War I. In 1917, the Communists overthrew the government of Nicholas II and, by 1922, had established the Union of the Soviet Socialist Republics, better known as the Soviet Union.

30. **1** The Bolshevik Party in 1917 gained the support of the peasant class because they promised them "Peace, Land, and Bread." Lenin's promise of "Peace, Land, and Bread" during the Bolshevik Revolution of 1917 was made in an effort to gain popular support to overthrow the government. When Russia entered World War I in 1914, the country was unprepared. By 1915, Russian casualties were almost 2 million. In March 1917, workers led food riots all across Russia. The Russian Revolution began when soldiers refused to fire on striking workers in St. Petersburg. Czar Nicholas II was forced to give up his throne. Leaders of the Duma, the Russian Parliament, set up a republic. This provisional government, headed by Prince Luvov, set up a western-style democratic government that guaranteed civil rights and freed political prisoners. The decision to continue the war and the inability to provide food resulted in the loss of support among the people. The Bolsheviks, a revolutionary group led by Lenin, promised "peace for the soldiers, land for the peasants, and bread for the workers." Lenin, who had been in exile when the March Revolution broke out, was sneaked into the country by the Germans, who used him to undermine the support of the provisional government. The majority of the Russian people were not Communists but were displeased with the government. In November 1917, the Bolsheviks seized control of the government and established the first communist nation in Europe.

WRONG CHOICES EXPLAINED:

(2) "Liberty, Equality, Fraternity" are terms associated with the French Revolution.

(3) and (4) The Bolsheviks never promised the abolition of the secret police or democratic reforms in all levels of government. The Bolsheviks were an elite group of revolutionaries who wanted to gain power and did not outline a program of civil liberties and democratic reforms. Under Bolshevism, or communism, the government had total control of all aspects of Soviet society.

31. **1** The time period in German history most accurately represented in this map is between World War I and World War II, from 1918 to 1939. On June 28, 1919, Germany signed the Versailles Treaty that officially ended World War I. According to the Treaty, Germany had to cede Alsace-Lorraine to France. France also gained control of the Saarland and mines as reparations. The Saar Basin was to be occupied for 15 years by the major powers, after which people living in the area could vote on which country they wanted to join. Germany was forced to give up a large strip of German land called the Polish Corridor to the newly created nation of Poland. This strip cut off East Prussia from the rest of Germany and gave Poland access to the Baltic Sea. In the 1930s, Adolf Hitler and the Nazi Party would gain support by blaming Germany's troubles on the Versailles Treaty. Hitler would promise to regain Germany's lost territories in Europe.

WRONG CHOICES EXPLAINED:

(2) The Berlin Conference took place between 1884 to 1885.

(3) The time period for the Congress of Vienna was from 1814 to 1815.

(4) The unification of Germany under Bismarck occurred from 1864 to 1871.

32. **2** The statement that describes one major aspect of a command economy is that most economic decisions are made by the government. A command economy is an economic system in which the central authority or government makes all the production decisions on what and how much to produce as well as sets the price of goods. Under communism, the Soviet Union developed a command economy in which the government officials (such as Gosplan, a state-planning commission) made all basic economic decisions. The government owned all businesses and allocated financial and other resources to any area it wanted to develop.

WRONG CHOICES EXPLAINED:

(1) In a Capitalist economy, supply and demand determine what will be produced.

(3) In a Socialist type of economy, the means of production are controlled by labor unions.

(4) A traditional economy is mainly agricultural.

33. **4** Ireland is an area once controlled by Britain, suffered a mass starvation in the 1840s, and became an independent Catholic nation in 1922. The main cause of the mass starvation in Ireland during the 19th century was the failure of the potato crop. In the 1840s, Ireland experienced one of the worst famines of modern history. The potato, introduced from the Americas, was the main source of food for most of the Irish. In 1845, a blight, or disease, destroyed the potato crop. Other crops, such as wheat and oats, were not affected. The British, who ruled Ireland, continued to require the Irish to ship these crops outside Ireland, leaving little for the Irish except the blighted potato. The result was the Great Hunger. Of a population of 8 million, about 1 million people died from starvation and disease over the next few years. Millions more emigrated to the United States and Canada. The Great Hunger left a legacy of Irish bitterness toward their British overlords. Throughout the 19th century, the Irish demands for self-rule intensified. The Irish quest for self-rule dragged on for decades. The existence of a large Protestant population in the northern part of Ireland posed problems for Irish independence. Back in the 16th century, when England became Protestant, the people of Ireland had remained Catholic. In an attempt to control Ireland, the English sent Protestant settlers to Ireland in the 1600s. These Protestants settled mainly in the north. In 1914, the British Parliament passed a home rule bill allowing self-rule for Ireland. The home rule bill was shelved when World War I began. In 1922, a Catholic independent nation of Ireland, known as the self-governing Irish-Free State, was established, but

the Protestant majority in northern Ireland (Ulster) remained under British rule. Many Catholics objected to the division of Ireland. The status of Northern Ireland has remained a controversial issue throughout the 20th and early 21st centuries.

WRONG CHOICES EXPLAINED:

(1), (2), and (3) None of these areas suffered mass starvation in the 1840s, and none of them is a Catholic nation.

34. **3** Totalitarian countries are characterized by government control of newspapers, radio, and television. Totalitarianism is a 20th-century system of government in which a one-party dictatorship regulates all aspects of the lives of citizens. By using modern technology, the totalitarian state can bombard the public with relentless propaganda, stressing the importance of the state over the individual. Hitler's Germany, Stalin's Soviet Union, and Mao's China were examples of totalitarian states. For example, in the Soviet Union, radios and loudspeakers blared into factories and villages. In movie theaters and schools, citizens heard about Communist successes and the evils of capitalism. Newsreels and newspapers proclaimed the misery of workers under capitalism and praised communism. The government controlled all the newspapers and what books were published. In totalitarian countries, the government expected obedience from everyone and achieved it through the effective use of terror. In all totalitarian countries, the needs of the state are more important than those of the individual.

WRONG CHOICES EXPLAINED:

(1) Totalitarian countries are not characterized by free and open discussions of ideas. Totalitarian countries do not allow for differences of opinions. The government controls all forms of public discussion or policy.

(2) Totalitarian countries are not characterized by a multiparty system with several candidates for each office. The only political party in the Soviet Union was the Communist Party, and the National Socialist Party was the only political party in Nazi Germany. Until 2003, the only political party in the totalitarian government of Saddam Hussein was the Ba'ath Party.

(4) Totalitarian governments do not provide for the protection of people's civil liberties. Totalitarian countries have no regard for the individual's civil liberties. The state determines what freedoms and liberties an individual possesses.

35. **4** The name that would best complete this partial outline is Kwame Nkrumah. The first African nation south of the Sahara to win freedom was the British colony of the Gold Coast. During the 1940s, Kwame Nkrumah was impatient with Britain's policy of gradual movement toward independence. In 1940, he worked to liberate the Gold Coast from the British. Nkrumah organized strikes and boycotts and was often imprisoned by the British government. In 1957, the Gold Coast won independence. Nkrumah,

who had emerged from prison to become prime minister of the new nation, named it Ghana after the ancient West African empire. Nkrumah pushed through expensive development plans and economic projects, such as new roads, new schools, and expanded health facilities. This costly project soon crippled the country and strengthened his opposition. In addition, Nkrumah was also criticized for spending too much time on Pan-African efforts and neglecting economic problems in his own country. In his dream of a United States of Africa, Nkrumah was inspired by the Pan-Africanist Marcus Garvey, who wanted to create an Africa ruled by Africans. In 1958, Nkrumah hosted the first Pan-African meeting in Africa. This led to the formation of the Organization of African Unity (OAU) in 1963. In 1966, while Nkrumah was in China, he was deposed. The army and police opposed his dictatorial policies. Nkrumah died in 1972.

WRONG CHOICES EXPLAINED:

(1) Atatürk (Mustafa Kemal) lived from 1881 to 1938. Atatürk means "Father of Turks." He was the first president of Turkey from 1923 to 1938. He introduced reforms to westernize Turkey and created a secular state based on western customs.

(2) Ho Chi Minh founded the Vietnamese Communist Party. He was a national leader who fought against French colonialism and the United States in the Vietnam War. He died in 1969.

(3) José de San Martin was a South American nationalist leader. He defeated the Spanish in Argentina and Chile in 1810 in the struggle to end the colonial rule of the Spanish.

36. **3** Since 1948, a major reason for the conflict between Arabs and Israelis is that each side claims sovereignty over the same land. The historic claim of the Israelis and Arabs to the same land has been a key issue in the continuing dispute between the two sides. The land currently called Israel was the home of the Jews until Rome destroyed the country in A.D. 70. Lacking a homeland, most of the Jews scattered throughout the world. After the expansion of Islam in the 7th century, the area fell under the control of the Arabs and later the Ottoman Turks. In 1917, the British promised the Jews a homeland in the same territory but not at the expense of the Arabs who were still living in the area. In 1947, the United Nations drew up a plan to divide the land, which was then called Palestine and was under British rule, into an Arab and a Jewish state. In 1948, Israel proclaimed its independence, but the Arabs refused to recognize the partition and invaded Israel. Israel won the war. More than a half million Arabs became refugees. These Arabs still want an Arab Palestinian state. Arabs have vowed to drive the Jews out and restore Palestine as an Arab nation. Arab-Israeli wars occurred in 1949, 1956, 1967, and 1973. All of these wars have failed to resolve the conflict between Arabs and Israelis.

WRONG CHOICES EXPLAINED:

(1) There are no large deposits of oil reserves under the disputed land between the Arabs and Israelis. The vast deposits of oil in the Middle East are located in Saudi Arabia.

(2) Although the United States has tried to be an honest broker in conflicts between the Arabs and Israelis, Arab nations believe that the U.S. favors Israel. The U.S. was the first country to recognize Israel's independence and has supported the country with economic and military aid. However, the United States has tried to resolve the conflict through the Camp David Accords of 1979 and the Middle East Peace Conference in 1991. Both of these efforts were designed to open up negotiations for agreement between Arabs and Israelis.

(4) The Israelis have not sought to control trade on the eastern end of the Mediterranean Sea. Since 1956, Egypt has controlled the Suez Canal. There have been no conflicts over Egyptian control of the canal, which connects trade with the Red Sea and the Mediterranean. In 1967, however, Egypt and her Arab allies did move to close the Gulf of Aqaba, Israel's outlet to the Red Sea. Egypt's action led to the Six-Day War and the defeat of Egypt and her Arab allies.

37. **4** In the 1980s, Mikhail Gorbachev's attempts to change the Soviet Union resulted in a series of economic and political reforms. In 1985, Gorbachev came to power in the Soviet Union. At age 54, he was the youngest Soviet leader since Stalin. He pursued new ideas and was eager to reform the government and the economy. Gorbachev realized that economic and social reforms could not occur without a free flow of ideas and information. He launched glasnost, or openness. He ended censorship and encouraged more freedom. The government allowed more churches to open, and Gorbachev released dissidents from prison. He also restructured the state economy in a process called perestroika. He backed some free-market reforms, including limited private enterprise. Gorbachev's policies had a widespread impact. Relations with the United States improved, and treaties reduced the threat of war.

WRONG CHOICES EXPLAINED:

(1) Gorbachev's attempts at change did not lead to an increase in tensions between India and the Soviet Union. The Soviet Union had supported India during the Cold War. India, as a democratic nation, encouraged Gorbachev's efforts at reform.

(2) Gorbachev's attempts at change did not strengthen the Communist Party. In the past, voters could vote only for candidates who were handpicked by the Communist Party. Under glasnost, voters could choose from a list of candidates for each office. Voters were no longer required to vote for the candidates selected by the powerful Communist bosses.

(3) Gorbachev's attempts at change did not result in a shift from producing consumer goods to producing heavy machinery. Gorbachev wanted the

Russian economy to produce more consumer good like televisions and washing machines instead of steel and iron products. By reducing the arms race, Gorbachev hoped to improve consumer production.

38. **2** The most valid conclusion based on the ecological cycle shown in this diagram is that the destruction of forests leads to soil erosion. The environmental group Green Peace has warned that the rain forests will be wiped out in 80 years if deforestation is not decreased. Some estimate that the world is losing more than 50 million acres of tropical rain forests each year. The destruction of the rain forests in places like Zaire and central Africa has left the remaining soil barren. Heavy rain wears away the nutrients from these cleared lands, and as the diagram shows, the remaining soil is of such poor quality that it produces few crops and long-term production is stagnated. In parts of Zaire and central Africa, much of the fertile soil has turned into deserts after years of low rainfall. The Amazon rain forest, which is the world's largest continuous area of rain forest, has experienced a 40 percent rise in its destruction during the past two years. This continued trend would accelerate global warming and pose great environmental dangers. Efforts have been made to halt the erosion of the soil, such as planting more trees and restricting cattle grazing. However, efforts have been hampered by the need for countries such as Brazil and Zaire to pay off their massive international debts.

WRONG CHOICES EXPLAINED:

(1), (3), and (4) None of these conclusions can be supported by the diagram. There is no information about increased grain yields, grain production impact on the environment, or how natural disasters impact grain production.

39. **1** The conclusion that can be drawn from these statements is that societies often modify their environment to meet their needs. The Aswan Dam, or Saad el Aali in Arabic, lies in the middle of the Egyptian desert. It captures the mighty Nile River in the world's third largest reservoir, Lake Nasser. Before the dam was built, the Nile River overflowed its banks once a year and deposited 4 million tons of nutrient-rich silt on the valley floor, making Egypt's otherwise dry land productive and fertile. However, there were some years when the river did not rise at all, causing widespread drought and famine. In 1952, Egyptian President Gamal Abdal-Nasser pledged to control his country's annual flood with a giant new dam across the Nile River. His plan worked. The Aswan Dam captures floodwater during rainy seasons and releases the water during times of drought. The dam also generates enormous amounts of electric power—more than 10 billion kilowatt-hours every year. That is enough electricity to power 1 million color televisions for 20 years. When completed in 2009, the Three Gorges Dam will be the largest hydroelectric dam. The dam will stretch more than 1 mile across the Yangtze River and soar 600 feet above the valley floor. It will be the largest concrete dam in the world. The purpose of the project is to generate power to keep

pace with China's economic growth. Chinese officials note that the dam will relieve the danger of flooding. In addition, navigation capacities on the river from Yichang to Chongging will be improved so that 10,000-ton fleets can make direct trips, which will improve commerce. Brazil's Tucuruí Dam, located at the lower Tocantins River and adjacent to the Amazon Basin, is the largest dam built in a tropical rain forest and is also the largest man-made lake to be built in such a place. It cost nearly $10 billion and flooded 1,000 square miles of woodland. Ninety percent of Brazil's energy comes from hydroelectric power. The dam was considered to be a cheaper alternative to importing fossil fuel. Since its completion in 1984, the Tucuruí Dam has changed the lives of indigenous people, displaced 40,000 individuals and destroyed the habitat of fishes and plants. The vast reservoir created by the dam is also a place where disease-bearing mosquitoes thrive and breed. According to the National Institute for Amazonian Research, the decomposing vegetation is contributing to one-sixth of Brazil's total greenhouse gas emissions.

WRONG CHOICES EXPLAINED:

(2), (3), and (4) None of these conclusions can be drawn from these statements. There is no information about monsoons, topography, or land development.

40. **4** The main idea of this Brazilian cartoon is that the United States wants to control its relationships with Latin America. Throughout the 20th century, the United States has been the dominant power in Latin America. The U.S., represented by the Uncle Sam figure in the cartoon, is demonstrating its influence in Brazil by even trying to control how soccer is played. Soccer is the dominant sport in Brazil. Recent events in Brazil have challenged the dominant role of the United States in Latin America. Luiz Inacio Luia da Silva was elected president of Brazil in 2003. Da Silva envisions a United South America that gains strength by drawing closer together in trade, much like the European Union. The United States has opposed these efforts because they threaten its own economic domination in the area. Da Silva has persuaded South Africa and India to join Brazil in a dialogue that will focus on social and economic issues. Da Silva is also courting China to become its next big trading partner. China and Brazil have signed a commercial accord covering agribusiness, technology, construction, and natural resources. Da Silva has also followed a more pragmatic approach in foreign policy. He has befriended Venezuelan President Hugo Chavez, who has been very critical of the United States. Da Silva, like Chavez, has criticized the U.S.-backed Free Trade Area of the Americas, which is designed to eliminate or reduce trade barriers among the nations in the Americas. Brazil has opposed this agreement and suggested a series of bilateral agreements to reduce tariffs on goods. Brazil has taken a leadership role in the World Trade Organization among the less-developed nations in seeking an end to agricultural subsidies and free trade on foreign products. The United States has

opposed an end to agricultural subsidies. These developments have begun to change the relationship between the United States and countries in Latin America.

WRONG CHOICES EXPLAINED:

(1), (2), and (3) None of these ideas are expressed in the cartoon.

41. **3** These headlines refer to events in the subcontinent of India. India and Pakistan are two countries on the subcontinent of India. Since the partitioning in 1947, India, which is predominantly Hindu, and Pakistan, which is mostly Muslim, have been at odds over Kashmir, located near India's northwest frontier. In 1947, Kashmir's Hindu prince signed the area over to India. However, its majority Muslim population wanted to be part of Pakistan. Although most of the people are Muslim, two-thirds of the territory is governed by India. In 1948, the U.N. Security Council called for a vote of the people of Kashmir to choose which country they wanted to join. A vote was never taken. In Indian-held regions, Muslim guerrillas have been fighting against Indian rule, leading to frequent flare-ups and border wars between Pakistan and India. During the Indian independence movement, many Muslims in India demanded a separate state of Pakistan to address concerns about their status as a religious minority. In 1906, the Muslim League was set up in India to protect Muslim interests. At their Lahore Conference in 1940, the Muslim League first officially proposed the partitioning of India into separate Hindu and Muslim nations. Most Muslims lived in the northwest and northeast of the subcontinent. When World War II ended, the British realized that they could no longer keep India. As independence approached, widespread rioting broke out between Hindus and Muslims in Calcutta, East Bengal, Bihar, and Bombay. In August 1946, four days of rioting left more than 5,000 people dead and 15,000 hurt. In 1947, the British parliament passed the Indian Independence Act. This act ended British rule in India but also provided for the partitioning or subdividing of the Indian subcontinent into two separate, independent nations. One nation was the Hindu-dominated India, and the other was Pakistan, with a Muslim majority. India tested its first nuclear bomb in 1974. Pakistan felt threatened, and it tried to acquire its own nuclear technology. In 1998, Pakistan and India both tested nuclear weapons. As the nuclear rivalry raised new fears, the leaders of the two nations met. They agreed to build bridges that would ease tensions and improve relations. The international community is fearful that India and Pakistan will rely entirely on nuclear weapons to maintain their security. Still, both countries face strong nationalist and religious pressure to use at least the threat of nuclear conflict in future confrontations.

WRONG CHOICES EXPLAINED:

(1), (2), and (4) None of these headlines refers to events in the regions listed. Latin America includes lands in the Western Hemisphere that were influenced by Spanish and Portuguese settlers. Sub-Saharan Africa includes nations from Mauritania to Nigeria. East Asia includes the countries of China, Korea, and Japan.

42. **3** The main idea of this 2002 cartoon is that East Timor is facing several dangers that threaten its existence as a new nation. In 1975, Indonesia seized the Portuguese colony of East Timor. Indonesia is the largest Muslim nation in the world, but East Timor is predominantly Catholic. Even before Indonesia took East Timor away from Portugal, a proindependence rebellion was underway in East Timor. Indonesia used military force to deal with this independence movement. More than 200,000 citizens of East Timor died as a result of their efforts to gain independence. In 1996, two activists from East Timor, Bishop Carlos Ximenes Beto and José Ramos-Horta, won the Nobel Peace Prize for their efforts to gain independence for their country. In 1999, Indonesia agreed to let the people of East Timor vote for or against independence. The vote was held under United Nations supervision and 80 percent of the people voted for independence. Pro-Indonesian militias went on a rampage. These soldiers destroyed East Timor's main cities. Many of the territory's 600,000 people fled into West Timor, still part of Indonesia. An Australian-led peacekeeping force helped restore order. Then, U.N. administrators came to help rebuild East Timor and prepare for independence. East Timor became an independent country in 2002. In 2002, Xanano Gusmao, who is pictured in the cartoon, was elected the new country's first president. Gusmao is a legend among his people. He fought armed rebellions against Indonesian rule for two decades and spent more than six years in prison and under house arrest. He was released in September 1999, just days after East Timor's landmark referendum vote on independence. Since taking office in 2002, Gusmao has made it clear that he supports amnesty for the pro-Indonesian militias that went on a rampage. This approach has put Gusmao at odds with his former political party, Fretelin (Revolutionary Front for an Independent East Timor). There have been reports of tension between the two, with Gusmao criticizing unnamed government members for leading a lavish lifestyle at the expense of the poor. In May 2006, growing street violence prompted Gusmao to take emergency control over the police and army in a bid to end the unrest.

WRONG CHOICES EXPLAINED:

(1), (2), and (4) None of these ideas is expressed in this cartoon.

43. **4** One way in which the Tang dynasty, the Gupta Empire, and the European Renaissance are similar is that they all included periods of cultural achievements. In the 600s, a general named Tang Taizong came to power and established the Tang dynasty (618 to 907). The Tang dynasty ruled an immense empire of more than 50 million people. The emperor provided a revival of scholarship and the arts. Every educated person was expected to write poetry. Tang artisans perfected the making of porcelain and invented block printing. They carved the text of a page into a block of wood. Then they

reproduced the page by inking the wood and pressing a piece of paper onto it. The Gupta Empire ruled from 320 to 550. After 200 years of civil war, the Gupta dynasty was able to unite much of India. The Gupta emperors organized a strong government that ensured peace and prosperity. This stable government provided a background for advances in learning and art. In literature, Gupta writers produced fine poems and dramas. The best-known poet and playwright was Kalidasa, whose play *Shakuntala* is still performed today. Architects built beautiful stone temples for Hindu worship. Hindu temples were designed to reflect cosmic patterns. The ideal shape was a square inscribed in circles to symbolize eternity. Hindu temples were filled with carvings in gold of gods and goddesses. Buddhists built stupas, large dome-shaped shrines containing the remains of holy people. In mathematics, Gupta mathematicians devised the concept of zero and developed the system of 10 numerals, which is still used today. These are known as Arabic numerals because other Arabs carried them from India to the Middle East to Europe. The European Renaissance, which started in Italy in the 15th century, began with a reemphasis on the Greco-Roman culture that had been generally neglected during the Middle Ages. Renaissance writers focused on reason, a questioning attitude, experimentation, and free inquiry, in contrast to the medieval concerns with faith, authority, and tradition. Renaissance writers encouraged society to examine the world around them. They hoped to use ancient learning to increase knowledge about their own time. The paintings of Michelangelo, Leonardo da Vinci, and Raphael along with the literary achievements of Dante demonstrate a faith in the creative ability of the traditions. The Tang dynasty, the Gupta Empire, and the European Renaissance were Golden Ages of cultural development.

WRONG CHOICES EXPLAINED:

(1) Religious unity was not a way in which the Tang dynasty, the Gupta Empire, and the European Renaissance were similar. During the Gupta Empire, India had both Hindu and Buddhist temples. Under the Tang dynasty, China followed Confucianism as well as Buddhism. During the European Renaissance, southern Europe remained Roman Catholic while many northern Germans and northern European nations during the Renaissance became Protestant.

(2) The Tang dynasty, the Gupta Empire, and the European nations during the Renaissance did not experience democratic reforms. During these periods, kings or emperors, ruled the countries.

(3) Economic isolation was not a policy followed during any of these periods. The Tang dynasty, the Gupta Empire, and the European Renaissance promoted trade with other nations. Trade expanded with nations in Asia and the Middle East during the Tang dynasty and the Gupta Empire.

44. **1** One similar goal shared by Simón Bolívar and Mohandas Gandhi was ending foreign control. Simón Bolívar, who was born to a wealthy Venezuelan Creole family in 1783, always envisioned an independent and

united Latin America, free from Spanish domination. As a young man, he studied in Europe. His love of freedom was strengthened by the ideas of the French Revolution. Before returning from Europe, Bolívar promised that he would not rest until he broke the chain put upon the people of Latin America by the Spanish. He became known as the "Liberator" for his role in the wars for independence against Spain. In 1819, he helped free Venezuela and by 1824, had secured the freedom of Colombia, Ecuador, Peru, and Bolivia. In the 1920s and 1930s, Mohandas Gandhi became the leader of the Indian nationalist movement that wanted independence from Great Britain. Gandhi was a pacifist who believed in the principle of *satyagraha,* which in English is called passive resistance or civil disobedience. Gandhi believed that one perfect civil resister was enough to win the battle of right and wrong. Gandhi launched his campaign of nonviolent civil disobedience to weaken the British government and its economic power in India. One effective method of protest was the boycott in which Indians refused to buy British cloth and other manufactured goods. Gandhi urged Indians to begin spinning their own cloth and used the spinning wheel as a symbol of his rejection of Western civilization. He also called on the people to refuse to attend government schools, pay taxes, and vote in elections. Gandhi used these nonviolent methods to show the British the futility of denying India its freedom. India would not achieve its independence until 1947, one year before Gandhi's assassination on January 30, 1948.

WRONG CHOICES EXPLAINED:

(1) Religious freedom was not a goal of either Simón Bolívar or Mohandas Gandhi. These men sought to gain political, not religious, freedom for their country. Gandhi encouraged greater tolerance for the Muslim minority in India, but political freedom was his main goal.

(3) Simón Bolívar and Mohandas Gandhi did not want to establish a limited monarchy. Both of them supported a democratic form of government.

(4) Neither of these men wanted to create collective farms. Bolívar wanted to establish land reforms that allowed peasants to own land. Gandhi wanted India to have home industries and reject industrialization.

45. **3** The Armenian Massacre, the "killing fields" of the Khmer Rouge, and Saddam Hussein's attacks against the Kurds are examples of human rights violations. Human rights are those rights, such as freedom of speech and press, held by all people by virtue of belonging to a civil society. According to the United Nations' Universal Declaration of Rights adapted in 1948, all people are entitled to basic liberties and freedom. The Armenian Massacre refers to the atrocities committed against the Armenian people of the Ottoman Empire during World War I. By the 1890s, roughly 2.5 million Christian Armenians had begun to demand their freedom. As a result, relations between the group and its Turkish ruler grew strained. Throughout the 1890s, the Turkish troops killed tens of thousands of Armenians. When World War I broke out, the Armenians pledged their support to Turkey's enemies.

In response, the Turkish government deported nearly 2 million Armenians between the years 1915 and 1918. Along the way, more than 600,000 died of starvation or were killed by Turkish soldiers. Women and children were abused, and the entire wealth of the Armenian people was expropriated. In 1975, the Khmer Rouge, led by Pol Pot, took control of Cambodia. Pol Pot renamed the country Kamphuchea. He instituted a reign of terror and tried to drive out all Western influence. From 1975 to 1979, he tried to establish a purely agrarian society. The Khmer Rouge forced people out of the cities and resettled them in the country. He and his followers killed off the educated classes of the country, monks, minority groups, technicians, and artists. An estimated 1.25 to 1.7 million Cambodians died from forced labor, starvation, or execution in the killing fields. In 1979, Vietnam invaded and occupied Cambodia. In 1993, the U.N. supervised general elections. Pol Pot died in the jungles of northern Cambodia in 1998. The Kurds are a nomadic people following their herds through the mountains and high plateaus of eastern Turkey, western Iran, and northern Iraq. The Kurds are the largest ethnic group in the Middle East without their own homeland. Throughout the 20th century, their struggle for political and cultural autonomy was opposed by the countries to which they have been scattered. The Turks and Iranians have persecuted them. Saddam Hussein, who was a dictator that ruled Iraq from 1971 to 2001, crushed any effort by the Kurds in northern Iraq to gain freedom. In the late 1980s, the Iraqis dropped poison gas on the Kurds, killing 5,000. Despite Hussein's defeat in the Gulf War of 1990, he brutally crushed the Kurdish rebellion, which forced more than 1 million of them to flee to other countries. The United States responded by establishing in northern Iraq a safe haven for Kurds and a Kurdish control zone of 4 to 5 million refugees. The Kurds hoped that the zone would eventually become the core of self-governing Kurdistan. The American invasion of Iraq in 2003 and the end of Saddam Hussein's government has allowed the Kurds to achieve basic human rights and has renewed the issue of an independent Kurdistan.

WRONG CHOICES EXPLAINED:

(1) Apartheid is an official policy of strict segregation of races. Apartheid was practiced in South Africa from 1945 until it was repealed in 1991.

(2) Enslavement refers to holding a person in servitude and considering the person as property with no basic rights.

(4) Forced collectivization was a pooling of land and labor in an attempt to increase efficiency. Joseph Stalin in Russia and Mao-Zedong in China used collectivization to boost agricultural production.

46. **2** In western Europe, the Middle Ages began after the collapse of the Roman Empire. The Middle Ages covers the 900-year period from the collapse of Rome in the 5th century to the middle of the 1400s. The fall of Rome resulted in a period of disorder in western Europe. The Roman roads deteriorated, leading to a decline in trade. As trade diminished, the cities lost population. There was no central government. In response, political and

social systems emerged, such as feudalism and manorialism, based on powerful lords and their holdings. The Roman Catholic Church preserved the elements of Roman civilization and assumed many functions of government. The Catholic Church emerged as a unifying force in western Europe and had great influence over economic, social, and religious life.

WRONG CHOICES EXPLAINED:

(1) The Mughal Empire ruled India from 1526 to 1837.
(3) The Ottoman Empire ruled from 1453 to 1918.
(4) The Byzantine Empire lasted from 330 to 1453.

47. **1** These executions occurred during the French Revolution. On July 14, 1789, the French people stormed the Bastille, which was a symbol of the Bourbon monarchy that had ruled the country for more than 200 years. The revolutionary slogan of "Liberty, Equality, and Fraternity" led to the overthrow of King Louis XVI and the establishment of a National Assembly with a written constitution and a limited monarchy. European nations denounced the revolution because they feared it would spread to their countries. These nations threatened to intervene to save the king. Fearful of an attack, the French declared war on other European countries. The Radicals, or Jacobins, gained control and turned France into a republic. King Louis XVI and his wife Marie Antoinette were beheaded by the new government. The Committee of Public Safety led by Maximilien Robespierre launched the Reign of Terror from 1793 to 1794 to save the revolution from foreign and domestic enemies. Robespierre believed that France could achieve a republic of virtue only through terror. The guillotine, which was considered more humane because it worked swiftly, became the symbol of the horrors of the Reign of Terror. By 1794, the public rejected violence, and Robespierre himself was executed, thus ending the Reign of Terror.

WRONG CHOICES EXPLAINED:

(2), (3), and (4) None of these executions apply to the Russian, Chinese, or Cuban Revolutions. Historians used the term Reign of Terror to describe the radical state of the French Revolution.

48. **3** The statement that is best supported by information found in this chart is that the Reign of Terror crossed social and economic boundaries. The chart shows that the Reign of Terror had no respect for class or social status. The clergy, nobility, middle class, working class, and peasants all lost their lives to the guillotine. Although the majority of victims were working class, peasants, and middle class, all members of French society suffered during the Reign of Terror.

WRONG CHOICES EXPLAINED:

(1) The clergy were not spared during the Reign of Terror. The chart shows that of those executed, 7 percent were members of the clergy.

(2) The Reign of Terror did not affect all classes equally. Only 15 percent of those killed were clergy and nobility. The working class, peasants, and the middle class comprised 84 percent of the people who were executed during the Reign of Terror.

(4) The working class, not the peasants, were the most frequent victims of the Reign of Terror. The chart shows that 4,389 members of the working class were executed compared with 3,961 peasants.

49. **3** This passage best illustrates circumstances that characterized the Commercial Revolution. The Commercial Revolution marked the change in the economies of Europe in the Middle Ages in which there was a growth of towns, banking systems, and trade among nations. As trade revived, merchants needed money to buy goods, so they borrowed money from moneylenders. In time, the need for capital or money for investments led to the growth of the banking system. Joint stock companies were sometimes formed to raise large sums of money. These ventures were privately owned companies that sold stocks to investors hoping to make a profit. The joint stock companies, as a form of business organizations, were the forerunners of the present-day corporations. Merchants also developed a system of insurance to help reduce costs. For a small fee, the underwriter would insure the merchants' shipments. Bankers also devised various new credit facilities. Bills of exchange for use in international trade enabled a merchant in one country to pay for goods purchased in another country. Banknotes or paper money issued by the banks were used as a convenient substitute for gold and silver. These new methods of doing business were part of the Commercial Revolution that transformed the medieval economy.

WRONG CHOICES EXPLAINED:

(1) The Crusades were religious wars between Christian Europe and the Muslims for control of the Holy Land. The Crusades lasted from 1096 to 1246.

(2) The Age of Reason is also known as the Enlightenment in 18th-century Europe. Enlightenment thinkers believed that one could use reason to understand the universe.

(4) The Scientific Revolution is the period in science during the 16th and 17th centuries. Scientists challenged traditional authority and used reason and observations to reach conclusions.

50. **1** The events in these headlines contributed most directly to the beginning of World War I. By 1914, Europe was divided into two large camps of secret alliances. The two most important alliances were the Triple Alliance, consisting of Germany, Austria-Hungary, and Italy, and the Triple Entente, consisting of Great Britain, France, and Russia. The purpose of these alliances was to preserve the balance of power. However, any dispute involving any of these countries threatened to involve all the others. The Balkans, which were a hotbed of nationalist rivalries, had created tension in the area.

The spread of nationalism had led some groups to break away from the Ottoman Empire and form new nations, including Bulgaria, Romania, and Serbia. Serbia, which had gained its independence in 1878 and had a large Slavic population, hoped to absorb the Slavs of the Balkan Peninsula. Austria-Hungary opposed Serbia's expansion because it feared rebellion among its multiethnic empire and was threatened by Serbia's growth. Serbia wanted to annex Bosnia-Herzegovina, which had a large Serbian population. Russia, the largest Slavic country, defended the rights of people of similar backgrounds to unite. By 1914, Russia's big brother policy of Pan-Slavism made her ready to support Serbia, its Slavic brother, against any threats. The spark that led to World War I was the assassination of Archduke Franz Ferdinand of Austria-Hungary on June 28, 1914, in Bosnia by a Serbian nationalist, Gavriol Princip. Archduke Ferdinand was the heir to the Austrian throne. The assassination set off a chain reaction that broke the peace of Europe. Austria-Hungary, supported by Germany, declared war on Serbia. Russia, which supported Serbia, declared war on Austria-Hungary. Russia turned to France, who promised its support against Germany and Austria-Hungary. On July 28, Austria-Hungary invaded Serbia, and on July 30, Russia came to the aid of Serbia. Germany, which was a member of the Triple Alliance, declared war on Russia and later on France. When Germany invaded Belgium on August 3 and violated Belgian neutrality, Great Britain declared war on Germany. By August 1914, the European continent was involved in World War I.

WRONG CHOICES EXPLAINED:

(2), (3), and (4) None of these events contributed to the outbreak of World War I. The Cold War began in 1945. The development of Communist rule in Europe extended from 1945 to the late 1980s. The strengthening of European monarchies was during the 16th and 17th centuries.

THEMATIC ESSAY: GENERIC SCORING RUBRIC

Score of 5:

- Shows a thorough understanding of the theme or problem
- Addresses all aspects of the task
- Shows an ability to analyze, evaluate, compare and/or contrast issues and events
- Richly supports the theme or problem with relevant facts, examples, and details
- Is a well-developed essay, consistently demonstrating a logical and clear plan of organization
- Introduces the theme or problem by establishing a framework that is beyond a simple restatement of the task and concludes with a summation of the theme or problem

Score of 4:

- Shows a good understanding of the theme or problem
- Addresses all aspects of the task
- Shows an ability to analyze, evaluate, compare and/or contrast issues and events
- Includes relevant facts, examples, and details, but may not support all aspects of the theme or problem evenly
- Is a well-developed essay, demonstrating a logical and clear plan of organization
- Introduces the theme or problem by establishing a framework that is beyond a simple restatement of the task and concludes with a summation of the theme or problem

Score of 3:

- Shows a satisfactory understanding of the theme or problem
- Addresses most aspects of the task or addresses all aspects in a limited way
- Shows an ability to analyze or evaluate issues and events, but not in any depth
- Includes some facts, examples, and details
- Is a satisfactorily developed essay, demonstrating a general plan of organization
- Introduces the theme or problem by repeating the task and concludes by repeating the theme or problem

Score of 2:

- Shows limited understanding of the theme or problem
- Attempts to address the task
- Develops a faulty analysis or evaluation of issues and events
- Includes few facts, examples, and details, and may include information that contains inaccuracies
- Is a poorly organized essay, lacking focus
- Fails to introduce or summarize the theme or problem

Score of 1:

- Shows very limited understanding of the theme or problem
- Lacks an analysis of evaluation of the issues and events
- Includes little or no accurate or relevant facts, examples, or details
- Attempts to complete the task, but demonstrates a major weakness in organization
- Fails to introduce or summarize the theme or problem

Score of 0: Fails to address the task, is illegible, or is a blank paper

PART II: THEMATIC ESSAY QUESTION

Throughout history, trade routes have had a major impact on nations and regions. The Mediterranean trade routes, dominated by Venice and Genoa in the 13th century, had a positive impact on European society. The Atlantic Slave Trade routes of the 16th century had a negative effect on the western coast of Africa.

According to legend, Venice was originally founded in the 5th century by Roman refugees after their land had been ravaged by the Huns led by Attila. These refugees settled among the marshes of the Po estuary along the Adriatic Sea in northeastern Italy.

The Byzantine Empire controlled most of the trade in the eastern Mediterranean. However, Venice, by the middle of the 12th century, had become a leading city bolstered by its powerful merchant fleet and overseas trade. Venice also benefited from the Fourth Crusade to Constantinople. In 1204, Venetians and Crusaders stormed Constantinople. Before sacking the city, merchants were able to bring back thousands of valuable relics that they later sold throughout Europe. Venetian merchants also gained control of the Byzantine trade routes and established a trade monopoly with Asia.

Renewed interest in products of the East, such as silk, perfume, and sugar, allowed Venice to serve as a link between western Europe and Asia. This bustling port city attracted traders from all over the world. These advantages made Venice one of the wealthiest city-states during the late Renaissance. At the peak of its power, Venice had 36,000 sailors operating 3,300 ships dominating the Mediterranean trade lanes. At its height, the Venetian Empire stretched from the Adriatic Sea in the east to Milan in the west.

The Venetian fleet carried European wheat, wine, lumber, and wool to eastern Mediterranean cities such as Alexandria and Constantinople. After goods arrived in Venice, traders took them over the Alps and up the Rhine River to Flanders. From there, other traders took the goods throughout Europe as far as areas along the Baltic Sea.

Like Venice, Genoa became a wealthy northern Italian city due to overseas trade. In the early 14th century, both Venice and Genoa built ships that were able to sail during the whole year. With these improvements, ships could transport more goods and could travel much quicker. The rise of Venice and Genoa gave a Christian Europe a crucial connection to the East and contributed to the rise of the Renaissance in these cities. Eventually, the spirit of the Renaissance, which led to a reawakened interest in the classical works of art, architecture, and literature of Greece and Rome, would spread to northern Europe.

The dominance of the trade routes by Venice and Genoa would also change the economic structure of these cities and, later, other European cities. A banking system developed as bankers made loans to kings and supported other commercial ventures that contributed to economic growth across Europe.

Venice and Genoa's control of the only practical route by which Asian goods reached Europe contributed to the high prices of these products. Many Europeans wanted to bypass the Mediterranean and trade directly with the East as a way to increase profits and end domination by Venice and Genoa. Thus, by the 1400s, European countries like France, Spain, Portugal, and England began the quest to seek ocean routes to Asia that would eventually lead to the discovery of the New World and shift the trade routes from the Mediterranean Sea to the Atlantic Ocean and end the domination by Venice and Genoa.

In the 1500s, the Atlantic Slave Trade began to fill the needs for labor on the large plantations in the Americas. At first, European colonists in the Americas forced Native Americans to work their profitable mines and plantations. As natives began dying by the millions from diseases brought from Europe, Europeans became desperate for new workers. Europeans looked to Africa to replenish their labor force. Many Africans had been exposed to various European diseases and had built up an immunity to them. Many Africans also had experience in farming and could be taught large-scale plantation work. In time, the buying and selling of Africans for work became a massive enterprise.

Each year, tens of thousands of enslaved Africans were traded across the Atlantic to work on tobacco and sugar plantations in the Americas. For enslaved Africans, the journey to the Americas was a horror. Once purchased, Africans were packed below the decks of slave ships. Hundreds of men, women, and children were crammed into a single vessel. Slave ships became floating coffins on which up to half of the Africans onboard died from disease or brutal mistreatment.

Many African rulers and merchants played a willing role in the Atlantic Slave Trade. However, as the slave trade grew, some African rulers voiced their opposition to the practice. King Nzinga Mbemba of the Congo in West-Central Africa, also known as Affonso, had originally participated in the slave trade. However, he soon realized its devastating effect on African societies. In 1526, he wrote a letter to the king of Portugal in which he protested the taking of Africans for enslavement. His pleas failed, and the slave trade continued and steadily grew. Lured by its profits, many African rulers continued to participate. As for African merchants, they simply developed new trade routes to avoid rulers who refused to cooperate.

It is estimated that by the mid-1800s, when the overseas slave trade was finally stopped, close to 11 million enslaved Africans had reached the Americas. Another 2 million probably died under the brutal conditions of the voyage between Africa and the Americas.

The Atlantic Slave Trade had a profound negative impact on West Africa. In Africa, numerous cultures lost generations of their fittest members, their young and able, to European traders and plantation owners. In addition, countless African families were torn apart. Many of them were never reunited. The slave trade devastated African societies by introducing guns to the continent. African rulers seeking to conquer new territories saw these firearms as more effective than spears. The African chiefs and kings traded guns for potential slaves, thus spreading war and conflict throughout Africa.

In West Africa, the loss of population resulted in some states disappearing forever. At the same time, new African states arose, whose way of life depended on the slave trade. The rulers of these new powerful states, like the Asante Kingdom, waged wars against other African states to gain control of the slave trade in their regions. The Atlantic Slave Trade destroyed the fabric of African society.

The Mediterranean trade routes and the Atlantic Slave Trade impacted society in different ways. The rise of the city-states of Venice and Genoa enabled Europe to expand and develop its civilizations. The Atlantic Slave Trade, in contrast, contributed to the decline of Africa's civilization. These positive and negative changes continue to impact the world in the 21st century.

PART III: DOCUMENT-BASED QUESTIONS

Part A: Short Answers

Document 1

The information shown on this map about the governments of Western Europe and Eastern Europe after World War II indicates that countries in Eastern Europe were Communist while countries in Western Europe were non-Communist.

Note: This response receives full credit because it correctly interprets the information on the map about the governments of Western and Eastern Europe after World War II.

Document 2a

Based on these broadcasts from Free Radio Rakoczi and Free Radio Petofi, two reasons the Hungarian people were asking for help in 1956 were:

(1) Soviet troops attacked Hungary.

(2) Hungary's revolution was failing and free radio in Hungary was being destroyed.

Note: This response receives full credit because it specifically cites information in the document to show why the Hungarian people were asking for help in 1956.

Document 2b

Based on this broadcast from Radio Moscow, one result of the Hungarian Revolution was a new government was formed under the leadership of Janos Kadar.

Note: This response receives full credit because it correctly states one result of the Hungarian Revolution.

Documents 3a and 3b

Based on this map and the Burkhardt photograph, one way the Cold War affected the city of Berlin was Berlin was divided into four sectors. West Berlin was non-Communist, and East Berlin was Communist.

Note: This response receives full credit because it specifically cites how the Cold War affected Berlin.

Document 4

According to Prime Minister Nehru, India's foreign policy in 1956 was nonalignment and to maintain friendly relations with all countries.

Note: This response receives full credit because it states the foreign policy of Prime Minister Nehru in 1956 as cited in the document.

Document 5

Based on Sook Nyul Choi's description, two ways the beginning of the Korean war affected the people of Korea were:

(1) Refugees found their way to Seoul.

(2) Traitors were killed.

Note: This response receives full credit because it cites specific information from the document to show how the beginning of the Korean War affected the people of Korea.

Documents 6a and 6b

Based on the information shown on these maps, one similarity in the way the Cold War affected Korea and Vietnam was that both countries were divided and wars occurred in both countries.

Note: This response receives full credit because it states one similarity that can be drawn from looking at both maps.

Documents 7a and 7b

Based on this map and President John F. Kennedy's address, one way the Cold War affected Cuba was that Soviet missiles were placed in Cuba.

Note: This response receives full credit because it states specific information on how the Cold War affected Cuba.

Document 8a

According to this document from the Library of Congress, an effect the Cold War had on Nicaragua in the 1980s was that compulsory military service was introduced and the Sandinistas were supported by Cuba and the Soviet Union.

Note: This response receives full credit because it notes the effect of the Cold War on Nicaragua in the 1980s.

Document 8b

According to Mark A. Uhlig, Violeta Chamorro hoped to bring to Nicaragua the political change of throwing the Sandinistas out of power and proclaiming democracy and freedom.

Note: This response received full credit because it states a political change that Violeta Chamorro hoped to bring to Nicaragua.

DOCUMENT-BASED QUESTION: GENERIC SCORING RUBRIC

Score of 5:
- Thoroughly addresses all aspects of the *Task* by accurately analyzing and interpreting at least **four** documents
- Incorporates information from the documents in the body of the essay
- Incorporates relevant outside information
- Richly supports the theme or problem with relevant facts, examples, and details
- Is a well-developed essay, consistently demonstrating a logical and clear plan of organization
- Introduces the theme or problem by establishing a framework that is beyond a simple restatement of the *Task* or *Historical Context* and concludes with a summation of the theme or problem

Score of 4:
- Addresses all aspects of the *Task* by accurately analyzing and interpreting at least **four** documents
- Incorporates information from the documents in the body of the essay
- Incorporates relevant outside information
- Includes relevant facts, examples, and details, but discussion may be more descriptive than analytical
- Is a well-developed essay, demonstrating a logical and clear plan of organization
- Introduces the theme or problem by establishing a framework that is beyond a simple restatement of the *Task* or *Historical Context* and concludes with a summation of the theme or problem

Score of 3:
- Addresses most aspects of the *Task* or addresses all aspects of the *Task* in a limited way, using some of the documents
- Incorporates some information from the documents in the body of the essay
- Incorporates limited or no relevant outside information
- Includes some facts, examples, and details, but discussion is more descriptive than analytical
- Is a satisfactorily developed essay, demonstrating a general plan of organization
- Introduces the theme or problem by repeating the *Task* or *Historical Context* and concludes by simply repeating the theme or problem

Score of 2:
- Attempts to address some aspects of the *Task*, making limited use of the documents
- Presents no relevant outside information
- Includes few facts, examples, and details; discussion restates contents of the documents

- Is a poorly organized essay, lacking focus
- Fails to introduce or summarize the theme or problem

Score of 1:
- Shows limited understanding of the *Task* with vague, unclear references to the documents
- Presents no relevant outside information
- Includes little or no accurate or relevant facts, details, or examples
- Attempts to complete the *Task*, but demonstrates a major weakness in organization
- Fails to introduce or summarize the theme or problem

Score of 0: Fails to address the *Task*, is illegible, or is a blank paper

Part B: Essay

The United States and the Soviet Union had cooperated to win World War II. However, conflicting interests and mutual distrust led to the Cold War. This continued state of tension between the United States and the Soviet Union affected many regions of the world, including Europe, Asia, and Latin America.

The Cold War began in 1945 and ended with the collapse of the Soviet government in 1991. The Cold War was a period of political and economic struggle between the nations of the West led by the United States and the Communist countries of the Soviet Union. The United States and other Western European countries considered communism an evil force creeping across Europe and threatening countries around the world. In 1946, Winston Churchill, the British prime minister who supported the United States, coined the phrase "Iron Curtain." Churchill proclaimed that an Iron Curtain had descended over Eastern Europe and that Europe was divided between those countries controlled by the Soviet Union and those who followed the West (Doc. 1). The Iron Curtain referred to the Soviet-made barrier that split Europe into Communist countries, like Hungary and Poland, and the non-Communist countries of France, Italy, and Great Britain.

The Cold War immediately affected Germany at the end of World War II. In 1945, Germany was divided into four zones controlled by Great Britain, France, the United States, and the Soviet Union. The Soviet Union stripped its zone, which became known as East Germany, of industrial resources. The United States, England, and France agreed to combine their sectors of Berlin to form what became known as West Berlin (Doc. 2a). They also planned to form an independent West German state by joining their zones of occupation. Although Berlin was located in East Germany, the Soviets controlled only one section, and the Western powers held the rest of the city, called West Berlin. Russia was fearful of a restored Germany. The Soviets reacted by closing all the highways and links to Berlin. The city was blockaded. It could not receive supplies by land. The United States and its allies decided to airlift supplies rather than break the blockade by sending land troops. The Berlin Airlift kept the people from starving by bringing tons of food, clothing, and fuel every day At the peak of the airlift, 13,000 tons landed on one day. After 321 days, in May 1949, the Soviets ended the blockade and once again opened the land routes to Berlin.

The United States policy, which became known as containment, was designed to give economic and military assistance to countries fighting against communism. In 1949, the United States and 12 other Western European nations formed the North Atlantic Treaty Organization as an alliance against communism. These nations pledged to support each other in case any member nation was attacked. The alliance was formed after the Berlin Airlift and the division of West Germany from Communist East Germany. In 1955, the Soviet Union formed the Warsaw Pact in response to the creation of NATO. The Warsaw Pact included the Soviet Union and seven of its satellites in Europe. It was a defensive alliance promising mutual military cooperation. The Warsaw Pact ended with the collapse of communism in 1991.

The dividing of Germany created tension between the United States and the Soviet Union. Between 1949 and 1961, more than 3 million East Germans fled to West Berlin. Most of these refugees escaped by going from East Berlin to West Berlin. Suddenly, on August 13, 1961, Premier Nikita Khrushchev of the Soviet Union ordered the construction of the Berlin Wall. The wall was made of concrete bocks and barbed wire (Doc 3b). It extended 28 miles along the border between East and West Germany, sealing off East Germany in violation of an existing agreement. The Berlin Wall became a symbol of the Cold War. By 1959, East German leaders could no longer count on support from the Soviet Union. A rising wave of protests forced the Communist East German government from power. On November 9, 1989, the new East German leaders allowed people to leave Germany. Within days, more than 2 million Germans crossed the border. The crowds were so huge that the government bulldozed new openings in the Berlin Wall. The Berlin Wall was torn down by joyous Germans.

The Cold War also affected the Soviet satellites in Eastern Europe. Joseph Stalin, the dictator of the Soviet Union, maintained a tight control over countries such as Poland and Hungary. After Joseph Stalin's death in 1953, Communist leaders in Hungary eased control for two years but imposed it again when Hungary did not achieve their economic goals. Bitter opposition to these tighter restrictions turned into a full-scale revolution. In 1956, Imre Nagy, the new Hungarian Communist prime minister, declared Hungary a neutrality and withdrew from the Warsaw Pact. This raised the fear that the Soviet Union was losing control of its satellite countries in Eastern Europe. In response, the Soviet Union poured in troops and tanks (Doc. 2a). Thousands of Hungarians died, and more than 100,000 Hungarian refugees fled to the United States. The Soviets deposed Nagy. Free Hungarian Radio Rakoczi and Free Radio Petofi pleaded for help, insisting that communism would continue to spread if the Soviets were not stopped by force (Doc. 2b).

Western European countries, as well the Uinted States, did nothing. After the Soviets removed Nagy, they installed a puppet regime under Janos Kadar, who reimposed strict control over Hungary (Doc. 2b).

The Cold War also affected regions like the subcontinent of India. After World War II, India and many other developing nations followed a policy of nonalignment (Doc. 4). India's policy of nonalignment during the Cold War means it did not support either the United States or the Soviet Union. Prime Minister Nehru believed that India could ease international tensions by following an independent course (Doc. 4). Under Nehru, India helped form a bloc of nonaligned nations. In that role, India arranged a prisoner of war exchange after the Korean War. India also played an active part in the United Nations peacekeeping missions in trouble spots around the world. Nehru's policy of nonalignment also allowed India to accept help from both the Untied States and Russia. The policy of nonalignment ended with the collapse of the Soviet Union in 1991.

Communism also affected the countries of China, Korea, and Vietnam in Asia. In 1949, the Communists took control of China. Mao Zedong, the Communist leader, had won the support of China's huge peasant population. The Communists pledged to distribute land to poor peasants and end oppression by landlords. The United States supported Chiang Kai Shek (Jiang Jieshi) because of his opposition to communism. The Chinese Communists established the People's Republic of China, and Jiang's forces fled to the island of Taiwan.

During the Cold War, Korea and Vietnam were divided into Communist and non-Communist states (Doc. 6a, 6b). In 1945, Korea, which had been a colony of Japan since 1910, was divided at the 38th parallel. North Korea was occupied by Soviet troops and South Korea by American troops. When the United States and Russia failed to agree regarding Korean unification and Russia refused to cooperate with U.N. election procedures, Korea remained divided. In the north, the People's Republic of Korea with its capital at Pyongyang kept close ties with the Soviet Union and China. South Korea, officially the Republic of Korea, maintained links with the United States. By mid-1949, both Soviet and American troops had withdrawn from Korea. On June 25, 1950, North Korean forces, hoping to unify the country under a Communist government, invaded South Korea. The United Nations Security Council, in the absence of the Soviet Union, condemned the invasion and organized an army to oppose it. Although 16 countries contributed troops to the U.N. forces, more than 90 percent of the soldiers came from the United States. Commanded by Douglas MacArthur, the U.N. forces drove the Communist Koreans back to North Korea and within six weeks had conquered most of North Korea. The Chinese Communists came to the aid of North Korea and forced the U.N. army to retreat (Doc. 6a). North Korean troops filled the streets of Seoul. With the aid of Russian and Chinese Communist tanks, many South Koreans were killed as traitors (Doc. 5). By the summer of 1951, the battle lines stabilized near the 38th-degree parallel. On July 27, 1953, the two sides agreed to stop fighting and accepted an armistice line that today continues to divide Korea at the 38th parallel. The Korean War, which lasted more than three years, resulted in the death of 5 million people.

The Cold War also affected Vietnam in Asia. At the end of World War II, Vietnamese forces under Ho Chi Minh occupied parts of North Vietnam. Ho Chi Minh, which means "He Who Enlightens," was the Vietnamese leader who was determined to build a Communist movement and win independence. When the French refused to recognize his new nation, he began a war to regain control. After eight years of bitter struggle, the French were defeated at Dien Bien Phu in 1954 and were forced to withdraw. The Geneva Agreement in 1954 divided Vietnam at the 17th parallel with elections to be held within two years to unite the country (Doc. 6b). Ho Chi Minh and his Communist followers established a government in the north. South Vietnam came under the control of the non-Communist government led by Ngo Dinh Diem. The Diem regime rejected plans for an all-Vietnamese election because he feared losing to the Communists. Diem claimed that honest elections were impossible in the north. The United States, fearful of a Communist takeover in South Vietnam, continued the struggle and provided military support to help South Vietnam. Although Minh died in 1969, the Vietnamese War continued. In 1975, Communist forces captured Saigon, the capital of South Vietnam, and Vietnam became a united country in 1975.

The ideological struggle of the Cold War would also impact the countries of Cuba and Nicaragua. In 1959, Fidel Castro overthrew the dictatorship of Fulgencio Batista and seized power. He denounced the United States as imperialistic, forbade elections, and nationalized American investments without compensation. The United States reacted by breaking off trade. In 1961, Castro proclaimed his intention to transform Cuba into a Communist state and threatened to expose communism to other Latin American countries. He wanted closer ties with the Soviet Union. The Cuban Missile Crisis of October 1962 developed when President John F. Kennedy announced that Castro was allowing the Soviet Union to build nuclear missile bases in his country, which was just 90 miles off the coast of Florida (Doc. 7a). If the plan succeeded, Soviet nuclear missiles would be within easy striking distance of major cities in the United States. President Kennedy blockaded Cuba and threatened to invade if the missiles were not withdrawn (Doc. 7b). After 13 days of intense negotiations, Premier Nikita Khruschev of the Soviet Union agreed to withdraw the missiles in exchange for a pledge by President Kennedy that the United States would not invade Cuba.

From 1936 to 1979, the Somoza family governed Nicaragua. The Somozas' regimes were repressive but had close ties to the United States because of their anti-Communist stance. In 1979, the Sandinistas, a group that included both reform-minded nationalists and Communists, overthrew the Somoza government. The Sandinistas were supported by Cuba and the Communist countries of Eastern Europe as well as the Soviet Union (Doc. 8a). The Sandinista Police and the Sandinista People's Army (EPS) were trained by these Communist countries. By the 1980s, the EPS forces were the best military forces in Central America (Doc. 8a). Under the Sandinistas, President Daniel Ortega introduced land reform and other socialist policies. They seized lands that belonged to wealthy Somoza supporters and turned them over to peasant groups. They also taught people to read and write and improved rural healthcare. However, the Sandinistas faced growing opposition from the upper- and middle-class Nicaraguans who had lost property to them and opposed the creation of a socialist dictatorship. With the help of the United States, which feared that Nicaragua might become a Communist state like Cuba, the Contras—forces that opposed the Sandinistas—fought a civil war that lasted over a decade and seriously weakened the economy. As the economic situation worsened, President Ortega agreed to hold free elections. In 1990, Violeta Chamorro, whose husband's murder had sparked the Sandinista revolution, challenged Daniel Ortega for the presidency. Chamorro ran as a moderate, challenged communism, and proclaimed the importance of democracy (Doc. 8b). Chamorro won the election as president, and the Sandinistas peacefully turned over power. Chamorro asserted that her victory would result in freedom spreading to Poland, Bulgaria, and Chile because it was "the hour of democracy" (Doc. 8b).

The Cold War was a worldwide struggle between forces of democracy represented by the United States and communism led by the Soviet Union. Although the two countries never fought each other, the tensions between them led to problems in Europe, Asia, and Latin America. Although the Cold War ended, the struggle between the United States and Russia would still influence the course of events in the world at the beginning of the 21st century.

Topic	Question Numbers	Total Number of Questions	Number Wrong	*Reason for Wrong Answer
U.S. AND N.Y. HISTORY				
WORLD HISTORY	2, 4, 5, 10, 14, 15, 17, 19, 21, 22, 23, 30, 33, 35, 37, 42, 43, 44, 45, 46, 47, 48, 50	23		
GEOGRAPHY	1, 3, 7, 8, 11, 12, 13, 16, 18, 28, 29, 31, 36, 39, 41	15		
ECONOMICS	20, 26, 27, 32, 38, 49	6		
CIVICS, CITIZENSHIP, AND GOVERNMENT	6, 9, 24, 25, 34, 40	6		

*Your reason for answering the question incorrectly might be (a) lack of knowledge, (b) misunderstanding the question, or (c) careless error.

Actual Items by Standard and Unit

	1 U.S. and N.Y. History	2 World History	3 Geography	4 Economics	5 Civics, Citizenship, and Gov't	Number
Methodology of Global History and Geography		2	1, 3			3
UNIT ONE Ancient World		4, 5	7, 8		6, 9	6
UNIT TWO Expanding Zones of Exchange		10, 14, 46	12, 13			5
UNIT THREE Global Interactions		17, 19	16	49		4
UNIT FOUR First Global Age		21, 22, 23		20	24, 25	6
UNIT FIVE Age of Revolution		47, 48	28, 29	26, 27, 32		7
UNIT SIX Crisis and Achievement (1900–1945)		30, 33, 50	31		34	5
UNIT SEVEN 20th Century Since 1945		35, 37, 45	36, 39, 41		40	7
UNIT EIGHT Global Connections and Interactions		42		38		2
Cross topical		15, 43, 44	11, 18			5
Total # of Questions		23	15	6	6	50
% of Items by Standard		46%	30%	12%	12%	100%

Examination June 2007

Global History and Geography

PART I: MULTIPLE CHOICE

Directions (1–50): For each statement or question, write in the space provided the *number* of the word or expression that, of those given, best completes the statement or answers the question.

Base your answer to question 1 on the map below and on your knowledge of social studies.

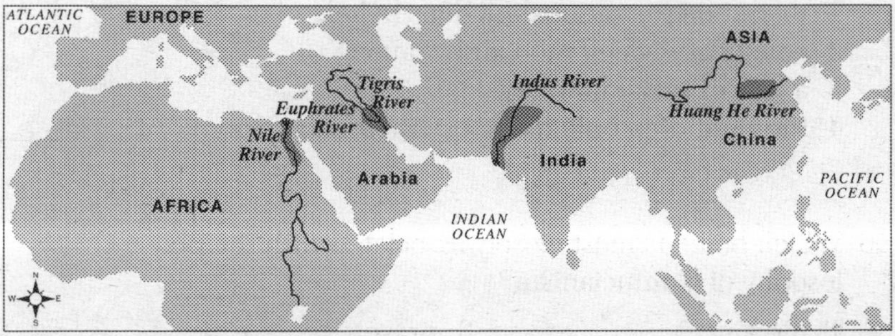

Source: Charles F. Gritzner, *Exploring Our World, Past and Present*, D. C. Heath and Company (adapted)

1 The main purpose of this map is to illustrate the location of

1 overseas trade routes
2 early belief systems
3 river valley civilizations
4 burial sites of ancient rulers

1 ____

2 Which social scientist specializes in studying issues such as the scarcity of resources and availability of goods?

1 anthropologist
2 sociologist
3 economist
4 archaeologist

2____

3 Which feature would most likely be shown on a physical map?

1 population density
2 vegetation zones
3 climate
4 mountain ranges

3____

4 Which society practiced direct democracy?

1 ancient Athens
2 dynastic China
3 Gupta Empire
4 early Egypt

4____

5 The caste system in India was characterized by

1 toleration for various religious beliefs
2 equality between men and women
3 a lack of social mobility
4 the right of people to choose their occupations

5____

6 Which belief is most closely associated with the philosophy of Confucianism?

1 nirvana
2 reincarnation
3 prayer
4 filial piety

6____

7 What was one result of large armies traveling great distances during the Crusades?

1 Europe's population severely declined.
2 Democracy in the Middle East grew.
3 Cultural diffusion increased.
4 Slavery was eliminated. 7_____

8 Constantinople was a thriving city in the 1200s mainly because of its location on a major trade route between

1 China and southern Africa
2 the Atlantic Ocean and the Baltic Sea
3 the Inca Empire and the Aztec Empire
4 Asia and eastern Europe 8_____

Base your answer to question 9 on the pictures below and on your knowledge of social studies.

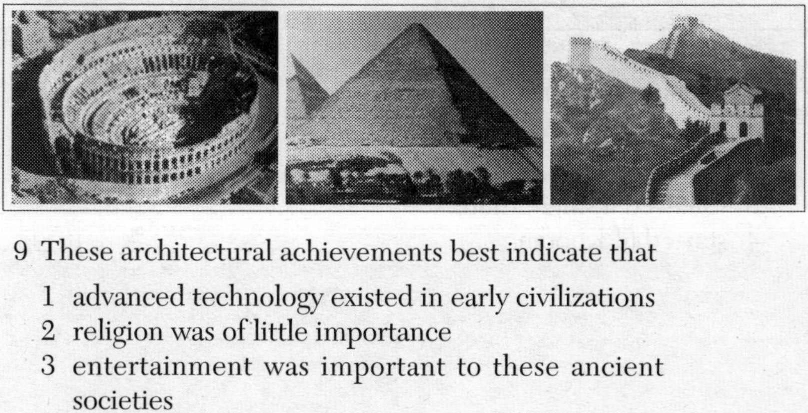

9 These architectural achievements best indicate that

1 advanced technology existed in early civilizations
2 religion was of little importance
3 entertainment was important to these ancient societies
4 trade routes existed between China and the Americas 9_____

Base your answer to question 10 on the map below and on your knowledge of social studies.

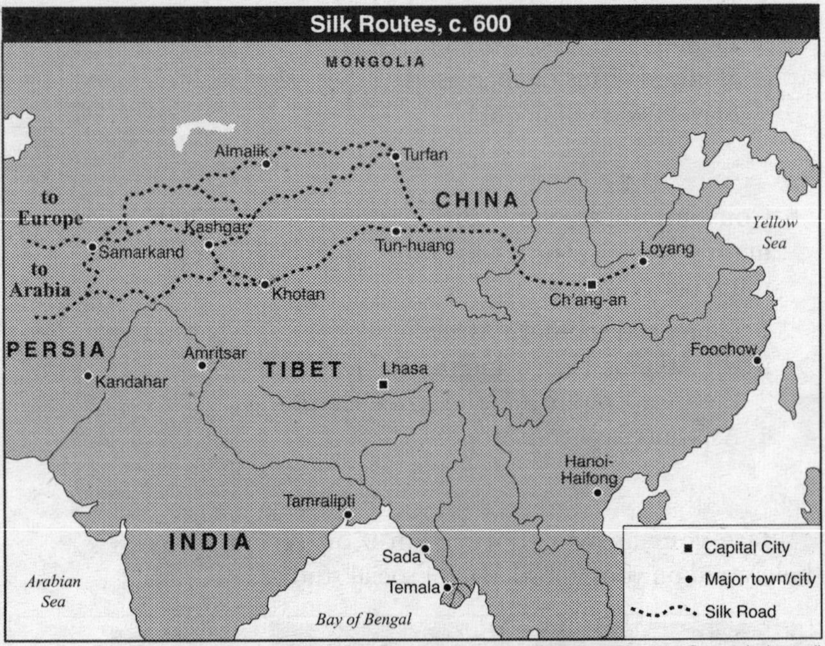

Source: *Asian History on File,* Facts on File, The Diagram Group (adapted)

10 This map shows that the Silk Road

1 crossed both Africa and Asia
2 was located primarily in Asia
3 followed a single route
4 started in Khotan

10_____

Base your answer to question 11 on the map below and on your knowledge of social studies.

West Africa, 800–1500

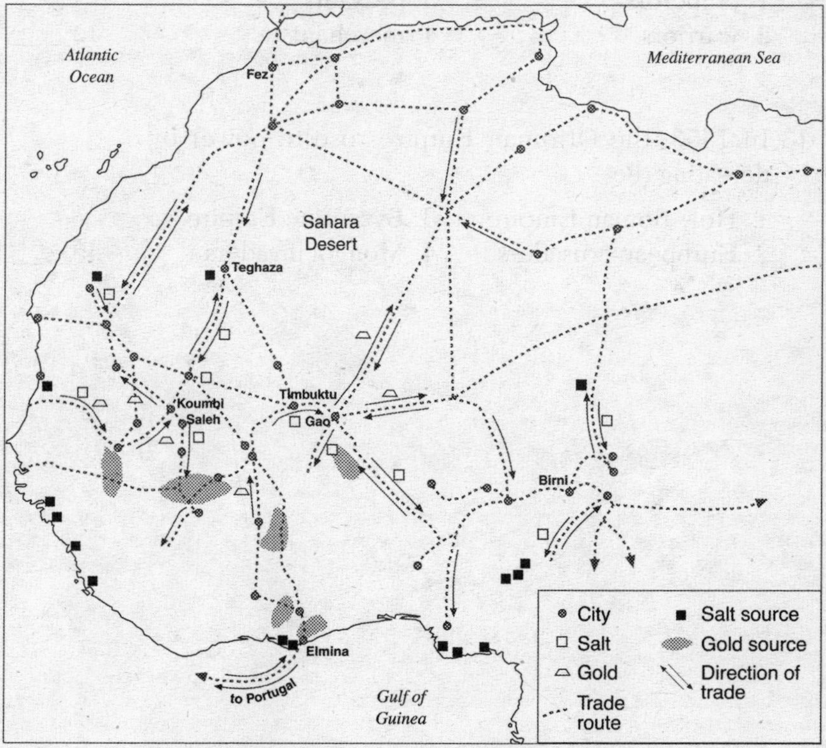

Source: Patrick K. O'Brien, ed., *Oxford Atlas of World History*, Oxford University Press (adapted)

11 Based on the map, which conclusion can best be drawn about this region?

1 The Sahara Desert acted as a barrier to trade.
2 Rivers served as the primary trade routes for the entire region.
3 The economy of the region was influenced by extensive trade connections.
4 Goods from the Gulf of Guinea were exchanged directly with English cities. 11____

12 The terms *Bushido*, *samurai*, and *daimyo* are most closely associated with which group in Japanese history?

1 emperors
2 warriors
3 peasants
4 merchants

12____

13 In 1453, the Ottoman Empire rose to power by defeating the

1 Holy Roman Empire
2 European crusaders
3 Byzantine Empire
4 Mongol invaders

13____

Base your answers to questions 14 and 15 on the map below and on your knowledge of social studies.

Source: *American History, Historical Outline Map Book,* Prentice Hall (adapted)

14 Which letter identifies the region in the Andes Mountains where many Inca settlements were located?

1 *A*
2 *B*
3 *C*
4 *D*

14____

15 The letter *C* indicates an area of Latin America that was colonized mostly by the

1 Dutch
2 Portuguese
3 English
4 French

15____

16 • Pope Leo authorizes the sale of indulgences, 1515
• Martin Luther posts the Ninety-five Theses, 1517

These events are most closely associated with the

1 Protestant Reformation
2 Crusades
3 Age of Reason
4 Puritan Revolution

16 ____

17 One contribution that John Locke made to Enlightenment philosophy was the idea that

1 absolute monarchies should continue
2 the punishment should fit the crime
3 individual rights should be denied
4 governments should be based on the consent of the people

17 ____

18 What was a major result of the Glorious Revolution?

1 Napoleon was restored to power.
2 England further limited its monarchy.
3 Oliver Cromwell became the leader of England.
4 The Spanish Armada was defeated.

18 ____

19 A study of the revolutions in Latin America in the 19th century would show that

1 religion was a major cause of the conflicts
2 Spanish-born peninsulares led most of the Latin American uprisings
3 nationalism had little influence on the outcome
4 events in North America and Europe influenced Latin Americans

19 ____

20 A major reason the Industrial Revolution began in England was that England possessed

1 a smooth coastline
2 abundant coal and iron resources
3 many waterfalls
4 numerous mountain ranges 20____

21 What was an immediate result of the mass starvation in Ireland in the late 1840s?

1 expansion of the Green Revolution to Ireland
2 acceptance of British rule by the Irish
3 migration of many Irish to other countries
4 creation of a mixed economy in Ireland 21____

22 Which individual is associated with the phrase *blood and iron* as related to the unification of Germany?

1 Otto von Bismarck
2 Giuseppe Garibaldi
3 Kaiser Wilhelm II
4 Count Camillo di Cavour 22____

23 Which statement would Social Darwinists most likely support?

1 Universal suffrage is a basic human right.
2 Political equality strengthens the effectiveness of government.
3 Stronger groups have the right to rule and control weaker groups.
4 Public education should be guaranteed to all members of a society. 23____

24 One similarity between the Sepoy Mutiny and the Boxer Rebellion is that they

1 opposed European imperialism
2 ended an established dynasty
3 resulted in the redistribution of land
4 instituted communist governments 24____

25 What was a direct result of World War I?

1 Nicholas II was named czar of Russia.
2 Germany lost its colonies in Africa and Asia.
3 Archduke Franz Ferdinand was assassinated by a terrorist.
4 The Ottoman Empire expanded. 25____

26 Which statement about both the Bolshevik Revolution in Russia and the rise of fascism in Germany and Italy is accurate?

1 Economic conditions led to political change.
2 Industrialization hindered national development.
3 Goals were achieved by peaceful means.
4 Communist ideals fueled both movements. 26____

27 The term *appeasement* is best defined as

1 an attempt to avoid conflict by meeting the demands of an aggressor
2 a period of peace and prosperity, resulting in cultural achievement
3 a declaration of war between two or more nations
4 an agreement removing economic barriers between nations 27____

Base your answer to question 28 on the map below and on your knowledge of social studies.

1937–1938

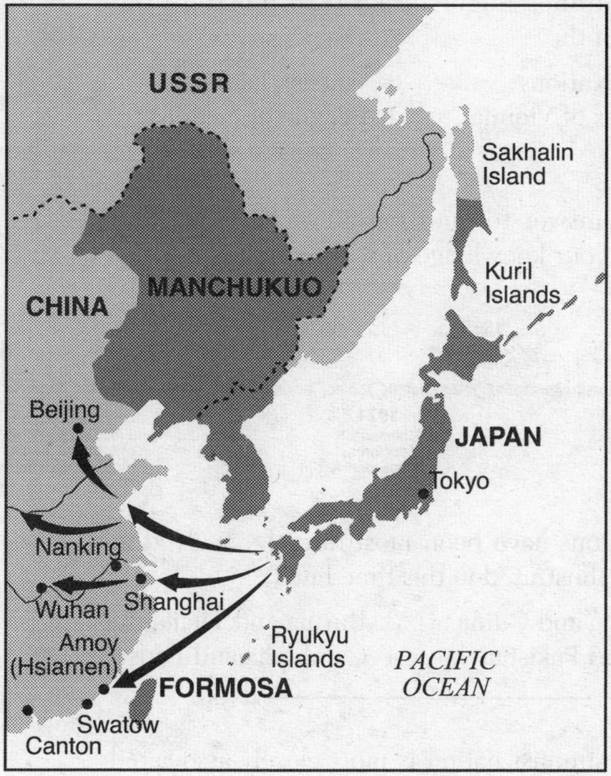

Source: Peter Stearns et al., *World Civilizations: The Global Experience*, Pearson Longman (adapted)

28 What is the best title for this map?

1 Dominance of Manchukuo
2 Japanese Imperial Expansion
3 East Asian Trade Routes
4 Natural Resources of China and Japan 28 ____

29 **"Mussolini Attacks Ethiopia" (1935)**
"Germany Takes the Rhineland Back" (1936)
"Germany and Russia Divide Poland" (1939)

These headlines might be used to illustrate the weakness of the

1 United Nations
2 Congress of Vienna
3 Warsaw Pact
4 League of Nations

29 ____

Base your answer to question 30 on the time line below and on your knowledge of social studies.

1965
Second war over Kashmir begins.
1972
Cease-fire signed.
1949
Cease-fire in Kashmir ends 1st war after independence.
1971
Bangladesh declares independence.
1992
Hindu mob destroys mosque at Ayodhya, begins Hindu-Muslim riots.

30 Which nations have been most directly involved in the events illustrated in this time line?

1 Mongolia and China
2 India and Pakistan
3 Burma and Thailand
4 Cambodia and Laos

30 ____

---

31 Which communist nation is most closely associated with the leadership of Ho Chi Minh and the surrender of Saigon?

1 North Korea
2 Soviet Union
3 Vietnam
4 People's Republic of China

31 ____

32 A similarity between the Polish group Solidarity in 1980 and the Chinese protesters in Tiananmen Square in 1989 is that both groups

1 supported movements for democracy
2 succeeded in ending communism
3 encouraged military occupation by the Soviet Union
4 favored increases in military spending

32____

33 The status of Hong Kong changed in July 1997 when the city

1 was returned to China
2 was closed to international trade
3 became an independent nation
4 adopted a capitalist economy

33____

34 Mikhail Gorbachev's reforms of perestroika and glasnost resulted in

1 an era of world peace and Soviet prosperity
2 conditions that helped lead to the breakup of the Soviet Union
3 a successful transition to a command economy in Russia
4 censorship of the news media in Russia

34____

35 The governments of Augusto Pinochet, Saddam Hussein, and Slobodan Milosevic are examples of

1 absolute monarchies
2 oppressive regimes
3 democratic republics
4 Islamic theocracies

35____

36 One way in which wars, religious conflict, and natural disasters are similar is that these situations may result in

1 the mass migration of people
2 economic stability
3 an increase in life expectancy
4 global warming

36 ____

Base your answers to questions 37 and 38 on the passage below and on your knowledge of social studies.

> . . . Above all, we want equal political rights, because without them our disabilities will be permanent. I know this sounds revolutionary to the Whites in this country, because the majority of voters will be Africans. This makes the White man fear democracy.
>
> But this fear cannot be allowed to stand in the way of the only solution which will guarantee racial harmony and freedom for all. It is not true that the enfranchisement [right to vote] of all will result in racial domination. Political division, based on colour, is entirely artificial and, when it disappears, so will the domination of one colour group by another. The ANC [African National Congress] has spent half a century fighting against racialism. When it triumphs it will not change that policy. . . .
>
> — Nelson Mandela, Speech at Rivonia Trial, 1964

37 This passage describes the opposition of the African National Congress to the

1 revival of colonialism
2 rivalries between tribes
3 practice of apartheid
4 introduction of a coalition government

37 ____

38 Which generalization can be supported by this passage?

1 Racism has disappeared in South Africa.
2 The African National Congress has changed its social goals.
3 Giving the vote to black Africans will result in racial domination.
4 Nelson Mandela opposed political division based on color. 38____

---

39 Kim Jong Il and Fidel Castro are 21st-century leaders who believe in the ideas of

1 Karl Marx
2 Adam Smith
3 Siddhartha Gautama
4 Jean-Jacques Rousseau 39____

Base your answers to questions 40 and 41 on the cartoon below and on your knowledge of social studies.

Source: Jeff Koterba, *Omaha World Herald,* 2003 (adapted)

40 What is the main idea of this 2003 cartoon?

1 There are problems to resolve on the road to peace.
2 Colin Powell has removed the stumbling blocks to peace.
3 Both groups have reached agreement on the road map for peace.
4 The road to peace has been carefully mapped.

40 ____

41 This 2003 cartoon illustrates the struggle between Palestinians and

1 Iraqis
2 Hamas
3 Egyptians
4 Israelis

41 ____

42 Which heading best completes the partial outline below?

I. ______________________
  A. Unification of Italy
  B. Formation of the Indian National Congress
  C. Founding of the Muslim League
  D. Breakup of Austria-Hungary

1 Tensions of the Cold War
2 Effects of Nationalism
3 Causes of World War II
4 Results of Economic Revolutions 42____

43 A. Crusades
B. Fall of the Roman Empire
C. Golden Age of Greece
D. Renaissance

Which sequence of letters places these events in the correct chronological order?

1 $A \rightarrow B \rightarrow C \rightarrow D$
2 $D \rightarrow C \rightarrow B \rightarrow A$
3 $C \rightarrow B \rightarrow A \rightarrow D$
4 $C \rightarrow D \rightarrow B \rightarrow A$ 43____

44 One way in which Asoka, Mansa Musa, and Suleiman the Magnificent are similar is that they

1 established republics
2 led nationalist movements
3 ruled during times of prosperity
4 discouraged scientific advancements 44____

Base your answers to questions 45 and 46 on the passage below and on your knowledge of social studies.

> . . . The power of God can be felt in a moment from one end of the world to the other: the royal power acts simultaneously throughout the kingdom. It holds the whole kingdom in position just as God holds the whole world.
>
> If God were to withdraw his hand, the entire world would return to nothing: if authority ceases in the kingdom, all lapses into confusion. . . .
>
> — Bishop Jacques-Benigne Bossuet

45 This passage describes the idea of

1 divine right rule
2 parliamentary democracy
3 Marxism
4 totalitarianism

45 ____

46 Which historical era is most closely associated with this passage?

1 Industrial Revolution
2 Agricultural Revolution
3 Age of Imperialism
4 Age of Absolutism

46 ____

Base your answer to question 47 on the cartoon below and on your knowledge of social studies.

Capitalism Will Crush Russia!

Source: Student Artwork, Shaneekwa Miller, Fashion Industries High School (adapted)

47 Which period of history is depicted in this cartoon?

1 Industrial Revolution
2 Age of Enlightenment
3 Age of Imperialism
4 Cold War

47 _____

48 Which situation best illustrates the concept of isolationism?

1 The Spanish government required that gold found in its colonies be brought directly to Spain.
2 Japan closed its ports to trade with other nations.
3 France, Germany, Belgium, and Great Britain negotiated to divide various areas of Africa into colonies.
4 The British ruled much of India through the control of local rulers. 48____

49 "Bombardment, barrage, curtain-fire, mines, gas, tanks, machine-guns, hand-grenades — words, words, but they hold the horror of the world."

— Erich Maria Remarque,
All Quiet on the Western Front

This quotation best describes the effects of the

1 technological developments used during World War I
2 formation of alliances in World War II
3 tension between the superpowers during the Cold War
4 protests against reforms during the Indian independence movement 49____

50 One similarity in the leadership of Simón Bolívar and Jomo Kenyatta is that both leaders

1 promoted European control over the Americas
2 became religious leaders of their countries
3 controlled large areas of land in the Americas
4 fought for independence from European control 50____

In developing your answer to Part II, be sure to keep these general definitions in mind:

(a) describe means "to illustrate something in words or tell about it"

(b) explain means "to make plain or understandable; to give reasons for or causes of; to show the logical development or relationships of"

(c) discuss means "to make observations about something using facts, reasoning, and argument; to present in some detail "

PART II: THEMATIC ESSAY QUESTION

Directions: Write a well-organized essay that includes an introduction, several paragraphs addressing the task below, and a conclusion.

Theme: Political Change

> Often, governments implement policies in an attempt to change society.

Task:

> Choose ***one*** example from global history where a government attempted to change society and
> - Describe the change the government wanted to bring about
> - Explain why the government wanted to make this change
> - Describe ***one*** specific policy the government used to try to bring about this change
> - Discuss the extent to which this change was achieved

You may use any example of governmental change from your study of global history. Some suggestions you might wish to consider include efforts to strengthen the Empire of Mali under Mansa Musa, Reformation in England under Henry VIII, westernization of Russia under Peter the Great, Reign of Terror during the French Revolution under Robespierre, Meiji Restoration in Japan under the Emperor Meiji, modernization of Turkey under Atatürk, five-year plans in the Soviet Union under Joseph Stalin, fascism in Italy under Benito Mussolini, and oil policies in Venezuela under Hugo Chávez. **Although you are *not* limited to these suggestions, you may *not* use communism under Mao Zedong or Deng Xiaoping as your example of governmental change.**

Do *not* use an example of governmental change in the United States as your answer.

Guidelines:

In your essay, be sure to:

- Develop all aspects of the task
- Support the theme with relevant facts, examples, and details
- Use a logical and clear plan of organization, including an introduction and a conclusion that are beyond a restatement of the theme

In developing your answers to Part III, be sure to keep these general definitions in mind:

(a) describe means "to illustrate something in words or tell about it"

(b) discuss means "to make observations about something using facts, reasoning, and argument; to present in some detail"

PART III: DOCUMENT-BASED QUESTION

This question is based on the accompanying documents. The question is designed to test your ability to work with historical documents. Some of these documents have been edited for the purposes of this question. As you analyze the documents, take into account the source of each document and any point of view that may be presented in the document.

Historical Context:

Throughout history, different economic systems have influenced specific nations, regions, and peoples. These systems include **manorialism** during the Middle Ages in Western Europe, **mercantilism** during the Age of Exploration, and **communism** in post–World War II China.

Task:

Using the information from the documents and your knowledge of global history, answer the questions that follow each document in Part A. Your answers to the questions will help you write the Part B essay in which you will be asked to

Choose ***two*** of the economic systems mentioned in the historical context and for ***each***

- Describe the characteristics of the economic system
- Discuss the impact of the economic system on a specific nation ***or*** region ***or*** on a group of people

Part A: Short-Answer Questions

Directions: Analyze the documents and answer the short-answer questions that follow each document in the space provided.

Document 1

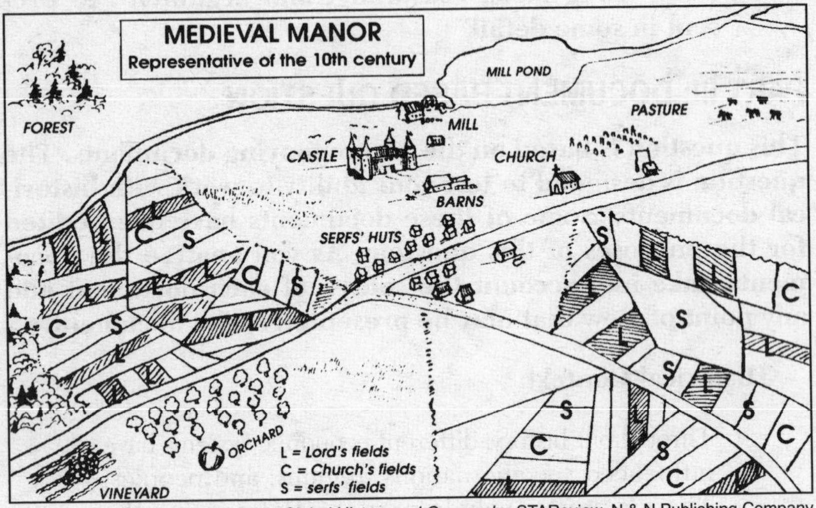

Source: Kime and Stich, *Global History and Geography*, STAReview, N & N Publishing Company

1 Based on this diagram, state ***one*** economic characteristic of the medieval manor. [1]

____

____

Document 2

Tenants on a manor owed services to their lord. Some of these services are listed below.

> . . . To carry manure for two days, with a cart and two oxen, receiving food as before [3 meals each day];
>
> To find a man to mow for two days receiving food as above; it is estimated that he can mow 1 1/2 acres in the two days;
>
> To gather and lift the hay so mown, receiving 2 meals for one man;
>
> To carry the lord's hay for one day with a cart and three of the tenant's own beasts, receiving 3 meals as before;
>
> To carry beans or oats for two days in the autumn, and wood for two days in the summer, in the same manner and with the same food as before; . . .

Source: S. R. Scargill-Bird, ed., *Custumals of Battle Abbey in the Reigns of Edward I and Edward II (1283–1312)*, The Camden Society (adapted)

2*a* Based on the *Custumals of Battle Abbey*, state ***one*** benefit the lord received under manorialism. [1]

____

____

b Based on the *Custumals of Battle Abbey*, state ***one*** benefit that tenants received under manorialism. [1]

____

____

Document 3

> . . . Of necessity, the manor was a self-sufficient economic unit in view of the overwhelming difficulties of transportation in the period. International trade was carried on only to serve the demands of the wealthy, and it was largely in the hands of aliens [different peoples]—Greeks, Jews, Moslems. Local society made almost no use of money. To the extent that local exchange was carried on, it was conducted by barter. The small amount of international trade precluded [ruled out] the need for gold coinage. The Carolingians minted only silver coins, which were all that was usually necessary when the smallest silver coin could buy a cow. When gold coins were needed, Byzantine and Moslem currency was used. . . .

Source: Norman F. Cantor, *The Civilization of the Middle Ages*, Harper Perennial

3 According to Norman Cantor, what are ***two*** ways manorialism influenced the economy of Europe? [2]

(1) ____

____

(2) ____

____

Document 4

The Mercantilist Argument for Colonial Expansion

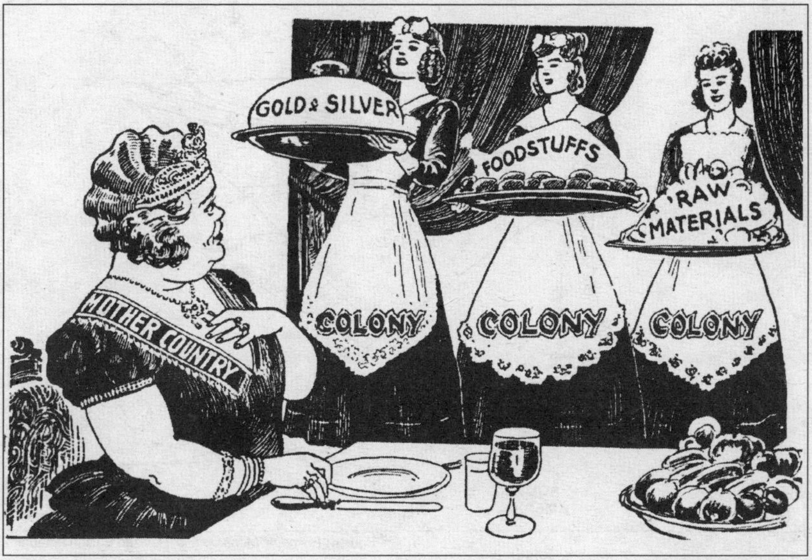

Source: Philip Dorf, *Our Early Heritage: Ancient and Medieval History*, Oxford Book Company (adapted)

4 According to this cartoon by Philip Dorf, what is ***one*** characteristic of mercantilism from the perspective of the mother country? [1]

____

____

Document 5

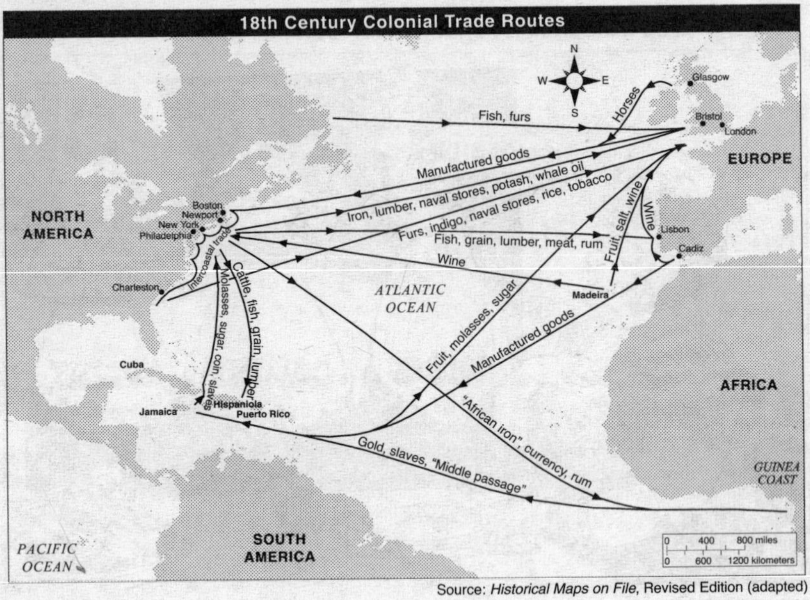

Source: *Historical Maps on File*, Revised Edition (adapted)

5 Based on this map, state ***one*** effect of the Atlantic trade. [1]

____

____

Document 6

This is an excerpt from a letter written in 1559 by Michele Soriano about Spain's interactions with its colonies in the Americas.

> . . . From New Spain are obtained gold and silver, cochineal, (little insects like flies,) from which crimson dye is made, leather, cotton, sugar and other things; but from Peru nothing is obtained except minerals. The fifth part of all that is produced goes to the king, but since the gold and silver is brought to Spain and he has a tenth part of that which goes to the mint and is refined and coined, he eventually gets one-fourth of the whole sum, which fourth does not exceed in all four or five hundred thousand ducats, although it is reckoned not alone at millions, but at millions of pounds. Nor is it likely that it will long remain at this figure, because great quantities of gold and silver are no longer found upon the surface of the earth, as they have been in past years; and to penetrate into the bowels of the earth requires greater effort, skill and outlay, and the Spaniards are not willing to do the work themselves, and the natives cannot be forced to do so, because the Emperor has freed them from all obligation of service as soon as they accept the Christian religion. Wherefore it is necessary to acquire negro slaves [enslaved Africans], who are brought from the coasts of Africa, both within and without the Straits, and these are selling dearer [more expensive] every day, because on account of their [enslaved Africans'] natural lack of strength and the change of climate, added to the lack of discretion [care] upon the part of their masters in making them work too hard and giving them too little to eat, they fall sick and the greater part of them die. . . .

Source: Merrick Whitcomb, ed., "The Gold of the Indies — 1559," *Translations and Reprints from the Original Sources of European History*, The Department of History of the University of Pennsylvania

6 According to Michele Soriano, what is ***one*** influence that gold and silver had on Spain? [1]

____

____

Document 7

This is an excerpt from Chapter 1, General Principles, of the 1954 "Constitution of the People's Republic of China."

> **Article 1** The People's Republic of China is a people's democratic state led by the working class and based on the alliance of workers and peasants. . . .
>
> **Article 6** The state sector of the economy is the socialist sector owned by the whole people. It is the leading force in the national economy and the material basis on which the state carries out socialist transformation. The state ensures priority for the development of the state sector of the economy.
>
> All mineral resources and waters, as well as forests, undeveloped land and other resources which the state owns by law, are the property of the whole people.
>
> **Article 7** The co-operative sector of the economy is either socialist, when collectively owned by the masses of working people, or semi-socialist, when in part collectively owned by the masses of working people. Partial collective ownership by the masses of working people is a transitional form by means of which individual peasants, individual handicraftsmen and other individual working people organize themselves in their advance towards collective ownership by the masses of working people. . . .

Source: *Constitutions of Asian Countries*, N. M. Tripathi Private

7 Based on these articles from the "Constitution of the People's Republic of China," state ***two*** characteristics of the communist economic system in China. [2]

(1) ____

____

(2) ____

____

Document 8

> In an attempt to break with the Russian model of Communism and to catch up with more advanced nations, Mao proposed that China should make a "great leap forward" into modernisation. He began a militant Five Year Plan to promote technology and agricultural self-sufficiency. Overnight, fertile rice fields were ploughed over, and factory construction work began. Labour-intensive methods were introduced and farming collectivised on a massive scale. The campaign created about 23,500 communes, each controlling its own means of production. But former farmers had no idea how to actually use the new factories and what was once fertile crop land went to waste on a disastrous scale. The Great Leap Forward was held responsible for famine in 1960 and 1961. Twenty million people starved, and Mao Zedong withdrew temporarily from public view.

Source: BBC News, Special Reports, China's Communist Revolution

8 Based on this BBC News article, what is ***one*** effect the Great Leap Forward had on China's economy? [1]

____

____

Document 9

This is an excerpt from the speech "We Shall Speed Up Reform" given by Deng Xiaoping on June 12, 1987.

> . . . China is now carrying out a reform. I am all in favour of that. There is no other solution for us. After years of practice it turned out that the old stuff didn't work. In the past we copied foreign models mechanically, which only hampered [blocked] the development of our productive forces, induced [caused] ideological rigidity and kept people and grass-roots units from taking any initiative. We made some mistakes of our own as well, such as the Great Leap Forward and the "cultural revolution" [Mao's policies], which were our own inventions. I would say that since 1957 our major mistakes have been "Left" ones. The "cultural revolution" was an ultra-Left mistake. In fact, during the two decades from 1958 through 1978, China remained at a standstill. There was little economic growth and not much of a rise in the people's standard of living. How could we go on like that without introducing reforms? So in 1978, at the Third Plenary Session of the Eleventh Central Committee, we formulated a new basic political line: to give first priority to the drive for modernization and strive to develop the productive forces. In accordance with that line we drew up a series of new principles and policies, the major ones being reform and the open policy. By reform we mean something comprehensive, including reform of both the economic structure and the political structure and corresponding changes in all other areas. By the open policy we mean both opening to all other countries, irrespective [regardless] of their social systems, and opening at home, which means invigorating [quickening] the domestic economy. . . .

Source: Deng Xiaoping, *Fundamental Issues in Present-Day China*, Foreign Languages Press, 1987

9 According to Deng Xiaoping, what were ***two*** ways Mao Zedong's economic policies influenced China? [2]

(1) ______________________________

____

(2) ______________________________

____

Part B: Essay

Directions: Write a well-organized essay that includes an introduction, several paragraphs, and a conclusion. Use evidence from *at least* ***four*** documents in your essay. Support your response with relevant facts, examples, and details. Include additional outside information.

Historical Context:

Throughout history, different economic systems have influenced specific nations, regions, and peoples. These systems include **manorialism** during the Middle Ages in Western Europe, **mercantilism** during the Age of Exploration, and **communism** in post–World War II China.

Task:

Using the information from the documents and your knowledge of global history, write an essay in which you

Choose ***two*** of the economic systems mentioned in the historical context and for ***each***

- Describe the characteristics of the economic system
- Discuss the impact of the economic system on a specific nation ***or*** region ***or*** on a group of people

Guidelines:

In your essay, be sure to:

- Develop all aspects of the task
- Incorporate information from *at least* ***four*** documents in the body of the essay
- Incorporate relevant outside information
- Support the theme with relevant facts, examples, and details
- Use a logical and clear plan of organization, including an introduction and conclusion that are beyond a restatement of the theme

Answers June 2007

Global History and Geography

Answer Key

PART I (1–50)

1. 3	**14.** 2	**27.** 1	**40.** 1
2. 3	**15.** 2	**28.** 2	**41.** 4
3. 4	**16.** 1	**29.** 4	**42.** 2
4. 1	**17.** 4	**30.** 2	**43.** 3
5. 3	**18.** 2	**31.** 3	**44.** 3
6. 4	**19.** 4	**32.** 1	**45.** 1
7. 3	**20.** 2	**33.** 1	**46.** 4
8. 4	**21.** 3	**34.** 2	**47.** 4
9. 1	**22.** 1	**35.** 2	**48.** 2
10. 2	**23.** 3	**36.** 1	**49.** 1
11. 3	**24.** 1	**37.** 3	**50.** 4
12. 2	**25.** 2	**38.** 4	
13. 3	**26.** 1	**39.** 1	

PART II: Thematic Essay See Answers Explained section.

PART III: Document-Based Essay See Answers Explained section.

Answers Explained

PART I

1. **3** The main purpose of this map is to illustrate the location of river valley civilizations. The fertile soil along the river valleys influenced the development of ancient civilizations. The first river valley civilization developed in Mesopotamia, in the regions located along the Tigris and Euphrates Rivers. Although the area was hot and dry, people learned how to irrigate the land by diverting water from these rivers. This irrigation allowed settlements to grow and increased food supplies. In Egypt, the land would be a desert without the Nile River. Each year, the overflowing of the Nile deposited fertile soil where it flooded that enabled farmers to grow large amounts of food, and also required a strong government to control this flooding. Like the Nile, the Tigris and Euphrates in Mesopotamia, the Indus River in India, and the Huang He (Yellow River) in China fostered the development of civilization. The overflowing of these rivers created rich deposits of fertile soil that encouraged permanent settlements, supporting these cultures' growth.

WRONG CHOICES EXPLAINED:

(1), (2), and (4) None of these answers can be supported by the map. The map does not provide any information about overseas trade routes among different civilizations, early belief or religious systems, or the burial sites of the ancient rulers of these civilizations.

2. **3** An economist is a social scientist who specializes in studying issues such as the scarcity of resources and the availability of goods. An economist studies how a society deals with the problems of scarcity of resources. The fundamental economic problem facing all societies is how people use their limited resources to satisfy their wants and needs. Scarcities arise because a society does not have enough resources to produce all the things people would like to have. An economist studies and analyzes how a society uses its limited resources to satisfy its needs.

WRONG CHOICES EXPLAINED:

(1) An anthropologist studies society's culture, which includes an examination of religion, legends, and festivals.

(2) A sociologist examines the social institutions of a society, such as family structure and social relationships.

(4) An archaeologist is a social scientist who studies the objects left by early people. Archaeologists use these objects to determine the type of civilization and government that a society developed during a particular period.

3. **4** A feature most likely to be shown on a physical map would be mountain ranges. A physical map shows features such as mountains, lakes, rivers, and elevation (height above sea level). The physical features of a place or region are called its topography.

WRONG CHOICES EXPLAINED:

(1) A population map shows *population density*—how many people live in each area on the map.

(2) Vegetation zones are features on a map that illustrate the plant life of a place or region.

(3) A climate map shows the average type of weather of different locations in the world. The climate map focuses on the temperature and rainfall in different regions.

4. **1** Ancient Athens was a society that practiced direct democracy. Under Pericles, who ruled Athens from 460 B.C. to 429 B.C., Athens had a direct democracy in which citizens themselves participated in the day-to-day running of the government, rather than doing so through elected representatives. In a funeral oration, Pericles spelled out the Athenian idea about democracy. He pointed out that power rested in the hands of the individuals, and that all citizens were equal before the law. Athenian democracy, however, was extremely limited. Only free male citizens who had been born in Athens had the right to participate in government. The majority of Athenians—including slaves, resident foreigners, and women—had no political rights. They could not vote, own property, or hold public office. Athens still gave a greater number of people a voice in government than any other culture of its time, becoming a model for other city-states.

WRONG CHOICES EXPLAINED:

(2) Dynastic China was governed by ruling families for many years. These dynastic families claimed that they had a "mandate from Heaven to rule the country."

(3) The Gupta Empire lasted in India from 320 A.D. to 535 A.D. In 320 A.D., a young warrior, Chandragupta I, set up the Gupta dynasty or ruling family. The Guptas expanded their control over northern India and brought peace and prosperity to their empire until its decline in 535.

(4) Early Egypt was ruled by a pharaoh. The pharaoh (king) was the absolute ruler and worshipped as the gods' earthly representative.

5. **3** The caste system in India was characterized by a lack of social mobility. Social mobility is the ability to move from one social class to another through education or improvement in income or occupation. The caste system, developed around 1500 B.C., was a rigid social system that was characteristic of traditional Hindu Indian society. Indian society was divided into four major groups based on occupation or birth. At the top of society were Brahmans, or priests; next came the rulers and warriors. The third class were

landowners, merchants, and herders. At the bottom of society were the peasants and servants who waited on the others. Below the castes were millions of despised persons who did menial labor and were called "untouchables." The caste system set up a strict social and religious order. A person was born into a certain caste, ranked within the system, and nothing could change that fact. Anyone who violated the caste system became an outcast from society.

WRONG CHOICES EXPLAINED:

(1) The caste system was not characterized by tolerance for various religious beliefs. It was based on strict segregation of the classes and was a social rather than religious belief system. However, the Hindu beliefs about rebirth and karma became closely tied to the caste system. Buddhism, introduced into India in the 6th century, differed from Hinduism and would battle the caste system for over a thousand years.

(2) The caste system rejected equality between men and women. Women were not considered equal to men in any of the four castes, and contact among different classes was strictly forbidden. Each person was to remain in his or her own hereditary caste.

(4) Under the caste system, people did not have the right to choose their own occupation. The caste in which a person was born determined his occupation, which he had to follow throughout his life.

6. **4** Filial piety is the belief most closely associated with the philosophy of Confucianism. According to the Chinese philosopher Confucius, filial piety is the duty and respect that children owe to their parents. Confucius, born in 551 B.C., was China's most influential philosopher. He stressed filial piety or respect for parents as the factor linking the three groups in the Chain of Humanity. For Confucius, the family represented society on a smaller scale. He stressed five key relationships: father to son, elder brother to younger, husband to wife, ruler to subject, friend to friend. Confucius believed that, except for friendship, none of these relationships was equal. Older people were superior to the young; men were superior to women. However, mothers of sons should be respected. The Confucian emphasis on filial piety and traditional customs became associated with ancestor worship.

WRONG CHOICES EXPLAINED:

(1) Nirvana is related to the religion of Buddhism. Buddhism is based on the philosophy of self-denial and meditation. By following the eightfold paths of Buddhism, an individual can escape the cycles of reincarnation and achieve nirvana, which is a state of eternal bliss or no unfulfilled desires.

(2) Reincarnation is a Hindu belief that the soul is reborn in various forms. Hindus believe that, at death, a person's soul is reborn as another living thing, becoming part of an endless cycle of rebirth.

(3) All belief systems promote prayer. However, prayer is a major idea associated with Islam and Christianity. In Islam, Muslims are expected to pray five times a day; in Christianity, prayer is one way in which Christians can talk to God.

7. **3** One result of large armies traveling great distances during the Crusades was that cultural diffusion increased. Cultural diffusion is the exchange of goods, ideas, customs, and technology from one group or region to another culture. The Crusades (1096–1246), which failed to permanently capture the Holy Land from the Muslims, led to an increase in European demands for Eastern goods. Returning Crusaders later brought back new fabrics, spices, and perfumes. Even before the Crusades, trade with the Byzantine Empire sparked European curiosity about goods from the East. Trade increased during the Crusades, and Italian merchants who had built fleets to transport Crusaders, used these same transports to keep trade routes open. Contact with the East spurred a new demand for luxury goods such as spices, sugar, melons, tapestries, silk, and other items that Europe had been unable to obtain. The increased trade and contact between Europe and the East also led to renewed interest in learning, as Europeans became aware of Greek and Roman civilizations and Arab advances in art, science, and literature. The renewed European curiosity also stimulated trade and broadened Europe's knowledge of the world.

WRONG CHOICES EXPLAINED:

(1) Europe's population did not severely decline due to the Crusades. The Crusades increased trade and led to the growth of towns in number and size, ultimately increasing population.

(2) Democracy did not grow in the Middle East as a result of the Crusades. The Crusades brought together rulers and nobles from all over Europe in a common cause to regain the Holy Land. These leaders did not believe in democracy and did not promote it as a goal in the Middle East. The Crusades left a bitter legacy of religious hatred behind them. Both Christians and Muslims committed atrocities in the name of religion.

(4) Slavery was not eliminated as a result of the Crusades. Slavery continued in many parts of the world until the 19th century. However, the Crusades did help many serfs in Europe to escape feudalism. Some serfs gained freedom by joining the Crusades. Other serfs fled to the growing cities and eventually became legally free.

8. **4** Constantinople was a thriving city in the 1200s mainly because of its location on a major trade route between Asia and eastern Europe. Located on a peninsula, Constantinople overlooks the Bosporus, the narrow strait between the Sea of Marmara and the Black Sea. A second strait, the Dardanelles, connects the Sea of Marmara to the Aegean Sea, which leads to the Mediterranean. Byzantine ships loaded with cargo sailed the Mediterranean and Black Seas. Merchants traded agricultural goods and furs from northern Europe for luxury goods from the East. Ships brought cloves and sandalwood from the East, pepper, copper, and gems from India, and silk from China to Constantinople's busy harbor, called the Golden Horn. Byzantine merchants shipped goods to Venice on the Adriatic Sea.

WRONG CHOICES EXPLAINED:

(1) Constantinople was not a major trade route between China and southern Africa. The Chinese city of Canton and the Silk Road were major trade routes between China and Africa in the 1200s.

(2) The Atlantic Ocean and the Baltic Sea did not become a major trade route until the 14th century. In the mid-1300s, Lubeck, Hamburg, and many other northern German towns were members of the Hanseatic League. This league eventually monopolized trade in the Baltic Sea and the Atlantic Ocean.

(3) Constantinople was never a major trade route between the Inca Empire and the Aztec Empire. Spain established its control over these empires in the 1500s and the trade routes extended across the Americas.

9. **1** These architectural achievements best indicate that advanced technology existed in early civilizations. These pictures show the architectural achievements of the Romans, Egyptians, and Chinese.

The Romans excelled in engineering. By using an improved form of concrete, the Romans were able to use features such as the arch and the dome to build many different types of structures. The first picture shown is the Colosseum, one of the greatest feats of Roman engineering and a model for all ages. The name comes from the Latin word *colossus*, meaning "gigantic." The Colosseum was constructed between 72–82 A.D. The stone amphitheater could seat 45,000 to 50,000 people, and was 157 feet high and 620 feet long. In its arena, both rich and poor cheered a variety of free, bloody spectacles presented for their entertainment. Gladiators fought each other to the death. Captured wild animals were hunted and killed. Christians were devoured by lions. The Colosseum had eighty entrances in all and their giant staircases allowed the building to be emptied in minutes.

The second picture of the pyramids illustrates the advanced technology of the Egyptian civilization. The Egyptians believed that their pharaoh or king ruled after his death. The pharaoh's resting place after death was an immense structure called a pyramid. The builders had no iron tools or wheeled vehicles. Workers quarried (cut) the stones, pulled them on sleds to the site, and hoisted them up ramps. The largest of the pyramids is the Great Pyramid at Giza, completed about 2556 B.C. The limestone for the Great Pyramid was hauled 400 miles upriver. Each perfectly-cut stone block weighed at least $2\frac{1}{2}$ tons, with some weighing up to 15 tons. More than two million of these blocks were stacked with precision to a height of 481 feet. The entire structure covers more than 13 acres. The pyramids reflect the strength of Egyptian civilization.

The third picture is the Great Wall of China, which was constructed during the Qin Dynasty from 221–206 B.C. by Shi Huangdi, which means "First Emperor." From the Yellow Sea in the east to the Gobi Desert in the west, the Great Wall twisted for a total distance of 1,400 miles. Pushing wheelbarrows (a Chinese invention), about one million peasants collected, hauled, and dumped millions of stones, dirt, and rubble to fill the core of the Great Wall. Slabs of cut stone on the outside of the wall enclosed a heap of pebbles on the inside. Each section of the wall rose to a height of 20-25 feet. The Great Wall of China is the only human-made feature on the earth that is visible from the moon. All of these achievements demonstrated the technological advancements of ancient civilizations.

WRONG CHOICES EXPLAINED:

(2), (3), and (4) None of these choices can be supported by these pictures. The pictures do not address the religion, entertainment, or trade routes of these different civilizations.

10. **2** This map shows that the Silk Road was located primarily in Asia. The Han Dynasty (206–220 A.D.) in China opened a trade route that became known as the Silk Road. This road through central Asia connected China to the Middle East, Rome, and other regions. Over these routes, China exported silk, iron, and bronze in exchange for gold, linen, cloth, glass, monkeys, and parrots. Contact with India led to the introduction of Buddhism, which became popular during the Han Dynasty. The Silk Road stretched for 4,000 miles, also linking China to the Fertile Crescent in southwestern Asia. Few traders, however, covered the entire distance. Goods were transported in stages from one set of traders to another. At the western end, trade was controlled by various people, including the Persians. The road became known as the Silk Road because traders made fortunes carrying silk to the West.

WRONG CHOICES EXPLAINED:

(1) The map does not show that the Silk Road crossed Africa and Asia. There is no reference on the map to any region in Africa.

(3) The Silk Road did not follow a single route. The map shows that the Silk Road began in China and passed through different routes in the north, such as Turfan, and branched off to Tun-huang.

(4) The Silk Road did not start in Khotan, which was a major town or branch on the Silk Road. The map shows that the Silk Road began in northern China near the region known as Loyang, which was one of the four great ancient capitals of China.

11. **3** Based on the map, the conclusion that can best be drawn about this region is that the economy of the region was influenced by extensive trade connections. The West African kingdoms of Ghana, Mali, and Songhai experienced economic prosperity in this region because they traded with many different nations. These kingdoms were located near the trans-Saharan trade routes, and each of them controlled trade routes for gold and salt. The Kingdom of Ghana, founded around 750 A.D., controlled a trading empire stretching over 100,000 square miles. They prospered from the taxes they imposed on the goods that entered or left their kingdom. Because the Ghana, or king, controlled such a vast region, the land became known simply as

Ghana. Large caravans from Ghana traveled north to Morocco, bringing nuts and farming produce. Gold from Ghana was traded for Saharan salt brought by Muslim traders. In 1242, Mali conquered Ghana and established a new empire. The rulers extended this empire by putting the gold and salt mines directly under their control. Mali's most famous leader was Mansa Musa, a convert to Islam who ruled from 1312 to 1337 A.D. and expanded Mali to about twice the size of Ghana. After his pilgrimage to Mecca, Musa brought many scholars and architects back to Mali. Under his rule, the city of Timbuktu became the center of learning and trade. The city attracted students from Europe, Asia, and Africa. The flourishing of trade, culture, and wealth sparked the interest of European rulers in African gold. At the end of the 15th century, Songhai replaced Mali as the most powerful West African kingdom. Like Ghana and Mali, it grew rich from trade across the Sahara Desert. Songhai became the largest of the West African kingdoms as trade expanded to Europe and Asia. In the late 1500s, invading armies from Morocco gained control of Songhai. The fall of Songhai marked the end of the great West African kingdoms.

WRONG CHOICES EXPLAINED:

(1) The map indicates that the Sahara Desert did not act as a barrier to trade. The map shows that the West African kingdoms traded with areas in the far north, as well as with Muslim traders who exchanged Saharan salt for other products.

(2) The map does not show that rivers served as the primary routes for the entire region. It shows the direction of the trade and what products were traded.

(4) The map shows that the goods from the Gulf of Guinea were exchanged or sent to Portugal, not England.

12. **2** Warriors are the group in Japanese history most closely associated with the terms *Bushido, samurai,* and *daimyo.* Under the Japanese feudal system, the emperor still ruled in name, but the powerful warrior nobles controlled the country. Under this system, the real power lay in the hands of the shoguns, or top military commanders. To provide military protection for their lands, noble landowners recruited samurai warriors. Samurai, which means "those who serve," were knights on horseback who swore an oath of loyalty to the emperor and the local daimyo, who had promised to support the shogun with this army. The samurai promised to follow a strict code of honor known as Bushido, or "the way of the warrior." Bushido emphasized the loyalty of the samurai to the daimyo. Honor was supremely important. If a samurai brought dishonor to his daimyo and betrayed the code of Bushido, he was expected to commit ritual suicide, an act called seppuku.

WRONG CHOICES EXPLAINED:

(1) The emperors in Japanese history under the feudal system were only figureheads and did not have any power.

(3) and (4) Neither of these choices is associated with these groups under the feudal system in Japan. There was a limited merchant class in feudal Japan and peasants were protected by the daimyo in exchange for their labor and land.

13. **3** In 1453, the Ottoman Empire rose to power by defeating the Byzantine Empire. During the early 1300s, the Ottomans, a nomadic group of Turkish people who were originally from Central Asia and who had converted to Islam, emerged as a powerful force in the world as they moved through Asia Minor and into the Balkans. In 1453, the Ottomans stunned Christian Europe by capturing Constantinople, ending the thousand-year-old Byzantine Empire. The Ottomans renamed the city Istanbul and made it the capital of their Muslim empire. For a time, they cut off European trade with Asia and took control of the Mediterranean. After 1453, the Ottoman Empire greatly expanded its size. The Ottomans conquered Egypt and North Africa and united the entire Muslim world under their rule, except for Persia and Afghanistan. In 1529, the Ottomans laid siege to Vienna but failed to capture the city. However, by the 1500s, the Ottomans had built the most powerful empire in the Middle East and Europe. At its peak, the Ottoman Empire reached across three continents, from southeastern Europe through the Middle East and North Africa.

WRONG CHOICES EXPLAINED:

(1) The Ottoman Empire did not rise to power by defeating the Holy Roman Empire. The Holy Roman Empire was created in 962 A.D., when the Pope crowned Otto I as emperor of Germany for his help in defeating rebellious Roman nobles. Later, Otto's successors took the title Holy Roman Emperor because they saw themselves as heirs to the emperors of ancient Rome. The Holy Roman Empire was a loose confederation of German states. In 1806, Napoleon abolished the Holy Roman Empire.

(2) European Crusades were religious wars between Christian Europe and Middle Eastern Muslims for control of the Holy Land, lasting from 1096 until 1246. The Ottoman Turks became a powerful force in the world when the Crusades ended.

(4) The Mongol invaders did not contribute to the rise of the Ottoman Empire. The Mongol invaders were fierce fighters who built the largest empire in the world during the 1200s. The Ottoman Empire did not emerge until the late 14th and 15th centuries.

14. **2** B is the letter that identifies the region in the Andes Mountains where many Inca settlements were located. The Inca Empire developed along the Andes Mountains and extended over much of present-day Peru, Ecuador, and Bolivia. It was connected by a remarkable 14,000-mile-long network of roads and bridges through rugged mountains and harsh deserts. These roads allowed the Incan emperor to control his vast empire. Cuzco was considered the center of the Inca Empire from the 14th century until the

Spanish conquests in 1533. The Incan capital was known for its fine streets, plazas, and palaces. At the center of the city stood the Temple of the Sun, its interior filled with gold. Although they had no iron tools and did not use the wheel, Incan builders fitted the huge blocks of stone so perfectly that they needed no mortar. Many of these buildings have remained intact, undisturbed by the region's earthquakes.

WRONG CHOICES EXPLAINED:

(1), (3), and (4) None of these regions are where the many Inca settlements were located. The Incas did not settle in Area A (Venezuela), Area C (Brazil), or Area D (Uruguay).

15. **2** The letter C indicates an area of Latin America that was colonized mostly by the Portuguese. With the Treaty of Tordesillas in 1494, the Pope divided America between Spain and Portugal by drawing a north-south line that placed Brazil under Portuguese rule. Portugal issued grants of land to Portuguese nobles, who developed the lands and shared profits with the crown. Landowners sent settlers to build towns, plantations, and churches. To make the colony profitable, the Portuguese turned to growing sugar, enslaving Native Americans at first, then turning to slaves from Africa. Nearly 40 percent of all Africans taken to the Americas went to Brazil. Brazil gained its independence from Portugal in the 19th century. Brazil is the only country in South America where Portuguese is the national language.

WRONG CHOICES EXPLAINED:

(1) The Portuguese expelled the Dutch from Brazil in 1630 when they tried to seize land and grow sugar. The Dutch moved to the Caribbean, where they set up sugar plantations.

(3) and (4) Neither the English nor the French colonized Brazil. The English and French colonized islands in the Caribbean.

16. **1** These events are most closely associated with the Protestant Reformation. The Protestant Reformation refers to the period beginning in 1517 when many Europeans broke away from the Roman Catholic Church. In 1515, Pope Leo X authorized the sale of indulgences to help offset the cost of rebuilding the Cathedral of St. Peter in Rome. Pope Leo X authorized Johann Tetzel, a Dominican monk, to preach and sell indulgences. Indulgences were certificates issued by the Church that reduced or even canceled punishment for a person's sins. People purchased indulgences and believed that this would ensure their admission to heaven. Martin Luther, a German monk, condemned the sale of indulgences and was critical of people who get wealthy from the money collected in Germany. On October 31, 1517, he posted his *95 Theses* on a church door in Wittenberg, a university town. In these statements, he challenged the sale of indulgences and other papal practices. Luther's attack struck a chord throughout Germany. His actions led to the Protestant Reformation, whose supporters broke away from

the Catholic Church. Martin Luther's demands for reform, which included a denial of papal authority and the belief that the Bible was the only guide for salvation, led to the establishment of many different Protestant churches throughout Europe. Powerful northern European and northern German rulers welcomed the revolt against Rome as a way of getting valuable Church property. Thus, many northern German rulers protected Luther from attack and punishment. The Protestant Reformation led to a series of religious wars in the 1520s between Catholics and Lutherans, ended by the Peace of Augsburg. This agreement, signed in 1555, allowed the rulers of a country to decide the religion of its people. Thus most of northern Europe and northern Germany became Protestant, and southern Europe remained mostly Catholic. The Protestant Reformation ended the religious unity of Europe, which had existed for almost a thousand years.

WRONG CHOICES EXPLAINED:

(2) The Crusades were so-called "Holy Wars" by which Christian Europe sought to regain the Holy Land from the Muslims. The Crusades lasted from 1096 A.D. to 1246 A.D.

(3) The Age of Reason is the time period associated with the generation that came of age between the publication of Newton's ideas in 1687 and the death of Louis XIV of France in 1715. The main idea of this era was that natural law and the scientific method could be used to examine and understand all aspects of society.

(4) The Puritan Revolution took place in England from 1642–1660. The Puritans, under the leadership of Oliver Cromwell, established a military dictatorship and beheaded the English King Charles I in 1649. Puritan rule ended in 1658 after the death of Cromwell.

17. **4** One contribution that John Locke made to Enlightenment philosophy was the idea that governments should be based on the consent of the people. John Locke was a 17th-century English philosopher who wrote *Two Treatises of Government* to justify the Glorious Revolution. He believed that all people in a "state of nature" were happy and that all people possess natural rights, including the right to life, liberty, and property. Locke claimed that people entered a social contract with their government to protect these rights. Locke proposed the idea that if a government does not protect these rights, the people have the right to overthrow it. Locke's ideas influenced Thomas Jefferson's Declaration of Independence and Jean-Jacques Rousseau's book, *The Social Contract*.

WRONG CHOICES EXPLAINED:

(1) Locke rejected the idea that absolute monarchies should continue. Locke supported the end of absolutism in England.

(2) Locke did believe that the punishment should fit the crime. However, he believed that an impartial judge would be fair in determining justice for the criminal rather than the victim. Locke's major contribution to the

Enlightenment was the idea that a social contract based on the consent of the people is the foundation of government.

(3) Locke did not believe that individual rights should be denied. He asserted that man had natural rights that could not be denied or controlled by the government.

18. **2** A major result of the Glorious Revolution was that England further limited its monarchy. The Glorious Revolution of 1689 refers to the non-violent transfer of power from James II to William and Mary of Orange. The British Parliament forced James II to abdicate because of his wish to become an absolute ruler and because of the fear that he would restore Catholicism. Parliament invited these monarchs to rule provided that they agreed to submit all legislation to Parliament for approval. As part of the bloodless Glorious Revolution in 1689, Parliament passed the Bill of Rights, which finally ended rule by divine right in England. The Bill of Rights was a set of acts to ensure the supremacy of Parliament over the monarchy. The acts included provisions that the king must meet regularly with Parliament, that the people were guaranteed basic civil liberties, and that the king could not suspend these rights, levy taxes, or maintain an army without the consent of Parliament. With the Bill of Rights, England became a constitutional monarchy in which a legislative body limited the monarch's powers.

WRONG CHOICES EXPLAINED:

(1) Napoleon was restored to power in France when he escaped from Elba in 1815. His return lasted only 100 days.

(3) Oliver Cromwell became the leader of England during the Puritan Revolution. The Puritan Revolution ended in 1660 when the British invited the Stuart King, Charles I, to return from exile and accept the throne.

(4) The defeat of the Spanish Armada by the British occurred in 1588. The Spanish defeat ended any prospect of Spain invading England.

19. **4** A study of revolutions in Latin America in the 19th century would show that events in North America and Europe influenced Latin Americans. The French and American Revolutions most influenced the 19th-century Latin American independence movements. In the 1700s, educated Creoles (natives of Spanish America of European descent) read the works of Voltaire, Rousseau, and Montesquieu. These Enlightenment writers supported the idea that people had the right to rebel against unjust rulers. The Creoles also watched American colonists defeat the British in 1783. They read translations of the Declaration of Independence and the Constitution. Some Creoles also traveled through Europe and were inspired by the ideas of the French Revolution. Simon Bolivar, who had studied in Europe and witnessed the reforms of the French Revolution, earned the title of "The Liberator" for his role in the struggle for Latin American independence. Bolivar's return in 1800 from Europe, by way of the United States, allowed him to study the American system of government. In a series of battles from 1810 to 1824,

Bolivar won freedom for the present-day countries of Venezuela, Colombia, Panama, Bolivia, and Ecuador from their European colonial rulers.

WRONG CHOICES EXPLAINED:

(1) Religion was not a major cause of these conflicts. The revolutionary leaders of Latin America were concerned with gaining independence from Spanish colonial rulers. Once they gained freedom, nationalist leaders in Latin America wanted to end the Church's power over education and reduce its vast landholdings in the country.

(2) Spanish-born peninsulares did not lead most of the Latin American uprisings. Educated Creoles—American-born descendents of Spanish settlers—were the main fighters for Latin American independence.

(3) Nationalism had a major, not a little, influence on the outcome. Nationalism is the belief that each group is entitled to its own nation. The revolutionary leaders of 19th-century Latin America were fighting to end Spanish colonial rule and establish their own nations.

20. **2** A major reason the Industrial Revolution began in England was that England possessed abundant coal and natural resources. Great Britain was rich in natural resources, including waterpower and coal to fuel steam power, and iron ore to make machines, tools, and buildings. Great Britain was also blessed with an abundance of rivers for inland transportation and trading, and good harbors for trade with the rest of the continent and the world. Its fleet of more than 6,000 merchant ships sailed to almost every part of the globe. This overseas trade gave Britain access to raw materials and markets. Both were essential to industrial growth.

WRONG CHOICES EXPLAINED:

(1) England does not have a smooth coastline. It has a long coastline of 2,000 miles (3,200 km). In the south and west, the coastline can be rocky with steep cliffs. The eastern coast is often flat.

(3) and (4) Neither of these reasons contributed to the Industrial Revolution in England. Great Britain is an island nation whose many natural harbors and rivers serve as a means of transportation and sources of power for factories. There were not that many waterfalls to provide power for the factories, and England does have numerous mountain ranges. Most of England consists of rolling hills with a chain of low mountains in the north.

21. **3** An immediate result of the mass starvation in Ireland in the late 1840s was the migration of many Irish to other countries. In the 1840s, Ireland experienced one of the worst famines in modern history. The potato, introduced from the Americas, was the main source of food for most of the Irish. In 1845, a "blight" (disease) destroyed the potato crop. Other crops, such as wheat and oats, were not affected. The British, who ruled Ireland, continued to require the Irish to ship these crops outside Ireland, leaving little for the Irish except the blighted potato. The result was the "Great Hunger." Of a population

of eight million, about a million people died from starvation and disease over the next few years. Millions more emigrated to the United States and Canada. In the 1850s, over a million Irish emigrated to the United States. By the middle of the 20th century, over 4.5 million had emigrated to the United States.

WRONG CHOICES EXPLAINED:

(1) The mass starvation in Ireland in the late 1840s did not lead to the Green Revolution. The Green Revolution is the use of 20th-century technological advances in agriculture to achieve increased food production on a limited parcel of land.

(2) The Great Hunger or mass starvation left a legacy of bitterness, not acceptance, of British rule. The anti-British attitude would continue throughout the 20th century.

(4) Ireland did not develop a mixed economy based on government regulation with private enterprise. The Irish economy was primarily agricultural, with little or no emphasis on industrial growth.

22. **1** Otto von Bismarck is associated with the phrase *blood and iron* relating to the unification of Germany. Otto von Bismarck was appointed Chancellor of Prussia in 1867. Over the next decade, Bismarck was a strong, practical leader who guided German unification. Bismarck believed that the only way to unify Germany was through "blood and iron." He had no faith in representative government and thought that the only way to unite the German states was through war. In seven years, Bismarck led Prussia into three wars. Each of these wars increased Prussia's presence and moved the German states closer to unity. In the Danish War (1864), Prussia, allied with Austria, seized territory from Denmark. In the Austro-Prussian War (1866), Prussia turned against Austria and defeated it within seven weeks; Bismarck annexed the North German states into Prussia. In the Franco-Prussian War (1870–1871), Bismarck used nationalism to rally the people against Napoleon III of France and easily defeated France. During this war, the southern German states were united with Prussia. In 1871, Germany became one nation.

WRONG CHOICES EXPLAINED:

(2) Giuseppe Garibaldi was an Italian national leader who conquered the Two Sicilies in 1860, helping to unite Italy.

(3) Kaiser Wilhelm I was proclaimed the first Emperor of the German Empire in 1871 by prime minister Otto von Bismarck.

(4) Count Camillo di Cavour was the Prime Minister of Piedmont Sardinia. With the help of the French, he promoted the unification of Italy in 1860.

23. **3** Social Darwinists would most likely support the statement that stronger groups have the right to rule and control weaker groups. Social Darwinism is the application to human societies of Charles Darwin's ideas about the evolution and survival of the fittest. Those who were the most fit for survival enjoyed wealth and success and were superior to others. Some Social

Darwinists expanded these ideas into racist thinking. They claimed that certain groups of people were fitter, brighter, stronger, and more advanced than others. They claimed that these superior races were intended by nature to dominate lesser people. Many Europeans used such arguments to justify the spread of imperialism in Africa and Asia during the late 19th century.

WRONG CHOICES EXPLAINED:

(1), (2), and (4) None of these statements would be supported by Social Darwinists. Social Darwinists did not believe in universal suffrage, political equality, or public education. Social Darwinists argued that natural selection was the basis for the right to suffrage, equality, and education. Those people who gained any rights were the fittest and enjoyed the benefits of their success. The poor or those deprived of any rights remained in this position because they were unfit.

24. **1** One similarity between the Sepoy Mutiny in India and the Boxer Rebellion in China is that they both opposed European imperialism. The Sepoys were Indian soldiers serving under British command. These soldiers were protesting the policies of the British East India Company. The British cartridges used by the Sepoys had to be bitten to remove the seal before inserting them in their guns. The coverings were said to be greased with pork and beef fat to make them waterproof. In 1857, the Sepoy soldiers refused to accept these cartridges. Both Hindus, who considered the cow sacred, and Muslims, who did not eat pork, were angry. The Sepoy Mutiny (rebellion) lasted more than a year. The British government sent troops to help the British East India Company. This was a turning point in Indian history. After 1858, the British government took direct control of India. Eventually, the British began educating and training Indians for a role in their own Indian government.

The Boxers were a secret society formed in China in 1899. Their goal was to drive out the foreigners who they felt were destroying China with their Western technology. In 1900, the Boxers attacked international communities in China, as well as foreign embassies in Beijing. In response, Western powers and Japan formed a multinational force of 25,000 troops. They crushed the Boxers and rescued the foreigners besieged in Beijing. Both of these rebellions were responses to Western imperialism.

WRONG CHOICES EXPLAINED:

(2) Neither of these events ended an established dynasty. India was not ruled by a dynasty. The Sepoy Rebellion led to stricter control by the British, who did not give India self rule until 1947. The Qing Dynasty (Manchu) in China ended in 1911.

(3) Neither the Sepoy Mutiny nor the Boxer Rebellion resulted in the redistribution of land. India began to address this issue when it gained independence in 1947. Mao Zedong began a redistribution of land when he and the Communist Party seized control of mainland China in 1949.

(4) Neither of these movements instituted communist governments. Communism was established in China in 1949.

25. **2** A direct result of World War I was that Germany lost its colonies in Africa and Asia. The Versailles Treaty was signed between Germany and the Allied powers on June 28, 1919. The treaty punished Germany, which lost substantial territory in Africa and the Pacific. All German territories in East and West Africa and the Pacific were declared mandates to be administered by the League of Nations. Under the peace agreement, the Allies (England and France) would govern these protectorates until they were judged ready for independence. Some former colonies, such as Tanzania, did not gain independence until 1962.

WRONG CHOICES EXPLAINED:

(1) World War I led to the end of the Russian government led by Czar Nicholas II. In March 1917, Czar Nicholas II was forced to abdicate and a new provisional government was established. In 1918, the communists, who took control of Russia, killed the Czar and his family.

(3) The assassination of Archduke Francis Ferdinand by a terrorist was the spark that led to World War I.

(4) The Ottoman Empire did not expand. It ended as a direct result of World War I. The Turks lost their territory in the Middle East and these areas were divided between England and France.

26. **1** A statement about both the Bolshevik Revolution in Russia and the rise of fascism in Germany and Italy that is accurate is that economic conditions led to political change. World War I created conditions in Russia that helped trigger the Bolshevik Revolution. In 1914, Russia was one of the World War I Allied powers that fought against Germany. However, Russia was not ready to fight a war. Russian soldiers lacked adequate supplies and weapons. Food was scarce and the transportation system broke down so often that needed supplies never made it to the front. By 1915, soldiers had little ammunition, rifles, or medical care. In March 1917, workers led food riots all across Russia. In St. Petersburg, when soldiers refused to fire upon the striking workers, Nicholas II, Czar of Russia, was forced to give up his throne and the leaders of the Duma, the Russian Parliament, set up a republic. This provisional government, headed by Prince Luvov, set up a western-style democratic government that guaranteed civil rights and freed political prisoners. The decision to continue the war and the continued inability to provide food resulted in the loss of support among the people. The Bolsheviks, a revolutionary group led by Vladimir Lenin, promised "peace for the soldiers, land for the peasants, and bread for the workers." Lenin, who had been in exile when the March Revolution broke out, was infiltrated into the country by the Germans, who used him to undermine support of the provisional government. In November 1917, the Bolsheviks seized control of the government. The Bolsheviks, who now changed their name to "Communists," made Russia the first communist nation in Europe.

The fascist governments of Benito Mussolini in Italy and Adolf Hitler in Germany came to power because these nations faced severe economic difficulties. After World War I, Italy and Germany faced widespread unemployment and inflation, leading to severe economic unrest. In the 1920s, it was reported in Germany that one loaf of bread cost 200 billion marks; four trillion marks were the equivalent of one U.S. dollar. Mussolini and Hitler gained support among the middle class and business leaders by promising to improve the economy. In Germany, the government's policy of simply printing money led to runaway inflation and destroyed the value of the life savings of many people. The inability of the Italian government and the Weimar Republic in Germany to command a majority in parliament made it difficult to solve each nation's economic problems. People in Russia, Italy, and Germany turned to these movements to solve their economic crises.

WRONG CHOICES EXPLAINED:

(2) Industrialization did not hinder the national development leading to the rise of the Bolsheviks and fascists. The Bolsheviks in Russia and the fascists in Germany and Italy gained support by promoting industrial development through government intervention and control.

(3) Neither the Bolsheviks nor the fascists gained control by peaceful means. The Bolsheviks gained control by violently overthrowing the Russian government in November 1917. The fascists in Germany and Italy achieved their goals by gaining political power and then suppressing all opposition.

(4) Lenin was a Bolshevik who promoted communism in Russia. Hitler in Germany and Mussolini in Italy promised to fight communism by their efforts to seize factories and redistribute land under the control of their respective governments.

27. **1** The term *appeasement* is best defined as an attempt to avoid conflict by meeting the demands of an aggressor. In Europe during the 1930s, several national leaders followed a policy of appeasement. These leaders agreed to the demands of an aggressor to preserve peace at any cost. During the 1930s, Italy and Germany sought to build new empires. In 1935, Italy invaded the African country of Ethiopia. The Ethiopian emperor, Haile Selassie, appealed to the League of Nations for help. Although the League condemned the attack, its members did nothing. Britain continued to let Italian troops and supplies pass through the British-controlled Suez Canal. Britain and France hoped to keep peace in Europe by giving in to Mussolini in Africa. By 1935, Hitler had rebuilt the German army in violation of the 1919 Versailles Treaty. In 1936, Hitler marched into the Rhineland, a 30-mile-wide zone on either side of the Rhine River that formed a buffer zone between Germany and France. The Versailles Treaty had required Germany to remove troops from this region. It was also an industrial area. The French were unwilling to risk war and the British urged peace. The Western democracies' weak response to Germany's initial victories encouraged Hitler to become more aggressive. In 1938, Hitler made Austria part of the German Reich. In September 1938, Hitler demanded that the Sudetenland—region in Czechoslovakia bordering Germany and inhabited by about three million

German-speaking people—be returned to Germany. The Czech government, a democracy under President Edward Benes, refused to yield. They asked for help from France. The Munich Conference, held on September 29, 1938, tried to resolve the problem. Germany, France, Britain, and Italy attended, but the Czechs were not invited. British Prime Minister Neville Chamberlain believed that he would preserve peace by giving in to Hitler's demands. The Western democracies agreed that Germany would have control of the Sudetenland; in exchange, Hitler pledged to respect Czechoslovakia's new borders. Less than six months after the Munich meeting, Hitler's troops took over the rest of Czechoslovakia and Mussolini seized Albania. In August 1939, England and France refused to give in to Hitler's demands that Poland return the former German port of Danzig; but appeasement had convinced Hitler that neither nation would risk war. On September 1, 1939, Hitler invaded Poland. Two days later, Britain and France honored their guarantee to Poland and declared war on Germany. World War II had started. Appeasement had failed to keep peace.

WRONG CHOICES EXPLAINED:

(2) The term Golden Age defines a period of peace and prosperity, resulting in cultural achievement.

(3) A declaration of war between two or more nations is known as international conflict.

(4) A trade agreement is a term used to describe an agreement removing economic barriers among nations.

28. **2** The best title for this map is Japanese Imperial Expansion. In 1905, the Russians and Japanese fought the Russo-Japanese war after the interests of the two nations conflicted in Korea. Japan, to the world's surprise, defeated Russia. The Treaty of Portsmouth provided for Japan's acquisition of the southern half of Sakhalin Island, and Russia's sphere of influence in southern Manchuria, a region north of Korea. In 1931, a group of Japanese army officers provoked an incident that would provide an excuse to seize Manchuria. The militaristic leaders of Japan wanted to build a Japanese empire. The empire would provide Japan with raw materials and markets for its goods. The military officers set explosives and blew up tracks on a Japanese-owned railroad line, claiming that the Chinese had committed the act. In "self-defense," the army attacked Chinese forces. Without consulting their own government, the Japanese military forces conquered all of Manchuria and set up a puppet state called Manchukuo. In 1937, the Japanese invaded the Chinese mainland and set off a full-scale war between Japan and China. Beijing and other northern cities, as well as the capital of Nanking (Nanjing), fell to the Japanese. The Japanese established a puppet government in the city. Their invasion of Nanking was so brutal that it became known as the "rape of Nanking." Between December 1937 and March 1938, the Japanese army murdered more than half of the 600,000 civilians and soldiers in the city. During this six-week carnage, an estimated 80,000 women

and girls were raped or mutilated. The Japanese continued to gain territory during the war with China. These territories provided additional resources for the Japanese industrial economy, as well as an area to support Japan's growing population.

WRONG CHOICES EXPLAINED:

(1), (3), and (4) None of these titles can be supported by the information on the map. There is no information about Japanese dominance of Manchukuo, East Asian trade routes, or the natural resources of China and Japan.

29. **4** These headlines might be used to illustrate the weakness of the League of Nations. In the 1930s, Germany and Italy sought to build new empires. The League of Nations was weak. Western countries were recovering from the Great Depression and did not want war. In 1935, Italy invaded the African country of Ethiopia. The Ethiopian emperor, Haile Selassie, appealed to the League of Nations for help. Although the League condemned the attack, its members did nothing. Britain continued to let Italian troops and supplies pass through the British-controlled Suez Canal. Britain and France hoped to keep peace in Europe by giving in to Mussolini in Africa. In 1936, Hitler marched into the Rhineland, a 30-mile-wide zone on either side of the Rhine River that formed a buffer zone between Germany and France. The Versailles Treaty had required Germany to remove troops from this industrialized region. The French were unwilling to risk war and the British urged peace. On September 1, 1939, Hitler invaded Poland. Two days later, Britain and France, without the backing of the League of Nations, honored their guarantee to Poland and declared war on Germany. As part of their Non-Aggression Pact of August 1939, Germany and Russia had agreed not to fight each other. In return for Russia's support, Germany allowed Russia to annex the eastern half of Poland, while Germany seized the western half. The weakness of the League of Nations led to the destruction of Poland and failed to prevent World War II.

WRONG CHOICES EXPLAINED:

(1) The United Nations was formed in 1945 to replace the League of Nations.

(2) The Congress of Vienna was a series of meetings from 1814 to 1815. European leaders sought to establish a lasting peace and security after the defeat of Napoleon.

(3) The Warsaw Pact was a military alliance formed in 1955 by the Soviet Union and seven of its eastern European satellite countries.

30. **2** India and Pakistan are the nations that have been most directly involved in the events illustrated in this time line. Since the partition of 1947, India, which is predominantly Hindu, and Pakistan, which is mostly Muslim, have been at odds over Kashmir, located on India's northwest frontier. In 1947, Kashmir's Hindu prince signed it over to India. However, its majority

Muslim population wanted to be part of Pakistan. Although most of the people are Muslim, two-thirds of the territory is governed by India. In 1948, the UN Security Council called for a vote of the people of Kashmir to choose which country they wanted to join. A vote was never taken. In Indian regions, Muslim guerrillas fought against Indian rule. Fighting between India and Pakistan ended with UN intervention. Since 1949, the cease-fire has been monitored by UN Military Observer Groups in India and Pakistan. In 1965, a second war over Kashmir began when Pakistan claimed that India was trying to manipulate elections in Kashmir and suppress the Muslim population. On July 2, 1972, India and Pakistan signed the Silma Accord, under which both countries agreed to respect the cease-fire line and to resolve differences over Kashmir by peaceful negotiations. The Silma Accord left the settlement of the Kashmir question to be resolved at an unspecified future date.

Rivalries between India and Pakistan also led to the creation of Bangladesh in 1971. West Pakistan and East Pakistan were separated by more than 1,000 miles of Indian territory. From culture to ethnic background, the two regions were different; only the Islamic religion united them. East Pakistan, or the Bengalis, had a larger population than the West, but its government was dominated by the Punjabis in the West. Rebellion broke out in April 1971. In December 1971, the Indian army lent its support to East Pakistan. When Pakistan tried to crush the rebels, a new nation, Bangladesh, was formed from East Pakistan. Millions of Bengalis also fled to India to escape the attempt by Pakistan to destroy them. India's support enabled the Bengalis to establish an independent nation.

Although many Muslims fled to Pakistan in 1947, about 100 million still live in India. In 1992, Hindu fundamentalists called for the destruction of a Muslim mosque in Ayodhya. This conflict touched off rioting and the mosque was destroyed. Recently, the report of Indian archaeologists that they found evidence of a Hindu temple under the ruins of a 16th-century mosque added to the tension between Hindus and minority Muslims.

WRONG CHOICES EXPLAINED:

(1), (3), and (4) None of these nations were directly involved in the events illustrated in this time line.

31. **3** Vietnam is a communist nation that is most closely associated with the leadership of Ho Chi Minh and the surrender of Saigon. Ho Chi Minh, which means "He Who Enlightens," was a Vietnamese leader who attended the Versailles Peace Conference in 1919 and called upon France to grant Vietnam independence. France refused. Disappointed, Ho Chi Minh was nevertheless determined to build a communist movement and win independence. During World War II, Ho formed the Viet Minh and used guerrilla warfare against the Japanese. By 1945, he controlled northern Vietnam, including Hanoi. In 1946, France set out to regain control of Vietnam. After eight years of bitter struggle, Ho's forces decisively defeated the French at Dienbienphu in 1954 and the French were forced to withdraw. However, the

United States continued the struggle because it wanted to prevent the communists from taking over in Vietnam. Ho died in 1969, but the fight for Vietnamese independence continued. In 1975, communist forces captured Saigon, the capital of South Vietnam, and renamed the city Ho Chi Minh City in his honor. Vietnam became a unified communist country in 1975.

WRONG CHOICES EXPLAINED:

(1), (2), and (4) None of these communist countries are associated with the leadership of Ho Chi Minh.

32. **1** One similarity between the Polish group Solidarity in 1980 and the Chinese protesters in Tiananmen Square in 1989 is that both groups supported movements for democracy. In 1980, economic hardships ignited strikers by shipyard workers. Led by Lech Walesa, they organized Solidarity, an independent trade union. It gained millions of members and demanded political changes. Under pressure from the Soviet Union, the Polish government outlawed the union in 1981 and arrested its leaders, including Walesa, who was released in 1982. In the late 1980s, Mikhail Gorbachev, leader of the Soviet Union, declared that he would not interfere in eastern Europe. By that time, Poland was introducing radical economic changes similar to Gorbachev's changes in the Soviet Union. The government also legalized Solidarity and in 1989, Poland held its first free election in 50 years. Solidarity candidates triumphed. Lech Walesa was elected president of Poland and the country was on the path of continued political changes in the next decade. In China, after the death of Mao Zedong in 1976, Deng Xiaoping, the new communist leader, introduced reforms to modernize the economy. The government was willing to grant economic but not political reforms. In April 1989, 100,000 students gathered in Tiananmen Square in Beijing to protest against official corruption, demand more civil liberties, and promote better conditions at Chinese universities. In the following weeks, factory workers joined the students and demonstrations spread to other cities. Some communist officials even expressed support for the students. After six tense weeks, Deng sent out tanks and troops to crush the demonstrations in Tiananmen Square. Many students were killed or wounded. The government hunted down all dissidents and stifled all political dissent.

WRONG CHOICES EXPLAINED:

(2) Solidarity helped end communism in Poland in 1989. The protesters in Tiananmen Square did not end communism in China. The Communist Party still controls China in 2007.

(3) Solidarity leaders, with the support of Pope John Paul II, did not encourage the military occupation by the Soviet Union and warned them not to invade. The Chinese communist government never encouraged any military intervention in China by the Soviet Union. They considered the Tiananmen Square problem an internal matter that was not the concern of any outside country.

(4) These movements were concerned with political changes. They were not directed toward any increase in military spending.

33. **1** The status of Hong Kong changed in July 1997 when the city was returned to the communist People's Republic of China. In 1842, Britain gained control of the island of Hong Kong after the Opium War when it defeated China. Under British rule, Hong Kong and nearby territories grew into a center of trade. In 1949, millions of refugees from the Chinese Revolution flooded Hong Kong, providing labor and capital to help the area. In the following years, Hong Kong became a world financial center, with many foreign banks and a busy stock market. In the 1980s, Britain and China decided that Hong Kong would return to mainland Chinese rule. China agreed not to change Hong Kong's social or economic system for 50 years and to allow the people a degree of self-government. Many residents are still nervous about China's power and the use of repressive measures against protesters. The people are fearful that China will try to incorporate the island into its communist system.

WRONG CHOICES EXPLAINED:

(2) Hong Kong was not closed to international trade after 1997. Hong Kong has become known as one of the "Asian tigers" because of its aggressive economic growth.

(3) Hong Kong did not become an independent nation after 1997. It is an island province of the People's Republic of China with a limited amount of self-rule.

(4) Hong Kong had a capitalist economy before 1997.

34. **2** Mikhail Gorbachev's reforms of *perestroika* and *glasnost* resulted in conditions that helped lead to the breakup of the Soviet Union. In 1985, Gorbachev came to power in the Soviet Union. At 54, he was the youngest Soviet leader since Stalin. He pursued new ideas and was eager to reform the government and the economy. Gorbachev realized that economic and social reforms could not occur without a free flow of ideas and information. He launched a policy of *glasnost* or "openness." He ended most censorship and encouraged more freedom. The government allowed more churches to open and released dissidents from prison. Gorbachev also restructured the state economy in a process called *perestroika*. He backed some free market reforms, including limited private enterprise. Gorbachev's policies had widespread impact. Relations with the United States improved and treaties reduced the threat of war. Glasnost led to unrest, however, in the multinational Soviet empire. In 1989, the Berlin Wall was torn down, leading to the eventual reunification of Germany. In 1991, the Baltic states of Estonia, Latvia, and Lithuania, which had been seized by Stalin during World War II, became independent. In Eastern Europe, countries such as Poland and Rumania broke out of the Soviet orbit. In August 1991, Gorbachev resigned and Boris Yeltsin eventually became the first directly-elected leader in

Russian history. On December 12, 1991, the government of the Soviet Union was replaced by a commonwealth of independent nations. The Soviet Union had ceased to exist.

WRONG CHOICES EXPLAINED:

(1) Gorbachev's program did not result in an era of world peace and Soviet prosperity. His policy of *perestroika*, or economic reform, did not bring about economic prosperity. Perestroika led to inflation and shortages of food and medicine. Gorbachev's policy of *glasnost* won support among western leaders for efforts to end the Cold War, but the political changes led to unrest and revolts among the Soviet satellite countries, such as Poland and Hungary, as well as the destruction of the Berlin Wall.

(3) Gorbachev's reforms were designed to transform the Russian economy into a market economy, not a command economy. He believed that Russia's economy, first established by Stalin under the Five Year Plan, needed to be reformed.

(4) Gorbachev's policy sought to end censorship, not promote censorship of the media.

35. **2** The governments of Augusto Pinochet, Saddam Hussein, and Slobodan Milosevic are examples of oppressive regimes. Augusto Pinochet was dictator and president of Chile from 1973 to 1990. In 1973, at the request of the legislative and judicial branches of government, Pinochet participated in a coup d'etat that deposed Marxist President Salvador Allende and established a military government. Arguing that Chile was under siege by communists, Pinochet implemented a series of security operations in which approximately 3,000 suspected terrorists or known dissidents were killed and about 30,000 were imprisoned and tortured. Pinochet remained in power until 1990 when he was defeated in a plebiscite that rejected the continuation of his rule. At the time of his death in 2006, around 300 criminal charges in Chile were still pending against Pinochet for alleged human rights abuses during his rule.

Saddam Hussein joined the Ba'ath socialist party in 1957. In 1958, Hussein had to go into Egyptian exile after taking part in a failed revolt against the premier of the Iraqi republic. Hussein returned in 1963 and took full power in 1971. He surrounded himself with family members, crushed all opposition, and became a dictator. In 1990, a human rights report stated that people were arrested for disloyalty and for spilling coffee on a newspaper photo of Hussein. Hussein also murdered family members who opposed his government. In 1988 and 1991, the government crushed Kurdish rebellions and forced more than a million Kurds and Iraqis to flee to other countries. Hussein remained the dictator of Iraq until his overthrow by United States and coalition forces in 2003. He was executed in 2006 after being found guilty of war crimes at his trial.

The breakup of Yugoslavia in 1991 and 1992 sparked ethnic violence in Bosnia among Serbs, Croatians, and Muslims. Slobodan Milosevic, the

Serbian Yugoslav president, began a policy of ethnic cleansing to destroy all non-Serbs. The Serbs already dominated most of Yugoslavia. Milosevic forcibly removed other ethnic groups from areas that Serbs controlled. Hundreds of thousands of Bosnians became refugees, living on food sent by the United Nations and charities. Many others were brutalized or killed. Milosevic also waged a brutal campaign of ethnic cleansing against Muslim Kosovars. In November 1999, NATO forces started a military campaign against Yugoslavia. Milosevic was forced to retreat and was ousted from power. In 2002 the International Court at the Hague tried Milosevic for crimes against humanity. He was the first head of state to face an international war-crimes court. He died of a heart attack in March 2006. His death precluded a verdict in his four-year trial, dashing any hopes that he would be held accountable for the deaths of more than 200,000 people.

WRONG CHOICES EXPLAINED:

(1) Absolute monarchies were governments where kings had supreme powers and control over the lives of the people in their country. In Europe, the Age of Absolutism reached its height during the 17th century.

(3) Democratic republics are systems of government in which the people rule through elected representatives.

(4) Islamic theocracies are systems of government ruled by religious leaders who believe that the government should be guided by the principles and values in the Koran.

36. **1** One way in which wars, religious conflicts, and natural disasters are similar is that these situations may result in the mass migration of people. In 1830, Polish nationalists fled for western Europe and the United States after the Russian army crushed their revolt. Several thousand Germans moved to cities in the United States after the failed German revolts of 1848. In the 1840s, the Irish potato famine led to the migration of millions to the United States and other parts of the world. In the 19th century, Russian Jews left eastern Europe to escape pogroms, and Italian farmers, suffering from poor economic conditions, migrated to other countries. Throughout history, religious conflicts have led to migration. In the 17th and 18th centuries, groups fled from Europe to America to escape persecution because of their religious beliefs as either Protestants or Catholics. In the 20th century, the establishment of India as an independent nation caused mass migration. During the summer of 1947, 10 million people were on the move in India. Muslims moved from the Hindu areas of India to the newly-independent Muslim state of Pakistan. Hindus in the area of Pakistan moved to Hindu-dominated states of India. In the process, over a million people were killed. Natural disasters such as hurricanes, earthquakes, and droughts in Asia, Africa, and the Americas have also contributed to migration. Drought conditions throughout many parts of Africa have forced the migration of many Africans to different parts of the world. The 2004 tsunami in the Pacific and Indian Oceans also forced many people to migrate. It has been estimated that

worldwide over 32.9 million people have been driven from their homes by war, persecution, and poverty, with 9.9 million officially listed as refugees by the United Nations.

WRONG CHOICES EXPLAINED:

(2) These situations have caused economic instability. The loss of millions of people due to these situations leads to a nation's loss of its educated elite and contributes to social problems as family life is undermined.

(3) These situations would lead to a decrease, not an increase, in life expectancy.

(4) These situations do not lead to global warming. Global warming is thought to be caused by changes in industrial production and the way we use our resources.

37. **3** This passage describes the opposition of the African National Congress to the practice of apartheid. Apartheid, an African word for "apartness," was an official policy of strict racial segregation that was practiced in South Africa. In 1948, the Nationalist Party came to power in South Africa. This party promoted Afrikaner or Boer South African nationalism. Their policy of apartheid banned social contacts between whites and blacks. It established segregated schools, hospitals, and neighborhoods. Black Africans resisted the control imposed by the white minority. The African National Congress (ANC), formed in 1912 to fight for blacks' rights, organized strikes to protest these racial policies. In 1964, Nelson Mandela, the leader of the ANC, was imprisoned for 27 years for his opposition to apartheid. In 1991, the policy of apartheid was repealed.

WRONG CHOICES EXPLAINED:

(1), (2), and (4) None of these choices are supported by this passage. Mandela does not describe his opposition to the revival of colonialism, rivalries between tribes, or the introduction of a coalition government.

38. **4** The generalization that can be supported by this passage is that Nelson Mandela opposed political division based on color. In 1990, Mandela, the imprisoned leader of the African National Congress, was released from prison. The end of apartheid in 1991 was the first step towards the creation of a new constitution that would grant political equality for all. In 1994, multicultural elections were held and the people chose Nelson Mandela as the first black South African president. As president, Mandela welcomed longtime foes into the government. Mandela's slogan was "Let us build together." He invited into the government Afrikaners who had once tyrannized the black majority. He advocated and wanted members of his party to accept a multiparty system. Even in Mandela's South Africa, the minority whites own three-fourths of the land, black unemployment is high, and the crime rate makes many cities unsafe. But South Africa's first black president did bring about a peaceful transition to democratic rule without violence and chaos.

WRONG CHOICES EXPLAINED:

(1) The passage does not indicate that racism has disappeared in South Africa. Mandela claims that South Africa must continue to struggle for equality.

(2) According to Mandela, the social goals of the African National Congress will not change its policy even when it triumphs.

(3) Mandela denies that giving the vote to black Africans will result in racial domination. He believes that equal political rights would guarantee freedom.

39. **1** Kim Jong Il and Fidel Castro are 21st-century leaders who believe in the ideas of Karl Marx. Karl Marx wrote the *Communist Manifesto* in 1848, which outlined the abuses of capitalism and predicted the inevitability of communism because of the laws of history. Marx believed that the workers of the world would unite in a worldwide revolution that would lead to the overthrow of the capitalist system. Marx's ideas inspired the leaders of North Korea and Cuba in their struggle against capitalist countries. Kim Jong Il is the Soviet-born leader of North Korea. He succeeded his father Kim Il-Sung, founder of North Korea, who died in 1994. Even when the Soviet and Chinese allies undertook economic reforms, North Korea clung to hardline communism. Under Kim Jong Il, the "Dear Leader," North Korea's economy is one of the world's most centrally planned and isolated. Failed government policies and terrible floods have repeatedly destroyed harvests, bringing widespread hunger. Massive international food deliveries have allowed the regime to escape mass starvation since 1995–1996. Kim has held onto power despite the misery and famine. Kim has also been criticized by world governments for human rights abuses carried out under his rule, as well as for North Korea's production of nuclear weapons in violation of the Nuclear Non-Proliferation Treaty. It has been reported that North Korea has concentration camps where up to 50,000 men, women, and children are detained and where human rights violations by guards include murdering babies born to inmates. Kim Jong Il is considered to be one of the most repressive rulers in the world. He personally directs every aspect of the state, even minor details such as the size of party leaders' homes and the delivery of gifts to his subordinates.

Fidel Castro, who was born in 1927, was the son of a wealthy Spanish Cuban farmer. He became involved in politics while studying law at the University of Havana. In 1959, Fidel Castro overthrew the dictatorship of Fulgencia Batista and seized power in Cuba. Throughout the 1950s, the United States had supported the unpopular dictator Batista. Castro denounced the United States as an imperialist country, forbade elections, and nationalized (seized for the Cuban government) American investments in Cuba without compensation. In 1961, Castro proclaimed his intention to transform Cuba into a communist state and threatened to export communism to other Latin American countries. He also established close ties with the Soviet Union, which had established a communist government in Russia in 1917. The close ties between Cuba and the Soviet Union ended in 1991 with the collapse of the Soviet Union. Castro's government is one of the last communist governments in the world. The aging Castro has refused to change his communist system of government or give up power after 48 years in office.

WRONG CHOICES EXPLAINED:

(2) Adam Smith was a social philosopher and economist who wrote *The Wealth of Nations.* Smith is considered the "Father of Capitalism."

(3) Siddhartha Gautama, who lived from 566 to 486 B.C., was the founder of Buddhism.

(4) Jean-Jacques Rousseau was the 19th-century French philosopher of the Enlightenment who wrote the *Social Contract.* He asserted that government is a social contract in which the people give power to the government to act for the good of the people.

40. **1** The main idea of this 2003 cartoon is that there are problems to resolve on the road to peace. The "road map to peace" is a plan proposed by the United States, the European Union, Russia, and the United Nations, to resolve the Israeli-Palestinian conflict. The U.S.-backed peace proposal was formally introduced by President Bush in June 2003 when he called for an independent Palestinian state living side by side with Israel. The Palestinians and Israelis accepted the basic outline of the plan. Both sides were required to take immediate steps to end violence and create conditions for lasting peace. The road map required the Palestinian Authority to make democratic reforms and abandon the use of terrorism. Israel had to immediately dismantle and end settlement activity of the Gaza Strip and West Bank as the Palestinian terrorist threat was removed. The road map comprises three goal-driven phases with the ultimate goal of a provisional Palestinian state at the end of 2003. The goal has not yet been achieved. The Israeli government says that the Palestinians failed to rein in the suicide bombers and gunmen of Hamas and other extremist groups. The Palestinians claim that Israel was not committed to ending settlement expansion. The plan also doesn't resolve issues, such as the borders of a Palestinian state or the status of Jerusalem. The plan leaves such final status open to subsequent negotiations. The plan also does not deal with the contentious issue of Palestinian refugees. According to international law, all refugees have the right to return to their place of origin. However, if all the Palestinian refugees who claim to come from Israel—a number estimated to be about 3.7 million people—try to return, it would quickly mean the end of the Jewish state. The current population of Israel is 6.4 million people with 5.2 million Jews. Many believe that the road map to peace is like the Oslo Accords of 1993, a framework for negotiations, not a set agreement. Recent conflict between Israel and Hezbollah in Lebanon, along with the success of Hamas in gaining control of the Gaza Strip, have severely strained the road map.

WRONG CHOICES EXPLAINED:

(2), (3), and (4) None of these ideas are expressed in the cartoon. There is no indication that Colin Powell has removed the stumbling blocks to peace, or that both groups have reached agreement, or that the road has been carefully mapped.

41. **4** This 2003 cartoon illustrates the struggle between Palestinians and Israelis. The people in the cartoon are: Secretary of State Colin Powell in the car; Prime Minister Mahmound Abbas, who took over the leadership of the Palestinian Authority after the death of Yasir Arafat in 2004; and Prime Minister Ariel Sharon, who is shown wearing a jacket with the Star of David, a symbol in the Israel flag. In January 2006, Sharon suffered a major stroke and slipped into a coma. Finance Minister Ehud Olmert became the interim prime minister in April 2006. Olmert has continued working on the difficult task of establishing peace in the Middle East.

WRONG CHOICES EXPLAINED:

(1), (2), and (3) None of these groups are illustrated in the cartoon.

42. **2** The heading that best completes the partial outline is "Effects of Nationalism." Nationalism is the belief that each group is entitled to its own nation or government. For many years, Italy was divided into a number of small states and was considered a geographic expression, rather than a united country. Italian nationalists like Giuseppe Mazzini called for a united country. In 1852, Count Camillo di Cavour became Prime Minister of Piedmont (also known as the Kingdom of Sardinia). He strengthened the country by promoting industry, enlarging the army, and improving agriculture. He was also successful in getting diplomatic assistance to free Italy from Austrian domination. In 1859, he secured a promise of support from Napoleon III of France if Austria attacked Sardinia. Cavour maneuvered Austria into war and with the help of France was successful in driving Austria out of northern Italy. Further to the south, Giuseppe Garibaldi and his volunteer army of 1,000 Red Shirts gained control of Naples and the Two Sicilies. Cavour joined Naples to enlarge the kingdom of Piedmont. By 1860, Italy had become a united nation. Cavour died in 1861 and is considered the "brains of Italian unification." Venice, and later Rome, joined Italy in 1866 and 1870, respectively.

The Indian National Congress was formed in 1885 by Hindu nationalists who began to call for gradual change in English policies toward the colony. The members of the party were mostly professional and business leaders who favored peaceful protest. They called for greater democracy in India, looked forward to self-rule, and urged more government jobs for India. Mohandas Gandhi became the leader of the Indian National Congress and developed a large following among India's peasants. Gandhi sought to end British rule not by violence, but with passive resistance, or civil disobedience. His followers boycotted England, refused to pay taxes, and disregarded British laws. Gandhi believed that passive resistance would compel Britain to withdraw from India. Indian leaders had hoped for independence after World War I but were disappointed by British opposition. After World War II, British leaders recognized that they were too weak to resist Indian demands for independence. In 1947, the British agreed to Indian independence.

In the 1930s, Muhammad Ali Jinnah, an Indian Muslim, led his religious group out of the Congress Party and formed the Muslim League. He was fearful that as India became closer to independence, they would be dominated by the Hindu majority. While millions of Muslims responded to Gandhi's campaigns of non-violence, tensions between Hindus and Muslims often erupted into violence. Muslims, led by Jinnah, told the British that they wanted their own separate state. Thus, when the British granted independence to India in 1947, the Muslim section of India became a separate independent nation, Pakistan.

World War I contributed to the breakup of Austria-Hungary. As a result of the war, the government in Austria-Hungary collapsed. Several new European nations were created out of the former empire: Austria and Hungary became independent nations; Czechoslovakia and Yugoslavia, two multinational states, were formed. The creation of these independent states ended the Austro-Hungarian empire.

WRONG CHOICES EXPLAINED:

(1), (3), and (4) None of these headings deal with nationalism and its effect on the world.

43. **3** The correct chronological order is Golden Age of Greece (460 B.C.); fall of the Roman Empire (476 A.D.); Crusades (1096–1246 A.D.); the Renaissance (14th to 17th century).

WRONG CHOICES EXPLAINED:

(1), (2), and (4) None of these choices are in correct chronological order.

44. **3** One way in which Asoka, Mansa Musa, and Suleiman the Magnificent are similar is that they ruled during times of prosperity. The first ruler to unite all of northern India was Chandragupta Maurya. In 321 B.C., he founded the Mauryan Empire, which controlled India for 140 years. Asoka was Chandragupta's grandson who ruled from 269 to 232 B.C. He began his reign with a series of military campaigns that enlarged the Mauryan Empire to include all of India except its southern tip. His victory against the southern tribes ended in the slaying of 100,000 captives. Asoka eventually became sickened by the bloodshed and converted to Buddhism. Asoka decided to win his people's loyalty by acts of kindness and by promoting the welfare of the people. He decided that all religions should live peacefully with one another. Asoka established an efficient bureaucracy that oversaw the building of roads and an irrigation system. He also built hospitals and sent teachers throughout the empire to promote education. After Asoka's death, the Mauryan Empire began to fall apart.

Mansa Musa was Mali's greatest ruler who ruled for 25 years, from 1312 to 1337 A.D. During his reign, he expanded Mali's borders to the Atlantic Ocean and conquered many Berber cities in the Sahara region to the north. He promoted peace and prosperity by opening up trade routes and protecting caravans with a powerful standing army. He also introduced Islam to Mali and enhanced the prestige of Mali through a famous pilgrimage to Mecca in 1324. Arab writers noted that he traveled in grand style. He took with him more than 1,200 slaves, each dressed in silk and carrying bars of gold. He gave away so much gold that the price of gold fell. At Mecca, he invited a skilled architect, As-Sahili, to return to Mali. He built mosques and other fine buildings in the capital of Timbuktu, which became the center of Muslim culture. The city had three universities and 50,000 residents at the height of its power. Ibn Battuta, a medieval Arab traveler, wrote in his book *The Rihala* that Mali was a kingdom based on justice and one in which there was security and peace.

The Ottoman Empire enjoyed its golden age under Suleiman, who ruled from 1520 to 1566. He was called "the Magnificent" by westerners and his own people knew him as "the Lawgiver." He modernized the army and conquered many new lands. He extended the Ottoman rule eastward into Mesopotamia as well as into Kurdistan and Georgia in the Caucasus Mountains. In the west, Suleiman advanced deeper into Europe and was able to gain control of nearly all of Hungary through diplomacy and conquest. Although he failed to capture the Austrian city of Vienna, the Ottomans ruled the largest, most powerful empire in both Europe and the West. Suleiman was a wise and capable ruler. He strengthened the government and improved the system of justice in the empire. As sultan, Suleiman had absolute power, but he ruled with the help of a grand vicar and council. He also chose able officials to run the larger bureaucracy and supervise everyday matters of government. As a Muslim, he based his law on the Sharia, the Islamic system of laws. Government officials worked closely with religious scholars who interpreted the law. The arts blossomed under Suleiman. Ottoman poets adapted Persian and Arab models to produce works in their own Turkish language. Ottoman painters, influenced by Persian artistic styles, produced detailed miniatures and illuminated manuscripts. Suleiman's rule was a golden age for the Ottoman Empire.

WRONG CHOICES EXPLAINED:

(1) These leaders created empires, not republics.

(2) None of these leaders led nationalist movements. These leaders were absolute rulers that sought to impose their will on the territories that they conquered or controlled.

(4) These leaders did not discourage scientific advancement. All of them promoted the arts and culture for their society. Science was not a major concern for them, but these rulers did not discourage learning which might lead to scientific growth.

45. **1** This passage describes the idea of rule by divine right. Divine right theory is the belief that the king or queen is God's earthly representative and receives all power directly from God to rule his subjects. Bishop Jacques Bossuet, who was tutor to the son of Louis XIV, King of France, summed up the theory in his book, *Universal History*. According to this way of thinking, the king was an agent of God and his authority to rule came directly from God. The king was entitled to unquestioning obedience and was responsible only to God. This divine right theory was used to justify absolute rulers in India, Spain, France, and Russia.

WRONG CHOICES EXPLAINED:

(2) A parliamentary democracy is a type of government in which the people elect representatives to the legislative branch of the government (Parliament) and the majority party in Parliament selects a prime minister from its ranks.

(3) Marxism is the political and economic theory developed by Karl Marx and Friedrich Engels in support of an economic interpretation of history. This view leads to the belief that history is a class struggle between the "haves" and the "have-nots."

(4) Totalitarianism is a system of government in which one group or set of groups control all aspects of the political, economic, and social life of a nation.

46. **4** The Age of Absolutism is the historical era most closely associated with this passage. The Age of Absolutism refers to the period in Europe and Asia during the 1500s and 1600s when kings sought to centralize their power. Absolute rulers had complete authority over their government and people.

WRONG CHOICES EXPLAINED:

(1) The Industrial Revolution was the period in Europe beginning around 1750 during which the means of production shifted from hand to machine.

(2) The Agricultural Revolution describes the changes in farming methods in England during the 1600s that dramatically increased farm production.

(3) The Age of Imperialism was the period from 1870 to 1914 when European nations extended political control over areas in Africa, Asia, and the Middle East.

47. **4** The Cold War is the period of history depicted in this cartoon. The Cold War was a period of tension and hostility between the United States and the Soviet Union (and its communist allies) that began at the end of World War II in 1945 and ended with the collapse of the Soviet Union in 1991. The Cold War was an ideological struggle between democracy and communism (represented in the cartoon by the Russian bear). During the Cold War, the United States and the Soviet Union competed for influence without an actual conflict. The opening gun of the Cold War was the Truman Doctrine of 1947 that was formed to fight communism. Under this doctrine,

the United States sent economic aid to Greece and Turkey to help withstand the communist threat. In 1947, the United States also proposed the Marshall Plan, also known as the European Recovery Act, to help rebuild European countries as a way to strengthen democratic governments against communism. The United States gave $17 billion in aid from 1947 to 1951. Although the United States also offered aid to Eastern Europe, Soviet Premier Joseph Stalin forbade these countries from accepting this aid. In 1948, Stalin tried to drive the Western Allies out of Berlin by closing all land routes bringing essential supplies between Berlin and the three Western zones. To thwart this Berlin Blockade, the Allies resorted to an airlift. For almost a year, the airlift provided more than two million West Berliners with food and supplies. In May 1949, after 321 days, the Soviets ended the blockade. In 1949, the United States, Canada, and nine western European nations formed the North Atlantic Treaty Organization (NATO), a defensive alliance designed to protect Europe from communist aggression. Member nations agreed to help each other if any member nation was attacked. The Cold War also led to the violation of the civil rights of many people. In the United States, Senator Joseph McCarthy charged that many Americans harbored communist sympathies. Government workers were expected to sign loyalty oaths and some workers were fired because they had been members of the Communist Party. The "Red Scare" created the fear that communism might spread to the United States.

WRONG CHOICES EXPLAINED:

(1), (2), and (3) None of these periods in history is depicted by this cartoon. The Industrial Revolution refers to changes brought about in society by the shift from hand to machine production. The Age of Enlightenment refers to 17th-century France and the emphasis on the importance of reason to understand society. The Age of Imperialism refers to the period from 1870 to 1914, when Europe expanded control over Africa, Asia, and the Middle East.

48. **2** A situation that best illustrates the concept of isolationism is when Japan closed its ports to trade with other nations. Isolationism is a policy of avoiding or limiting involvement in the affairs of other nations. After the Tokugawa shoguns gained power in 1603, they re-imposed centralized feudalism, closed Japan to foreigners, and forbade Japanese to travel abroad. The Tokugawa shoguns banned all European merchants except the Dutch. The nation's only window to the world was through the Dutch, who were allowed limited trade at Nagasaki. For two hundred years, Japan developed in isolation, and this policy had far-reaching effects. Gradually, Japan fell behind Europe in science, technology, and military power. On the other hand, isolation gave Japan a long period of peace and stability.

WRONG CHOICES EXPLAINED:

(1) Mercantilism was an economic policy by which the Spanish government required that gold found in its colonies be brought directly to Spain.

(3) Imperialism is illustrated when France, Germany, Belgium, and Great Britain negotiated to divide various areas of Africa into colonies. These negotiations took place at the Congress of Berlin in 1871.

(4) Indirect rule was the concept by which the British ruled much of India through control of local rulers.

49. **1** This quotation best describes the effects of the technological developments used during World War I. The quotation from this book describes the grueling effect of modern technology on soldiers in World War I. World War I, which lasted from 1914 to 1918, is considered to be the first truly technological war. The technology developed during World War I resulted in vastly increased military casualties. The automatic machine gun, the tank, the submarine, poison gas, and the airplane increased the number of deaths. The mounted machine gun made it possible for a few gunners to mow down waves of dismounted soldiers. In one five-month battle, more than one million soldiers were killed. By 1918, there were artillery pieces able to shell Paris from 70 miles away. More than 8.5 million people died in the war, and more than 17 million were wounded.

WRONG CHOICES EXPLAINED:

(2), (3), and (4) None of these choices is described in this quotation. The formation of alliances, the tension between the superpowers during the Cold War, and protests against reforms during the Indian independence movement are all events that took place after the end of World War I.

50. **4** One similarity in the leadership of Simon Bolivar and Jomo Kenyatta is that both leaders fought for independence from European control. Simon Bolivar, who was born to a wealthy Venezuelan Creole family in 1783, always envisioned an independent and united Latin America, free from Spanish domination. As a young man, he studied in Europe. His love of freedom was strengthened by the ideas of the French Revolution. Before returning from Europe, Bolivar promised that he would not rest until he broke the chains put upon the people of Latin America by the Spanish. He became known as "the Liberator" for his role in the wars for independence against Spain. In 1819, Bolivar helped free Venezuela and, by 1824, had also secured the freedom of Colombia, Ecuador, Peru, and Bolivia.

Jomo Kenyatta was a nationalist leader of Kenya. After World War II, Kenyatta, who had been educated and living in England, became a spokesman for Kenya's independence. In 1947, Kenyatta was chosen as the leader of the Kenyan African Union, a political movement for independence. Other Africans formed a group that the Europeans called the Mau Mau. This secret group was made up of Kikuyu farmers who were forced out of the highlands by the British, who had passed laws to ensure British domination. The goal of the Mau Mau was to force the British off the land. They began to carry out attacks against European settlers, such as burning farms and destroying livestock. Kenyatta, who was Kikuyu, had no connection to the

Mau Mau but refused to condemn these actions. The British took military action against the movement and jailed Kenyatta, whom they accused of leading the movement. More than 10,000 Kenyans were killed during the struggle for independence. In 1963, Britain granted Kenya its independence. Kenyatta was elected the first prime minister and held office until his death in 1978. He worked hard to unite all the different ethnic and language groups in the country.

WRONG CHOICES EXPLAINED:

(1) Simon Bolivar rejected European control over the Americas. He believed that the Americas should be free of European or Spanish domination. Jomo Kenyatta was devoted to promoting freedom in Africa.

(2) Both of these men were nationalist leaders who became political, not religious, leaders of their countries.

(3) Neither of these men controlled large areas of land in the Americas. Bolivar supported freedom for the people of Latin America and Kenyatta focused on African freedom, not domination.

THEMATIC ESSAY: GENERIC SCORING RUBRIC

Score of 5:
- Shows a thorough understanding of the theme or problem
- Addresses all aspects of the task
- Shows an ability to analyze, evaluate, compare and/or contrast issues and events
- Richly supports the theme or problem with relevant facts, examples, and details
- Is a well-developed essay, consistently demonstrating a logical and clear plan of organization
- Introduces the theme or problem by establishing a framework that is beyond a simple restatement of the task and concludes with a summation of the theme or problem

Score of 4:
- Shows a good understanding of the theme or problem
- Addresses all aspects of the task
- Shows an ability to analyze, evaluate, compare and/or contrast issues and events
- Includes relevant facts, examples, and details, but may not support all aspects of the theme or problem evenly
- Is a well-developed essay, demonstrating a logical and clear plan of organization
- Introduces the theme or problem by establishing a framework that is beyond a simple restatement of the task and concludes with a summation of the theme or problem

Score of 3:
- Shows a satisfactory understanding of the theme or problem
- Addresses most aspects of the task or addresses all aspects in a limited way
- Shows an ability to analyze or evaluate issues and events, but not in any depth
- Includes some facts, examples, and details
- Is a satisfactorily developed essay, demonstrating a general plan of organization
- Introduces the theme or problem by repeating the task and concludes by repeating the theme or problem

Score of 2:
- Shows limited understanding of the theme or problem
- Attempts to address the task
- Develops a faulty analysis or evaluation of issues and events
- Includes few facts, examples, and details, and may include information that contains inaccuracies
- Is a poorly organized essay, lacking focus
- Fails to introduce or summarize the theme or problem

Score of 1:
- Shows very limited understanding of the theme or problem
- Lacks an analysis of evaluation of the issues and events
- Includes little or no accurate or relevant facts, examples, or details
- Attempts to complete the task, but demonstrates a major weakness in organization
- Fails to introduce or summarize the theme or problem

Score of 0: Fails to address the task, is illegible, or is a blank paper

PART II: THEMATIC ESSAY QUESTION

Throughout history, governments have implemented policies in an attempt to change conditions in their society. In the 1600s, Russia was still a medieval state, untouched by the Renaissance and largely isolated from western Europe. One of the leaders who tried to push Russia forward on the road to becoming a great modern power was Peter the Great. Throughout his 36-year rule, he constantly strove to ensure that Russia become more modern. He embarked on a policy of Westernization, the adoption of Western ideas, technology, and culture. His goal was to make Russia a great power.

Although Peter the Great came to the Russian throne in 1682 at the age of 10, he did not take control of the government until seven years later. Peter was not well educated, but his immense curiosity played a role in how he ruled. In the late 17th century, Peter traveled to European cities to observe their political, social, and economic practices. He took back to Russia not only his observations on life in western Europe, but also a group of scholars, soldiers, and noblemen whom he had recruited and gathered throughout his travels. He would use these people and his observations to modernize Russia.

One of Peter the Great's most sweeping reforms was that of the Russian army. Before Peter's reign, the army was feeble, with part-time soldiers who were unskilled in modern military techniques. To improve Russia's military, Peter required that all noblemen serve either in the army or in civil service. In recognition of the skilled nature of many Western armies, Peter set up schools and universities to teach modern military techniques. Peter established a standing army of 200,000 men, mainly commoners, who were required to serve in the military.

In addition to changes in Russia's military, Peter the Great felt it necessary to centralize his power, and he did so by bringing all Russians—including the Orthodox Church—under his control. He insisted that all of Russia would follow the European calendar, with the New Year starting on January 1, rather than on September 1. In response to practices he had observed while in western Europe, Peter insisted that nobles (minor royalty such as dukes and barons) shave their beards and dress in modern, Western-style clothing, in place of their old-fashioned robes and beards. Women were no longer required to veil their faces in public and were not required to seclude themselves in their houses. He invited women to his lavish parties, much to the disapproval of many citizens. In addition, Peter put an end to arranged marriages.

By the end of Peter the Great's reign, Russia had made great strides in many other areas. He increased the number of factories in Russia and encouraged the exportation of Russian goods. Peter was responsible for making potatoes the staple crop of Russia. He simplified the Russian alphabet and developed Russia's system of education by forming academies to study and teach mathematics, engineering, and science.

The greatest symbol of Peter's reign was the capital city of St. Petersburg. Located near the Baltic coast, St. Petersburg was a lavish city built mainly because Peter forced thousands of serfs to drain the swamps near the city.

Many of these serfs died in the process, but after their work was done, Peter brought Italian architects and artisans to design a "Western" city.

Despite these numerous reforms and advances, Peter the Great was not entirely successful in modernizing Russia. For example, he failed to gain a warm-water port that could remain open year-round. During his 36-year rule, Peter and his army were constantly engaged in battle, yet Peter's territorial gains were minimal at best.

Peter the Great's biggest failure was his reliance on serfdom. The serfs who had helped to build his "window to the West" were actually holding Russia back from true modernization. As Peter continued to bring Western ideas into Russia, the divide between the uneducated poor and the educated elite widened. There was great hatred of Peter among those who were forced to work the land as serfs, since they saw no benefits to Peter's modernization. By clinging to a system of serfdom that had long been abolished in the rest of Europe, Peter the Great failed to fully modernize and Westernize Russia.

PART III: DOCUMENT-BASED QUESTIONS

Part A: Short Answers

Document 1

The diagram shows that an economic characteristic of the medieval manor was that fields were divided between the lords, the church, and the serfs.

Note: This response receives full credit because it correctly identifies one of the economic characteristics of the medieval manor as shown by the diagram with the letters, "L," "C," and "S."

Document 2a

Based on the *Custumals of Battle Abbey,* one benefit the lord received under manorialism was that tenants used their own beasts to carry hay and performed services for their lord.

Note: This response receives full credit because it correctly states a benefit the lord received under manorialism.

Document 2b

Based on the *Custumals of Battle Abbey,* one benefit that tenants received under manorialism was that they received two meals for one man when hay was gathered and lifted.

Note: This response receives full credit because it specifically cites one of the benefits the tenants received under manorialism.

Document 3

According to Norman Cantor, two ways manorialism influenced the economy of Europe are:

1. Local societies had almost no use for money and barter was used to conduct local trade.

2. International trade was largely in the hands of the Greeks, Jews, and Moslems.

Note: This response receives full credit because it identifies two ways manorialism influenced the economy of Europe.

Document 4

According to this cartoon by Philip Dorf, one characteristic of mercantilism from the perspective of the mother country was that colonies provided gold, silver, and raw materials.

Note: This response receives full credit because it states a characteristic of mercantilism from the perspective of the mother country.

Document 5

Based on this map, one effect of the Atlantic trade was that European nations received raw materials from the Americas and manufactured goods were sent from Europe to the colonies.

Note: This response receives full credit because it shows the effect of the Atlantic trade based on the map.

Document 6

According to Michele Soriano, one influence that gold and silver had on Spain was that the king got rich from millions of pounds of gold and silver from Spain.

Note: This response receives full credit because it cites the way in which gold and silver had an influence on Spain.

Document 7

Based on these articles from the "Constitution of the People's Republic of China," two characteristics of the communist economic system in China are:

1. It is based on an alliance of workers and peasants.
2. The state sector of the economy is owned by the whole people.

Note: This response receives full credit because it cites two characteristics of the communist economic system in China.

Document 8

Based on this BBC News article, one effect the Great Leap Forward had on China's economy was that fertile land went to waste on a disastrous scale and twenty million people starved.

Note: This response receives full credit because it specifically cites information from the document to show the effect of the Great Leap Forward on China's economy.

Document 9

According to Deng Xiaoping, two ways Mao Zedong's economic policies influenced China are:

1. China remained at a standstill during the two decades from 1958 through 1978.
2. There was very little growth in the standard of living.

Note: This response received full credit because it states the ways in which Mao Zedong's economic policies influenced China.

DOCUMENT-BASED QUESTION: GENERIC SCORING RUBRIC

Score of 5:
- Thoroughly addresses all aspects of the *Task* by accurately analyzing and interpreting at least **four** documents
- Incorporates information from the documents in the body of the essay
- Incorporates relevant outside information
- Richly supports the theme or problem with relevant facts, examples, and details
- Is a well-developed essay, consistently demonstrating a logical and clear plan of organization
- Introduces the theme or problem by establishing a framework that is beyond a simple restatement of the *Task* or *Historical Context* and concludes with a summation of the theme or problem

Score of 4:
- Addresses all aspects of the *Task* by accurately analyzing and interpreting at least **four** documents
- Incorporates information from the documents in the body of the essay
- Incorporates relevant outside information
- Includes relevant facts, examples, and details, but discussion may be more descriptive than analytical
- Is a well-developed essay, demonstrating a logical and clear plan of organization
- Introduces the theme or problem by establishing a framework that is beyond a simple restatement of the *Task* or *Historical Context* and concludes with a summation of the theme or problem

Score of 3:
- Addresses most aspects of the *Task* or addresses all aspects of the *Task* in a limited way, using some of the documents
- Incorporates some information from the documents in the body of the essay
- Incorporates limited or no relevant outside information
- Includes some facts, examples, and details, but discussion is more descriptive than analytical
- Is a satisfactorily developed essay, demonstrating a general plan of organization
- Introduces the theme or problem by repeating the *Task* or *Historical Context* and concludes by simply repeating the theme or problem

Score of 2:
- Attempts to address some aspects of the *Task*, making limited use of the documents
- Presents no relevant outside information
- Includes few facts, examples, and details; discussion restates contents of the documents

- Is a poorly organized essay, lacking focus
- Fails to introduce or summarize the theme or problem

Score of 1:

- Shows limited understanding of the *Task* with vague, unclear references to the documents
- Presents no relevant outside information
- Includes little or no accurate or relevant facts, details, or examples
- Attempts to complete the *Task*, but demonstrates a major weakness in organization
- Fails to introduce or summarize the theme or problem

Score of 0: Fails to address the *Task*, is illegible, or is a blank paper

Part B: Essay

Since the origins of civilization, economic systems have influenced the development of historical events. Manorialism in medieval Europe and mercantilism during the Age of Exploration had a great effect on the growth of nations, regions, and people. These two economic systems had a major impact on Europe, as well as Africa and the Americas.

After the collapse of the Roman Empire in western Europe in 476 A.D., the political system of feudalism was developed to provide protection for the people. Manorialism was the economic aspect of feudalism that developed in medieval Europe prior to the Renaissance. The manor or lord's estate was the heart of the medieval economy, which was built on agriculture. Most manors usually covered a few square miles. A typical manor included a few dozen one-room huts clustered close together in a village (Doc. 1). Nearby stood a watermill to grind grain, a tiny church, and the manor house. The field surrounding the village was divided into narrow strips. Each family had strips of land in different fields so that good and bad lands were shared evenly. The manor was largely a self-sufficient community. The peasants produced everything that they and their lord needed for daily life—from food and clothing to simple furniture and tools (Doc. 1).

The manor system was based on the peasants and lords being tied together by mutual rights and obligations. The lord provided the serfs with housing, strips of land, and protection from bandits. In return, serfs tended the lord's land, cared for his animals, and performed other tasks to maintain the estate. Although the lord provided some meals for the peasants who lifted hay (Doc. 2), the peasants or serfs paid dearly for the right to live and grow crops on the lord's land. Peasants had to work at least two to three days plowing the land in the summer or perform other services such as carrying manure, beans, oats, and wood (Doc. 2). Peasants also had to pay a tax on all grain ground in the lord's mill. Any attempt to dodge taxes by baking bread elsewhere was treated as a crime.

For peasants, life on the manor was difficult and often harsh. They were not free, but they were not slaves. Unlike slaves, serfs could not be bought, sold, or traded to another lord. Yet, serfs could not lawfully leave the manor on which they were born. They were bound to the soil. They worked long hours and few peasants lived past the age of 35. Most peasant men and women rarely traveled far from their own manor. Their lives were controlled by the lord of the manor.

Weddings could take place only with the lord's consent and the peasants had to pay a tax on marriage. In spite of such hardships, the lives of the peasants were held together by the common thread of Christianity. Their celebrations, marriages, births, and holidays, such as Christmas and Easter, were centered in the Roman Catholic Church.

As manors became more self-sufficient, the need for trade and outside products declined. Inadequate roads and bridges also made commerce difficult (Doc. 3). Since manors were self-sufficient, money had largely disappeared from medieval Europe. Barter meant that products such as grain, honey, eggs, or chickens could be used as currency.

However, there was some revival of trade among the wealthy noble Carolingians of the Frankish Empire in western Europe. Charlemagne was the most notable ruler of the family, who reigned from 766–814 A.D. Under the Carolingians, only the wealthy were able to get luxury items, such as glass, spices, and textiles. Trade was largely in the hands of Greeks, Jews, and Moslems, and the only currency used was supplied by the Byzantine and Moslem Empires (Doc. 3). The manorialism system would dominate western Europe until the middle of the 11th century and was one of the factors that contributed to its lack of economic growth and development.

The Age of Exploration, from about 1400 to 1600, brought about national economic changes. The fierce competition for trade and overseas expansion in Africa and the Americas among European nations led to the adoption of a new economic system known as mercantilism. Mercantilists supported several basic ideas. They believed that a nation's wealth was measured in gold and silver treasure (Doc. 4). To build a supply of gold and silver, mercantilists insisted that a nation must export more goods than it imports or establish a favorable balance of trade.

Overseas empires were central to the mercantile system. Colonies existed for the benefit of the mother country (Doc. 4). They provided the raw materials that could not be found in the home country, such as wood and fur (Doc. 4). In addition to playing the role of supplier, the colonies also served as a market for manufactured goods (Doc. 5). A nation's ultimate goal under mercantilism was to become self-sufficient, like the medieval manor.

To achieve the goals of mercantilism, European nations passed strict laws regulating trade with their colonies. Colonies could not set up their own industries to manufacture goods. They were also forbidden to buy goods from foreign countries. In addition, only ships from the parent country or the colonies themselves could be used to send goods in or out of the colonies.

These strict regulations led to the rise of the Triangular Trade. Africans transported to the Americas were part of this trans-Atlantic trading network. Over one trade route, Europeans transported manufactured goods to the west coast of Africa. These traders exchanged goods for captured Africans. The Africans were then transported across the Atlantic Ocean. The voyage from Africa to the Americas on the slave ships was called the Middle Passage (Doc. 5). Conditions were terrible on the ships. Millions of Africans died during this trip from disease, brutal mistreatment, or suicide. Those who survived were sold in the West Indies to work on plantations.

Merchants then bought sugar, coffee, and tobacco in the West Indies and sailed back to Europe to sell these products. On other triangular routes, merchants carried rum and other goods from New England colonies to Africa. There, they were exchanged for Africans. The traders then transported the Africans to the West Indies and sold them for sugar and molasses. They then sold these goods to rum producers in New England (Doc. 5). The triangular trade encompassed a network of trade routes crisscrossing northern and southern colonies, as well as the West Indies, England, Europe, and Africa. The network carried a variety of products, including furs, fruit, and lumber, as well as millions of African people.

The Atlantic slave trade had a profound impact on Africa, causing the decline of some African states and the rise of others. In West Africa, the loss of countless numbers of young women and men resulted in some small states disappearing forever. At the same time, there arose new African states whose way of life depended on the slave trade. The rulers of these powerful states waged war against other Africans so that they could gain control of the slave trade in their region and reap the profits. These conditions destroyed much of the social and economic structure of Africa.

The mercantile system also had a great impact on Spain and its colonies, known collectively as New Spain. The Spanish king became very powerful because he received a large portion of the gold that was mined in the Americas (Doc. 6). The influx of gold and silver from the New World contributed to Spain's growth as a major power in the 16th century. However, the large quantities of gold and silver from the New World affected the economy of Spain, as well as western Europe. Since there was more money in circulation, it drove up prices and led to inflation.

Spain's conquests in the Americas directly affected the population of Native Americans. The Spanish monarchs granted the conquistadors *encomiendas*, the right to demand labor or tribute from Native Americans. The conquistadors used this system to force Native Americans to work under brutal conditions. Those who resisted were hunted down and killed. Disease, starvation, and cruel treatment destroyed about 80 percent of the Native American population. Native Americans, however, were freed from this forced labor when they converted to Christianity (Doc. 6).

Through the efforts of Spanish priests like Bartolome de las Casas, laws were eventually passed to end abuses against Native Americans. However, to fill the labor shortage, Africans were then imported to work on the plantations. The Spanish began bringing Africans as slave laborers to the Americas in the 1530s (Doc. 6). It is estimated that the Spanish enslaved over one million Africans to work on plantations in their colonies.

In Spanish America, the mix of diverse people gave rise to a new social structure. The blending of Native Americans, Africans, Europeans, and traditions resulted in a new American culture. At the top of colonial society were *peninsulares*, people born in Spain. Peninsulares filled the highest positions in both colonial government and the Catholic Church. Next came Creoles, American-born descendants of Spanish settlers. Creoles owned most of the plantations, ranches, and mines. Other social groups reflected the mixing of the population. They included *mestizos*, people of mixed Native American and European descent, and mulattoes, people of African and European descent. Native Americans and people of African descent formed the lowest social classes. This structured social division would contribute to the oppression of the lower classes that continued well into the 18th and 19th centuries.

Manorialism in the Middle Ages and mercantilism during the Age of Exploration had major impacts on the world. Although these systems provided an economic structure of strict rules and regulations promoting order in society, they also created many negative consequences that destroyed the social structure of many regions. In the 21st century, some regions, especially in Latin America and Africa, are still trying to overcome the lingering problems caused by these two economic systems.

Topic	Question Numbers	Total Number of Questions	Number Wrong	*Reason for Wrong Answer
U.S. AND N.Y. HISTORY				
WORLD HISTORY	5, 6, 7, 9, 12, 13, 16, 19, 22, 24, 25, 29, 30, 34, 39, 40, 41, 42, 43, 44, 46, 47, 49	23		
GEOGRAPHY	1, 3, 8, 10, 11, 14, 15, 20, 28, 31, 33, 36	12		
ECONOMICS	2, 21, 26, 48	4		
CIVICS, CITIZENSHIP, AND GOVERNMENT	4, 17, 18, 23, 27, 32, 35, 37, 38, 45, 50	11		

*Your reason for answering the question incorrectly might be (a) lack of knowledge, (b) misunderstanding the question, or (c) careless error.

Actual Items by Standard and Unit

	1 U.S. and N.Y. History	2 World History	3 Geography	4 Economics	5 Civics, Citizenship, and Gov't	Number
Methodology of Global History and Geography			1, 3	2		3
UNIT ONE Ancient World		5, 6, 9, 12	10		4	6
UNIT TWO Expanding Zones of Exchange		7	8			2
UNIT THREE Global Interactions		16	11			2
UNIT FOUR First Global Age		13, 46	14, 15		18, 45	6
UNIT FIVE Age of Revolution		19, 22, 24, 25	20	21, 48	17, 23	9
UNIT SIX Crisis and Achievement (1900–1945)		29, 49	28	26	27	5
UNIT SEVEN 20th Century Since 1945		34, 39, 40, 41, 47	31, 33		32, 35, 37, 38	11
UNIT EIGHT Global Connections and Interactions		30	36			2
Cross topical		42, 43, 44			50	4
Total # of Questions		23	12	4	11	50
% of Items by Standard		40%	32%	18%	10%	100%

Examination August 2007

Global History and Geography

PART I: MULTIPLE CHOICE

Directions (1–50): For each statement or question, write in the space provided the *number* of the word or expression that, of those given, best completes the statement or answers the question.

1 Which source of information is considered a primary source?

1 travel diary of Ibn Battuta
2 modern novel about the Golden Age of Islam
3 textbook on the history of North Africa
4 dictionary of English words adapted from Arabic 1 ____

2 Which continent's economic and political development has been influenced by the Andes Mountains and the Amazon River?

1 Asia
2 Africa
3 Europe
4 South America 2 ____

3 • Planting wheat and barley
• Domesticating animals
• Establishing permanent homes and villages

At the beginning of the Neolithic Revolution, the most direct impact of these developments was on

1 religion and government
2 transportation and trade
3 diet and shelter
4 climate and topography 3____

4 • Kushites adapted Egyptian art and architecture.
• Greeks adopted Phoenician characters for an alphabet.
• Arabs used the Indian mathematical concept of zero.

These actions are examples of

1 filial piety
2 cultural diffusion
3 scientific research
4 ethnocentrism 4____

5 Which belief system is most closely associated with the terms *Eightfold Path*, *Four Noble Truths*, and *nirvana*?

1 Buddhism
2 Christianity
3 Judaism
4 Shinto 5____

6 . . ."If a man has knocked out the teeth of a man of the same rank, his own teeth shall be knocked out. If he has knocked out the teeth of a plebeian (commoner), he shall pay one-third of a mina of silver.". . .

— Code of Hammurabi

Which statement is supported by this excerpt from Hammurabi's code of laws?

1 All men are equal under the law.
2 Fines are preferable to physical punishment.
3 Law sometimes distinguishes between social classes.
4 Violence must always be punished with violence. 6____

7 Confucianism had a strong impact on the development of China mainly because this philosophy

1 established a basic structure for military rule
2 provided a basis for social order
3 contained the framework for a communist government
4 stressed the importance of the individual 7____

8 The terms *masters*, *apprentices*, and *journeymen* are most closely associated with the

1 encomienda system of Latin America
2 guild system of Europe in the Middle Ages
3 civil service system of China during the Tang dynasty
4 caste system of India 8____

Base your answers to questions 9 and 10 on the map below and on your knowledge of social studies.

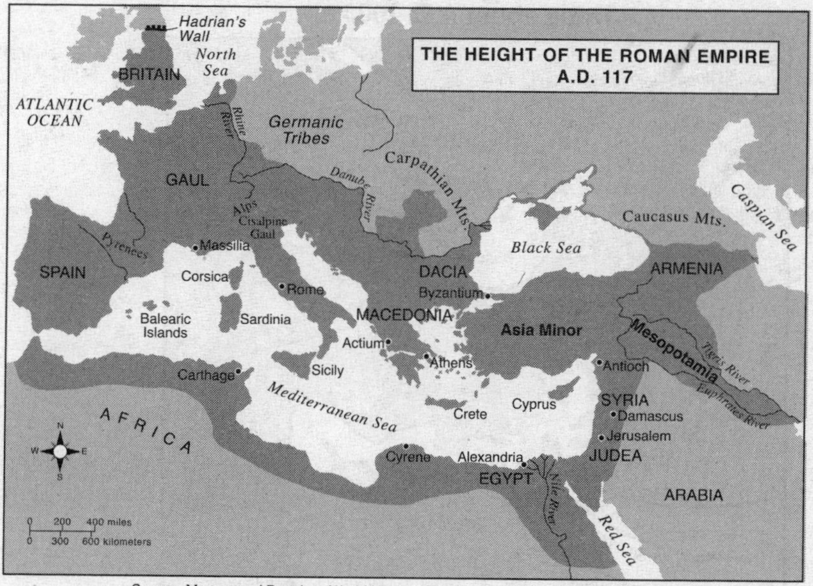

Source: Mazour and Peoples, *World History: People and Nations*, Harcourt Brace Jovanovich (adapted)

9 Which statement is best supported by the information on this map?

1 The Roman Empire extended over three continents.
2 Rivers kept invaders out of the Roman Empire.
3 Alexandria served as the eastern capital of the Roman Empire.
4 Carthage was eventually destroyed by the Romans. 9____

10 Based on the information provided by this map, which body of water was most likely the center of Roman trade?

1 Red Sea
2 Black Sea
3 Atlantic Ocean
4 Mediterranean Sea 10____

Base your answers to question 11 on the map below and on your knowledge of social studies.

Trade about A.D. 1000

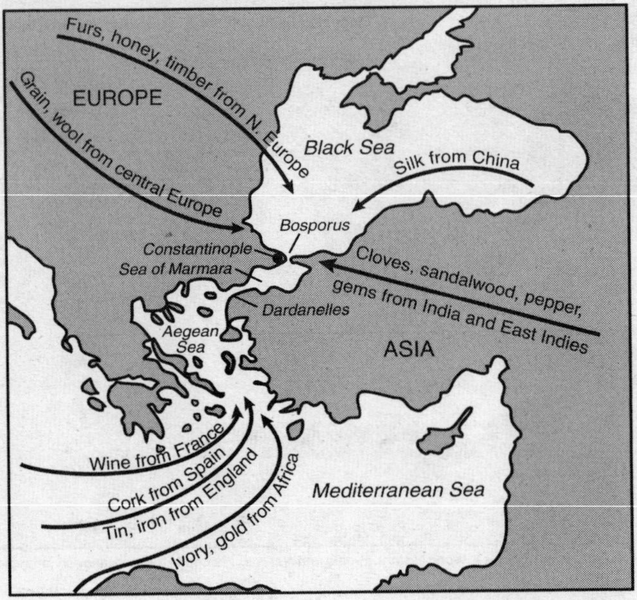

Source: Farah and Karls, *World History, The Human Experience*, Glencoe/McGraw-Hill (adapted)

11 Based on the information provided by this map, which statement about Constantinople is accurate?

1 Africans traded more goods in Constantinople than in any other area.
2 Constantinople was a city located on the Mediterranean Sea.
3 Gold was the primary commodity that China sent to Constantinople.
4 Constantinople was an important trading center. 11 ____

12 One major characteristic of the Renaissance period is that the

1 Catholic Church no longer had any influence in Europe
2 manor became the center of economic activity
3 classical cultures of Greece and Rome were revived and imitated
4 major language of the people became Latin 12____

13 ". . . Therefore those preachers of indulgences are in error, who say that by the pope's indulgences a man is freed from every penalty, and saved; . . ."

— Martin Luther

Which period in European history is most directly related to this statement?

1 Age of Exploration
2 Scientific Revolution
3 Crusades
4 Protestant Reformation 13____

14 The economies of the western African civilizations of Ghana, Mali, and Songhai relied on

1 industrial growth
2 shipbuilding
3 textile production
4 trans-Saharan trade routes 14____

15 A major reason for Zheng He's voyages during the 15th century was to

1 promote trade and collect tribute
2 establish colonies in Africa and India
3 seal off China's borders from foreign influence
4 prove the world was round 15____

16 What was one effect of the Columbian exchange?

1 rapid decline in European population
2 economic instability in China and Japan
3 introduction of new foods to both Europe and the Americas
4 spread of Hinduism into Latin America 16 ____

17 From the 15th to the 18th centuries, absolute monarchs of Europe and Asia sought to

1 increase the power of the Catholic Church
2 centralize their political power
3 redistribute land to the peasants
4 strengthen feudalism 17 ____

Base your answers to question 18 on the map below and on your knowledge of social studies.

Asia — 1294

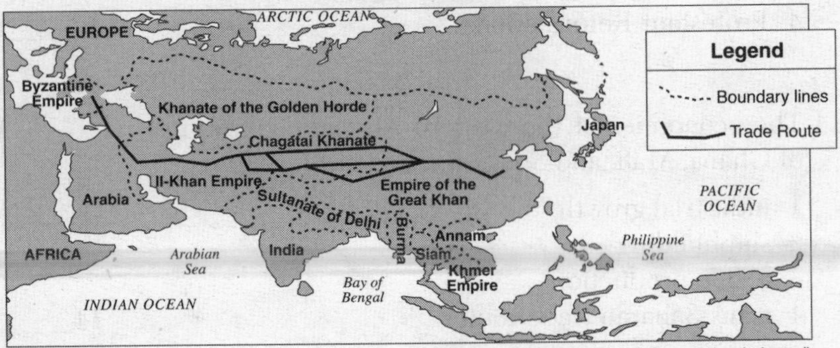

Source: GeoSystems Global Corporation (adapted)

18 Which group of people ruled much of Asia during the period shown on this map?

1 Mongol
2 Indian
3 Japanese
4 European 18 ____

19 Which person is credited with saying "L'état, c'est moi" (I am the state)?

1 Louis XIV
2 John Locke
3 Karl Marx
4 Queen Isabella

19____

20 Seventeenth-century scholars Galileo Galilei and René Descartes faced serious challenges to their scientific theories because their ideas

1 were based on the Bible
2 contradicted traditional medieval European beliefs
3 relied only on teachings from non-Christian cultures
4 were not supported by scientific investigations

20____

21 Which statement expresses an idea of the Enlightenment?

1 The king is sacred and answers only to God.
2 History is a continuous struggle between social classes.
3 Those who are the most fit will survive and succeed.
4 All individuals have natural rights.

21____

22 The breakdown of traditions, increased levels of pollution, and the expansion of slums are negative aspects of

1 militarism
2 collectivization
3 pogroms
4 urbanization

22____

23 Which heading best completes this partial outline?

> I. ______________________
>
> A. Rivalries between powerful countries over colonies
>
> B. Breakup of large empires
>
> C. Demand for self-determination by ethnic groups

1 Reasons for Communist Revolutions
2 Effects of Nationalism
3 Methods of Propaganda
4 Formation of Democratic Governments 23 ____

Base your answer to question 24 on the passage below and on your knowledge of social studies.

> . . . The factory owners did not have the power to compel anybody to take a factory job. They could only hire people who were ready to work for the wages offered to them. Low as these wage rates were, they were nonetheless much more than these paupers could earn in any other field open to them. It is a distortion of facts to say that the factories carried off the housewives from the nurseries and the kitchens and the children from their play. These women had nothing to cook with and [nothing] to feed their children. These children were destitute [poor] and starving. Their only refuge was the factory. It saved them, in the strict sense of the term, from death by starvation. . . .
>
> — Ludwig von Mises, *Human Action, A Treatise on Economics*, Yale University Press

24 Which statement summarizes the theme of this passage?

1 Factory owners created increased hardships.
2 Factory owners preferred to use child laborers.
3 The factory system allowed people to earn money.
4 The factory system created new social classes. 24____

---

25 What was one impact of industrialization on Japan during the Meiji Restoration?

1 Japan became more isolated from world affairs.
2 Demand for natural resources increased.
3 Japan became a colonial possession of China.
4 Traditional practices of Bushido were reintroduced. 25____

Base your answer to question 26 on the map below and on your knowledge of social studies.

Eastern Asia in 1914

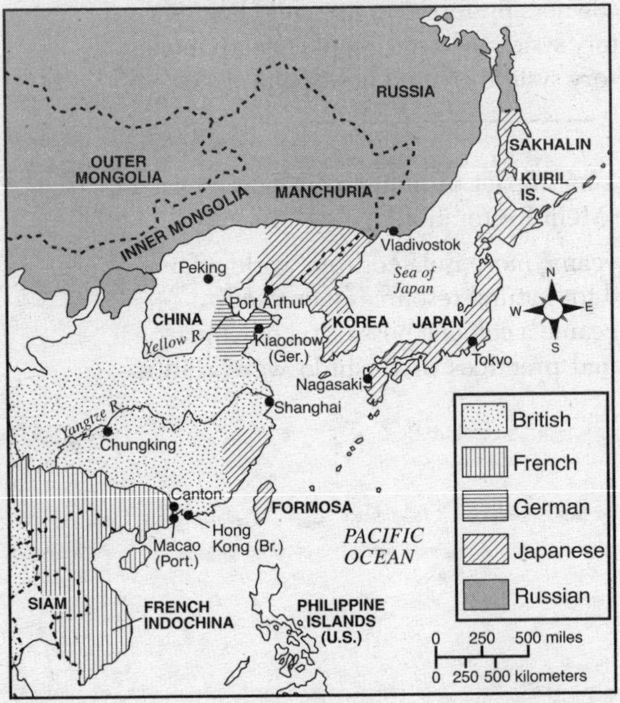

Source: Robert Feeney et al., *Brief Review in Global Studies*, Prentice Hall (adapted)

26 This map illustrates the concept of

1 ethnocentrism
2 socialism
3 containment
4 imperialism

26____

---

27 Which region was described as "the powder keg of Europe" prior to World War I?

1 Iberian Peninsula
2 British Isles
3 Balkan Peninsula
4 Scandinavia

27____

Base your answer to question 28 on the passage below and on your knowledge of social studies.

> . . . In order to obtain Arab support in the War, the British Government promised the Sherif of Mecca in 1915 that, in the event of an Allied victory, the greater part of the Arab provinces of the Turkish Empire would become independent. The Arabs understood that Palestine would be included in the sphere of independence.
>
> In order to obtain the support of World Jewry, the British Government in 1917 issued the Balfour Declaration. The Jews understood that, if the experiment of establishing a Jewish National Home succeeded and a sufficient number of Jews went to Palestine, the National Home might develop in course of time into a Jewish State. . . .
>
> — Summary of the Report of the Palestine Royal Commission, 1937

28 Which conclusion is best supported by this passage?

1 The British made no promises to either the Arabs or the Jews.
2 The Arab-Israeli conflict can be traced in part to British promises.
3 The United Nations did not try to prevent conflict in the Middle East.
4 Only the Jews were promised an independent state in Palestine. 28____

29 • Led the Russians in a second revolution (1917)
• Promised "Peace, Land, and Bread"
• Established the New Economic Policy (NEP)

Which leader is being described by these statements?

1 Czar Nicholas II
2 Nikita Khrushchev
3 Vladimir I. Lenin
4 Mikhail Gorbachev 29____

Base your answer to question 30 on the passage below and on your knowledge of social studies.

> . . . A weary, exhausted, nerve-racked group of men it was indeed that, about noon November 1, assembled in a gully north of Sommerance [France] to rest and dig in for the night. The artillery was still firing furiously, but the enemy's barrage [bombardment] had ceased very suddenly about 10:00 a.m. and now only occasional shells from long-range rifles would explode in the vicinity. The weather was gloomy and the moist air chilled one to the bones. Yet it was with that meticulous [methodical] care that is characteristic of worn-out men, that we prepared our foxholes, carrying boards and iron sheeting from abandoned machine-gunners' dugouts in order to make our "houses" as comfortable as possible, even though only for one night. . . .
>
> Source: William L. Langer, *Gas and Flame in World War I*, Knopf/Borzoi

30 Which means of warfare is described in this passage?

1 guerilla
2 nuclear
3 biological
4 trench

30 ____

---

31 A major goal of Joseph Stalin's five-year plans was to

1 encourage communist revolutions in the colonies of the European powers
2 transform the Soviet Union into an industrial power
3 expand the Soviet Union's borders to include warm-water ports
4 reduce the amount of foreign aid coming from the Western Hemisphere

31 ____

Base your answer to question 32 on the chart below and on your knowledge of social studies.

NAZI RISE TO POWER
World War I
• German war debts
• Loss of German colonies
• Wish for revenge
Weak Government
• Doubts about Weimar Republic
• Quarrels among political groups
• Wish to return to strong leader like the Kaiser
Economic Problems
• Inflation
• Worldwide depression
• Unemploy-ment

Source: *Guide to the Essentials of World History,* Prentice Hall (adapted)

32 Based on the information in this chart, which situation gave rise to Nazi power in Germany?

1 global prosperity and trade
2 success of the Weimar Republic
3 political and economic instability
4 expansion of Germany's colonial empire 32____

Base your answer to question 33 on the passage below and on your knowledge of social studies.

> . . . "We may anticipate a state of affairs in which two Great Powers will each be in a position to put an end to the civilization and life of the other, though not without risking its own. We may be likened to two scorpions in a bottle, each capable of killing the other, but only at the risk of his own life.". . .
>
> — J. Robert Oppenheimer, July 1953

33 This statement expresses concern about the

1 threats to the environment by developed and developing economies
2 differences between command and market economies
3 economic costs of World War II
4 dangers of the Cold War

33 ____

Base your answer to question 34 on the cartoon below and on your knowledge of social studies.

Sending Forth Another Dove

Source: Herblock, May 13, 1941 (adapted)

34 The main idea of this 1941 cartoon is that Japan, Italy, and Germany

1 had formed an alliance for peace
2 were determined to defeat communism
3 had supported a peaceful international solution
4 were committed to aggression 34 ____

35 At the end of World War II, the British decided to partition the Indian subcontinent into the nations of India and Pakistan. What was a primary reason for this division?

1 India had adopted a policy of nonalignment.
2 Religious differences had led to conflicts between Hindus and Muslims.
3 Most of India's valuable resources were located in the south.
4 British India's Muslim minority controlled most of India's banking industry. 35____

Base your answer to question 36 on the graph below and on your knowledge of social studies.

World Petroleum Reserves

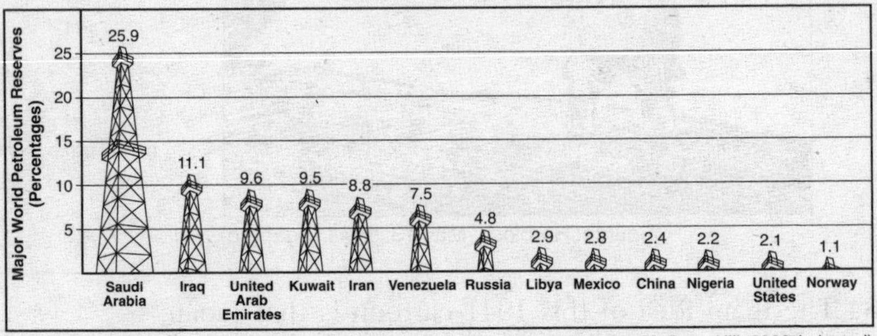

Source: John T. Rourke, *International Politics on the World Stage*, McGraw-Hill, 2003 (adapted)

36 Which conclusion is best supported by the information provided on this graph?

1 The United States has adequate petroleum reserves to meet future needs.
2 Nations lacking major petroleum reserves cannot industrialize.
3 Overproduction of petroleum products has caused inflation in the Middle East.
4 Most of the world's largest petroleum reserves are located in the Middle East. 36____

Base your answer to question 37 on the cartoon below and on your knowledge of social studies.

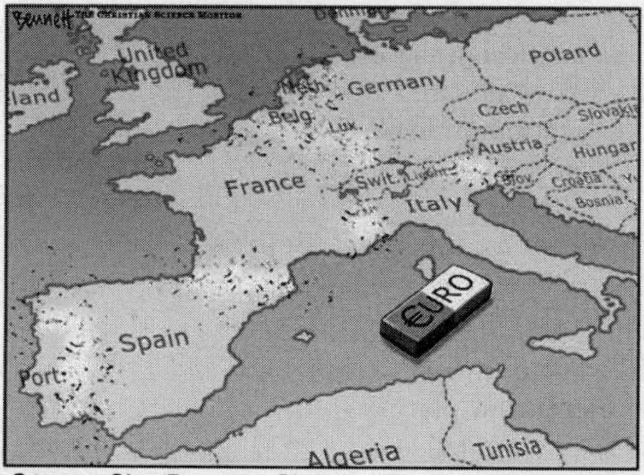

Source: Clay Bennett, *Christian Science Monitor*, 2002

37 What does this cartoon suggest about the introduction of the EURO in Europe?

1 Additional countries were created.
2 Isolation among nations increased.
3 Communist economic policies were adopted.
4 Economic barriers between nations decreased. 37 ____

38 The Four Modernizations of Deng Xiaoping in the 1970s and 1980s resulted in

1 an emphasis on the Five Relationships
2 a return to Maoist revolutionary principles
3 a move toward increased capitalism
4 the end of the communist system of government 38 ____

39 One way in which Ho Chi Minh, Fidel Castro, and Kim Jong Il are similar is that each

1 set up democratic governments
2 used Marxist political principles
3 overthrew a ruling monarch
4 promoted Confucian principles 39____

40 In the late 20th century, the Green Revolution had the greatest impact on

1 grain production in India
2 political freedom in Russia
3 economic reforms in Cuba
4 traditional customs in Japan 40____

Base your answer to question 41 on the illustration below and on your knowledge of social studies.

A European View

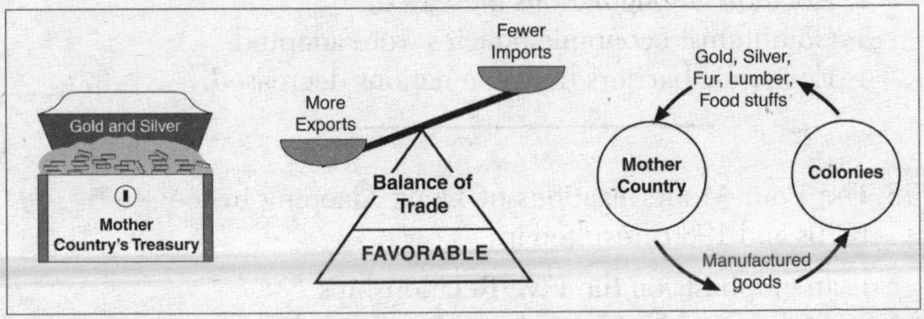

41 Which policy is portrayed in this illustration?

1 nonalignment
2 laissez-faire capitalism
3 perestroika
4 mercantilism 41____

Base your answer to question 42 on the cartoon below and on your knowledge of social studies.

Source: Dana Summers, *The Orlando Sentinel* (adapted)

42 What is the main idea of this cartoon?

1 The original causes of apartheid have not been eliminated.
2 Apartheid improved race relations in South Africa.
3 Peace can be achieved by nonviolence.
4 Hate is caused by poverty. 42____

---

43 Ethnic cleansing in Bosnia, the killing fields of Cambodia (Kampuchea), and the dirty war in Argentina are all examples of

1 nationalist revolts
2 human rights violations
3 international terrorism
4 religious conflicts 43____

44 Studying the architectural features of the Parthenon, Notre Dame Cathedral, and the Taj Mahal provides information about the

1 beliefs and values of a given culture
2 climatic changes in an area
3 19th-century use of technology
4 influence of Chinese design 44____

45 Which geographic factor had the most influence on the development of Inca society and Japanese society?

1 frequent monsoons
2 large deserts
3 mountainous topography
4 tropical climate 45____

Base your answer to question 46 on the diagram below and on your knowledge of social studies.

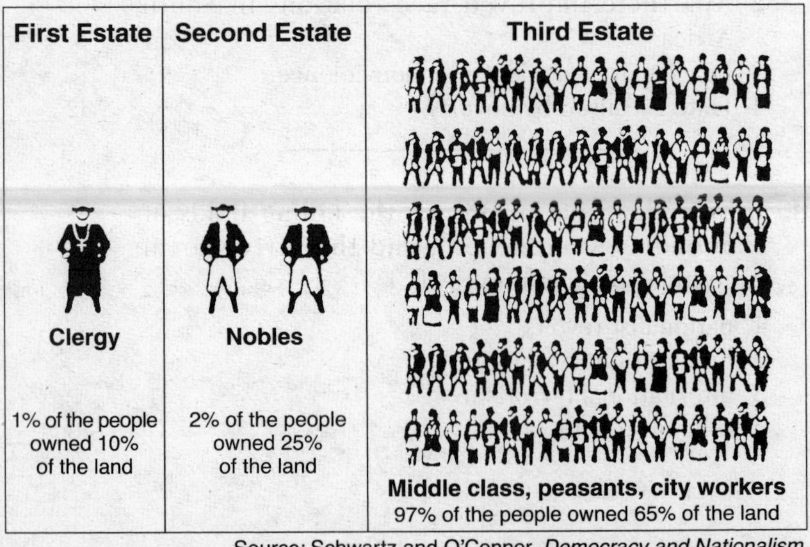

Source: Schwartz and O'Connor, *Democracy and Nationalism*, Globe Book Company (adapted)

46 Which revolution resulted from the division of society shown in this diagram?

1 Puritan (1642)
2 French (1789)
3 Mexican (1910)
4 Russian (1917) 46____

47 The golden ages of the Roman, Byzantine, and Ottoman Empires can be attributed in part to

1 cultural isolation
2 stable governments
3 command economies
4 distinct social classes 47____

48 One way in which Simón Bolívar, Jomo Kenyatta, and Mohandas Gandhi are similar is that each

1 led a nationalist movement
2 used nonviolent tactics
3 supported imperialism
4 opposed communism 48____

49 Which factor most hindered the efforts of both Napoleon and Hitler to conquer Russia?

1 climate
2 fortifications
3 advanced technology
4 lack of ports 49____

50 One way in which the Sepoy Mutiny in India, the Zulu resistance in southern Africa, and the Boxer Rebellion in China are similar is that each resulted from

1 government policies of ethnic cleansing
2 attempts by democratic forces to overthrow the monarchy
3 native reaction to foreign interference in the region
4 government denial of access to fertile farmland 50____

In developing your answer to Part II, be sure to keep these general definitions in mind:

(a) describe means "to illustrate something in words or tell about it"
(b) discuss means "to make observations about something using facts, reasoning, and argument; to present in some detail"

PART II: THEMATIC ESSAY QUESTION

Directions: Write a well-organized essay that includes an introduction, several paragraphs addressing the task below, and a conclusion.

Theme: Political Systems

Political systems have affected the history and culture of nations and societies.

Task:

Choose ***two*** different political systems and for ***each***
- Describe the characteristics of the political system
- Discuss how the political system has affected the history ***or*** culture of a specific nation or society

You may use any political systems from your study of global history. Some suggestions you might wish to consider include absolute monarchy, constitutional monarchy, parliamentary democracy, direct democracy, theocracy, communism, and fascism.

You are *not* limited to these suggestions.

Do *not* use the United States as an example of a nation or society.

Guidelines:

In your essay, be sure to:

- Develop all aspects of the task
- Support the theme with relevant facts, examples, and details
- Use a logical and clear plan of organization, including an introduction and a conclusion that are beyond a restatement of the theme

In developing your answers to Part III, be sure to keep these general definitions in mind:

discuss means "to make observations about something using facts, reasoning, and argument; to present in some detail"

PART III: DOCUMENT-BASED QUESTION

This question is based on the accompanying documents. The question is designed to test your ability to work with historical documents. Some of these documents have been edited for the purposes of this question. As you analyze the documents, take into account the source of each document and any point of view that may be presented in the document.

Historical Context:

Throughout history, natural resources such as water, coal, oil, and diamonds have both helped and hindered the development of nations and regions.

Task:

Using information from the documents and your knowledge of global history, answer the questions that follow each document in Part A. Your answers to the questions will help you write the Part B essay, in which you will be asked to

- Discuss how natural resources have helped ***and/or*** hindered the development of specific nations ***or*** regions

Do *not* use the United States as the specific nation or region.

Part A: Short-Answer Questions

Directions: Analyze the documents and answer the short-answer questions that follow each document in the space provided.

Document 1

Earliest Civilizations, 3500 – 1500 BC

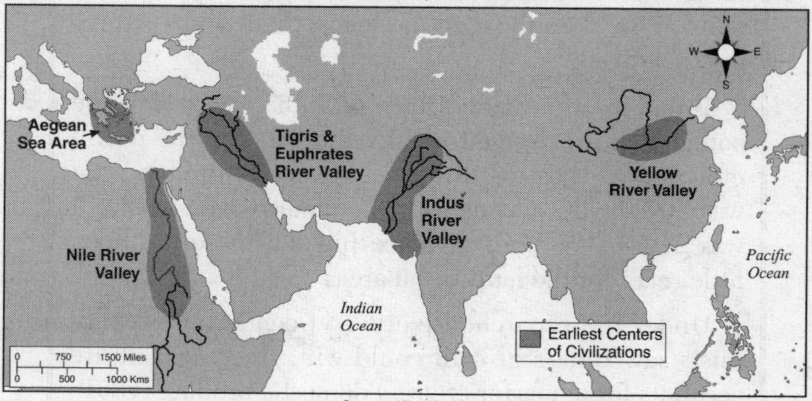

Source: *Historical Maps on File,* Revised Edition, Facts On File (adapted)

1 Based on this map, identify ***one*** geographic feature that influenced the location of early centers of civilization. [1]

____

____

Document 2a

"Farmers in India Await the Rains, and Despair"

REWARI, India—When the monsoon rains that sweep across India every year failed to arrive in late June, the farmers here began to worry. Now, as they scan the empty blue skies for signs of clouds, their worry is turning to despair.

Broad swaths [wide areas] of India are seeing the country's worst drought in 15 years. Here in the northern state of Haryana, the level of rainfall until July 24 was 70% below average; for the country as a whole, it was 24% below normal. Since July 24, there has been little relief for the hardest-hit areas.

Under these parched [very dry] conditions, economists say, India's growth could wilt, since agriculture accounts for a quarter of gross domestic product [GDP] and sustains [supports] two-thirds of the nation's billion-strong population. Before the drought, economists were expecting agricultural expansion of around 2% and GDP growth of 4.5% to 6% in the current fiscal year, which began April 1. Now they are predicting that agricultural production will remain stagnant or even turn negative, shaving something like half a percentage point off overall economic growth. . . .

Source: Joanna Slater, *The Wall Street Journal*, August 6, 2002

2*a* Based on this excerpt by Joanna Slater, state ***one*** negative impact the lack of rain has had on the economy in India. [1]

____

____

Document 2b

"Indian Monsoon Drenches the Land; Marketers Drench the Consumer"

BOMBAY, India—One year after a crippling drought, plentiful rains are sweeping across India— and delivering a flood of good news for its economy.

Agriculture's contribution to India's gross domestic product [GDP], its total output of goods and services, has declined over the past decade as the service and industrial sectors have grown. Nevertheless, the showers are a relief for farmers, who depend on the monsoon to irrigate their crops. They are also a boon [benefit] to sales of everything from tractors to shampoo; a good harvest puts more money in the pockets of rural consumers, improving the fortunes of companies ranging from Anglo-Dutch Unilever to Honda Motor Co. of Japan to South Korea's Samsung Electronics Co.

Agriculture still sustains two-thirds of India's billion-strong population and contributes a quarter of its GDP, which economists predict will expand by as much as 6.5% in the fiscal year ending next March, partly because of the abundant rains and the resurgent [recovered] farm sector. . . .

Source: Joanna Slater, *The Wall Street Journal*, July 24, 2003

2*b* Based on this excerpt by Joanna Slater, state ***one*** positive impact that abundant levels of rain have had on the economy in India. [1]

____

____

Document 3

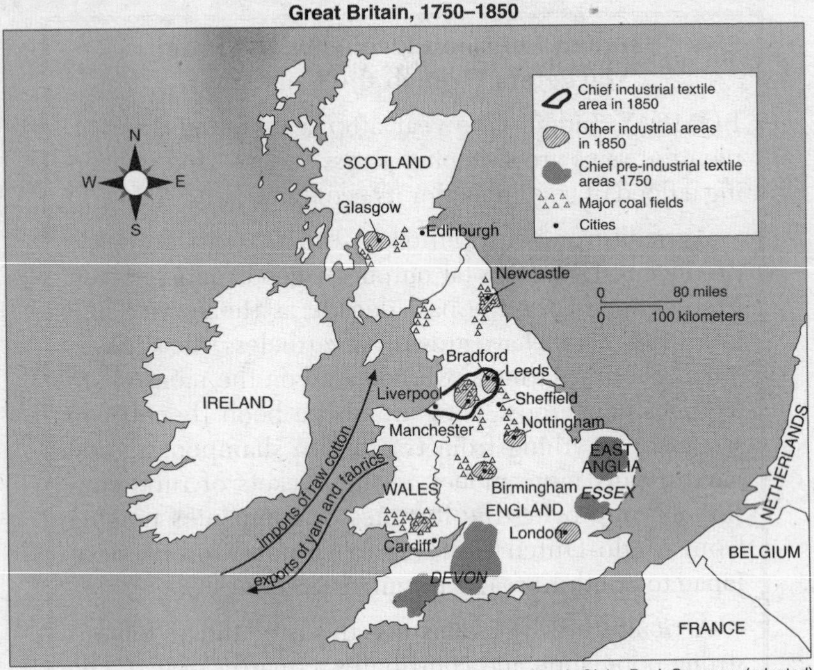

Source: Holt and O'Connor, *Exploring World History Workbook*, Globe Book Company (adapted)

3 Based on this map, state ***one*** way that coal affected the development of Great Britain between 1750 and 1850. [1]

____

____

Document 4

> . . . The lives of factory workers in Manchester, and in the other new industrial cities rising up around Britain, were shaped by the burning of coal just as the coal miners' lives were shaped by the digging of it. Coal made the iron that built the machines the workers operated as well as the factories they worked in, and then it provided the power that made the machines and factories run. Coal gas provided the lights the workers toiled [worked] under, letting their work day start before dawn and end after dusk. When they left the factory doors, they would walk through a city made of coal-fired bricks, now stained black with the same coal soot that was soiling their skin and clothes. Looking up, they would see a sky darkened by coal smoke; looking down, a ground blackened by coal dust. When they went home, they would eat food cooked over a coal fire and often tainted with a coal flavor, and with each breath, they would inhale some of the densest coal smoke on the planet. In short, their world was constructed, animated, illuminated, colored, scented, flavored, and generally saturated by coal and the fruits [results] of its combustion. . . .

Source: Barbara Freese, *Coal: A Human History*, Perseus Publishing

4 According to Barbara Freese, what are ***two*** effects that coal had on factory workers in the industrial cities of Great Britain during the Industrial Revolution? [2]

(1) ____

____

(2) ____

____

Document 5

Kuwait became a major supplier of oil during the late 1940s and the 1950s. Kuwait made a deal with foreign oil companies in return for payments. This money changed the way many people earned a living in Kuwait and led to a change in Kuwait's economic infrastructure.

> . . .The government's efforts to modernize the City of Kuwait resulted in a construction boom, particularly in the period 1952 to 1965. Foreign planning consultants, architects, engineers, construction firms, and labor planned and created a city with the best material and technologies the industrial world could supply. In contrast to the land acquisition program, however, government outlays in this period to create social overhead capital did generate considerable economic activity. In addition to a great many public buildings, commercial centers, apartment blocks, and suburban community projects built in the period, the following were also constructed:
>
> 1. 176 government schools and 32 private schools.
> 2. 8 hospitals, 2 sanatoria [treatment centers], 37 dispensaries and health centers, 148 school dispensaries and 9 centers for preventive medicine.
> 3. 1,100 kilometers of paved roads.
> 4. A number of electric power stations and an expansive network for distribution and street lighting laid; between 1956 and 1965, installed capacity increased from 30,000 kwh to 370,000 kwh. . . .

Source: Jacqueline S. Ismael, "The Economic Transformation of Kuwait," *The Politics of Middle Eastern Oil*, Middle East Institute

5 According to Jacqueline S. Ismael, what are ***two*** ways Kuwait used its oil resources to improve the city of Kuwait? [2]

(1) ____

____

(2) ____

____

Document 6

"I can't see a reason to go to war with Iraq...."

Source: Michael Ramirez, *Los Angeles Times,* January, 2003 (adapted)

6 Based on Michael Ramirez's cartoon, in what way did Iraqi oil contracts influence the French government in 2003? [1]

____

____

Document 7

. . . When De Beers discovered diamonds in Botswana in 1969, the government had been independent for three years, and the men running it were traditional chiefs who owned cattle. They came from a desert culture where people have to scrimp and save to survive the long, dry season.

During three decades, Botswana's leaders have carefully guided what became the world's fastest-growing economy. They invested in roads, schools and clinics. In stark contrast to the rulers of Angola and Congo, they created an African nation devoted to improving the lives of its people. In 1965, only about half of primary school-aged children attended school. Today, 90 percent of that group is enrolled. Life expectancy, which was less than 50 at independence, is now near 70.*

Phones work in Botswana, potholes get repaired, garbage gets picked up, and a lively press pokes fun at the government without fear. At $3,600 per year, the gross national product per capita is seven times higher than the average for sub-Saharan Africa. The standard of living is higher than in South Africa, Turkey or Thailand.

"Diamonds are not devils," said Terry Lynn Karl, professor of political science at Stanford and author of "The Paradox of Plenty," (University of California Press, 1997), a book about the poisonous mix of natural resources, big money and thieving elites in developing countries. "What matters is that there be a tradition of good government and compromise in place prior to the exploitation of these resources.". . .

* Correction: The United Nations says that because of AIDS, the figure has fallen sharply and is 41, no longer close to 70.

Source: Blaine Harden, "Africa's Gems: Warfare's Best Friend," *New York Times*, April 6, 2000, Correction published April 17, 2000

7 According to Blaine Harden, what are ***two*** ways the sale of diamonds affected Botswana? [2]

(1) ______________________________

____

(2) ______________________________

____

Document 8

In 1980, diamonds were discovered at Gope in the Central Kalahari Game Reserve (CKGR). Since 1997, the government of Botswana has been removing the Bushmen from this area. Many wish to return to their traditional homelands.

> . . . In a recent court case concerning the Bushmen's right to return to their ancestral lands, Tombale assured the court that the evictions had nothing to do with diamonds. This was strange, because the bushmen's lawyers had never mentioned diamonds. They were just defending the Gana and Gwi Bushmen's right to live on lands they had occupied for thousands of years.
>
> And yet when Margaret Nasha said in February 2002 that the relocation of the Gana and Gwi was not unprecedented she cited an example of people being relocated 'to give way for projects of national interest' in Jwaneng. They were, in fact, relocated to make way for a diamond mine.
>
> As Botswana's foreign minister Mompati Merafhe has explained: 'Many Bushmen have been removed because of economic interests. In Orapa, my area, a great chunk of people were removed because of the mine. Botswana is where it is today because of this facilitation. These people are no exception.'. . .
>
> Meanwhile, back in the Kalahari the Botswana government has been parcelling up the CKGR into diamond concessions and sharing them out between De Beers, the Australian-based company BHP Billiton and the Canadian outfit Motapa Diamond Inc. And by November last year virtually the entire game reserve, bar [except for] a small bite-sized chunk in the northwest, had been dished out.

> So either the government has pulled off a fat scam by selling dud concessions to three unsuspecting multinationals — or it's lying. . . .

Source: "Why are the Bushmen being evicted?"
The Ecologist, September 2003

8 Based on this excerpt from *The Ecologist*, state ***one*** impact the 1980 discovery of more diamonds has had on the people of Botswana. [1]

____

____

Part B: Essay

Directions: Write a well-organized essay that includes an introduction, several paragraphs, and a conclusion. Use evidence from at least ***five*** documents in your essay. Support your response with relevant facts, examples, and details. Include additional outside information.

Historical Context:

Throughout history, natural resources such as water, coal, oil, and diamonds have both helped and hindered the development of nations and regions.

Task:

Using the information from the documents and your knowledge of global history, write an essay in which you

- Discuss how natural resources have helped ***and/or*** hindered the development of specific nations ***or*** regions

Do *not* use the United States as the specific nation or region.

Guidelines:

In your essay, be sure to:

- Develop all aspects of the task
- Incorporate information from *at least* ***five*** documents
- Incorporate relevant outside information
- Support the theme with relevant facts, examples, and details
- Use a logical and clear plan of organization, including an introduction and conclusion that are beyond a restatement of the theme

Answers August 2007

Global History and Geography

Answer Key

PART I (1–50)

1. 1	**14.** 4	**27.** 3	**40.** 1
2. 4	**15.** 1	**28.** 2	**41.** 4
3. 3	**16.** 3	**29.** 3	**42.** 1
4. 2	**17.** 2	**30.** 4	**43.** 2
5. 1	**18.** 1	**31.** 2	**44.** 1
6. 3	**19.** 1	**32.** 3	**45.** 3
7. 2	**20.** 2	**33.** 4	**46.** 2
8. 2	**21.** 4	**34.** 4	**47.** 2
9. 1	**22.** 4	**35.** 2	**48.** 1
10. 4	**23.** 2	**36.** 4	**49.** 1
11. 4	**24.** 3	**37.** 4	**50.** 3
12. 3	**25.** 2	**38.** 3	
13. 4	**26.** 4	**39.** 2	

PART II: Thematic Essay See Answers Explained section.

PART III: Document-Based Essay See Answers Explained section.

Answers Explained

PART I

1. **1** A source of information considered a primary source is the travel diary of Ibn Battuta. Primary sources are original records of an event. Primary sources include official documents and firsthand accounts of events by people who witnessed or participated in these developments. Primary sources include letters, reports, and photographs by people involved in the events. Ibn Battuta was born in Morocco in 1304 and spent 27 years of his life traveling through Muslim lands. His writings provide the Western world with a positive view of the Muslims in Southeast Asia, China, Meçca, and Timbuktu.

WRONG CHOICES EXPLAINED:

(2), (3), and (4) None of these answers are primary sources. A novel about the Golden Age of Islam, a textbook on the history of North Africa, and a dictionary of English words adapted from Arabic are examples of secondary sources. Novels are works of fiction and are typically not based on true facts. Textbooks and dictionaries are secondary sources that obtain information from primary sources.

2. **4** A continent whose economic and political development has been influenced by the Andes Mountains and the Amazon River is South America. The Andes are the world's longest mountain range. These mountains have created barriers to the movement of people and contributed to regionalism or strong local traditions dividing the people of South America within their country or region. The Andes Mountains divided Colombians and Venezuelans. This geographic division was one of the reasons that Simon Bolivar, known as the liberator of South America, was unable to achieve his dream of unity among the nations of the region in the 19th century.

Beginning in the snowy Andes Mountains in Peru, the Amazon River flows eastward, and at least 1,000 tributaries pour into the Amazon on its journey to the Atlantic Ocean. The Amazon carries more water than any other river in the world. Because the Amazon is both deep and wide, ocean-going ships can sail 1,000 miles upriver as far as Manaus, Brazil. Smaller vessels can carry cargoes as far as Iquitos, Peru, which is 2,300 miles from the mouth of the Amazon. Until the 1950s, few people lived along the river. The hot, humid climate as well as the seasonal flooding and thick vegetation made settlements difficult. Since then, many settlers have moved into the region to develop its rich resources. Today, ships haul lumber and livestock along the Amazon from the interior to the coast. Unfortunately, these economic developments threaten the ecological balance in the Amazon Basin, which is the site of the world's largest rain forest.

WRONG CHOICES EXPLAINED:

(1), (2), and (3) None of these continents were influenced by the Andes Mountains and the Amazon River. Neither of these geographic features is located in these regions of the world.

3. **3** At the beginning of the Neolithic Revolution, the most direct effect of these developments was on diet and shelter. About 10,000 years ago, people began to change from hunters and gatherers to producers of food. They discovered how to grow food and to herd or domesticate animals. Anthropologists believe that these changes may have occurred in parts of southwest Asia, where wild wheat and barley were plentiful. People noticed that they could spread the seeds of these plants to grow crops. They also learned how to herd animals, such as goats, sheep, and cattle. These discoveries meant that people no longer had to search for food, there would be an abundance of food, and permanent settlements could be established. As these settlements or villages grew, people needed to work together. Skilled occupations developed, and there was a need for government to establish order. These developments created a more complex society. These advances are referred to as the Neolithic Revolution, or the Agricultural Revolution, because farming and domestic animals changed the way people lived.

WRONG CHOICES EXPLAINED:

(1) The Neolithic Revolution did not have the most direct effect on religion and government. The people continued to follow their polytheistic religion, or the belief in many gods. Some types of informal government had existed during the Stone Age when people moved from area to area. However, during the Neolithic era some men gained prestige as warriors and chiefs.

(2) The Neolithic Revolution did not have the most direct effect on transportation and trade. Traditional economies were based on agriculture, and farmers did not trade or travel beyond their local settlements.

(4) Climate and topography were not affected by the Neolithic Revolution. During this time, farmers made effective use of physical features of the area so they could continue to farm.

4. **2** These actions are examples of cultural diffusion. Cultural diffusion is the exchange of goods, ideas, customs, and technology between one group or region and another. Kushites lived south of Egypt along the Nile River. Egypt dominated Kush from 2000 to 1000 B.C. Egyptian armies raided and occupied Kush for a brief period. The people of Kush learned about Egyptian civilization through trade. The Kushites adopted the Egyptian idea of god-king, and built temples and pyramids like those in Egypt. They also adopted Egyptian hieroglyphics. In 750 B.C. the Kushites conquered the Nile Valley, but their rule over Egypt was short-lived.

The Phoenicians were one of the earliest trading empires of the ancient Middle East. They set up small city-states along the eastern Mediterranean coast and earned a living through commerce and trade. It is estimated that as many as 300 Phoenician cities were set up along the Mediterranean coasts of Europe and Africa. Phoenician merchants needed a simplified kind of writing to keep records. Cuneiform with its 600 symbols was too cumbersome. The Phoenicians discovered a way to keep records using 22 symbols. The Phoenician writing system first appeared around 900 B.C. Soon it was carried to trading centers along the Mediterranean world. About 800 B.C., the Greeks adopted the Phoenician alphabet and added four other symbols. This alphabet was then passed to the Western world.

During the two centuries of Gupta rule, which is sometimes known as the golden age of Hindu culture, lasting from 320 to 535 A.D., Indian mathematicians and scholars developed the concept of zero and the decimal system based on the number 10. In the late 7th century, after the death of Muhammad, the founder of Islam, Muslim armies conquered the Indus Valley, and by 100, the Arabs had created a Muslim empire on the subcontinent with its capital at Delhi. Between 700 and 1350, Arab merchants built a vast trading network across the Muslim world. Trade spread both products and technology. Arab scholars studied Indian mathematics before making their contributions. They borrowed the concept of zero and the decimal system and developed Arabic numbers, which were eventually adapted worldwide.

WRONG CHOICES EXPLAINED:

(1) Filial piety is the duty and respect that children owe to their parents according to the Chinese philosopher Confucius.

(3) Scientific research is the use of a step-by-step approach that emphasizes experimentation and observation to test and prove results.

(4) Ethnocentrism is the belief that one's culture or standards are superior to those of other societies.

5. **1** Buddhism is the belief system that is most closely associated with the terms *Eightfold Path, Four Noble Truths,* and *nirvana.* The religion of Buddhism began in India around 600 B.C. Prince Siddhartha Guatama (563–487 B.C.) is considered the founder of Buddhism. Siddhartha Guatama lived his youth in comfort and luxury. Upset by the human suffering that he saw beyond the palace, he left his wealth and set out in search for truth. While meditating under a special tree, he found the answer to his questions and was therefore referred to as the Buddha, or the Enlightened One. The central philosophy of Buddhism revolves around the Four Noble Truths, which are that all of life is suffering and that suffering is caused by a desire for riches and a long life. One way to eliminate suffering is to eliminate desire. A person can eliminate desire only by following the Eightfold Path of righteous living. The Eightfold Path consists of giving up material pleasure, controlling emotions, meditating selflessly, respecting all living things, acquiring knowledge, cultivating goodness, speaking the truth, and acting generously. If Buddhists follow these rules, they will enter into nirvana, a state in which the soul merges with the universe and is released from the endless cycles of reincarnation.

WRONG CHOICES EXPLAINED:

(2) Christianity is a belief system based on the teachings of Jesus Christ that began in the Middle East about 2,000 years ago.

(3) Judaism is a monotheistic religion of the Hebrews whose spiritual and ethical principles are rooted in the Old Testament of the Bible and in the Talmud.

(4) Shintoism is a Japanese religion that stresses the connection between people and the forces of nature. In the 18th century, it became the national religion of Japan, extolling nationalism, ancestor worship, and divinity of the emperor.

6. **3** The statement that is supported by this excerpt from Hammurabi's code of laws is that laws sometimes distinguish between social classes. Hammurabi, ruler of the Babylonians, developed the first written law codes around 1705 B.C. Hammurabi's Code consisted of 282 sections dealing with most aspects of daily life. It clearly stated which actions were considered violations and assigned a specific punishment for each. Hammurabi's Code was designed to ensure order, strengthen the government, protect the weak, and establish the legal rights of citizens. Instead of fining violators, the code enacted what the Bible later expressed as an "eye for an eye" and a "tooth for a tooth." Although the codes set standards of justice, not all social classes were treated equally under the law. A sharp division of classes provided harsher punishments for an offense against a noble or priest than for the same offense against a common person such as an artisan, merchant, or slave. One of the codes said that if someone stole cattle belonging to members of the court, he would have to pay 30 times the price. However, if the cattle belonged to a free man, he would have to pay only 10 times the price. These examples as well as the excerpt reinforce the class distinctions existing under the law.

WRONG CHOICES EXPLAINED:

(1) This excerpt would support the statement that men were not equal under the law by showing that there were stricter punishments for the poor than for the rich.

(2) and (4) Neither of these statements can be supported by this excerpt. There is no reference to fines that are preferable to physical punishment or to the fact that violence must always be punished with violence.

7. **2** Confucianism had a strong effect on the development of China mainly because this philosophy provided a basis for social order. Confucius, who lived between 551 and 479 B.C., was one of China's greatest philosophers and formulated an ethical code of behavior. The purpose of this code was to improve society and to build and maintain good government. He believed that harmony could be achieved by the proper behavior of each member of a family or society. He taught that individuals should be guided by the following virtues: careful observance of ancient traditions; reverence for learning;

respect for honesty; devotion to parents, family, and friends; obedience to the rulers; and respect for ancestors. He believed that these traditions could help maintain social peace and harmony. Each person's social role brought a number of obligations. If everyone fulfilled these roles by meeting their responsibilities, people and society would be in harmony. Confucius's followers collected his sayings and put them in a book titled *The Analects*.

WRONG CHOICES EXPLAINED:

(1) Confucianism did not establish a basic structure for military rule. Confucius stressed the importance of obedience to good government ruled by an emperor, not a military leader.

(3) Confucianism did not contain any framework for a communist government. Mao Zedong established communism in China in the 20th century. Under his leadership, the communists rejected Confucianism.

(4) Confucianism did not stress the importance of the individual. Each individual's role in society had to be in harmony with society. Confucius claimed that the good of society was more important than the needs of the individual.

8. **2** The terms *masters, apprentices,* and *journeymen* are most closely associated with the guild system of Europe in the Middle Ages. In medieval towns, merchants and artisans formed associations known as guilds made up of people who worked at the same occupation. They were similar to today's labor unions. In medieval towns, guilds controlled all wages and prices in their craft. The craft guilds strictly regulated the training and advancement of workers. The apprentice, or beginning worker, bound himself for a seven-year period, generally without pay, to a master craftsman. The master supported him and taught him the craft, social manners, and morals. After this period, the apprentice might be promoted to the journeyman class. The journeyman could be employed in any shop in return for a daily wage. If he passed a test by producing a masterpiece, whether it was a shoe, barrel, or sword, he advanced to the master class. Journeymen whose products met guild standards were welcomed into the guild as masters. The master craftsman could open his own shop where he was both a worker and owner. The guild system provided a framework of economic structure for life in medieval towns.

WRONG CHOICES EXPLAINED:

(1) The *encomienda* system of Latin America was established by the Spanish government in the Americas and enabled the colonists to tax or get labor from the Native Americans.

(3) The civil service system of China during the Tang dynasty was established for those people who wanted to hold public office. People had to pass difficult examinations emphasizing Confucian philosophy. Rulers set up schools that prepared male students to take these exams. This system provided China with a highly educated ruling class.

(4) The caste system of India is a division of society into four major groups based on occupation or birth. The caste system is a rigid social system that was characteristic of Hindu Indian society.

9. **1** The statement best supported by the information on this map is that the Roman Empire extended over three continents. At the height of the Roman Empire in 117 A.D., Rome extended control in Europe over Gaul, Spain, and Britain. In North Africa, Rome dominated Carthage and Egypt. Rome also controlled parts of Asia Minor.

WRONG CHOICES EXPLAINED:

(2), (3), and (4) None of these statements can be supported by the information on the map.

10. **4** Based on the information provided by this map, the Mediterranean Sea is the body of water that is most likely the center of Roman trade. During the height of the Roman Empire, the government expanded its control over the prosperous trade routes throughout the Mediterranean. For several centuries, the Mediterranean was a Roman lake surrounded on all sides by the empire, with Rome dominating the entire Mediterranean basin. Trade flowed freely from distant parts such as Carthage, Greece, and the Nile Valley, and brought wealth to the empire via the Mediterranean Sea. *Mare Nostrum* (Latin for "Our Sea") was the affectionate Roman name for the Mediterranean Sea.

WRONG CHOICES EXPLAINED:

(1), (2), and (3) None of these choices can support the fact that they were the center of Roman trade. The Red Sea provided commerce in the eastern part of the empire. Neither the Black Sea nor the Atlantic Ocean provided trade with Rome.

11. **4** Based on the information provided by this map, the statement about Constantinople that is accurate is that Constantinople was an important trading center. Located on a peninsula, Constantinople overlooked the Bosporus, the narrow strait between the Sea of Marmara and the Black Sea. A second strait, the Dardanelles, connects the Sea of Marmara and the Aegean Sea, which leads to the Mediterranean. Byzantine ships loaded with cargo sailed the Mediterranean and Black seas. Merchants traded agricultural goods from central Europe, such as grain, and fur from northern Europe for luxury goods from Africa and the East. Ships brought cloves and sandalwood from the East, pepper and gems from India, gold and ivory from Africa, and silk from China to Constantinople. The busy harbor city of Constantinople became known as the Golden Horn.

WRONG CHOICES EXPLAINED:

(1) The map does not provide any information to indicate that Africans traded more goods to Constantinople than to any other area.

(2) The map shows that Constantinople was near the Bosporus, not the Mediterranean Sea.

(3) The map shows that silk, not gold, was the primary commodity that China sent to Constantinople. Africa shipped gold to Constantinople.

12. **3** One major characteristic of the Renaissance period is that the classical cultures of Greece and Rome were revived and imitated. The Renaissance, which in French means "rebirth," was a period of artistic and cultural achievement in Europe from the 14th to the 16th century. The Renaissance began with a reemphasis on the Greco-Roman culture that had been neglected during the Middle Ages. Renaissance writers focused on reason, a questioning attitude, experimentation, and free inquiry, in contrast to the medieval approach that emphasized faith, authority, and tradition. Renaissance writers looked to the teachings of Plato and Socrates as their guides and began to question the teachings of Aristotle, whose philosophy had influenced life in the Middle Ages. Renaissance artists rejected the medieval form of art and initiated the classical works of Greece and Rome. Their art was very realistic; the artists studied the human anatomy in detail and worked from live models. They also studied the technique of three-dimensional perspective. The artistic achievements of Leonardo's *Last Supper* and *Mona Lisa* and Michelangelo's *Pieta* and *David* are considered masterpieces of Western art.

WRONG CHOICES EXPLAINED:

(1) During the Renaissance, the Catholic Church still had influence in Europe. Church leaders supported many artistic projects, such as the Sistine Chapel and the Duomo in Florence. However, during the Renaissance, people began to question the absolute authority of the church and the abuses that had developed over the years. The questioning attitude led to the Protestant Reformation and the end of religious unity in Europe.

(2) The manor was the center of economic activity during the Middle Ages, not the Renaissance.

(4) During the Renaissance, the vernacular, the national language of a country, replaced Latin as the major language of the people.

13. **4** The Protestant Reformation is the period in European history that is most directly related to this statement. The Protestant Reformation refers to the period beginning in 1517 when Martin Luther, a German monk, posted the Ninety-five Theses to the door of the church at Wittenberg on All Hallows' Eve. Luther denied the pope's supremacy and proclaimed the Bible as the final authority in religious matters. He also condemned a number of Catholic religious practices, such as the selling of indulgences. Indulgences were certificates issued by the Catholic Church that reduced or even canceled punishment for a person's sins. Luther preached that people could gain salvation by faith alone. He claimed that faith in God was the only way to gain heaven. Luther's attack on the Catholic Church ended Europe's religious

unity and led to the establishment of many different Protestant churches throughout Europe.

WRONG CHOICES EXPLAINED:

(1) The Age of Exploration was the period from 1400 to 1600, during which European monarchs sent explorers to find new trade routes, resources, and land in Asia, Africa, and the Americas.

(2) The Scientific Revolution was a period in science during the 16th and 17th centuries in which scientists challenged traditional authority. Scientists began to reach conclusions based on observations and reason, not faith.

(3) The Crusades were religious wars between Christian Europe and the Muslims for control of the Holy Land. The Crusades lasted from 1096 A.D. to 1246 A.D.

14. **4** The economies of the western African civilizations of Ghana, Mali, and Songhai relied on trans-Sahara trade routes. These west African kingdoms experienced economic prosperity because they all traded with many other nations. These kingdoms were near the trans-Sahara trade routes, and each of them controlled the trade routes of gold and silver. The Kingdom of Ghana, which was founded around 750 A.D., controlled a trading empire that stretched over 100,000 square miles. They prospered from the taxes they imposed on the goods that entered or left their kingdom. Because the Ghana, or king, controlled such a vast region, the land became known by the name of its ruler—Ghana. Large caravans from Ghana traveled north to Morocco, bringing nuts and farming produce. Gold from Ghana was traded for Saharan salt brought by Muslim traders. In 1242, Mali conquered Ghana and established a new empire. The rulers extended its empire by putting the gold and salt mines directly under their control. Mali's most famous leader was Mansa Musa, a convert to Islam who ruled from 1312 A.D. to 1337 A.D. and expanded Mali to about twice the size of Ghana. Under his rule, the city of Timbuktu became the center of learning and trade. The city attracted students from Europe, Asia, and Africa. The flourishing of trade, culture, and wealth sparked European rulers' interest in African gold. At the end of the 15th century, Songhai replaced Mali as the most powerful west African kingdom. Like Ghana and Mali, it grew rich from trade across the Sahara Desert. Songhai became the largest of the west African kingdoms as trade expanded to Europe and Asia. In the late 1500s, invading armies from Morocco gained control of Songhai. The fall of the kingdom of Songhai marked the end of great west African kingdoms.

WRONG CHOICES EXPLAINED:

(1), (2), and (3) None of these choices influenced the economies of these western African civilizations. They were not involved in shipbuilding because they traded by land routes. None of these economies had the natural resources necessary for industrial growth or textile production. These African civilizations depended on trading gold and salt for prosperity.

15. **1** A major reason for Zheng He's voyages during the 15th century was to promote trade and collect tribute. In 1405, before Europeans began to sail beyond their borders, Zheng He, a Chinese Muslim admiral, launched the first of seven voyages of exploration. Some of his expeditions included as many as 62 ships, carrying more than 25,000 sailors, with some ships measuring 400 feet long. His earliest voyages were to Southeast Asia and India. Later, he traveled as far as Arabia and eastern Africa. Zheng's goal was to impress the world with the power and splendor of Ming China and to expand China's tribute system. Everywhere he went, Zheng distributed gifts such as gold, silver, silk, and scented oils to show Chinese superiority. As a result, more than 16 countries sent tribute to the Ming court. Many envoys traveled to China. In the wake of these voyages, Chinese merchants settled in Southeast Asian and Indian trading centers.

WRONG CHOICES EXPLAINED:

(2) Zheng He did not establish colonies in Africa and Asia. He wanted to promote trading centers, not permanent colonies. The Chinese did not promote colonization.

(3) Zheng He's voyages were not designed to seal off China's borders from foreign influence. He wanted to expand trade with Asia and Africa. After his death, in 1453, the Ming emperor ended overseas exploration and withdrew into isolation.

(4) Zheng He's voyages did not seek to prove that the world was round. He traveled to promote commerce and trade.

16. **3** One effect of the Columbian exchange was the introduction of new foods to both Europe and the Americas. The voyages of Christopher Columbus began a vast cultural exchange between the two hemispheres. In 1493, Columbus returned to Spain with new plants and animals that he had found in the Americas. When Columbus returned to the Americas later in 1493 with some 1,200 settlers, he brought with him a collection of European animals and plants, including horses, cattle, and pigs. The Columbian exchange had begun. Ships brought a wide array of products that Europeans, Asians, and Africans had never seen before, including plants such as tomatoes, squash, pineapples, tobacco, and cocoa beans (chocolate). Perhaps the most important foods brought from the Americas to the rest of the world were corn and potatoes. Over time, both crops became an important and steady part of diets throughout the world. The planting of the white potato in Ireland and the first sweet potato in China greatly changed the lives of the people in those countries. The introduction of new foods from the Americas also frightened people. Italians thought it was harmful to eat tomatoes, and officials in Burgundy, France, banned the potato. They thought that eating too many potatoes caused leprosy. Few events transformed the world like the Columbian exchange.

WRONG CHOICES EXPLAINED:

(1) The Columbian exchange did not lead to a rapid decline in European population. European population expanded from the 15th century onward but was developing more slowly by the end of the 19th century.

(2) The Columbian exchange did not contribute to economic stability in China and Japan. The Chinese and Japanese had isolated themselves from the West. Some of these crops became part of their diet, but their economies did not depend upon them for survival.

(4) The Columbian exchange did not spread Hinduism into Latin America. Columbus spread Catholicism in Latin America.

17. **2** From the 15th to the 18th century, absolute monarchs of Europe and Asia sought to centralize their political power. *Absolutism* refers to a political system in which the monarch (king or queen) has supreme power and control without limits over the lives of the people in their country. In England, France, Spain, and Russia, the kings expanded power at the expense of the nobles. In England, the Tudor dynasty, which ruled from 1500 to 1603, strengthened the power of the monarchy. Although Parliament held sessions, it was effectively dominated by the Tudors. Under the leadership of Henry VII, Henry VIII, and Elizabeth I, there was expanded governmental authority over the nation. Henry VIII increased his power by replacing the Catholic Church with the Anglican Church, which was controlled by the king. In France, the Bourbon family, who ruled for more than 200 years, established the foundation of absolutism. Louis XIV of France represented the height of absolutism. He ruled France from 1643 to 1715 and claimed to rule by the divine right of kings. To illustrate this attitude, it is claimed that he said, "L'état, c'est moi," which means, "I am the state." Louis XIV is often referred to as the Sun King. The Hapsburg monarchs of Austria and Spain also established absolute rule in their countries. In Spain, the king increased power by destroying the power of the nobles and enacted laws without the Cortes, the Spanish legislature. In Russia, the Romanov family established control in 1613 and ruled for more than 300 years. Peter the Great, who ruled from 1682 to 1715, established absolute control by creating a strong army loyal to him, extending control over the Russian Orthodox Church and ruthlessly crushing all opposition.

In the last half of the 1500s, Akbar the Great ruled the powerful Mughal empire in India. Akbar strengthened the centralized government. He conquered neighbors in Muslim and Hindu states, uniting all of northern India under his rule. He also set out to unite his Muslim and Hindu subjects through a policy of religious toleration. To govern his large empire more efficiently, Akbar divided it into twelve provinces. Akbar sent well-trained imperial officials to supervise local government, enforce laws, and ensure the collection of taxes. Akbar's successors, however, were not strong rulers, and Mughal power declined during the late 1600s.

WRONG CHOICES EXPLAINED:

(1) Absolute monarchs did not increase the power of the Catholic Church. In France, the Bourbon family and the Hapsburg family dominated the church, and the religious leaders were dependent on the monarchs for their power. In England, the Tudor family supported the Anglican Church over the Catholic Church. The Catholic Church was never very influential in either Russia or India.

(3) None of the absolute monarchies redistributed land to the peasants. Under these absolute monarchies, the land was owned by either the ruling families or members of the nobility.

(4) Absolute monarchies did not strengthen feudalism. These rulers destroyed the power of the local nobles by forcing them to swear loyalty to the king, not local leaders.

18. **1** The Mongols were the group of people who ruled much of Asia during the period shown on the map. The information provided by the map indicates that in 1294, the Mongols controlled territory from eastern China to eastern Europe. The Mongols of central Asia were skilled riders, fierce fighters, and raiders. During the 1200s, the Mongols established the largest land empire in the world under the Mongol leader Genghis Khan (1167–1227), which means "Universal Ruler" or "World Emperor." He was able to unite the different tribes and build a powerful empire. With his organized and disciplined armies, Khan invaded China and gained control of Beijing and captured the Muslim states of central Asia. After his death in 1227, his successors drove armies south, east, and west out of inner Asia. After conquering northern China, the Mongols invaded Korea. They leveled the Russian city of Kiev, conquered Moscow, destroyed Poland, added Hungary to their empire, and reached the banks of the Adriatic Sea. In 1279, Kublai Khan, the grandson of Genghis Khan, completed the entire conquest of China and established the Yuan dynasty, which ruled China for less than a century until 1368. Under Kublai Khan, the Mongols ruled China, Korea, Tibet, and Vietnam, as well as territory in eastern Europe. Their empire extended from central Asia to eastern Europe.

WRONG CHOICES EXPLAINED:

(2), (3), and (4) None of these groups ruled Asia during the period shown on the map. There is no reference to any of them on the map.

19. **1** Louis XIV is the person credited with saying, "L'état, c'est moi" (I am the state). Louis XIV, who ruled France from 1643 to 1715, believed in the divine right of kings. The divine-right theory of kings was the belief that the king was an agent of God and that his authority to rule came directly from God. Louis XIV said, "I am the state" and took the sun as his symbol of power. He ruled without the Estates-General, which is the French Parliament, and crushed all opposition to his government. During his 72-year

reign, France became the center of culture and Louis built the Versailles palace, which became the perfect symbol of the Sun King's wealth and power.

WRONG CHOICES EXPLAINED:

(2) John Locke was a 17th-century English philosopher who proposed the social contract theory. According to his theory, a king ruled with the consent of the people and his power was not unlimited. If a king violated the rights of his people, they had a right to overthrow him.

(3) Karl Marx was a 19th-century philosopher who believed in Communism. In his book, the *Communist Manifesto,* Marx claims that the state will wither away and the government will become unnecessary.

(4) Queen Isabella of Castile was the queen of Spain whose marriage to Ferdinand V of Aragon in 1469 helped to pave the way for a unified state.

20. **2** Seventeenth-century scholars Galileo Galilei and René Descartes faced serious challenges to their scientific theories because their ideas contradicted traditional medieval European beliefs. In 1543, Nicholas Copernicus proposed a heliocentric, or sun-centered, model of the universe. He said that the planets revolved around the sun. Most scholars rejected Copernicus' theory because it contradicted the teachings of the Catholic Church and the teaching of Ptolemy, which claimed that the earth was the center of the universe. In 1609, an Italian, Galileo Galilei, built his own telescope and observed the night skies. His discovery of moons circling a planet convinced him that the Copernican theory about the earth revolving around the sun was correct. Since the moons revolved around Jupiter, Galileo realized that not all heavenly bodies revolved around the earth. It was possible that some planets did move. In 1632, Galileo published his ideas. Galileo's discoveries caused an uproar. The Catholic Church banned the book and condemned him because his ideas challenged the Christian teaching that the heavens were fixed and unmoving. In 1633, Pope Urban VIII brought Galileo to trial in Rome before the Inquisition. Urban's threat of torture forced Galileo to publicly state that the earth stood motionless at the center of the universe.

René Descartes was a French mathematician in the late 16th and early 17th century who stressed scientific experimentation and observation to understand the world. He challenged the scholarly tradition of the medieval universities that sought to make the physical world fit into the teachings of the church. In his *Discourse on Method,* Descartes explains how he decided to discard all traditional authorities and search for provable knowledge. His famous statement, "I think, therefore I am," laid the foundation for the Scientific Revolution that challenged the traditional authority of the Catholic Church in Europe.

WRONG CHOICES EXPLAINED:

(1) Galilei and Descartes did not base their ideas on the Bible but challenged church leaders to prove them through experimentation.

(3) These men did not rely only on teachings from non-Christian culture. Their theories were based upon observation of the world in which they lived.

(4) The theories of Galilei and Descartes were supported by extensive scientific investigation. These men insisted that their theories were based on reason, not faith.

21. **4** A statement that expresses an idea of the Enlightenment is that all individuals have natural rights. The Enlightenment was an intellectual and cultural movement of the 18th century that tied together the ideas of the Scientific Revolution. The writers and philosophers of the Enlightenment believed that science and reason could explain the laws of human society. They insisted that, just as there were natural laws to govern the physical universe, there must be natural laws to govern human society. John Locke, an Enlightenment thinker of the late 1600s, believed that all people possessed natural rights. These rights include the right to life, liberty, and property. Like the French Enlightenment writer Rousseau, Locke argued that people form governments to protect their rights. Enlightenment writers believed that government was based on a social contract and that if a government did not protect these individual rights, people had the right to overthrow it. Governments were established to protect the natural rights of people.

WRONG CHOICES EXPLAINED:

(1) The divine-right theory of government contains the idea that the king is sacred and answers only to God.

(2) Communism is the belief that history is a continuous struggle between social classes.

(3) Darwinism expresses the idea that those who are the most fit will survive and succeed.

22. **4** The breakdown of traditions, increased levels of pollution, and the expansion of slums are negative aspects of urbanization. Urbanization is the development of cities caused by the movement of people from rural areas in search of jobs and better opportunities. In 1900, Bombay (Mumbai) had a population of 1.5 million people. By the end of that century, the population had grown to more than 10 million. By 2024, it is projected that nearly 54 percent of Africans will live in urban areas. In modern cities, people's traditional values and beliefs are often weakened. In cities, people tend to live with nuclear families rather than with their extended families. Traditional bonds of lineage became less important. Urban dwellers find it hard to understand customs and traditions of village life. For example, the caste system in India is weaker in urban areas than rural areas. Women often have more opportunities for change in cities. Marriage customs are changing since the young prefer to choose their own mates rather than accept arranged marriages. Many people cannot afford to live in cities. They settle in shantytowns or makeshift shacks that become slum areas. These areas of increased population lack sewer systems, electricity, and other basic services. Crowded conditions

often lead to water pollution and other environmental effects. Lagos in Nigeria, Calcutta in India, and Mexico City in Mexico are just some of the cities that are suffering from pollution and environmental problems because they have been unable to cope with the waves of migration from rural areas.

WRONG CHOICES EXPLAINED:

(1) Militarism is a policy that glorifies the armed forces and supports aggressive military actions.

(2) Collectivization is a system under Communism in which many small farms are combined into large farms and operated by the government and worked by the peasants. Joseph Stalin began this policy in Soviet Russia during the late 1920s.

(3) Pogroms are organized attacks or persecutions against minority groups, particularly against the Jews in Czarist Russia.

23. **2** The heading that best completes this partial outline is "Effects of Nationalism." Nationalism creates a strong feeling of pride in and devotion to one's country. This feeling led to rivalries among powerful colonial countries over colonies. During the late 19th century, France, Germany, and other nations competed for colonies and economic power. France and Germany competed for colonial gains in Africa. Germany wanted to prevent the French from gaining Morocco. Great Britain resented Germany for blocking her efforts at creating a Cape–Cairo railway.

Nationalism led to the breakup of large empires. After World War II, Great Britain had hoped to maintain control of its vast holdings but was too weak to defend its possessions. The demise of the British Empire began in 1947, when India declared its independence. In Africa, England was forced to give up its control over the Gold Coast, which became known as Ghana in 1957, and had to relinquish control over most of its other colonies in Africa during the 1960s. In the 1950s, the French were forced to end their control over Indochina, which included Cambodia, Laos, Thailand, and Vietnam, as well as Morocco, Tunisia, and Algeria. Within two decades of the conclusion of World War II, the European colonial empires had been dismantled.

After many of these colonies gained independence, they had to struggle with ethnic groups that sought their self-determination. In India, there has been continued tension between Hindus and Muslims, which led to the creation of the independent state of Pakistan, which is predominantly Muslim. The partition of India in 1947 did not bring peace. Independence set off mass migration of Muslims fleeing India and Hindus fleeing Pakistan. Millions were killed crossing the borders. Tensions between Muslims and Hindus still exist and continue to erupt into violence. Sheiks who live in the state of Punjab have continued to demand self-rule for their provinces. In the early 1980s, Sikh separatists occupied the Golden Temple in Amistar to express their demands. The Indian government was forced to send military troops to reassert their control. In Africa, the Europeans established the most colonial boundaries. These boundaries were made without consideration for the traditional territories and ethnic groups. Nigeria is one of the many nations where tribalism has led to civil war. More than 200 ethnic groups live within the border of Nigeria. During the struggle for independence, several of the large groups fought for power. Among these groups were the Muslim Hausa and Fulani people in the north and the Christian Ibo and Yoruba people in the south. In 1966, a massacre of 20,000 Ibos took place. At the time, Hausa dominated the government. In 1967, the Ibos declared their region independent, calling it Biafra. A war raged for several years. Nigeria was able to end the war but not before nearly one million people had been killed in the war or died of starvation. Military rulers led Nigeria during the 1970s and took it over again in the mid-1980s. In 1999, Nigeria elected its first civilian government, but ethnic nationalism still exists in the country. The struggle for self-determination also led to ethnic tension in Rwanda between the Hutu and the Tutsi in the 1990s, as well as in such Southeastern Asian countries as Indonesia.

WRONG CHOICES EXPLAINED:

(1), (3), and (4) None of these headings address the topic contained in this partial outline.

24. **3** The statement that summarizes the theme of this passage is that the factory system allowed people to earn money. The passage points out that despite the poor pay, the industrial age brought about material benefits by creating jobs for wages that many of the workers would not be able to earn in any other field. The roles of women and children were forced to change in the new industrial society. Farming families had all worked the land together. Artisans, who had worked in their homes, now became separated from the home workplace. Women, who had worked at home, were now forced to seek employment outside the home. Employers preferred women because they could adapt more easily to the machines and many times earned less than the men. Since children had helped with farm work, parents accepted the idea of child labor. The wages of many of these children were needed to keep their families from starving. Despite the problems created by the Industrial Revolution, low wages and dismal conditions, the industrial age helped to raise the living standards of people over time as conditions improved for the workers.

WRONG CHOICES EXPLAINED:

(1), (2), and (4) None of these statements summarizes the theme of this passage. No references are made to the hardships created by the factory owners, to whether the factory owners preferred child laborers, or to whether the factory system created new social classes.

25. **2** One effect of industrialization on Japan during the Meiji Restoration was that the demand for natural resources increased. During the Meiji period from 1862 to 1912, the Japanese adapted the Western model of industrialization. Japan ended feudalism and began to modernize by selectively

borrowing from the West. The goal of the Meiji leader was to create a rich country and a strong military. Until the 1800s, Japan's limited resources and its relatively small size had little effect on the country. However, the Meiji Restoration industrialized Japan, creating the need for raw materials, especially cotton, iron ore, coal, and oil. It wanted to gain markets for its manufactured goods. Japanese nationalists also wanted to replace European imperialism with Asian imperialism. In 1895, Japan defeated China in a war and forced the Chinese to give up their claims to Korea. They also gained Taiwan and won special trading privileges. In 1910, Japan annexed Korea and forced its people to build railroads and roads for Japan's benefit. The Japanese took half of Korea's yearly rice crop to support Japanese expansion. In the 1920s and 1930s, the Japanese leaders developed the East Asia Co-Prosperity Sphere. Its aim was to conquer east Asia by taking raw materials. In 1931, Japan invaded Manchuria, a northern province of China, which was rich in coal, iron, and fertile soil. The Japanese argued that they had won Manchuria in the same way the Western nations had gained their colonies. By 1932, they had gained control of the area, begun to build hydroelectric plants, and created a sizable iron and steel industry, thereby increasing Japan's economy and military power. In the 1940s, the Japanese invaded French Indochina as well as the former Dutch East Indies (Indonesia). These areas provided the Japanese military with the important natural resources of rubber and oil. Japanese foreign policy led to conflict with Great Britain and the United States, and eventually to the attack on Pearl Harbor on December 7, 1941. This attack led to the United States involvement in World War II.

WRONG CHOICES EXPLAINED:

(1) The Japanese did not become more isolated from world affairs. The Meiji Restoration ended Japan's isolation from the world. During this period, Japanese leaders sent students abroad to learn from Western countries and brought in foreign experts to improve their industry.

(3) The Japanese did not become a colonial possession of China. The Japanese invaded China and took control of Manchuria.

(4) The Japanese sought to do away with the traditional practices of Bushido or the code of conduct for the samurai warrior of the feudal period. The Japanese wanted to model their army on the Prussian model.

26. **4** This map illustrates the concept of imperialism. Imperialism is a policy whereby one nation or a number of nations dominate the political, economic, and social life of a foreign country, region, or area. This map shows that the British, French, Germans, Japanese, and Russians extended their control over east Asia in 1914. The period that this refers to is known as the Age of Imperialism. Britain controlled Hong Kong, Canton, and other areas in China, and the French dominated French Indochina. The Germans controlled Kiaochow, and the Japanese dominated Korea, Port Arthur, and the Kuril and Sakhalin islands. Russia extended its control over Manchuria and parts of Mongolia. Imperialism allowed stronger nations to control weaker nations.

WRONG CHOICES EXPLAINED:

(1) Ethnocentrism is the belief that one's culture or standards are superior to those of other societies.

(2) Socialism is a system in which the government, not the individual, operates all the essential means of production.

(3) Containment is a policy that the United States followed toward the Soviet Union during the Cold War. The goal of the policy was to prevent the spread of Communism in the world.

27. **3** The Balkan Peninsula was the region described as "the powder keg of Europe" before World War I. The Balkans earned this title because of their nationalist rivalries. The Balkans—which refers to the mountainous peninsula in the southeastern corner of Europe—was home to an assortment of ethnic groups. The Ottoman Empire's control over the Balkans had weakened over time, and its power was in decline. Some groups had succeeded in breaking away from their Turkish rulers. These people had formed new nations, including Bulgaria, Greece, Montenegro, Romania, and Serbia. Nationalism was a powerful force in these countries. Each group wanted to extend its borders. Serbia, which declared its independence in 1878, had a large Slavic population and hoped to absorb all the Slavs of the Balkan Peninsula and join in an alliance with Russia. Serbia wanted control of Bosnia and Herzegovina, two provinces that would give landlocked Serbia an outlet to the Adriatic Sea. However, these provinces were Ottoman provinces administered by Austria-Hungary. Austria opposed Serbia's expansion because it feared rebellion among its own multiethnic empire and felt threatened by Serbia's growth. In addition, both Russia and Austria-Hungary had hoped to fill the power vacuum created by the Ottoman decline in the Balkans. In 1908, Austria took over Bosnia and Herzegovina. Serbian rulers were outraged, and the Russians offered full support. However, Russia was unprepared for war. Russia and Serbia had to back down when Germany stood firmly behind Austria. In 1914, tensions in the Balkans were once again on the rise. In 1912, Serbia had emerged victorious from several local conflicts. These conflicts brought Russia and Serbia closer together and intensified the hatred of Russia and Serbia for Austria-Hungary. The explosion that set off the Balkan powder keg and led to World War I was the assassination of Archduke Ferdinand of Austria-Hungary on June 28, 1914, by a Serbian nationalist.

WRONG CHOICES EXPLAINED:

(1) The Iberian Peninsula in southwestern Europe is occupied by Spain and Portugal.

(2) The British Isles are a group of islands off the northwestern coast of Europe. The group consists of two main islands, Great Britain and Ireland, and numerous smaller islands.

(4) Scandinavia is in the northern part of Europe. It consists of the countries of Norway, Sweden, and Denmark.

28. **2** The conclusion best supported by this passage is that the Arab-Israeli conflict can be traced in part to British promises. As the report shows, during World War I the British made two sets of vague promises. It promised to support Arab demands for their own kingdom in former Ottoman lands, including Palestine. In 1917, Arthur Balfour, the British foreign secretary, wrote to Lord Rothschild, the head of the English branch of a prominent banking family and a Zionist leader, promising to support the establishment of national homes for the Jewish people in Palestine. The British had issued the Balfour Declaration to win the support of European Jews and the Jews living in the United States. The declaration noted, however, that nothing should be done that harmed or injured the civil and religious rights of the existing non-Jewish communities in Palestine. These communities were Arab. In 1922, the British received the League of Nations mandate over Palestine. By 1938, more than 500,000 Jews had migrated to Palestine. They built new towns, restored desert lands to fertility, and started industries. As Jews poured into the land of Palestine, tensions between the two groups developed. Nationalists, who desired an Arab Palestine, and peasants and nomads, who feared the loss of traditional ways, resented Jewish settlers. The tensions between the two communities set the stage for conflict between Arab and Jewish nationalists. Arab nationalists continued to battle Zionists over a land the Arabs call Palestine and the Jews call Israel.

WRONG CHOICES EXPLAINED:

(1) The report shows that the British made promises to both the Arabs and the Jews.

(3) There is no reference to the United Nations in this report, which was issued in 1937. The United Nations was created in 1945 and became involved in the Middle East in 1947.

(4) The report indicates that the British promised the Jews as well as the Arabs an independent state in Palestine.

29. **3** Vladimir I. Lenin is the leader being described by these statements. Vladimir Lenin is considered the father of Russian Communism, a dynamic speaker who was able to attract the support of the people. When Russia entered World War I in 1914, the country was unprepared. By 1915, Russian casualties were almost two million. In March 1917, workers led food riots all across Russia. The Russian Revolution began when soldiers refused to fire on striking workers in St. Petersburg. Nicholas II was forced to give up his throne, and leaders of the Duma, the Russian parliament, set up a republic. This provisional government, headed by Prince Luvov, set up a Western-style democratic government that provided for guaranteed civil rights and freed political prisoners. The decision to continue the war and the inability to provide food resulted in the loss of support among the people. The Bolsheviks, a revolutionary group led by Lenin, promised "peace for the soldiers, land for the peasants, and bread for the workers." Lenin, who had been in exile when the March Revolution broke out, was sneaked into the country

by the Germans, who used him to undermine the support of the provisional government. In November 1917, the Bolsheviks seized control of the government. The majority of the Russian people were not Communists, but were displeased with the government. In November 1917, the Bolsheviks seized control of the government and established the first Communist nation in Europe. Lenin ended private ownership of land and distributed land to the peasants. Workers gained control of the factories and mines. However, the civil war that lasted more than three years resulted in economic disaster. Lenin was forced to adapt the New Economic Policy. Under this plan, private ownership was permitted, as well as small-scale manufacturing and agriculture. The government, however, still continued to control banks, large industry, and foreign trade. This change in policy helped the economy to recover. Lenin died in 1924, but his leadership enabled the Communist Revolution to survive in Russia.

WRONG CHOICES EXPLAINED:

(1) Czar Nicholas II was the last ruler of Russia and was forced to abdicate power in 1917.

(2) Nikita Khrushchev was the Communist leader of Russia who began the process of de-Stalinization in 1956. He was forced from power in 1964.

(4) Mikhail Gorbachev was the Soviet leader of the Communist Party who ruled from 1986 to 1991. He resigned from power when the Soviet Union collapsed in 1991.

30. **4** Trench warfare is described in this passage. *Trench warfare* is the term used to describe warfare along the Western front in World War I. The Allies (England, France, and Russia) and Central Powers (Germany, Austria, and Turkey) created a vast system of trenches stretching from the Swiss frontier to the English Channel. Life in the trenches was not glamorous, as soldiers roasted in the summer and froze in the winter. Sanitary conditions were horrible: Soldiers shared their food with rats and their beds with lice. Between the two trenches, there was "no-man's-land," and troops occasionally were sent over the top to attack the enemy trenches. The casualties were staggering. The British lost 60,000 per day and a total of 400,000 men at the Battle of Somme in 1916. Erich Remarque's great novel *All Quiet on the Western Front* (1929) describes the horrors of trench warfare.

WRONG CHOICES EXPLAINED:

(1) Guerilla warfare is fighting carried on through hunt-and-run raids.

(2) Nuclear warfare is the use of atomic weapons to fight a war.

(3) Biological warfare is the use of weapons, such as poison gas, or the use of germs and viruses, producing chemicals to destroy the enemy.

31. **2** A major goal of Joseph Stalin's Five-Year Plans was to transform the Soviet Union into an industrial power. In 1928, Joseph Stalin, who became leader of the Soviet Union after the death of Lenin in 1924, launched

the first of a series of Five-Year Plans to make Russia into an industrial giant. Stalin believed that the Soviet Union would be unable to stand up to the capitalist countries unless it modernized rapidly. Stalin established a command economy in which the government made all the economic decisions. Stalin poured resources into building steel mills, dams, and hydroelectric power. He set high goals for coal and oil production. New factories were built to produce chemicals, tractors, and other machines. By 1930, Soviet production in oil, coal, and steel had increased rapidly.

WRONG CHOICES EXPLAINED:

(1) Stalin's Five-Year Plans focused on creating economic changes in the Soviet Union, not Communist revolutions in the colonies of the European powers.

(3) Stalin's Five-Year Plans sought to make the Soviet Union economically independent and did not include any steps to expand the Soviet Union's borders to include warm-water ports.

(4) Stalin's Five-Year Plans did not seek to reduce the amount of foreign aid coming from the Western Hemisphere. Western nations never sent foreign aid to the Soviet Union. The goal of the Five-Year Plans was economic advancement without help from the West.

32. **3** Based on the information in this chart, political and economic instability was what gave rise to Nazi power in Germany. The Treaty of Versailles contained many harsh provisions that caused bitterness among the German people. Germany had to accept full responsibility for the war and pay huge reparations, or large sums of money, for all war damages. The reparations covered not only the destruction caused by the war, but also pensions for millions of Allied soldiers, or their widows, and families. The total cost of German reparations was more than $30 billion. The treaty severely limited the size of the German military forces. It also returned Alsace-Lorraine to France, removed hundreds of square miles of territory from western and eastern Germany, and stripped Germany of its overseas colonies. Adolf Hitler and the Nazis exploited this bitterness and focused on nationalists who were unable to accept defeat in World War I. Hitler pledged to tear up the Treaty of Versailles and denounce the German war-guilt clause. He demanded the return of Germany's colonies and European territories. He defended Germany's right to rearm and claimed that the German armies had been stabbed in the back, mainly by Jews and Communists, and not defeated by the Allies. After World War I, Germany faced widespread unemployment, and inflation created severe economic unrest. Hitler gained the support among the middle class and business leaders by promising to improve the economy. The government policy of simply printing money led to runaway inflation and destroyed many people's life savings. In the early 1920s, it was reported that four trillion marks were equivalent to one dollar. The Great Depression of 1929 added to the economic unrest. The inability of the Weimar Republic to command a majority in the parliament made it difficult

to solve the nation's economic problems and maintain law and order. The fear of Communism also created support for the Nazis. By fighting socialists and Communists, Hitler and the Nazis won the support of the industrialists and landowners. From these wealthy and influential people, Hitler secured the funds for his military forces and jobs for his followers. All of these factors contributed to the rise of Nazism in Germany.

WRONG CHOICES EXPLAINED:

(1) The chart indicates that Germany did not enjoy global prosperity and trade. The chart indicates that Germany suffered severe economic problems.

(2) The chart shows that the Weimar Republic was a weak government and could not deal with the political problems of the nation.

(4) The information in the chart shows that Germany did not expand, but lost its colonial empire.

33. **4** This statement expresses concern about the dangers of the Cold War. The Cold War was a period of tension and hostility between the United States and the Soviet Union that began after the end of World War II in 1945 and ended with the collapse of the Soviet Union in 1991. The Cold War triggered an arms race, with both sides producing huge arsenals of nuclear weapons. In this passage, Robert Oppenheimer, an American physicist, who was responsible for the development of the atomic bomb and is considered the father of the atomic bomb, believed nuclear war could destroy both sides. He argued for international control of nuclear weapons to avert nuclear war between the United States and the Soviet Union. However, neither side wanted to stop. The Soviet Union and the United States each claimed they wanted the power to deter the other from launching nuclear weapons. The Cold War created a nuclear balance of terror.

WRONG CHOICES EXPLAINED:

(1), (2), and (3) None of these choices are described in the passage. There is no reference to a threat to the environment, differences between command and market economies, or the economic costs of World War II.

34. **4** The main idea of this 1941 cartoon is that Japan, Italy, and Germany were committed to aggression. Aggression is the forceful action taken by nations to secure territorial gains. The cartoon represents the Rome-Berlin-Tokyo Axis, which was formed in 1940. These three countries agreed not to stop one another from making foreign conquests. Throughout the 1930s, Japan, Italy, and Germany took aggressive actions to pursue their goal for empires. They scorned peace and glorified war. In 1931, Japanese military leaders seized Manchuria in pursuit of their goal for empires. When the League of Nations condemned the aggression, Japan withdrew from the organization. Japan's easy success strengthened the militarists within the government. In 1937, Japanese armies overran much of eastern China. Once again, Western protests had no effect. In 1935, Italy invaded the African

country of Ethiopia. The Ethiopian emperor, Haile Selassie, appealed to the League of Nations for help. Although the League condemned the attack, its members did nothing. Britain continued to let Italian troops and supplies pass through the British-controlled Suez Canal. Britain and France hoped to keep peace in Europe by giving in to Mussolini in Africa. In 1936, Hitler marched into the Rhineland. The Treaty of Versailles had required Germany to remove troops from this region. The Rhineland was a 30-mile-wide zone on either side of the Rhine River and formed a buffer zone between Germany and France. It was also an industrial area. The French were unwilling to risk war, and the British urged peace. In 1938, Hitler made Austria part of the German Reich. In September 1938, Hitler demanded that the Sudetenland—a region in Czechoslovakia bordering on Germany and inhabited by about three million German-speaking people—be given to Germany. The Czech government, a democracy under President Edward Benes, refused to yield. They asked for help from France. The Munich Conference held on September 29, 1938, tried to resolve the problem. Officials from Germany, France, Britain, and Italy attended, but the Czechs were not invited. British Prime Minister Neville Chamberlain believed that he could preserve peace by giving in to Hitler's demands. The Western democracies agreed that Germany would seize control of the Sudetenland, and within six months of the Munich meetings, Hitler's troops took over the rest of Czechoslovakia and Mussolini seized Albania. In August 1939, England and France refused to give in to Hitler's demand that Poland return the former German port of Danzig. On September 1, 1939, Hitler invaded Poland. Two days later, Britain and France honored their guarantee to Poland and declared war on Germany. World War II had started. By the beginning of 1941, Germany dominated all of Western Europe except Great Britain. Italy had extended control in the Mediterranean, and the Japanese Empire included the Philippines and the British colonies of Burma, Hong Kong, and Malaya, and had taken control of French Indochina.

WRONG CHOICES EXPLAINED:

(1) This alliance was formed as an alliance of aggression, not peace.

(2) and (3) Neither of these ideas is contained in the cartoon.

35. **2** At the end of World War II, a primary reason for the division of the Indian subcontinent into the nations of India and Pakistan was that religious differences had led to conflicts between Hindus and Muslims. Hinduism is the major religion of India. The Muslims, a distinct minority, had invaded India in 700 and by 1200 had established a Muslim empire in northern India. However, unlike other invaders, the Muslims had never been absorbed into Hindu society. The difference between the two religions was too great. The Hindus believe in many gods. Islam is based on the belief in one God. Islam teaches that all Muslims are equal before God. Hinduism supports a caste system. Muslims were always a small percentage of the population. For example, in 1940, there were approximately 350 million Hindus

and about 100 million Muslims. Initially, the Muslims and Hindus cooperated in their campaign for independence from Great Britain. However, Muslims grew distrustful of the Indian National Congress, which had been formed in 1885 to promote independence, because the organization was mostly Hindu. In 1906, the Muslim League was set up in India to protect Muslim interests. The leader of the Muslim League, Muhammad Ali Jinnah, insisted that the Muslims resign from the National Congress Party. The Muslim League said that they would never accept India's independence if it meant rule by the Hindu-dominated Congress Party. At their Lahore Conference in 1940, the Muslim League first officially proposed the partition of India into separate Hindu and Muslim nations. Most Muslims lived in the northwest and northeast of the subcontinent. When World War II ended, the British realized that they could no longer keep India. As independence approached, widespread rioting broke out between Hindus and Muslims in Calcutta, East Bengal, Bihar, and Bombay. In August 1946, four days of rioting left more than 5,000 people dead and 15,000 hurt. In 1947, the British parliament passed the Indian Independence Act. This act ended British rule in India but also provided for the partition or subdivision of the Indian subcontinent into two separate, independent nations. One nation was the Hindu-dominated India and the other was Pakistan, with a Muslim majority. Muhammad Ali Jinnah became governor general of Pakistan. This partition led to an explosion of violence between Muslims and Hindus. Although India and Pakistan had promised each other religious tolerance, distrust and fear were deep rooted. Close to one million died in the fighting. To escape death, millions of Muslims fled India to Pakistan and millions of Hindus left Pakistan. An estimated 15 million people took part in this mass migration that led to the establishment of separate states for the Hindus and Muslims. The inability of the British to resolve these differences led to the creation of these nations.

WRONG CHOICES EXPLAINED:

(1) India adapted a policy of nonalignment in dealing with the United States and the Soviet Union during the Cold War. Under this policy, India would not support either the United States or Russia. Nonalignment was never designed to deal with issues of religious differences between Muslims and Hindus.

(3) Most of India's valuable resources are in the north, not the south. Northern India is rich in coal as well as limestone, manganese, and copper.

(4) The British India Muslim minority never controlled a majority of India's banking industry. The Hindu majority dominated the economy of India.

36. **4** A conclusion that is best supported by the information provided on this graph is that most of the world's largest petroleum reserves are in the Middle East. The top five world petroleum reserves are in the Middle Eastern countries of Saudi Arabia (25.9 million), Iraq (11.1 million), United Arab Emirates (9.6 million), Kuwait (9.5 million), and Iran (8.8 million).

Venezuela, which has 7.5 million reserves of oil, is a Latin American country, and Russia, which has a reserve of 4.8 million, is a European country. The combined reserves of Venezuela, Russia, Libya, Mexico, China, Nigeria, the United States, and Norway do not equal the total reserves of Saudi Arabia.

WRONG CHOICES EXPLAINED:

(1), (2), and (3) None of these conclusions can be supported by the information provided on this graph.

37. **4** This cartoon suggests about the introduction of the euro in Europe that economic barriers between nations decreased. The European Union was established in 1992 by the Maastricht Treaty. The goal of the European Union has been to end all tariff barriers and ensure the free movement of goods among member nations. There are 25 EU members consisting of Western European nations and former Russian satellites. The euro is the European Union's single currency. It became the official currency of EU members in 2002. The following 12 member states use the euro: Belgium, Germany, Spain, France, Ireland, Italy, Luxembourg, the Netherlands, Austria, Portugal, Finland, and Greece. Other EU members, England, Sweden, and Denmark, did not replace their currencies. However, these three members along with the rest of the world do accept euros. The ability of these nations to trade freely has enabled the European Union to have the largest gross domestic product in the world. The euro Monetary Union is a single market in which people, goods, services, and capital move with minimal restrictions. Their goal is to create the framework for economic growth and stability.

WRONG CHOICES EXPLAINED:

(1) The cartoon does not suggest that the use of the euro led to the creation of additional countries.

(2) The cartoon suggests that there was greater interdependence rather than isolation among nations.

(3) There is no data to support the idea that Communist policies were adopted after the introduction of the euro. Since the collapse of Communism in 1991, Russia and her former satellite countries have turned to capitalism.

38. **3** The Four Modernizations of Deng Xiaoping in the 1970s and 1980s resulted in a move toward increased capitalism. In 1976, Deng Xiaoping, the Communist leader of China, introduced the Four Modernizations, a program that advanced technology, agriculture, industry, and defense. Under this plan, the government set up special enterprise zones where foreigners could own and operate businesses. Citizens also were allowed to set up small businesses. In agriculture, the responsibility system replaced the commune. Peasant families were allotted plots of farmland. The government took a share of their crops, but the family could sell the rest on the free market. Deng reforms brought a surge of growth and a better standard of living for some Chinese.

WRONG CHOICES EXPLAINED:

(1) The Four Modernizations did not emphasize the Five Relationships. They focused on economic reforms, not the ideas contained in the Five Relationships.

(2) Deng did not return to Maoist revolutionary principles. Deng was a practical reformer who was interested in improving industrial output, not revolutionary principles.

(4) The Four Modernizations did not result in the end of the Communist system of government. Deng's program was designed to improve the economy and to keep the Communist system of strict political control in China.

39. **2** One way in which Ho Chi Minh, Fidel Castro, and Kim Jong Il are similar is that each used Marxist political principles. Karl Marx wrote the *Communist Manifesto* in 1848, outlining the abuses of capitalism and predicting the inevitability of Communism because of the laws of history. Marx believed that the workers of the world would unite in a worldwide revolution that would lead to the overthrow of the capitalist system. Marx's ideas inspired the leaders of Vietnam, Cuba, and North Korea in their struggle against capitalist countries.

Ho Chi Minh (1890–1969) was a nationalist and Communist leader who sought independence for Vietnam. He fought against French colonialism in Vietnam. Ho Chi Minh (which means "He Who Enlightens") turned to the Communists for help in his struggle. During the 1930s, his Indo-Chinese Communist Party led revolts and strikes against the French, who jailed Vietnamese protesters and sentenced Ho, the party leader, to death. Ho fled his death sentence and continued to lead the nationalist movement from exile. He returned to Vietnam in 1941, a year after the Japanese seized control of the country. He and other nationalists founded the Viet Minh (Independence League). The Japanese left in 1945, but the French wanted to retain their former colony. However, in 1945, Ho announced Vietnam's independence from the French. He joined together with Vietnamese nationalists and Communists to fight the French. After the French were defeated in 1954, he continued his struggle against the United States, which wanted to prevent the Communists from taking over South Vietnam. In 1975, the Communist forces took over Saigon, the capital of South Vietnam, and renamed it Ho Chi Minh City. Vietnam was finally united.

Fidel Castro, who was born in 1927, was the son of a wealthy Spanish Cuban farmer. In 1959, Fidel Castro overthrew the dictatorship of Fulgencia Batista and seized power in Cuba. Throughout the 1950s, the United States had supported the unpopular dictator Batista. Castro denounced the United States as imperialist, forbade elections, and nationalized American investments in Cuba without compensation. In 1961, Castro proclaimed his intention to transform Cuba into a Communist state. He also established close ties with the Soviet Union, which had established a Communist government in Russia in 1917. The close ties between Cuba and the Soviet Union ended in 1991 with the collapse of the Soviet Union. Castro's government is one of the last

Communist governments in the world. The aging Castro has refused to change his Communist system of government or give up power after 48 years in office.

Kim Jong Il is the Soviet-born leader of North Korea. He succeeded his father, Kim Il-Sung, founder of North Korea, who died in 1994. Even when the Soviet and Chinese allies undertook economic reforms, North Korea clung to hard-line Communism. Under Kim Jong Il, the "Dear Leader," the North Korean economy is one of the world's most centrally planned and isolated economies. Failed government policies and terrible floods destroyed harvests, bringing widespread hunger. Massive international food deliveries have allowed the regime to escape mass starvation since 1995–96. Kim has held on to power despite the misery and famine. Kim has also been criticized by world governments for human rights violations. Kim Jong Il is considered one of the most repressive rulers in the world. He personally directs every aspect of the state, even minor details such as the size of party leaders' homes and the delivery of gifts to his subordinates.

WRONG CHOICES EXPLAINED:

(1) All of these leaders have established dictatorships and rejected the principle of democratic governments.

(3) None of these leaders overthrew a ruling monarch. Kings ruled none of these countries in the 20th century. These leaders overthrew corrupt dictators or inept leaders.

(4) None of these leaders promoted Confucian principles that emphasized tradition, obedience, and respect for education and the family. Communism established the supremacy of the state over anyone in society.

40. **1** In the late 20th century, the Green Revolution had the greatest effect on grain production in India. The *Green Revolution* is the term used to describe the worldwide transformation of agriculture that led to a significant increase in agricultural production between the 1940s and 1960s. This transformation occurred as a result of programs of agricultural research and development. The term *Green Revolution* is applied to successful agricultural experiments in many Third World countries. It was most successful in India. In the 1960s, the Indian government began its Green Revolution program of plant breeding, irrigation, development, and financing of agrochemicals. India developed new strains of high-yield seeds, mainly wheat and rice. The Green Revolution resulted in a record grain output of 131 million tons in 1978–79. By 1987, India was producing 150 million tons. This established India as one of the world's biggest agricultural producers. By the 1980s, India had become an exporter of food grains. The Green Revolution helped India keep pace with its population growth.

WRONG CHOICES EXPLAINED:

(2) The Green Revolution did not affect political freedom in Russia. The Green Revolution was designed to improve agricultural production, not political freedom.

(3) The Green Revolution did not influence economic reforms in Cuba. Since the 1960s, the Communist government of Fidel Castro has not been successful in improving agricultural production in Cuba. The Green Revolution was used primarily in Third World countries in Asia and Africa.

(4) Traditional customs in Japan were not greatly affected by the Green Revolution. The Meiji Restoration of the late 19th century and the Japanese economic miracle after World War II affected traditional customs of Japan.

41. **4** Mercantilism is a policy portrayed in this illustration. During the 16th to 18th century, European monarchs supported mercantilism as a way of strengthening their national economies in the quest for trade and empires. Mercantilists believed that the wealth of a nation was measured by its supply of gold and silver and that the nations had to maintain a favorable balance of trade by exporting more goods than they imported. Colonies existed for the benefit of the mother country. They provided the raw materials not available in Europe and enriched the mother country by serving as markets for manufactured goods. European nations passed strict navigation laws to ensure that colonies traded only with the mother country.

WRONG CHOICES EXPLAINED:

(1) Nonalignment, which some Third World nations followed during the Cold War, is the policy of not supporting either the United States or the Soviet Union.

(2) Laissez-faire capitalism is an economic policy that supports the belief that there should be a "hands-off" or limited government involvement with private business.

(3) *Perestroika* was the term used to describe Mikhail Gorbachev's effort to reform the Russian economy in the 1980s. The goal was to promote private enterprise instead of a strict government-planned economy.

42. **1** The main idea of this cartoon is that the original causes of apartheid have not been eliminated. Apartheid was the official policy of strict segregation of the races practiced in South Africa. This policy was instituted in 1948. International pressure and the leadership of Nelson Mandela led to the repeal of apartheid in 1990. In 1994, the people chose Nelson Mandela as the first black South African president. The present leader of South Africa is Thabo Mbeki, who succeeded Mandela as president in December 1997 and was reelected for a second term in April 2004. The cartoon points out that nearly 13 years after the end of apartheid, South Africa is still not getting to the roots of its social problems. Leaders in government, businesses, and civil society still do not understand the problems created by the years of apartheid. South Africa has one of the highest rates of income inequality in the world. The white South African minority still tends to be considerably wealthier than the rest of the population. The country's majority black population still has a substantial number of rural inhabitants who lead largely impoverished lives. The unemployment rate of 36 to 42 percent in South

Africa is one of the highest in the world and is highest among black Africans. President Mbeki has sought to improve conditions, but problems continue to persist. Although the country made a remarkable peace transition to democracy, the majority of people continue to live in poverty and mass unemployment. Both urban and rural poor lack basic services, suffer from AIDS, and endure unacceptable levels of crime and violence.

WRONG CHOICES EXPLAINED:

(2), (3), and (4) None of these ideas are contained in the cartoon.

43. **2** Ethnic cleansing in Bosnia, the killing fields of Cambodia (Kampuchea), and the dirty war in Argentina are all examples of human rights violations. Human rights, such as freedom of expression, life, and liberty, are those freedoms that all people are entitled to as members of society.

The breaking up of Yugoslavia in 1991 and 1992 sparked ethnic violence in Bosnia among Serbs, Croatians, and Muslims. Slobodan Milosevic, the Yugoslav president, who was Serbian, began a policy of ethnic cleansing to destroy all non-Serbs. The Serbs dominated Yugoslavia. Milosevic forcibly removed other ethnic groups from the areas that Serbia controlled. Hundreds of thousands of Bosnians became refugees living on food sent by the United Nations and charities. Others were brutalized or killed. Milosevic also waged a brutal campaign of ethnic cleansing against Muslim Kosovans. In November 1990, NATO forces started a military campaign against Yugoslavia. Milosevic was forced to retreat and was ousted from power. The International Court of Justice at The Hague put him on trial, but he died of a heart attack after five years in prison in 2006.

In 1975, the Khmer Rouge led by Pol Pot took control of Cambodia. He instituted a reign of terror and tried to drive out all Western influence. From 1975 to 1979, he tried to establish a purely agrarian society. Pol Pot forced people out of the cities and resettled them in the country. It is estimated that 1.5 to 1.7 million Cambodians, or nearly one-third of the population, died from forced labor, starvation, or execution in the killing fields. In 1979, he fled into the jungles of Cambodia after an invasion by Vietnam, which led to the collapse of the Khmer Rouge government. Pol Pot was never brought to justice and died of natural causes in 1998 under house arrest.

The "dirty war" (1976–83) was a seven-year campaign by the Argentine government against suspected dissidents and subversives. Many people, both opponents of the government as well as innocent people, "disappeared" in the middle of the night. They were taken to secret government detention centers where they were tortured and eventually killed. These people are known as *los desaparecidos* or "the disappeared." After the death of the controversial president Juan Peron in 1974, his wife and vice president, Isabel Peron, assumed power. However, she was not very strong politically, and a military junta led a coup against her and removed her from office. This military junta maintained its grip on power by cracking down on anybody whom they believed was challenging their authority. Casualty counts from this war range from 10,000 to 30,000 people. Although the military dictatorship carried out its war against suspected domestic subversives throughout its entire existence, it was ironically a foreign foe that brought the regime to an end. In the early 1980s, it became clear to both the world and the Argentine people that the government was behind the tens of thousands of kidnappings. The junta, facing increasing opposition over its human rights record, as well as mounting allegations of corruption and its defeat by the British in the war over the Falkland Islands, was forced to restore basic civil liberties. The dirty war ended when Raul Alfonsin's civilian government took control of the country on December 10, 1983.

WRONG CHOICES EXPLAINED:

(1) These events were not nationalist revolts. Ethnic cleansing, the killing fields, and the dirty war were efforts by these groups to deprive people of their basic rights.

(3) None of these actions are examples of international terrorism. These groups did not seek to promote force or violence in other countries. They sought to use organized force to promote their control in their respective region or country.

(4) Not all of these events are examples of religious conflicts. In Cambodia, the issue was on establishing an agrarian society and the dirty war in Argentina was designed to protect the military leaders. It was only in Bosnia that religious differences contributed to conflict. Ethnic cleansing led to the forcible removal of Muslims by Christian Serbs.

44. **1** Studying the architectural features of the Parthenon, Notre Dame cathedral, and the Taj Mahal provides information about the beliefs and values of a given culture.

During the golden age of Greece, which developed in the 5th century B.C., Athenian culture reached new heights. Through the efforts of Pericles, a leading Athenian statesman, Athens became the cultural center of Greece. Architects built the Parthenon, which reflected a belief in the beauty and order of the universe. The Parthenon is regarded as an enduring symbol of ancient Greece and Athenian democracy.

In the Middle Ages, when the Catholic Church was the dominant institution in society, medieval people expressed their intensely religious spirit by constructing awe-inspiring cathedrals. The Cathedral of Notre Dame in Paris, built in the 12th century, is considered one of the finest examples of Gothic architecture. A key feature of Gothic architecture was the flying buttresses, or stone supports outside the church. These supports allowed builders to construct higher walls and leave space for stained-glass windows. The new Gothic churches soared to incredible heights. Their tall spires, lofty ceilings, and enormous windows carried the eye upward to the heavens. Many medieval people believed that Gothic architecture allowed the brilliance of God's sunlight to shine in churches and enlighten the faithful. Cities all over Europe competed to build grander, taller cathedrals. Notre Dame and other Gothic cathedrals, such as Westminster Abbey in London, were built to pay tribute to the greater glory of God.

The Taj Mahal is a mausoleum in Agra, India. The Mughal emperor Shah Jahan commissioned it as a mausoleum for his favorite wife, Mumtaz Mahal. Overcome with grief after her death at the age of 39, he ordered the white marble to be as beautiful as she was. Construction began in 1632, and more than 20,000 artisans worked on the monument before it was completed in 1648. The Taj Mahal is generally considered the finest example of Mughal architecture, a style that combines elements of Persian, Turkish, Indian, and Islamic architectural styles. Although the white-domed marble mausoleum is the most familiar part of the monument, the Taj Mahal is actually an integrated complex of structures. The Taj Mahal stands as the greatest monument of the Mughal empire.

WRONG CHOICES EXPLAINED:

(2) All of these buildings provide information about the culture and not climatic changes in an area.

(3) All of these buildings were constructed centuries before the use of 19th-century technology.

(4) Confucianism did not influence the architectural features of any of these buildings. The Parthenon was built to honor the goddess Athena. Notre Dame reflected the ideas of Catholicism. The Taj Mahal was a memorial to the emperor's wife.

45. **3** The geographic factor that had the most influence on the development of the Inca society and Japanese society was mountainous topography. The mountain ranges of the Andes in Peru and the rough terrain of Japan limited the amount of arable lands for farming to coastal plains and river valleys. The Incas and Japanese use terrace farming to adapt to the surrounding geography. Terrace farming is a method of growing crops on the side of hills or mountains by planting on graduated terraces built into the slopes. Peru's coastal valleys are almost rainless, but where enough water came down their rivers, the Incan farmers used every inch of available land for cultivation, including the river delta near the sea and the narrow plains leading to the Andes Mountains. Villages were built where they would not intrude on the cropland. Farmers usually raised two crops a year. This degree of production was possible because of the network of irrigation canals that the Incas developed more than 2,000 years ago. More than four-fifths of Japan is mountainous, and the Japanese have developed intensive farming methods to ensure that they use every available piece of land. They have drained marshes, swamps, and deltas and carved terraces into the steep hillside to help make use of their limited farmlands. In much of Japan, farmers harvest two crops a year. Like the Incas, the Japanese developed an irrigation system that flooded the rice paddies with water to ensure increased food production.

WRONG CHOICES EXPLAINED:

(1) Frequent monsoons are not an important geographic factor that influenced Inca and Japanese society. India and Southeast Asian countries are most affected by monsoons.

(2) There were no large deserts that influenced Inca and Japanese society. The Japanese, like the Incas of Peru, are mostly influenced by large mountain ranges.

(4) Neither of these societies is in a tropical climate area.

46. **2** The French Revolution (1789) resulted from the division of society shown in this diagram. From the Middle Ages to just before the French Revolution, the people of France were divided into three estates based mainly on their social class. The clergy of the Catholic Church represented about 1 percent of the population but owned about 10 to 15 percent of the land. They paid no direct taxes to the government. The clergy of the First Estate included bishops and abbots but not the parish priests. The Second Estate included the titled nobility and landowners in France. They represented less than 2 percent of the population but owned about 20 percent of the land. They were also exempt from taxes. The Third Estate was composed of the middle class, urban city workers, and peasant farmers who made up 97 percent of the population but owned only about 60 to 70 percent of the land. The majority of the Third Estate were the peasants who lived on the land. The bulk of the taxes fell on the Third Estate. These inequalities among the three classes created the dissatisfaction that contributed to the French Revolution.

WRONG CHOICES EXPLAINED:

(1), (3), and (4) None of these revolutions resulted from the division of society as shown in the diagram. The diagram describes the social division of French society in 1789. There are no references to conditions in England at the time of the Puritan Revolution in 1642 or social divisions in either Mexico in 1910 or Russia in 1917.

47. **2** The golden ages of the Roman, Byzantine, and Ottoman empires can be attributed in part to stable governments.

The Roman Empire existed from 27 B.C. until its fall in the west in 476 A.D. At its height in 117 A.D., the empire extended over three continents. For more than 200 of these years, Roman military might helped to keep the *Pax Romana*, or Roman Peace. This period of peace and stability contributed to Rome's golden age in art and science. The stability of the empire enabled Rome to construct military roads, aqueducts, and bridges still in use today. The famous amphitheater, the Coliseum, was built during this period of peace and prosperity. Roman writers, like Cicero and Virgil, also produced famous works of literature that are still read today.

Although the Roman Empire fell in the west in 476 A.D., the Eastern Empire survived and became known as the Byzantine Empire. The Roman Empire had been divided since the late 200s A.D. As German invaders weakened the western half, power shifted to the east. By 300, the emperor Constantine had built a new capital on the site of the Greek city of Byzantium, which he renamed Constantinople. The Byzantine Empire, as it came to be called, drew its name from the ancient site of the Greek colony of Byzantium. The extent of the Byzantine Empire varied over the centuries but at its core remained the Balkan Peninsula and Asia Minor. The empire collapsed when Constantinople fell to the Ottoman Turks in 1453. The Byzantine Empire blended Greek, Roman, and Christian influences and produced art and architecture that have lasted through the centuries. During the rule of Emperor Justinian (527–565), the Byzantine Empire was at its peak. Justinian organized the ancient laws of Rome. His collection became the body of civil law known today as the Justinian Code. The Justinian Code has influenced the legal system of Western Europe as well as the United States. During Justinian's golden age, the famous church of Santa Sophia was erected, a noteworthy example of Byzantine architecture and art.

In 1453, the Ottoman Turks captured Constantinople and overthrew the Byzantine Empire. Over the next 200 years, backed by military advances, the Ottomans built a large and powerful empire in Europe and the Middle East. Although the Ottoman Empire survived into the 20th century, it began to decline by the middle of the 17th century. The golden age of the Ottoman Empire was during the reign of Suleiman the Magnificent, who ruled from 1520 to 1566. He improved the government and the system of justice in his empire. Art also blossomed under Suleiman. Ottoman poets adapted Persian and Arab models to produce works in their own Turkish language. The royal architect, Sinan, designed hundreds of mosques and palaces. He compared his most famous building, the Selimiye Mosque at Edirne, to the greatest church of the Byzantine Empire.

All of these empires experienced golden ages because the stability of their government provided an environment of peace and progress.

WRONG CHOICES EXPLAINED:

(1) These empires experienced a golden age because they rejected cultural isolation and wanted contact with the world.

(3) Command economies are associated with totalitarian government. Absolute monarchs ruled these empires, and they allowed individuals to grow food for their own benefit.

(4) These empires did have distinct social classes during their golden ages. However, the lower classes never contributed to the arts, science, and literature during this period. Strong, stable governments led by powerful rulers made these golden eras possible.

48. **1** One way in which Simón Bolívar, Jomo Kenyatta, and Mohandas Gandhi are similar is that each led a nationalist movement.

Simón Bolívar was a Latin American revolutionary leader who earned the title "the Liberator" for his role in the struggle for independence from Spanish domination. By 1824, he had liberated his native Venezuela, as well as Colombia, Peru, Ecuador, and Bolivia, from Spanish rule. Bolívar tried to combine Enlightenment political ideas of the French Revolution, ideas from Greece and Rome, and his own original thinking. The result was a system of democratic ideas that influenced revolutions in Latin America. Simón Bolívar sought to incorporate these democratic ideals into the government of Venezuela.

Jomo Kenyatta was the nationalist leader of Kenya. After World War II, Kenyatta, who had been educated and living in England, became a spokesman for Kenya's independence. In 1947, Kenyatta was chosen as the leader of the Kenyan African Union, a political movement for independence. Other Africans formed a group that the Europeans called the Mau Mau. This secret group was made up of Kikuyu farmers who were forced out of the highlands by the British, who had passed laws to ensure their own domination. The goal of the Mau Mau was to force the British off the land. They began to carry out attacks against European settlers, such as burning farms and destroying livestock. Kenyatta, who was Kikuyu, had no connection to the Mau Mau but refused to condemn these actions. The British took military action against the movement and jailed Kenyatta, whom they accused of leading the movement. More than 10,000 black Kenyans and 100 white Kenyans were killed during the struggle for independence. In 1963, Britain granted Kenya its independence. Kenyatta was elected the first prime minister, and he held office until his death in 1978. He worked hard to unite all the different ethnic and language groups in the country.

Mohandas Gandhi became the leader of the Indian nationalist movement that wanted independence from Great Britain. Gandhi was a pacifist who believed in the principle of *satyagraha*, which in English is called "passive resistance" or "civil disobedience." Gandhi believed that one perfect civil resister was enough to win the battle of right and wrong. Gandhi launched his campaign of nonviolent civil disobedience to weaken the British government and its economic power in India. One effective method of protest was the boycott in which Indians refused to buy British cloth and other manufactured goods. Gandhi urged Indians to begin spinning their own cloth and used the spinning wheel as a symbol of his rejection of Western civilization. He also called on the people to refuse to attend government schools, pay taxes, and vote in elections. Gandhi used these nonviolent methods to show the British the futility of denying India its freedom. India did not achieve its independence until 1947, shortly before Gandhi's assassination on January 30, 1948.

WRONG CHOICES EXPLAINED:

(2) Gandhi was the only one of these leaders who used nonviolent tactics. Bolívar and Kenyatta used military means to achieve their goals.

(3) All of these men opposed imperialism. They rejected the idea that a foreign country should dominate their nations.

(4) Simón Bolívar believed in democracy. He died in 1830, 18 years before the *Communist Manifesto* was published in England. Neither Kenyatta nor Gandhi opposed Communism. Kenyatta visited Russia in the 1930s and

sympathized with the ideals of Communism. Gandhi was an advocate for socialism and Communism. However, he rejected class war as incompatible with nonviolence.

49. **1** The factor that most hindered the efforts of both Napoleon and Hitler to conquer Russia was the climate.

The severe winters combined with the large size of Russia contributed to Napoleon's defeat. In June 1812, Napoleon decided to invade Russia when Czar Alexander I withdrew from the Continental System that forbade European countries to trade with England. Alexander I refused to stop selling grain to Britain. Leading a huge army of 600,000 men, Napoleon marched into Russia. Czar Alexander pulled back his troops and refused to be trapped in a battle, causing Napoleon to overextend his supply lines. As the Russians retreated, they adapted a scorched-earth policy of burning crops and villages. Desperate soldiers deserted the French army to search for scraps of food. When Napoleon captured Moscow in September, he found the city in ashes: Russian patriots had probably destroyed most of the city. By October, when the czar did not make a peace offer, Napoleon was too late to advance and perhaps too late even to retreat. He could not feed and supply his troops through the long Russian winter and ordered his starving army to retreat. The 1,000-mile retreat from Moscow turned into a desperate battle. Russian raiders attacked Napoleon's ragged army. Soldiers staggered through the snow and dropped in their tracks as the temperatures fell to 35 degrees below zero. A French soldier noted that many of the soldiers were walking barefoot, using pieces of wood as canes, but that their feet were frozen so hard, they sounded like wooden clogs. By the middle of December, when the last survivors crossed the border out of Russia, Napoleon had lost three-fourths of his army. The 1,000-mile retreat from Moscow was a disaster and Napoleon's first great military defeat.

In June 1941, Hitler launched a major attack against Russia called Operation Barbarossa, which was named after the German king who had participated in the First Crusade during the 11th century. By October 1941, Hitler's army of more than 3 million men had surrounded Leningrad in the north, which was within 25 miles of Moscow. Russia did not collapse. The German invaders were not prepared for the cold Russian winter. Germans, in summer uniform, froze to death as the temperature plummeted to 20 degrees below zero. Their fuel and oil froze as trucks and weapons became useless. The Russians fought valiantly at the siege of Leningrad, which lasted 90 days. More than 1.5 million citizens died during this siege, and some inhabitants even resorted to cannibalism. Hitler then turned south to try to take Stalingrad. Russian troops and a freezing winter caused the German invaders to surrender. The Germans lost more than 300,000 men. After the Battle of Stalingrad in 1943, the Russian army slowly began to drive the Germans out of the Soviet Union.

The harsh Russian winters contributed to the failure of both Napoleon and Hitler to conquer Russia.

WRONG CHOICES EXPLAINED:

(2), (3), and (4) None of these factors hindered the efforts of Napoleon and Hitler to conquer Russia. Russia did not have any large fortifications to prevent Napoleon and Hitler's advances through the country. Neither Napoleon nor Hitler had advanced technology that could be used effectively in Russia. The Russian invasion was a land exercise, and a lack of ports did not influence any military planning by either Napoleon or Hitler.

50. **3** One way in which the Sepoy Mutiny in India, the Zulu resistance in southern Africa, and the Boxer Rebellion in China are similar is that each resulted from native reaction to foreign interference in the region.

The Sepoys were Indian soldiers serving under British command. These soldiers were protesting the policies of the British East India Company. The British cartridges used by the Sepoys had to be bitten to remove the seal before they could be inserted into their guns. The coverings were greased with pork and beef fat. In 1857, the Sepoy soldiers refused to accept these cartridges. Both Hindus, who considered the cow sacred, and Muslims, who did not eat pork, were angry. The Sepoy Mutiny (Rebellion) lasted more than a year. The British government sent troops to help the British East India Company. This was a turning point in Indian history. After 1858, the British government took direct control of India. Eventually, the British began educating and training Indians for a role in their own Indian government.

The Zulus had migrated into southern Africa in the 1500s. In the early 1800s, they emerged as a major force under Shaka. He built a powerful empire northeast of the Orange River. Shaka's war disrupted life across southern Africa. Groups defeated by the Zulus fled to safety, forcing others in their paths to move on. While the Zulus were moving southward, the Boers, Dutch farmers, were moving northward from the tip of South Africa. The Dutch had settled at Cape Town in 1652. In the early 1800s, the Cape Colony passed from the Dutch to the British. Many Boers resented British laws that abolished slavery and interfered in their way of life. To escape British rule, the Boers retreated on the "Great Trek" northward. The Boers set up two independent states in the 1850s, the Orange Free States and the Transvaal inlands, which the Zulus had recently conquered. Battles between the Zulus and Boers for control of the area continued for decades. Finally, the British joined the struggle and the superior firearms of the Europeans enabled them to win key battles. The Zulu land became a part of British-"controlled land in 1857.

The Boxers were a secret society formed in 1899. Their goal was to drive out the foreigners who were destroying China with their Western technology. In 1900, the Boxers attacked foreign communities in China as well as foreign embassies in Beijing. In response, Western owners and Japan formed a multinational force of 25,000 troops. They crushed the Boxers and rescued the foreigners besieged in Beijing.

All of these rebellions were nationalist attacks against Western imperialism.

WRONG CHOICES EXPLAINED:

(1) None of these rebellions resulted from government policies of ethnic cleansing. The Sepoy Mutiny, Zulu resistance, and Boxer Rebellion were designed to prevent foreign countries from destroying either the culture or the territorial integrity of their areas.

(2) None of these rebellions resulted from attempts by democratic forces to overthrow the monarchy. These events resulted from Western nations' efforts to control these countries.

(4) Government denial to fertile farmland did not contribute to any of these rebellions. The failure of Western nations to respect the political and cultural heritage of these groups led to these rebellions or resistance movements.

THEMATIC ESSAY: GENERIC SCORING RUBRIC

Score of 5:
- Shows a thorough understanding of the theme or problem
- Addresses all aspects of the task
- Shows an ability to analyze, evaluate, compare and/or contrast issues and events
- Richly supports the theme or problem with relevant facts, examples, and details
- Is a well-developed essay, consistently demonstrating a logical and clear plan of organization
- Introduces the theme or problem by establishing a framework that is beyond a simple restatement of the task and concludes with a summation of the theme or problem

Score of 4:
- Shows a good understanding of the theme or problem
- Addresses all aspects of the task
- Shows an ability to analyze, evaluate, compare and/or contrast issues and events
- Includes relevant facts, examples, and details, but may not support all aspects of the theme or problem evenly
- Is a well-developed essay, demonstrating a logical and clear plan of organization
- Introduces the theme or problem by establishing a framework that is beyond a simple restatement of the task and concludes with a summation of the theme or problem

Score of 3:
- Shows a satisfactory understanding of the theme or problem
- Addresses most aspects of the task or addresses all aspects in a limited way
- Shows an ability to analyze or evaluate issues and events, but not in any depth
- Includes some facts, examples, and details
- Is a satisfactorily developed essay, demonstrating a general plan of organization
- Introduces the theme or problem by repeating the task and concludes by repeating the theme or problem

Score of 2:
- Shows limited understanding of the theme or problem
- Attempts to address the task
- Develops a faulty analysis or evaluation of issues and events
- Includes few facts, examples, and details, and may include information that contains inaccuracies
- Is a poorly organized essay, lacking focus
- Fails to introduce or summarize the theme or problem

Score of 1:
- Shows very limited understanding of the theme or problem
- Lacks an analysis of evaluation of the issues and events
- Includes little or no accurate or relevant facts, examples, or details
- Attempts to complete the task, but demonstrates a major weakness in organization
- Fails to introduce or summarize the theme or problem

Score of 0: Fails to address the task, is illegible, or is a blank paper

PART II: THEMATIC ESSAY QUESTION

Throughout history, political systems have been instrumental in shaping the history and culture of nations and societies. Absolute monarchy in France in the 17th and 18th century and Communism in Russia in the 20th century have had a tremendous effect on the development of these two nations.

As Europe emerged from the Middle Ages, monarchs grew increasingly powerful. The decline of feudalism, the rise of cities, and the growth of national kingdoms provided the foundation for the rise of absolutism or absolute monarchs in Europe in the 17th and 18th century. Absolute monarchs regulated everything from religious worship to social gatherings. They created new government bureaucracies to control their countries' economic lives. Their goal was to free themselves from limitations imposed by the nobility and representative bodies, such as parliament.

In Europe, Louis XIV of France was the epitome of an absolute monarch. Inheriting the throne in 1643 as a five-year-old child, Louis XIV ruled France for 72 years and was one of the most powerful rulers in the nation's history. After the death of Cardinal Mazarin, his closest adviser, in 1661, Louis XIV took control of the government himself. He became his own prime minister and adopted the ideal of the divine right of kings. According to Bishop Jacques Bossuet, one of Louis' advisers, the king was chosen by God to rule, and only God had the authority over the king, not a parliamentary body or a group of nobles. The divine-right theory provided the justification for the absolute sovereignty of Louis and entitled the king to unquestioning obedience. Louis' statement, "L'état, c'est moi" (I am the state), represents his belief that there was no higher authority that could ever control him. Louis took the sun as the symbol of his absolute power. Just as the sun stands at the center of the solar system, so the king stood at the center of the nation.

During his reign, Louis never called a meeting of the Estates-General, the medieval council made up of representatives of all French social classes. The Estates-General did not meet between 1614 and 1789. In addition, Louis weakened the power of the nobles by excluding them from his councils. He expanded the power of government officials, called the intendants, who collected taxes and administered justice. To keep power under his control, Louis made sure that local officials communicated regularly with him.

During Louis XIV's reign, France became a dominant power in Europe. European countries envied France's success in industry and agriculture. Jean Baptiste Colbert (1619–83), Louis' able finance minister, helped revive trade and the economy. Although he did not invent the system of mercantilism, he rigorously applied it to France. To advance prosperity, Colbert promoted good farming methods, internal improvements (roads and canals), support of both old and new industries, and the creation of a strong merchant marine, which enabled France to establish trading posts in North America and Asia. Colbert's goal was to make France self-sufficient by centralizing the economy through government control of trade and industry.

Louis XIV also sought to control religion, believing that more than one religion could not exist and that religious unity was essential for absolute control. In 1685, he revoked the Edict of Nantes, which had granted French Protestants (Huguenots) religious toleration. He destroyed Huguenot schools and churches and took away their civil rights. The Huguenots escaped France and settled in Holland, England, and America. Many of those who fled were craftsmen and businesspeople, and their loss hurt the French economy.

Louis kept France at war for much of the time that he ruled. He pursued an aggressive foreign policy, wanting France to achieve its natural boundaries along the Rhine River. To this end, Louis created a personal army that was employed by the state instead of the nobles. Louis used this highly disciplined army to enforce his policies at home and abroad.

The reign of Louis XIV is considered the golden age of France. French became the language of polite society and replaced Latin as the language of diplomacy and scholarship. Louis, who was referred to as the Grand Monarch, was a strong patron of the arts. He loved the stage and encouraged writers like Moliere, Racine, and Louis De Rouvroy Saint-Simon to pursue their crafts. The French style of classicism and fashion were the models for all of Europe.

Louis XIV's palace at Versailles influenced the architectural style of Europe. It was built 12 miles outside of Paris at a cost of more than $100 million and filled with 1,400 fountains. This palace served as a fundamental tool of state policy under Louis. He was able to control the nobles, who were forced to live at Versailles, and also used the elaborate architecture to impress his subjects and foreign visitors. Versailles became a reflection of French genius. Peter the Great of Russia and Frederick the Great of Prussia would try to model their palaces on the one in Versailles. By the time of Louis' death in 1715, France was the leading nation on the European continent. However, his extravagant lifestyle at Versailles burdened the peasants with taxes, and the long war emptied the treasury, drained the country's manpower, and held back France's economic development. The French monarchy would not survive even a century after his death.

Communism in Russia was a political system that affected the nation's history for 84 years. The father of Communism was Karl Marx, who explained his ideas in the *Communist Manifesto* (1848). Marx claimed that history was a class struggle between the wealthy capitalists of the Industrial Revolution and the working class or proletariat. The injustices of poverty created by the Industrial Revolution would eventually force the workers to overthrow capitalism and create their own society. Then, the proletariat would take control of all the means of production and establish a classless society in which wealth and power would be equally shared. In Russia, Marx's ideas would lead to a Communist dictatorship.

In 1917, Valdimir Lenin, considered the father of Russian Communism, followed the ideas of Marx but adapted them to the Russian situation. For example, Marx had said that urban workers would rise on their own to overthrow the capitalist system. Russia, however, did not have a large urban working class. Lenin suggested that an elite group of reformers, the Bolsheviks, would guide the revolution in Russia. In 1917, Lenin guided the overthrow of the government by the Bolsheviks, now called Communists.

The Bolsheviks distributed land to the peasants and gave workers control of the factories and mines. However, from 1918 to 1921, Lenin faced a civil war with the forces loyal to the czar (king) of Russia for control of the country. By 1922, Lenin and the Communists had gained control of Russia. The Communists then created the Union of the Soviet Socialist Republic, also called the Soviet Union.

After Lenin's death in 1924, Joseph Stalin emerged as a leader of Russia and turned the Soviet Union into a totalitarian state. In this form of government, a one-party dictatorship attempted to regulate every aspect of the lives of its citizens. Stalin used terror and brutality to rule Russia from 1927 to 1953. For example, in the 1930s, fearful that the Communist Party members were plotting against him, Stalin launched the Great Purge. During Stalin's Reign of Terror from 1934 to 1938, he accused thousands of people of crimes against the government. Many of the accused were executed, exiled, or sent to prison camps. It is estimated that Stalin ordered the death of more than 15 million people.

Stalin also exercised control over the economy. He established a command economy in which government officials made all basic economic decisions. In 1928, Stalin introduced his first Five-Year Plan of centralized government to increase industrial and agricultural production to transform the Soviet Union into an industrial giant. Emphasis was placed on heavy industry, whereas consumer goods were neglected. In the 1930s, Soviet production of oil, coal, steel, and military goods increased. Factories, hydroelectric power stations, and railroads were built across the nation.

Despite this progress, most Russians remained poor and endured a low standard of living. Soviet central planning created shortages of consumer goods as well as products of poor quality. Stalin financed his Five-Year Plans by forcing peasants to give up their small farms and live on state-owned farm or collectives, which were large farms owned and operated by peasants or groups. The government controlled prices and farm supplies, and set production quotas. Many peasants resisted collectivization. They killed farm animals, destroyed tools, and burned crops. Stalin crushed all opposition, and the government seized the land of those who resisted and sent farmers to prison labor camps. The results of Stalin's agricultural policies were devastating. Mass starvation resulted in the Ukraine, where opposition to collectivization was especially strong. More than five million people died from starvation.

Although Stalin would transform the Soviet Union into a superpower, the Soviet Union was never able to provide its people and satellite countries in Eastern Europe with the consumer goods and political democracy that existed in Western Europe. In 1985, these conditions allowed Mikhail Gorbachev to introduce changes in Russia that led to the end of Communism.

The political system of absolutism in France and Communism in Russia have affected these countries. The absolutism of Louis XIV succeeded in creating a nation whose cultural and social changes still influence the world today. The legacy of Communism continues to affect Russia in the 21st century.

PART III: DOCUMENT-BASED QUESTIONS

Part A: Short Answers

Document 1

Based on this map, one geographic feature that influenced the location of early centers of civilization was that some civilizations were in river valleys and bodies of water.

Note: This response receives full credit because it correctly identifies from the map a geographic feature influencing the early centers of civilization.

Document 2a

Based on this excerpt by Joanna Slater, one negative effect the lack of rain has had on the economy in India is that the drop in agricultural production will hurt the overall economic growth.

Note: This response receives full credit because it correctly shows the negative effect of the lack of rain on the Indian economy.

Document 2b

Based on this excerpt by Joanna Slater, one positive effect of abundant levels of rain on the economy in India is that monsoon rain helps the expansion of agriculture and gives more money to rural consumers.

Note: This response receives full credit because it specifically cites a positive way in which the abundant level of rain helps the economy of India.

Document 3

Based on this map, one way that coal affected the development of Great Britain between 1750 and 1850 is that the location of new industrial areas near coal fields helped their expansion to the northern part of Great Britain.

Note: This response receives full credit because it cites a way in which coal affected the development of Great Britain between 1750 and 1850.

Document 4

According to Barbara Freese, two effects that coal had on factory workers in the industrial cities of Great Britain during the Industrial Revolution are as follows:

1. Coal provided power for the machines operated by workers.
2. Coal dust tainted the factory workers' clothes, skin, and food.

Note: This response receives full credit because it gives two effects of coal upon the factory workers in the industrial cities of Great Britain during the Industrial Revolution.

Document 5

According to Jacqueline S. Ismael, two ways Kuwait used its oil resources to improve the city of Kuwait are as follows:

1. A number of electric power stations were built.
2. Many public buildings were built, such as hospitals, schools, and health centers.

Note: This response receives full credit because it correctly states two ways Kuwait used its oil resources to improve the city.

Document 6

Based on Michael Ramirez's cartoon, a way in which Iraqi oil contracts influenced the French government in 2003 was that the contracts contributed to its opposition to the war.

Note: This response receives full credit because it cites the way in which the Iraqi oil contracts influenced the French government in 2003.

Document 7

According to Blaine Harden, two ways the sale of diamonds affected Botswana are as follows:

1. It helped raise the standard of living of the people.
2. The money from diamonds was invested in roads, schools, and clinics.

Note: This response receives full credit because it cites two effects of the sale of diamonds upon the country of Botswana.

Document 8

Based on this excerpt from *The Ecologist,* one effect the 1980 discovery of more diamonds has had on the people of Botswana is that, like the Bushmen, the people were relocated or evicted to make way for a diamond mine.

Note: This response receives full credit because it shows how the 1980 discovery of more diamonds has affected the people of Botswana.

DOCUMENT-BASED QUESTION: GENERIC SCORING RUBRIC

Score of 5:

- Thoroughly addresses all aspects of the *Task* by accurately analyzing and interpreting at least **four** documents
- Incorporates information from the documents in the body of the essay
- Incorporates relevant outside information
- Richly supports the theme or problem with relevant facts, examples, and details
- Is a well-developed essay, consistently demonstrating a logical and clear plan of organization
- Introduces the theme or problem by establishing a framework that is beyond a simple restatement of the *Task* or *Historical Context* and concludes with a summation of the theme or problem

Score of 4:

- Addresses all aspects of the *Task* by accurately analyzing and interpreting at least **four** documents
- Incorporates information from the documents in the body of the essay
- Incorporates relevant outside information
- Includes relevant facts, examples, and details, but discussion may be more descriptive than analytical
- Is a well-developed essay, demonstrating a logical and clear plan of organization
- Introduces the theme or problem by establishing a framework that is beyond a simple restatement of the *Task* or *Historical Context* and concludes with a summation of the theme or problem

Score of 3:

- Addresses most aspects of the *Task* or addresses all aspects of the *Task* in a limited way, using some of the documents
- Incorporates some information from the documents in the body of the essay
- Incorporates limited or no relevant outside information
- Includes some facts, examples, and details, but discussion is more descriptive than analytical
- Is a satisfactorily developed essay, demonstrating a general plan of organization
- Introduces the theme or problem by repeating the *Task* or *Historical Context* and concludes by simply repeating the theme or problem

Score of 2:

- Attempts to address some aspects of the *Task*, making limited use of the documents
- Presents no relevant outside information
- Includes few facts, examples, and details; discussion restates contents of the documents

- Is a poorly organized essay, lacking focus
- Fails to introduce or summarize the theme or problem

Score of 1:
- Shows limited understanding of the *Task* with vague, unclear references to the documents
- Presents no relevant outside information
- Includes little or no accurate or relevant facts, details, or examples
- Attempts to complete the *Task*, but demonstrates a major weakness in organization
- Fails to introduce or summarize the theme or problem

Score of 0: Fails to address the *Task*, is illegible, or is a blank paper

Part B: Essay

Throughout global history, a region's or nation's natural resources have influenced its development in both a positive and negative way. Rivers and waters have had an effect on ancient civilizations. Coal influenced Great Britain during the Industrial Revolution. Oil continues to affect the Middle East. Diamonds have shaped the development of Botswana.

The Nile River was at the heart of the Egyptian civilization (Doc. 1). The ancient Greek historian Herodotus called Egypt "the gift of the Nile," because the land would have been a desert without the Nile waters. The yearly flooding soaked the land and deposited layers of silt that kept the land fertile for agriculture. As villages grew along the riverbanks and farmers perfected their skills, they produced more food, allowing the population to grow. As villages prospered, strong leaders united villages into kingdoms. The Egyptian civilization prospered because the Nile served as a trade route and was used as a highway. The yearly flooding of the Nile also forced the Egyptians to develop the first calendar, dividing the year into 365 days, because it was important for them to keep track of the time between floods to plan for the harvest season. Egyptian architects and engineers built magnificent pyramids and temples along the Nile River.

To the north and east of Egypt, the Fertile Crescent, a crescent-shaped region of good farmland created by the Tigris and Euphrates rivers, stretched from the Persian Gulf to the Mediterranean. In this area, great civilizations arose, giving the Fertile Crescent the name "the cradle of civilization" (Doc. 1). In the eastern end of the Fertile Crescent lies Mesopotamia. Social scientists believe that the first civilizations developed along the banks of the Tigris and Euphrates rivers (present-day Iraq). This valley region was called Mesopotamia from the Greek word meaning "the land between the rivers." The Tigris and Euphrates rivers flooded Mesopotamia every year. As the floodwaters receded, it left a thick red, rich, new layer of mud called silt. In this rich new soil, farmers could plant enormous quantities of wheat and barley. The fertile land of the valley attracted farmers from the neighboring regions.

In time, their descendants produced the surplus food needed to support the growing population.

The first civilization in Mesopotamia was Sumer. About 5,000 years ago, villages along the river valley had grown into busy cities. With few natural barriers, the area became the crossroads where people mingled and traded. People gathered to exchange material items as well as ideas. Many archeologists have found goods from as far away as Egypt and India in the rubble of Sumerian cities. Since the rivers allowed for easy transportation, Sumeria became a center of learning. Baghdad was a major center. Sumerians made important contributions to the world. They invented the wheel and the sailboat and developed the first tools of copper and bronze. The Sumerians developed a system of early writing known as cuneiform, a form of symbol writing on clay tablets. The Sumerians were also the world's first city builders. They built walled cities and stepped pyramids known as ziggurats.

The mixing of trade and ideas also led to the development of other civilizations, such as the Babylonians and the Lydians. Hammurabi, a powerful Babylonian ruler, conquered all of Mesopotamia. He is best known for his set of laws called the Code of Hammurabi. This was the first major collection of laws in history. The Lydians were the first to replace the system of barter with coins or money. These government coins facilitated the transaction of business. The regions near the river valley became a mecca for different people who exchanged cultural ideas, which contributed to prosperity and allowed knowledge to spread.

Chinese history began along the Huang He (Yellow River) valley, where Neolithic people learned to farm (Doc. 1). The Huang He wanders for thousands of miles across northern China before emptying into the Yellow Sea. Its name comes from the loess, or fine blown yellow soil, that it carries eastward from Siberia and Mongolia. As in other river valley civilizations, the need to control the river through large water projects led to the rise of a strong central government. However, the Huang He has had a negative effect on the valley surrounding it. Although it provides food and water for its people, the Huang He has earned the name River of Sorrow because of its irregular flooding pattern and its difficult navigation. After heavy rains, the river overflowed its banks. Chinese peasants labored constantly to build and repair dikes that would keep the river from overflowing. If the dikes broke, floodwater burst all over the land. Such disasters destroyed the crops and brought mass starvation.

As in other river valley civilizations, when the Indus River flooded, it deposited rich soil along the banks. Food surpluses allowed people to build cities. Archeologists have found the remains of impressive cities such as Harappa and Mohenj-Daro that demonstrated the achievements of the first Indian civilization in the Indus River Valley.

The rivers and seas influenced Greek civilization in the Aegean Sea area (Doc. 1). Because the Greek peninsula extended out toward numerous islands, the sea and trading became an integral part of Greek civilization. The Aegean and Mediterranean seas were important links to the rest of the world. The Greeks exchanged goods as well as ideas and technology. For example, the Greeks adapted the Phoenician alphabet for their own use. They also established colonies in the eastern part of the Mediterranean area, such as Sicily, western Turkey, and Crete. Since Greece is a mountainous peninsula, it led to the development of independent city-states, such as Athens and Sparta, and was a main reason that Greece never formed a large, unified empire.

Like the rivers and waterways, monsoons have had a major effect on India. The monsoons are seasonal winds that dominate the climate of India. The word *monsoon* means "seasons" in Arabic. The monsoons are the key to life in India. In the months before the wet seasons, farmers plant seeds in the dry, sun-baked earth. The seeds must take root before the summer downpours. The results can be devastating if the monsoons are late or below average. In 2002, the northern part of India received rainfall that was 70 percent below average and the country, as a whole, was 24 percent below average (Doc. 2a). Many economists believe that these dry conditions will hurt India's GDP since agriculture accounts for 25 percent of the economy and supports two-thirds of the nation's billion-strong population (Doc. 2a). The drought resulted in a decline of .5 percent of overall economic growth in 2002.

However, the monsoons have also had a positive effect on India. They provide irrigation for crops and stimulate other parts of the economy, from the sale of tractors to shampoo. In 2003, a year after a crippling drought, abundant rains enabled the economy to expand by close to 6.5 percent (Doc. 2b).

Great Britain was greatly affected by its natural resource of coal. Coal was one of the factors that enabled Great Britain to become the first country to industrialize. Many of the industrial areas were near coal fields such as Leeds, Liverpool, New Castle, and Cardiff (Doc. 3). Because of its coal supply, Britain was able to have enough energy to run the steam engine, which was invented by James Watt. This helped to supply the energy to run machines and factories and textile mills, which were the foundation of the Industrial Revolution (Docs. 3 and 4). Coal-powered factories helped to end the domestic system and led to the development of the factory system. The use of coal led to the development of industries such as steamboats and railroads and enabled Great Britain to become a world power.

The abundance of coal also created many conditions that affected people in a negative way. Coal mining was dangerous, and there was a constant threat of mine collapse. Coal also affected workers' respiratory systems (Doc. 4). Coal-burning factories contributed to acid rain and other environmental problems. Freidrich Engels referred to the industrial city of Manchester as "Hell on Earth" because of the pollution and soot that came from the coal-producing factories. Coal was also used for lighting, which extended the workers' hours from before sunrise until after sunset (Doc. 4).

Another region greatly influenced by its natural resources is the Middle East. The Middle East has about 67 percent of the world's total proven oil resources. Kuwait has the third-largest reserves of petroleum behind Saudi

Arabia and Iraq. During the 1940s and 1950s, Kuwait became a major supplier of oil, and its profits changed the way people earned a living (Doc. 5). The government used the oil profits to modernize the city of Kuwait, resulting in a construction boom from 1952 to 1965 (Doc. 5). The government also helped build many public buildings and commercial centers (Doc. 5). The citizens of Kuwait also benefited from the government's effort to establish a more comprehensive health system as well as more public and private schools.

Oil has also been used as a political weapon. Kuwait and other oil-exporting countries united in 1960 to control prices and production by forming OPEC (Organization of Petroleum Exporting Countries). In 1973, during the Yom Kippur War, these countries demonstrated their power. OPEC severely limited oil exports to the United States and other countries that supported Israel. Prices skyrocketed, affecting the Western economies by slowing growth. Oil played a role when the United States asked the United Nations to support war with Iraq in 2003. Many claim that France refused because of its dependence on Iraq for oil (Doc. 6). Another major concern has been that oil has led to environmental problems like burning oil wells in Kuwait and oil spills. The excess dependence on oil has also been linked to global warming.

Diamonds, as other natural resources, have influenced the development of nations. Botswana in Africa is the world's leading producer of gem-quality diamonds that account for 70 percent of its export earnings. Diamond mining, like oil production in Kuwait, has enabled the government of Botswana to invest in roads, schools, and clinics (Doc. 7). It increased the gross national product, which has helped raise the standard of living for the people of Botswana. In 1965, only about half of the primary-school-age children attended school. Today, almost 90 percent are enrolled (Doc. 7). When Botswana received its independence, its life expectancy improved from 50 to 70. However, the UN has lowered that figure to about 41 because of the AIDS crisis in Botswana.

Diamonds have also caused problems for the people of Botswana. The discovery of more diamonds in 1980 led to the forced relocation of Bushmen to make way for diamond mines (Doc. 8). These steps have resulted in court cases for the Bushmen, who had lived on the land for centuries. Some believe that the struggle for control of diamond mining has led to neo-colonialism. The Botswanian government has divided the Central Kalahari Game Reserve among the multinational diamond corporation De Beers, the Australian-based company BHP Billiton, and the Canadian outfit Motapa Diamond Inc. This division will result in a loss of revenue and control by Botswana (Doc. 8).

The struggle over diamond mining has led to the use of children as soldiers and other abuses of human rights in neighboring countries. The country of Sierra Leone terrorizes its citizens with systematic mutilation of men, women, and children. Sierra Leone has suffered terrible social and economic costs as a result of its civil war and fighting over diamond control. Throughout the 10-year civil war that began in 1991, fighting centered around the diamonds. The Revolutionary United Front composed of fighters from Sierra

Leone and Liberia realize that whoever controls the diamond mines controls Sierra Leone, because the profits from smuggled diamonds funded its attack. Efforts to end the conflict had been unsuccessful. The war between 1991 and 2001 claimed more than 75,000 lives and caused 500,000 people from Sierra Leone to become refugees. The economy of Sierra Leone has also been cheated out of millions of dollars in the form of illegal diamonds.

Natural resources have greatly affected the development of regions or nations throughout history. Water and trade allowed for the rise of ancient civilizations. Coal deposits enabled Great Britain to industrialize during the 18th century. In the 21st century, monsoons continue to influence the Indian economy, oil shaped the development of Kuwait, and diamonds are changing the lives of people in Botswana. All of these natural resources have proven to both help and hinder the economic and political growth of these areas.

Topic	Question Numbers	Total Number of Questions	Number Wrong	*Reason for Wrong Answer
U.S. AND N.Y. HISTORY				
WORLD HISTORY	1, 3, 4, 5, 7, 8, 12, 13, 15, 17, 20, 23, 28, 29, 30, 33, 34, 39, 42, 43, 44, 46, 47, 48, 50	25		
GEOGRAPHY	2, 9, 10, 11, 16, 18, 22, 26, 27, 35, 36, 37, 45, 49	14		
ECONOMICS	14, 24, 25, 31, 38, 40, 41	7		
CIVICS, CITIZENSHIP, AND GOVERNMENT	6, 19, 21, 32	4		

*Your reason for answering the question incorrectly might be (a) lack of knowledge, (b) misunderstanding the question, or (c) careless error.

Actual Items by Standard and Unit

	1 U.S. and N.Y. History	2 World History	3 Geography	4 Economics	5 Civics, Citizenship, and Gov't	Number
Methodology of Global History and Geography		1				1
UNIT ONE Ancient World		3, 4, 5, 7	2, 9, 10		6	8
UNIT TWO Expanding Zones of Exchange		8	11	14		3
UNIT THREE Global Interactions		12, 13	18			3
UNIT FOUR First Global Age		15, 17	16, 45	41	19	6
UNIT FIVE Age of Revolution		20, 46	26	24, 25	21	6
UNIT SIX Crisis and Achievement (1900–1945)		29, 30, 34	27			4
UNIT SEVEN 20th Century Since 1945		28, 33, 39, 42, 43	35, 36, 37	31, 38	32	11
UNIT EIGHT Global Connections and Interactions			22	40		2
Cross topical		23, 44, 47, 48, 50	49			6
Total # of Questions		25	14	7	4	50
% of Items by Standard		50%	28%	14%	8%	100%

Examination June 2008

Global History and Geography

PART I: MULTIPLE CHOICE

Directions (1–50): For each statement or question, write in the space provided the *number* of the word or expression that, of those given, best completes the statement or answers the question.

Base your answer to question 1 on the announcement below and on your knowledge of social studies.

Discovery

OF

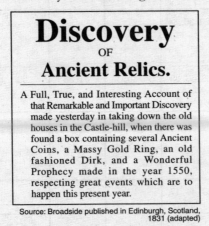

Ancient Relics.

A Full, True, and Interesting Account of that Remarkable and Important Discovery made yesterday in taking down the old houses in the Castle-hill, when there was found a box containing several Ancient Coins, a Massy Gold Ring, an old fashioned Dirk, and a Wonderful Prophecy made in the year 1550, respecting great events which are to happen this present year.

Source: Broadside published in Edinburgh, Scotland, 1831 (adapted)

1 Which term best describes the items mentioned in this announcement?

1 icons
2 fossils
3 artifacts
4 replicas

1 _____

2 One way in which South Korea, Saudi Arabia, and India are geographically similar is that each is located on

1 an island
2 an archipelago
3 an isthmus
4 a peninsula

2____

3 Which statement represents a characteristic of democracy?

1 Religious leaders control government policy.
2 Citizens are the source of power in government.
3 The government limits the thoughts and actions of the people.
4 The laws of the government are made by influential military officers.

3____

4 The Bantu cleared the land, then fertilized it with ashes. When the land could no longer support their families, the Bantu moved further south. By 1110 B.C., the Bantu had spread their rich culture throughout central and southern Africa.

Which agricultural technique is described in this passage?

1 irrigation
2 terrace farming
3 slash-and-burn
4 crop rotation

4____

5 Which ancient civilization is associated with the Twelve Tables, an extensive road system, and the poets Horace and Virgil?

1 Babylonian
2 Greek
3 Phoenician
4 Roman

5____

6 The term *feudalism* is best defined as a

1 holy war between Christians and Muslims
2 process in which goods are traded for other goods
3 division of political power between three separate branches
4 system in which land is exchanged for military service and loyalty 6____

7 Which title best completes the partial outline below?

I. ________________
A. Incorporation of European and Arabic ideas in architecture
B. Preservation of Greco-Roman ideas
C. Spread of Orthodox Christianity into Russia
D. Development of Justinian Code

1 Age of Discovery
2 Byzantine Empire
3 Persian Empire
4 Crusades 7____

Base your answer to question 8 on the illustration below and on your knowledge of social studies.

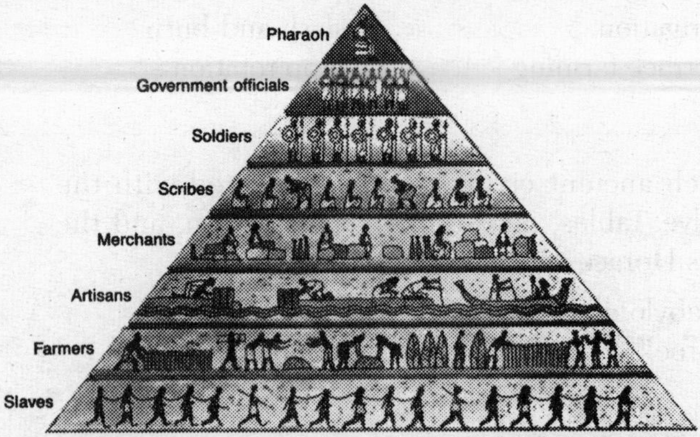

Source: Barry K. Beyer et al., *The World Around Us: Eastern Hemisphere*, MacMillan Publishing (adapted)

8 Based on the information in this illustration, which statement about the society of ancient Egypt is accurate?

1 The women had equal status to the men.
2 The social structure was hierarchical.
3 Social mobility was unrestricted.
4 Soldiers outnumbered farmers. 8____

9 Which statement about the Mongol Empire is accurate?

1 The Mongols developed a highly technological society that emphasized formal education.
2 European monarchies became a model for the early Mongol governments.
3 Pax Mongolia led to regional stability, increasing trade on the Silk Road.
4 The Mongols adopted Roman Catholicism as the official religion of the empire. 9____

10 Which period in European history is most closely associated with Leonardo da Vinci, Michaelangelo, William Shakespeare, and Nicolaus Copernicus?

1 Early Middle Ages
2 Renaissance
3 Age of Absolutism
4 Enlightenment 10____

11 What was one of the primary reasons for the spread of the bubonic plague?

1 increase in trade
2 colonization of the Americas
3 development of the manorial system
4 economic decline 11____

12 Which situation is considered a cause of the other three?

1 Religious unity declines throughout Europe.
2 The Catholic Counter-Reformation begins.
3 The power of the Roman Catholic Church decreases.
4 Martin Luther posts the Ninety-five Theses. 12____

Base your answer to question 13 on the table below and on your knowledge of social studies.

Population of the Largest Medieval Cities in 1250 and 1450

The 10 largest cities in 1250		The 10 largest cities in 1450	
1 Hangchow	320,000	1 Peking	600,000
2 Cairo	300,000	2 Vijayanagar	455,000
3 Fez	200,000	3 Cairo	380,000
4 Kamakura	200,000	4 Hangchow	250,000
5 Pagan	180,000	5 Tabriz	200,000
6 Paris	160,000	6 Canton	175,000
7 Peking	140,000	7 Granada	165,000
8 Canton	140,000	8 Nanking	150,000
9 Nanking	130,000	9 Paris	150,000
10 Marrakesh	125,000	10 Kyoto	150,000

Source: Tertius Chandler, *Four Thousand Years of Urban Growth*, St. David's University Press (adapted)

13 Which statement can best be supported by the information in this table?

1 The population of Paris increased between 1250 and 1450.
2 The populations of Cairo and Nanking were higher in 1250 than in 1450.
3 The population of most large cities exceeded one million people in 1450.
4 The population of Peking increased more than the population of Canton between 1250 and 1450. 13____

Base your answer to question 14 on the passage below and on your knowledge of social studies.

> It would be wrong to call the Ottoman Empire a purely Islamic state. It was not. It was a state that claimed some kind of an attachment, some kind of allegiance to Islam, but combined it with other forms of heritage from the Byzantine tradition or from the Turkic tradition that did not really correspond to Islam. So they always had this very, very pragmatic approach to Islam.
>
> —Professor Edhem Eldem, Bogazici University, NPR News, *All Things Considered*, August 18, 2004

14 This author is suggesting that during the Ottoman Empire

1 religion was mingled with historic traditions
2 most people belonged to minority religions
3 rulers tried to separate politics from religion
4 rulers operated under a strict set of laws 14____

---

15 • Foreign rulers were overthrown.
• Admiral Zheng He established trade links.
• Civil service exams were reinstated.

These events in history occurred during the rule of the

1 Mughal dynasty in India
2 Abbasid dynasty in the Middle East
3 Ming dynasty in China
4 Tokugawa shogunate in Japan 15____

16 What was the primary economic policy used by the Spanish with their Latin American colonies?

1 embargoes
2 tariffs
3 boycotts
4 mercantilism 16____

17 In *Two Treatises of Government*, John Locke wrote that the purpose of government was to

1 keep kings in power
2 regulate the economy
3 expand territory
4 protect natural rights 17____

Base your answer to question 18 on the map below and on your knowledge of social studies.

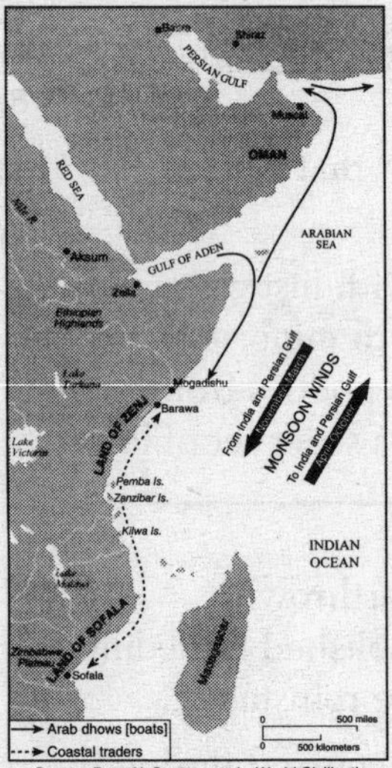

Source: Peter N. Stearns et al., *World Civilizations: The Global Experience*, Pearson (adapted)

18 Which generalization is best supported by the information on this map?

1 No trade occurred between East Africa and the Persian Gulf region.
2 The monsoon winds influenced trade between East Africa and India.
3 Trading states developed primarily in the interior of East Africa.
4 Trade encouraged the spread of Islam from East Africa to Arabia. 18____

Base your answer to question 19 on the summaries of the "New Laws" quoted below and on your knowledge of social studies.

> . . . Art. 31. All Indians held in encomienda by the viceroys, by their lieutenants, royal officers, prelates, monasteries, hospitals, religious houses, mints, the treasury, etc., are to be transferred forthwith to the Crown. . . .
>
> Art. 38. Lawsuits involving Indians are no longer to be tried in the Indies, or by the Council of the Indies, but must be pleaded before the King himself. . . .
>
> —New Laws issued by Emperor Charles V, 1542–1543

19 One purpose of these laws was to

1 reduce local authority and increase central control
2 increase religious authority and limit secular influences
3 guarantee citizenship to Indians while supporting traditional practices
4 promote economic development while expanding political rights for Indians 19____

---

20 One major effect of Napoleon's rule of France was that it led to

1 an increase in the power of the Roman Catholic Church
2 massive emigration to the Americas
3 trade agreements with Great Britain
4 a restoration of political stability 20____

21 Which idea is most closely associated with laissez-faire economics?

1 communes
2 trade unionism
3 subsistence agriculture
4 free trade 21____

22 In the 19th century, a major reason for Irish migration to North America was to

1 gain universal suffrage
2 avoid malaria outbreaks
3 flee widespread famine
4 escape a civil war 22____

23 A major goal of both the Sepoy Mutiny in India and the Boxer Rebellion in China was to

1 rid their countries of foreigners
2 expand their respective territories
3 receive international military support
4 restore an absolute monarch to the throne 23____

24 Early exploration of Africa by Europeans was hindered by the

1 lack of natural resources in Africa
2 alliances between African kingdoms
3 isolationist policies of European monarchs
4 many different physical features of Africa 24____

25 Which action taken by the Meiji government encouraged industrialization in 19th-century Japan?

1 building a modern transportation system
2 limiting the number of ports open to foreign trade
3 forcing families to settle on collective farms
4 establishing a system of trade guilds 25____

26 One goal of the League of Nations was to

1 promote peaceful relations worldwide
2 stimulate the economy of Europe
3 bring World War I to an end
4 encourage a strong alliance system 26____

27 • Five-year plans
• Collectivization of agriculture
• Great Purge

Which individual is associated with all these policies?

1 Adolf Hitler
2 Joseph Stalin
3 Deng Xiaoping
4 Jawaharlal Nehru

27____

28 Japan's invasion of Manchuria, Italy's attack on Ethiopia, and Germany's blitzkrieg in Poland are examples of

1 military aggression
2 appeasement
3 containment
4 the domino theory

28____

29 Which statement about the worldwide Depression of the 1930s is a fact rather than an opinion?

1 Political leaders should have prevented the Depression.
2 Germany was hurt more by the Treaty of Versailles than by the Depression.
3 The economic upheaval of the Depression had major political effects.
4 World War I was the only reason for the Depression.

29____

30 Which group was accused of violating human rights in the city of Nanjing during World War II?

1 Americans
2 Chinese
3 Japanese
4 Germans

30____

31 One way in which the Hitler Youth of Germany and the Red Guard of China are similar is that both organizations

1 required unquestioning loyalty to the leader
2 helped increase religious tolerance
3 hindered imperialistic goals
4 led pro-democracy movements

31____

32 • French intent to recolonize Indo-China after World War II
• United States desire to prevent the spread of communism
• United States support for the French in Southeast Asia

These ideas are most closely associated with the

1 causes of the conflict in Vietnam
2 reasons for the Nationalist settlement of Taiwan
3 factors that led to the Korean War
4 results of the Marshall Plan 32____

33 Which country is most closely associated with the terms *pass laws*, *homelands*, and *white minority rule*?

1 El Salvador
2 South Africa
3 Iran
4 Israel 33____

Base your answer to question 34 on the photograph below and on your knowledge of social studies.

Mahatma Gandhi demonstrating cotton-spinning on his own *charka* in Mirzapur, 1925.

Source: Stanley Wolpert, *Gandhi's Passion: The Life and Legacy of Mahatma Gandhi*, Oxford University Press

34 During the Indian independence movement, the activity shown in this photograph inspired the Indian people to

1 stop buying British goods
2 reject Muslim rule
3 join the Indian army
4 expand British textile manufacturing 34____

Base your answers to questions 35 and 36 on the passage below and on your knowledge of social studies.

> . . . (1) Internally, arouse the masses of the people. That is, unite the working class, the peasantry, the urban petty bourgeoisie and the national bourgeoisie, form a domestic united front under the leadership of the working class, and advance from this to the establishment of a state which is a people's democratic dictatorship under the leadership of the working class and based on the alliance of workers and peasants.
>
> (2) Externally, unite in a common struggle with those nations of the world which treat us as equals and unite with the peoples of all countries. That is, ally ourselves with the Soviet Union, with the People's Democracies and with the proletariat and the broad masses of the people in all other countries, and form an international united front. . . .

Source: Mao Tse-Tung [Mao Zedong], *Selected Works*, Volume Five, 1945–1949, New York International Publishers

35 In this passage, Mao Zedong is suggesting that China

1 create a government under the leadership of industrialists
2 give up its independence and become a part of the Soviet Union
3 rely on the United Nations for economic aid
4 join with the Soviet Union as a partner in communism

35____

36 In this passage, Mao Zedong is using the ideas of

1 Thomas Malthus
2 Adam Smith
3 Karl Marx
4 Jiang Jieshi (Chiang Kai-Shek)

36____

Base your answer to question 37 on the time line below and on your knowledge of social studies.

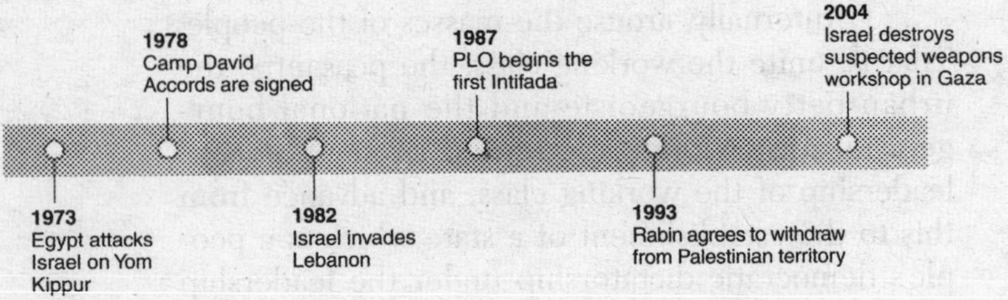
1978
Camp David
Accords are signed
1987
PLO begins the
first Intifada
2004
Israel destroys
suspected weapons
workshop in Gaza
1973
Egypt attacks
Israel on Yom
Kippur
1982
Israel invades
Lebanon
1993
Rabin agrees to withdraw
from Palestinian territory

37 Which conclusion can be drawn from this time line?

1 Israel withdrew from the Camp David Accords.
2 The Palestinian army is superior to the Israeli army.
3 Long-lasting peace in the Middle East has been difficult to achieve.
4 Neighboring countries have not been involved in the Arab-Israeli conflict. 37 ____

---

38 The destruction of the Berlin Wall and the breakup of the Soviet Union signify the

1 end of the Cold War
2 collapse of the Taliban
3 strength of the Warsaw Pact
4 power of the European Union 38 ____

39 In the 20th century, urbanization affected the developing nations of Africa, Asia, and Latin America by

1 reducing literacy rates
2 weakening traditional values
3 strengthening caste systems
4 increasing the isolation of women 39 ____

40 Which statement about the impact of the AIDS epidemic in both Africa and Southeast Asia is most accurate?

1 Life expectancy in both regions is declining.
2 The availability of low-cost drugs has cured most of those infected.
3 The introduction of awareness programs has eliminated the threat of the disease.
4 Newborn babies and young children have not been affected by the disease. 40____

41 In August 1990, Iraq invaded Kuwait. The United Nations response led to the Persian Gulf War of 1991. This response is an example of

1 détente
2 empire building
3 totalitarianism
4 collective security 41____

42 One similarity between the Roman Empire and the Ottoman Empire is that both

1 reached their height of power at the same time
2 developed parliamentary governments
3 ensured equality for women
4 declined because of corruption in government 42____

43 Which statement regarding the impact of geography on Japan is most accurate?

1 Large plains served as invasion routes for conquerors.
2 Arid deserts and mountains caused isolation from Asia.
3 Lack of natural resources led to a policy of imperialism.
4 Close proximity to Africa encouraged extensive trade with Egypt. 43____

Base your answer to question 44 on the map below and on your knowledge of social studies.

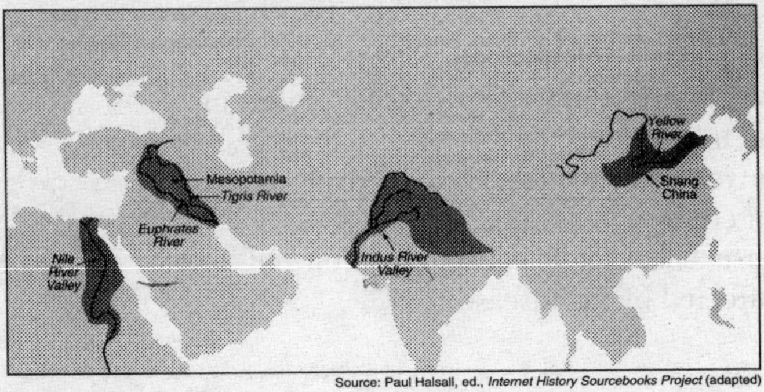

Source: Paul Halsall, ed., *Internet History Sourcebooks Project* (adapted)

44 Which revolution led to the development of these civilizations?

1 Industrial
2 Neolithic
3 Green
4 Commercial

44____

---

45 The Age of Exploration led directly to the

1 establishment of European colonies
2 start of the Puritan Revolution
3 invention of the magnetic compass
4 failure of the Congress of Vienna

45____

46 Which revolution was caused by the factors shown in this partial outline?

I. ______________________________
A. Bankruptcy of the treasury
B. Tax burden on the Third Estate
C. Inflation
D. Abuses of the Old Regime

1 Russian
2 Mexican
3 French
4 Cuban

46____

47 One way in which José de San Martin, Camillo Cavour, and Jomo Kenyatta are similar is that each leader

1 made significant scientific discoveries
2 led nationalist movements
3 fought against British imperialism
4 became a communist revolutionary 47____

48 One way in which Vladimir Lenin's New Economic Policy and Mikhail Gorbachev's policy of perestroika are similar is that both

1 allowed elements of capitalism within a communist economic system
2 strengthened their country's military defenses
3 supported censorship of news and of personal correspondence
4 increased tensions during the Cold War 48____

49 Which set of events in 19th- and 20th-century Chinese history is in the correct chronological order?

1 Great Leap Forward → Opium Wars → Long March → Four Modernizations
2 Four Modernizations → Long March → Opium Wars → Great Leap Forward
3 Opium Wars → Long March → Great Leap Forward → Four Modernizations
4 Long March → Four Modernizations → Great Leap Forward → Opium Wars 49____

50 A study of Spain during the late 1400s, the Balkan States during the early 1900s, Rwanda during the 1990s, and Central Asia today shows that

1 civil disobedience is an effective way to bring about change
2 people have been encouraged to question tradition
3 colonial rule has a lasting legacy
4 ethnic conflicts have been a recurring issue in history 50____

In developing your answer to Part II, be sure to keep these general definitions in mind:

(a) <u>explain</u> means "to make plain or understandable; to give reasons for or causes of, to show the logical development or relationships of"

(b) <u>discuss</u> means "to make observations about something using facts, reasoning, and argument; to present in some detail"

PART II: THEMATIC ESSAY QUESTION

Directions: Write a well-organized essay that includes an introduction, several paragraphs addressing the task below, and a conclusion.

Theme: Belief Systems

> The world has many different belief systems. Each is distinctive, but all greatly influenced the lives of their followers and the society in which the belief system was practiced.

Task:

> Choose ***two*** major belief systems and for ***each***
> - Explain key beliefs ***and/or*** practices
> - Discuss an influence the belief system had on the lives of its followers or the society in which it was practiced

You may use any example from your study of global history. Some suggestions you might wish to consider include animism, Buddhism, Christianity, Confucianism, Daoism, Islam, Judaism, legalism, and Shinto.

You are *not* limited to these suggestions.

Do *not* use the United States as the focus of your answer.

Guidelines:

In your essay, be sure to:

- Develop all aspects of the task
- Support the theme with relevant facts, examples, and details
- Use a logical and clear plan of organization, including an introduction and a conclusion that are beyond a restatement of the theme

In developing your answers to Part III, be sure to keep these general definitions in mind:

(a) <u>describe</u> means "to illustrate something in words or tell about it"

(b) <u>discuss</u> means "to make observations about something using facts, reasoning, and argument; to present in some detail"

PART III: DOCUMENT-BASED QUESTION

This question is based on the accompanying documents. The question is designed to test your ability to work with historical documents. Some of these documents have been edited for the purposes of this question. As you analyze the documents, take into account the source of each document and any point of view that may be presented in the document.

Historical Context:

Genocide, threats to the environment, and ***weapons of mass destruction*** are problems that the world has had to face. Various attempts have been made by the international community and its members to address and resolve these problems.

Task:

Using the information from the documents and your knowledge of global history, answer the questions that follow each document in Part A. Your answers to the questions will help you write the Part B essay in which you will be asked to

Select ***two*** problems mentioned in the historical context and for ***each***

- Describe the problem
- Discuss attempts made to address ***and/or*** resolve the problem

Part A: Short-Answer Questions

Directions: Analyze the documents and answer the short-answer questions that follow each document in the space provided.

Document 1

Raphael Lemkin created the term genocide. He sent a letter to the *New York Times* editor explaining the importance of the concept of genocide.

Genocide Before the United Nations

TO THE EDITOR OF THE NEW YORK TIMES:

The representatives of Cuba, India and Panama to the United Nations Assembly have brought forth a resolution which calls upon the United Nations to study the problem of genocide and to prepare a report on the possibilities of declaring genocide an international crime and assuring international cooperation for its prevention and punishment and also recommending, among others, that genocide should be dealt with by national legislation in the same way as other international crimes. . . .

International Concept

The concept of genocide thus is based upon existing and deeply felt moral concepts. Moreover, it uses as its elements well defined and already existing legal notions and institutions. What we have to do is to protect great values of our civilization through such accepted institutions adjusted to a formula of international law which is ever progressing. Because of lack of adequate provisions and previous formulation of international law, the Nuremberg Tribunal had to dismiss the Nazi crimes committed in the period between the advent of Nazism to power and the beginning of the war, as "revolting and horrible as many of these crimes were," to use the expression of the Nuremberg judgment.

It is now the task of the United Nations to see to it that the generous action of the three member states should be transferred into international law in order to prevent further onslaughts [attacks] on civilization, which are able to frustrate the purposes of the Charter of the United Nations. . . .

Source: Raphael Lemkin, *New York Times*, Nov. 8, 1946 (adapted)

1 According to Raphael Lemkin, what is ***one*** way the world community can address the problem of genocide? [1]

____

____

Document 2a

. . . In 1948, the fledgling UN General Assembly adopted an international Convention on the Prevention and Punishment of the Crime of Genocide, which came into force in 1951. That convention defines genocide as "acts committed with intent to destroy, in whole or in part, a national ethnic, racial or religious group," including inflicting conditions calculated to lead to a group's destruction. . . .

After the horrors of the Holocaust were revealed, the mantra [slogan] of the time became "never again." But it would take four decades, with the creation of the International Criminal Tribunal for the former Yugoslavia in 1994, before the international community would finally come together to prosecute the crime of genocide again.

Why did it take so long, despite atrocities and mass killings in Cambodia, East Timor, and elsewhere? . . .

Source: Irina Lagunina, "World: What Constitutes Genocide Under International Law, and How Are Prosecutions Evolving?," Radio Free Europe/Radio Liberty, 9/10/2004

2*a* According to Irina Lagunina, what was ***one*** criticism of the international community's response to genocide? [1]

____

____

Document 2b

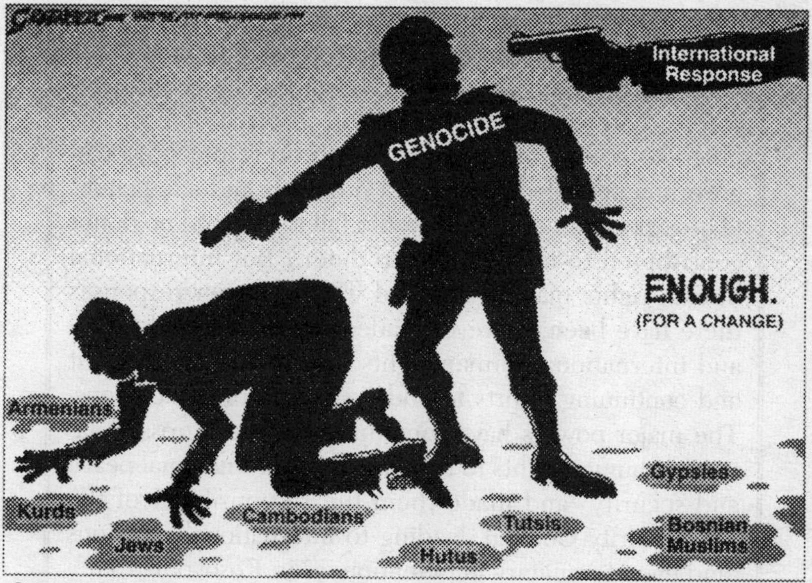

Source: Steve Greenberg, *Seattle Post-Intelligencer,* March 29, 1999 (adapted)

2*b* Based on this 1999 cartoon, identify ***two*** specific groups that have been victims of genocide. [1]

(1) ______________________________

(2) ______________________________

Document 3

. . . Undeniably, there have been terrible human rights failures—in Cambodia, Bosnia, Rwanda. There, and elsewhere, national constitutions and international norms failed to deter; international institutions and powerful governments failed to respond promptly and adequately. (The expectation that they would fail to respond no doubt contributed to their failure to deter.) But international human rights may be credited with whatever responses there have been, however inadequate, however delayed; and international human rights inspired all subsequent and continuing efforts to address the terrible violations. The major powers have sometimes declared gross violations of human rights to be "threats to international peace and security" and made them the responsibility of the UN Security Council, leading to international sanctions (and even to military intervention, as in Kosovo in 1999). International tribunals are sitting to bring gross violators to trial; a permanent international criminal tribunal to adjudicate [judge] crimes of genocide, war crimes, and crimes against humanity is being created. Various governments have moved to support international human rights and made their bilateral and multilateral influence an established force in international relations. . . .

Source: Louis Henkin, "Human Rights: Ideology and Aspiration, Reality and Prospect," *Realizing Human Rights*, St. Martin's Press, 2000

3 Based on this document, state ***one*** attempt made to address the problem of genocide. [1]

____

____

Document 4

At the dawn of the twenty-first century, the Earth's physical and biological systems are under unprecedented strain. The human population reached 6.3 billion in 2003 and is projected to increase to about 9 billion in the next half century. The United Nations estimates that one-third of the world's people live in countries with moderate to high shortages of fresh water and that this percentage could double by 2025. Many of the world's largest cities are increasingly choked by pollution. As carbon dioxide and other greenhouse gases build in the atmosphere, the average surface temperature of the Earth has reached the highest level ever measured on an annual basis. The biological diversity of the planet is also under heavy stress. Scientists believe that a mass extinction of plants and animals is under way and predict that a quarter of all species could be pushed to extinction by 2050 as a consequence of global warming alone. Without question, the human impact on the biosphere will be one of the most critical issues of the century. . . .

Source: Norman J. Vig, "Introduction: Governing the International Environment," *The Global Environment: Institutions, Law, and Policy*, CQ Press, 2005 (adapted)

4 According to Norman J. Vig, what are ***two*** environmental problems that pose a threat to the world? [2]

(1)____

____

(2)____

____

Document 5

Desertification is a major environmental problem. Nearly one-quarter of the Earth's land is threatened by this problem. China is one of those areas.

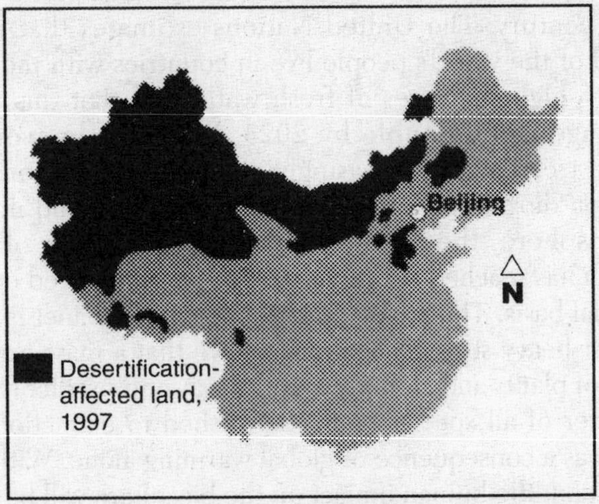

Source: China National Committee for the Implementation of the U.N. Convention to Combat Desertification (adapted)

Whipped by the wind, sand from Sky Desert swept through this village [Longbaoshan] last month like sheets of stinging rain, clattering against dried corn husks and piling up in small dunes against buildings.

Longbaoshan, a farming community about 40 miles northwest of Beijing, stands on the front line of China's losing war against the country's advancing deserts. Driven by overgrazing, overpopulation, drought and poor land management, they are slowly consuming vast areas of the country in a looming ecological disaster.

Official figures tell a frightening story.

Between 1994 and 1999, desertified land grew by 20,280 square miles. Desert blankets more than a quarter of China's territory. Shifting sands threaten herders and farmers in a nation with one-fifth of the world's population and one-fifteenth of its arable land. Scientists warn of calamity if the government fails to stop the sands.

"Pastures, farmland, railroads and other means of transportation will be buried under sand," said Dong Guangrong, a research fellow in environmental engineering at the Chinese Academy of Sciences. "People will be forced to move." . . .

In March, the worst sandstorm in a decade blinded the capital, painting the sky yellow and engulfing 40-story buildings as visibility dropped to less than a football field. Beijingers gritted their teeth as a seasonal storm known as the Yellow Dragon dumped 30,000 tons of sand on the city. People on the street covered their mouths with surgical masks or their faces with scarves in a futile attempt to keep the sand out. . . .

Officials here are trying to stop the sands by building green buffers. A project intended to protect Beijing in advance of the 2008 summer Olympic Games involves reclaiming desertified land in 75 counties. . . .

Source: Frank Langfitt, "Desertification," *The Post-Standard*, May 13, 2002 (adapted)

5*a* Based on this document, state ***one*** problem desertification poses in China. [1]

____

____

b Based on this document, state ***one*** attempt the Chinese officials have made to address the problem of desertification. [1]

____

____

Document 6

Selected Efforts to Preserve the Environment

1972	Stockholm—United Nations Conference on Human Environment—beginning of organized international effort to safeguard the environment
1973	The Convention on International Trade in Endangered Species of Wild Fauna and Flora (CITES)—restricts trade in 5,000 animal and 25,000 plant species
1987	Montreal Protocol—binding agreement on protection of the ozone layer
1992	Rio de Janeiro "Earth Summit"—produced treaties on climate change and biodiversity
1994	The World Conservation Union (IUCN)—published a revised Red List of endangered and threatened species, creating a world standard for gauging threats to biodiversity
1997	Kyoto Protocol—negotiated an agreement on obligations to reduce greenhouse gases in the atmosphere
2004	European Union—issued its first-ever pollution register containing data on industrial emissions and representing a "landmark event" in public provision of environmental information
2006	United Nations General Assembly—declared the International Year of Deserts which led to the United Nations Convention to Combat Desertification

Source: "Environmental Milestones," World Watch Institute (adapted)

6 Based on this document, identify ***two*** ways the international community has attempted to address environmental problems. [2]

(1) ____

____

(2) ____

____

Document 7

The Twentieth Century's Deadly Yield

Weapons of mass destruction generally refer to biological, chemical, and nuclear weapons.

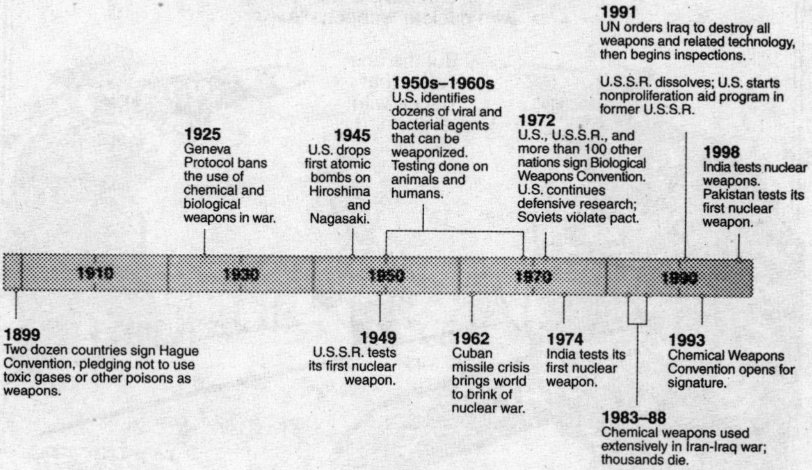

1991
UN orders Iraq to destroy all weapons and related technology, then begins inspections.
U.S.S.R. dissolves; U.S. starts nonproliferation aid program in former U.S.S.R.
1950s–1960s
U.S. identifies dozens of viral and bacterial agents that can be weaponized. Testing done on animals and humans.
1925
Geneva Protocol bans the use of chemical and biological weapons in war.
1945
U.S. drops first atomic bombs on Hiroshima and Nagasaki.
1972
U.S., U.S.S.R., and more than 100 other nations sign Biological Weapons Convention. U.S. continues defensive research; Soviets violate pact.
1998
India tests nuclear weapons. Pakistan tests its first nuclear weapon.
1910
1930
1950
1970
1990
1899
Two dozen countries sign Hague Convention, pledging not to use toxic gases or other poisons as weapons.
1949
U.S.S.R. tests its first nuclear weapon.
1962
Cuban missile crisis brings world to brink of nuclear war.
1974
India tests its first nuclear weapon.
1993
Chemical Weapons Convention opens for signature.
1983–88
Chemical weapons used extensively in Iran-Iraq war; thousands die.

Source: "Weapons of Mass Destruction," *National Geographic*, November 2002 (adapted)

7*a* Using the information on this time line, identify ***one*** way a weapon of mass destruction was used. [1]

____

____

b Using the information on this time line, identify ***one*** attempt made to address a problem related to weapons of mass destruction. [1]

____

____

Document 8

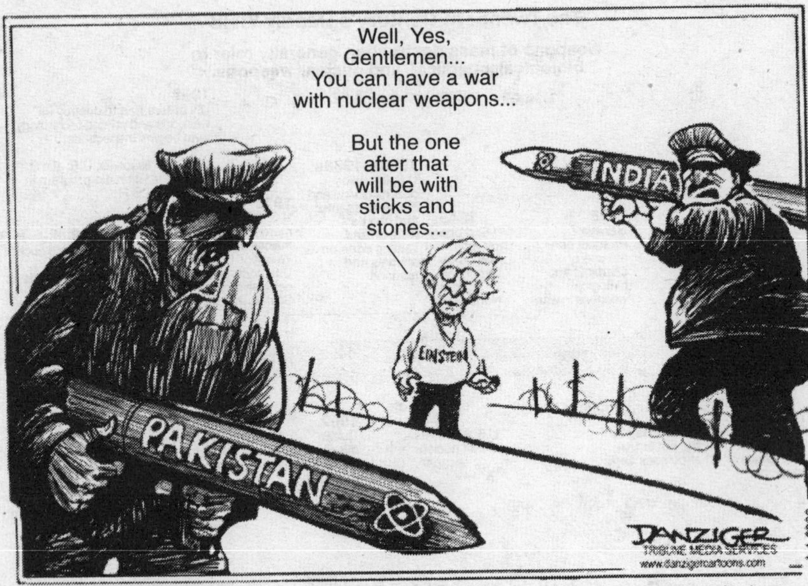

Source: Jeff Danziger, Tribune Media Services, January 4, 2002 (adapted)

8 Based on this cartoon, state ***one*** reason nuclear weapons pose a threat to the world community. [1]

____

____

Document 9

Civilian uranium is found at nonmilitary sites. It is used to conduct scientific and industrial research or to produce radioisotopes for medical purposes. This uranium can also be used to make highly enriched uranium (HEU), which is used in nuclear weapons.

Overview/Securing Civilian Uranium 235

- Terrorists who acquired less than 100 kilograms of highly enriched uranium (HEU) could build and detonate a rudimentary but effective atomic bomb relatively easily. HEU is also attractive for states that seek to develop nuclear weapons secretly, without having to test them.
- Unfortunately, large quantities of HEU are stored in nuclear research facilities worldwide—especially in Russia, often under minimal security.
- The U.S. and its allies have established programs to bolster security measures, convert reactors to use low-enriched uranium (which is useless for weapons) and retrieve HEU from research-reactor sites around the world. Dangerous gaps remain, however.
- High-level governmental attention plus a comparatively small additional monetary investment could go a long way toward solving the problem for good.

Source: Glaser and von Hippel, "Thwarting Nuclear Terrorism," *Scientific American*, February 2006

9 Based on this article by Glaser and von Hippel, state an attempt being made by the United States and its allies to improve the security of highly enriched uranium (HEU). [1]

____

____

Part B: Essay

Directions: Write a well-organized essay that includes an introduction, several paragraphs, and a conclusion. Use evidence from *at least* ***four*** documents in your essay. Support your response with relevant facts, examples, and details. Include additional outside information.

Historical Context:

Genocide, threats to the environment, and weapons of mass destruction are problems that the world has had to face. Various attempts have been made by the international community and its members to address and resolve these problems.

Task:

Using the information from the documents and your knowledge of global history, write an essay in which you

> Select ***two*** problems mentioned in the historical context and for ***each***
> - Describe the problem
> - Discuss attempts made to address ***and/or*** resolve the problem

Guidelines:

In your essay, be sure to:

- Develop all aspects of the task
- Incorporate information from *at least* ***four*** documents
- Incorporate relevant outside information
- Support the theme with relevant facts, examples, and details
- Use a logical and clear plan of organization, including an introduction and conclusion that are beyond a restatement of the theme

Answers
June 2008
Global History and Geography

Answer Key

PART I (1–50)

1. 3	**14.** 1	**27.** 2	**40.** 1
2. 4	**15.** 3	**28.** 1	**41.** 4
3. 2	**16.** 4	**29.** 3	**42.** 4
4. 3	**17.** 4	**30.** 3	**43.** 3
5. 4	**18.** 2	**31.** 1	**44.** 2
6. 4	**19.** 1	**32.** 1	**45.** 1
7. 2	**20.** 4	**33.** 2	**46.** 3
8. 2	**21.** 4	**34.** 1	**47.** 2
9. 3	**22.** 3	**35.** 4	**48.** 1
10. 2	**23.** 1	**36.** 3	**49.** 3
11. 1	**24.** 4	**37.** 3	**50.** 4
12. 4	**25.** 1	**38.** 1	
13. 4	**26.** 1	**39.** 2	

PART II: Thematic Essay See Answers Explained section.

PART III: Document-Based Essay See Answers Explained section.

Answers Explained

PART I

1. **3** *Artifacts* is the term that best describes the items mentioned in this announcement. Artifacts are objects made by human beings. They include tools; weapons, such as a dirk; pottery; clothing; and jewelry. By analyzing artifacts, archaeologists draw conclusions about how people dressed, what work they did, or how they worshipped.

WRONG CHOICES EXPLAINED:

(1) Icons are holy images of Christ, the Virgin Mary, or saints venerated in the Eastern Orthodox Church.

(2) Fossils are evidences of early life preserved in rocks. Human fossils often consist of fragments of teeth, skulls, or other bones. Paleontologists who study fossils use complex techniques to date ancient fossil remains and rocks.

(4) Replicas are exact reproductions of items or works of art by original artists.

2. **4** One way in which South Korea, Saudi Arabia, and India are geographically similar is that each is on a peninsula. A peninsula is a piece of land that is surrounded by water on three sides. Korea is a peninsula attached to the eastern mainland of Asia between China and Japan. The Yellow Sea is to its west. To the east are the Korean Strait and the Sea of Japan. Koreans call the Sea of Japan the East Sea. The Korean peninsula is divided into two nations, North and South Korea.

Saudi Arabia is the largest nation on the Arabian Peninsula. The Arabian Peninsula is a vast plateau that is about one-third the size of the United States. Saudi Arabia borders on several bodies of water, including the Red Sea, the Arabian Sea, and the Persian Gulf.

India is a landmass in southern Asia. South Asia is a large triangular peninsula that juts southward from the continent of Asia. The Arabian Sea lies to the west, the Indian Ocean to the south, and the Bay of Bengal to the east. These bodies of water set India apart from other regions but have not isolated it.

WRONG CHOICES EXPLAINED:

(1) An island is a body of land surrounded entirely by water and is smaller than a continent.

(2) An archipelago is a chain or group of islands.

(3) An isthmus is a narrow strip of land joining two large land areas or a peninsula to a mainland.

3. **2** A statement that represents a characteristic of democracy is that citizens are the source of power in government. A democracy is a form of government in which people have supreme power. The government can act only by and with their consent. In the form of a democracy called a republic, the people choose the leaders who represent them.

WRONG CHOICES EXPLAINED:

(1) A theocracy is a nation in which religious leaders control government policy.

(3) and (4) Neither of these statements are characteristic of a democracy. A totalitarian system or a dictatorship is a form of government limiting the thoughts and actions of the people, or one in which the laws of government are made by influential military officers.

4. **3** Slash-and-burn is the agricultural technique described in this passage. The Bantu practiced slash-and-burn farming. They cut the trees or grasses and burned them to clear a field. The remaining ashes fertilized the soil. Farmers planted for a year or two, then moved on to another area of land. After several years, the trees and grass grew back and other farmers repeated the process of slashing and burning. Although the Bantu spread their culture, their farming methods exhausted the land.

WRONG CHOICES EXPLAINED:

(1) Irrigation is an agricultural technique that supplies the land with water by artificial means, such as sprinklers or drip irrigation through small-diameter tubes. The goal of an irrigation system is to produce plant growth.

(2) Terrace farming is a system that the Incas and Japanese adapted to their rugged hilly environment. Terraces or step-like ridges constructed on mountain slopes helped the soil retain water and prevented it from being washed downhill in heavy rains. With terrace farming, the Incas and the Japanese were able to increase the productivity of their land.

(4) Crop rotation is a system of growing different crops in a field each year to preserve the fertility of the land.

5. **4** The Romans were the ancient civilization associated with the Twelve Tables, an extensive road system, and the poets Horace and Virgil. The Twelve Tables of Rome were developed in 450 B.C., and were the first written laws of the Roman Republic. The laws were an attempt by the plebeians to ensure that the Roman judges did not favor one class over another. The laws were displayed in the market and for the first time made it possible for plebeians to appeal judgments handed down by patrician judges, who were members of the wealthy class.

The Roman Empire dominated the world from 27 B.C. to about 476 A.D. A complex system of roads linked the empire throughout the Mediterranean from Spain to parts of Asia Minor. In the north, the Roman Empire spread to France as well as parts of Britain. The Roman roads were essential for the growth of the Roman Empire because they enabled the Romans to move armies, trade goods, and communicate news. At its peak, the Roman road system spanned 53,819 miles and contained about 372 links. The Romans became very good at constructing roads for military, commercial, and political reasons. They were intended primarily as carriage roads, the means of carrying material from one location to another. These long highways were very important in maintaining both the stability and expansion of the empire.

Horace (65–8 B.C.) wrote *Odes*, which focused on the life of ordinary Romans. In his poems, he praised the early Roman virtues of simplicity, courage, and reverence. He asserted that Rome needed these virtues to maintain its strength. Virgil (70–19 B.C.) wrote the epic poem *The Aeneid*, relating the adventures of Aeneas, whose descendants were believed to have founded the Roman race. Virgil extolled Rome's greatness.

WRONG CHOICES EXPLAINED:

(1) The Babylonian empire, which lasted from about 3000 to 1800 B.C., is associated with the Code of Hammurabi as well as a form of writing known as *cuneiform*.

(2) The Greek civilization began around 1750 B.C. and existed until about 133 B.C. The Greeks are associated with the development of democracy and with such writers as Socrates, Plato, and Aristotle.

(3) The Phoenician civilization prospered from about 1200 to 800 B.C. It was made up of small city-states in the lands known today as Lebanon and Syria. The Phoenicians were seafaring merchants who carried valuable goods across the Mediterranean. Their most important contribution was the alphabet, developed to record business transactions. The Phoenician alphabet was the basis for the alphabet we use today.

6. **4** The term *feudalism* is best defined as a system in which land is exchanged for military service and loyalty. During the early Middle Ages in Europe, the central government could not protect its subjects from local warfare or foreign invasion. Thus, small farmers surrendered their lands to powerful local nobles in exchange for their promise of protection. This system became known as feudalism. Feudalism helped people survive the breakdown of central government and order. Feudalism was characterized by key social, economic, and political relationships. A major social feature of feudal society was the development of a strict class structure based on the control of land and military power. There was a rigid class distinction in which the king was at the top and the peasant or serf was at the bottom. Everyone had a well-defined position in medieval European society. Feudal society was sharply divided into the land-holding nobles, the upper class, and the great mass of peasants or serfs. People were born as serfs, knights, or lords, and could not change their social position. Local nobles or lords were given lands by their rulers or kings in exchange for military service. These lords had small armies of their own made up of knights, armed warriors on horseback. During the Middle Ages, most people lived on the manor, which was the

noble's estate, and the serfs gave their lords part of the harvest for the use of the land. In return, the lords protected the serfs from outside attackers.

WRONG CHOICES EXPLAINED:

(1) The Crusades refer to the holy wars between Christians and Muslims for control of the Holy Land. The Crusades lasted from 1096 to 1246 A.D.

(2) Barter is the process in which goods are traded for other goods.

(3) Separation of powers refers to the division of political power among three separate branches of the Executive, Legislative, and Judiciary. The U.S. Constitution has a system of separation of powers.

7. **2** The title that best completes the partial outline is the "Preservation of Greco-Roman Ideas." The Byzantine Empire drew its name from the ancient Greek city of Byzantium. After the fall of Rome in 476 A.D., the Byzantine Empire was regarded as the heir to Roman power and traditions. The Byzantine Empire remained a political and cultural force for nearly 1,000 years after the fall of Rome. To Europe, it was a symbol of the power and glory of Rome long after the Roman Empire had faded. Emperor Justinian (527–565 A.D.) preserved Roman law. He set up a team of scholars to gather and organize the ancient laws of Rome, a collection of laws that became known as the Justinian Code. The Code served as the basis of law for many medieval rulers. Byzantine architecture combined the features of Greco-Roman and Persian architecture by devising a rectangular building topped by a round dome. Saint Sophia, the famous church erected in Constantinople in the 6th century by Emperor Justinian, is an example of Byzantine architecture. In 863 A.D., the Byzantine Empire introduced Orthodox Christianity to Russia. The Byzantine emperor sent two Greek monks, Cyril and Methodius, to convert the Slavic people. These missionaries adapted the Greek alphabet to translate the Bible into the Slavic language. The Cyrillic alphabet, named after Cyril, became the written language of Russia. It is still used today in Russia and the Ukraine. In 988 A.D., Prince Vladimir and all his subjects converted to Orthodox Christianity. Kiev, which was already linked to Byzantium by trade, now looked to Constantinople for religious guidance. Byzantine culture represented a continuation of classical knowledge, especially its Greek and Hellenistic aspects. The Byzantine Empire preserved Greek science, philosophy, and literature. When the empire declined in the 1400s, some of the ancient texts of Greece were carried to the West and helped to stimulate the revival of learning during the later Middle Ages and the Renaissance.

WRONG CHOICES EXPLAINED:

(1) The Age of Discovery refers to the period from 1400 to 1600. It was the era in which European monarchs sent explorers to find new trade routes, resources, and land in Asia, Africa, and the Americas.

(3) The Persian Empire lasted from 2000 to 100 B.C. At its height, it stretched more than 3,000 miles from the Nile to the Indus River. Darius was

the ruler who unified the Persian Empire by building a network of public roads. In 570 B.C., the ruler Zoroaster introduced a new religion known as *Zoroastrianism*. This religion taught that there were only two gods: the god of truth and goodness and the god of darkness and evil.

(4) The Crusades were a series of religious wars between Christians and Muslims from the late 1000s to the mid-1200s.

8. **2** Based on the information in this illustration, the statement about the society of ancient Egypt that is accurate is that the social structure was hierarchical. A hierarchical society is a system of ranking people within a particular society. The illustration shows that Egypt was shaped like a pyramid. The pharaoh or king, as well as his family, was at the top. Below him were other members of the upper class, including government officials, priests, and army commanders. The next tier of the pyramid contained merchants and the artisans. At the base of the pyramid was the biggest group, the peasant farmers. Beneath the peasants were the slaves. Slaves, usually captives from foreign wars, served in the homes of the rich or worked in the gold mines of upper Egypt.

WRONG CHOICES EXPLAINED:

(1) The illustration does not show any information that women had equal status to the men. Women in Egyptian society had many of the same rights as men. For example, wealthy or middle-class women could own and trade property, enter business deals, and obtain a divorce. However, women were not completely equal to men. They were excluded from being scribes or government officials.

(3) The illustration does not provide information about whether social mobility was unrestricted. Egyptians were not locked into their social classes. Lower-class Egyptians could gain high status through marriage or success in their jobs. Some slaves could even earn their freedom as a reward for their service.

(4) The illustration shows that soldiers did not outnumber farmers. Farmers were one of the largest class groups in ancient Egypt.

9. **3** The statement about the Mongol Empire that is accurate is that the Pax Mongolia led to regional stability, increasing trade on the Silk Road. Around 1200, the Mongols swept out of the grasslands of Central Asia to build the largest land empire in the world. They ruled people from China, Russia, Eastern Europe, and India. The Mongols imposed law and order across much of Eurasia. The Mongolian strong discipline and control over vast areas contributed to stability, which led to the period known as the Pax Mongolia (Mongol Peace); this allowed for an exchange of goods and ideas between the East and the West. The Mongol Peace made the caravan trade route along the Silk Road safe for travel and trade. Through the Silk Road, traders transported Chinese silk and porcelain, which continued to be desired in Europe and western Asia. Other Chinese products and inventions

that went west were the printing press, gunpowder, the compass, and playing cards. During the rule of Kublai Khan (1260–1294) foreign merchants were invited to visit China. Most of them were Muslims from India, central Asia, and Persia. The most famous European to visit China was Marco Polo, the Venetian trader. With his father and uncle, he traveled by caravan on the Silk Road and arrived at the court of Kublai Khan in 1275. Before returning home, he spent 17 years in China, where he marveled at the technological superiority of the Chinese, such as the use of gunpowder and coals, which was little known in Europe. His writings about that country's fabulous cities and its wealth aroused Western interest in trading with them.

WRONG CHOICES EXPLAINED:

(1) The Mongols did not develop a highly technological society that emphasized formal education. The Mongol rulers ruled with tolerance and respected academics and artists, but they did not establish any formal educational structure promoting technology.

(2) European monarchies did not become a model for the early Mongol rulers. During the rise of the early Mongol rulers in the 1200s, Europe was in its feudal period where local, rather than central, rulers controlled regions. The Mongols looked to the leadership of the eastern empires such as China or India.

(4) The Mongols never adopted Roman Catholicism as the official religion of the empire. The Mongols allowed different religions, such as Buddhism, Christianity, Islam, Judaism, and Confucianism.

10. **2** The Renaissance is the period in European history that is most closely associated with Leonardo da Vinci, Michelangelo, William Shakespeare, and Nicolaus Copernicus. The Renaissance, which in French means "rebirth," was a period of artistic and cultural achievement in Europe from the 14th to the 16th century. The Renaissance began with a reemphasis on the Greco-Roman culture that had been neglected during the Middle Ages. Renaissance writers focused on reason, a questioning attitude, experimentation, and free inquiry, in contrast to the medieval approach that emphasized faith, authority, and tradition. Renaissance artists rejected the medieval form of art and imitated the classical works of Greece and Rome. Their art was very realistic. The artists studied the human anatomy in detail and worked from live models. They also studied the techniques of three-dimensional perspective. Leonardo da Vinci is considered the ideal Renaissance man. He was skilled as a painter, sculptor, architect, musician, engineer, and scientist. Da Vinci's *Last Supper* and *Mona Lisa* are considered masterpieces.

Michelangelo was also a many-sided Renaissance genius. He was talented as a painter, sculptor, poet, and architect. He painted biblical scenes and figures on the ceiling of the Sistine Chapel in the Vatican. His *Pieta* and *David* are still considered the best examples of the artistic achievements of the Renaissance.

William Shakespeare was an English writer who is considered the greatest poet and playwright of all time. Shakespeare's best-known plays, which include *Hamlet*, *Macbeth*, and *Romeo and Juliet*, have endured for centuries. His dramas explore the full range of human activities and emotions.

Nicholas Copernicus (1473–1543) was the Polish astronomer who helped promote the Scientific Revolution. Copernicus stated that the earth and other planets revolved around the sun. This teaching contradicted Church teaching, which said the earth was the center of the universe. The scientific community would accept Copernicus' conclusions only after his death.

WRONG CHOICES EXPLAINED:

(1) The Early Middle Ages is also known as the Dark Ages. The period lasted from the 5th to the 10th century. It was a time of disorder and decline.

(3) The Age of Absolutism was a period in Europe and Asia during the 1500s and 1600s when rulers sought to centralize their power. These rulers established complete control of the government and the lives of the people and the nation.

(4) The Enlightenment, also known as the Age of Reason, was a period in Europe in the 18th century. Enlightenment thinkers believed that one could use reason to understand the universe. They also rejected traditional ideas based on authority.

11. **1** One of the primary reasons for the spread of the bubonic plague was the increase in trade. The plague began in Asia. Traveling the trade lanes, it infected most of Asia and the Muslim world. Flea-infested rats that carried the disease crept on board Italian trading ships in Asia Minor and spread the plague into Europe. In 1347, a fleet of Genovese merchant ships arrived in Sicily carrying a dreaded cargo. This disease became known as the Black Death because of the purplish or blackish spots produced on the skin. The disease swept through Italy. From there it followed the trade routes to France, Germany, England, and other parts of Europe. It is estimated that the Black Death killed one-third of the population of Europe, or about 75 million people. The increased trade between European countries and the Middle East helped to make the Black Death of 1347 one of the worst plagues in European history.

WRONG CHOICES EXPLAINED:

(2) The colonization of the Americas was not a primary reason for the spread of the bubonic plague. Europeans did not colonize the Americas until the later half of the 15th century. The bubonic plague spread throughout Europe in the 14th century.

(3) The development of the manorial system did not affect the spread of the bubonic plague. The manorial system was an economic system structured around the lord's manor or estate. The manors were self-sufficient, and the lords and serfs did not trade with groups outside of their estate or manor.

(4) Economic decline was one of the major effects of the plague but was not a reason for the spread of the disease. The economic effects of the plague were enormous. Town populations fell, trade declined, and production diminished as there were fewer workers to produce goods.

12. **4** A situation that is considered a cause of the other three is the posting of the Ninety-five Theses by Martin Luther. On October 31, 1517, Martin Luther, a German monk, posted his Ninety-five Theses on a church door in Wittenberg, a university town. In these statements, he challenged the sale of indulgences and other papal practices. Luther's attack struck a chord throughout Germany. His actions led to the Protestant Reformation because its supporters protested against the Catholic Church. Martin Luther's demands for reform, which included a denial of papal authority and the belief that the Bible was the only guide for salvation, led to the establishment of many different Protestant churches throughout Europe. Powerful northern Europeans and northern German rulers welcomed the revolt against Rome as a way of getting valuable Church property. Thus, many northern German rulers protected Luther from attack. As the Protestant Reformation continued to spread, the Catholic Church took a number of actions known as the *Counter-Reformation*. The purpose of the Counter-Reformation was to strengthen the Catholic Church as well as to keep Catholics from converting to Protestantism. Pope Paul II called the Council of Trent to guide the reform movement. The Council, which met on and off for twenty years, reaffirmed traditional Catholic practices and worked to end abuses in the Church. The Protestant Reformation led to a series of religious wars in the 1520s between Catholics and Lutherans, which led to the Peace of Augsburg. This agreement, signed in 1555, allowed the rulers of a country to decide the religion of the people. Thus, most of northern Europe and northern Germany became Protestant and southern Europe remained Catholic. The Protestant Reformation ended Europe's religious unity, which had existed for almost a thousand years.

WRONG CHOICES EXPLAINED:

(1), (2), and (3) All of these choices are the direct result of Martin Luther's posting of the Ninety-five Theses.

13. **4** "The population of Peking increased more than the population of Canton between 1250 and 1450" is the statement that can best be supported by the information in this table. According to the table, the population of Peking increased from 140,000 to 600,000 people, an increase of 475,000, whereas the city of Canton grew from 140,000 to 175,000, an increase of only 25,000 people.

WRONG CHOICES EXPLAINED:

(1) The population of Paris decreased between 1250 and 1450. The city of Paris lost 10,000 people.

(2) The populations of Cairo and Nanking were higher in 1450 than in 1250. In 1250, Cairo had a population of 300,000, and the city had gained 80,000 residents by 1450. In 1250, Nanking had a population of 130,000, which increased to 150,000 by 1450.

(3) None of the large cities exceeded 1 million people in 1450. The largest city was Peking, which had a population of 600,000.

14. **1** This author is suggesting that during the Ottoman Empire religion was mingled with historic traditions. The Ottoman Turks, people from central Asia, emerged as the rulers of the Islamic world in the 13th century. In 1453, they succeeded in capturing Constantinople, capital of what remained of the Byzantine Empire. By the 1500s, the Ottomans had built the largest, most powerful empire in the Middle East and Europe. At its peak, the Ottoman Empire reached across three continents from southeastern Europe through the Middle East and North Africa. The Ottomans ruled a vast area that included many diverse people with many religions. However, in accordance with Islamic law, the Ottomans granted freedom of worship to other religious communities, particularly Christians and Jews. They treated these communities as *millets* or nations. They allowed each to follow its own religious laws and educate its people as long as they obeyed Ottoman law. This patchwork system kept conflict among people of the various religions to a minimum.

WRONG CHOICES EXPLAINED:

(2), (3), and (4) None of these statements can be supported by this passage. The author does not discuss information about minority religions or whether rulers separated politics from religion or operated under a strict set of laws.

15. **3** These events in history occurred during the rule of the Ming dynasty in China. In 1368, peasant leader Zhu Yuan led a rebellion that successfully overthrew the foreign rule of the Mongols and established the Ming dynasty. The Ming dynasty ruled China from 1368 to 1644. During the first several decades of the 1400s, the Chinese admiral Zheng He established trade links with many distinct commercial centers. His earliest voyages were to Southeast Asia and India. Later, he traveled as far as Arabia and eastern Africa. Some of his expeditions included as many as 62 ships carrying more than 25,000 sailors, with some ships measuring 400 feet long. His voyages demonstrated to the world the power of Ming China. However, after Zheng He's death in 1433, the Ming emperor banned the building of large oceangoing ships and China halted its voyages of exploration. During the Ming dynasty, rulers enacted reforms to improve the government. They brought back the civil service system. In this system, candidates had to pass a difficult exam. Once again, Confucian learning became important because knowledge of Confucian classics was a key part of the exam. Ming leaders also established a board of censors to eliminate corruption in the bureaucracy.

WRONG CHOICES EXPLAINED:

(1) The Mughal dynasty ruled India from 1526 to 1837. The most famous Mughal was Akbar the Great (1542–1605). He united northern India under his rule. He promoted trade, and his policy of toleration for Hindus promoted peace and prosperity.

(2) Abu Al-Abbas founded the Abbasid dynasty in 750, which ruled until the mid-1200s. The Abbasid rule ended Arab domination of Islam. The Abbasid court ruled from Baghdad.

(4) The Tokugawa shogunate in Japan came to power in 1603 and brought peace and stability to Japan for 300 years. The shogun rulers barred all Japanese from traveling abroad and cut off trade with Europe.

16. **4** Mercantilism was the primary economic policy used by the Spanish with their Latin American colonies. Mercantilism was an economic policy that Spain adapted in the 15th and 16th centuries in their quest for trade and colonies. To make the empire profitable, Spain closely controlled its economic activities, especially trade. Colonies could export raw materials for the mother country and could buy only Spanish-manufactured goods. Laws forbade colonists from trading with other European nations or even with other Spanish colonies. Spanish colonies in the Americas kept the wealth flowing back into the home country because colonies ensured a favorable balance of trade. Spain (the mother country) was exporting more goods to the colonies than it was importing. This favorable balance of trade increased the wealth of the nation that was measured by the supply of gold and silver. The most valuable resources shipped from Spanish America to Spain were gold and silver.

WRONG CHOICES EXPLAINED:

(1) Embargoes are policies adopted by nations that impose a ban or complete halt on trade with other countries.

(2) Tariffs are taxes on imported goods.

(3) Boycotts are refusals to buy certain goods or services.

17. **4** In *Two Treatises of Government*, John Locke wrote that the purpose of government was to protect natural rights. John Locke was a 17th-century English philosopher who wrote *Two Treatises of Government* to justify the Glorious Revolution. He believed that all people in the state of nature were happy and that all people possess natural rights. These rights include the right to life, liberty, and property. Locke claimed that people entered a social contract with a government to protect these rights. If a government does not protect these rights, the people have the right to overthrow it. Locke's ideas influenced Thomas Jefferson's Declaration of Independence and Jean-Jacques Rousseau's book *The Social Contract*.

WRONG CHOICES EXPLAINED:

(1) Locke did not believe that the purpose of government was to keep kings in power. He claimed that the obligation of the government was to serve the people, not the rulers in power.

(2) The main purpose of the *Two Treatises of Government* was to address the natural rights of the people. Locke did not discuss the role of government and the economy.

(3) The *Two Treatises of Government* deals with distribution of political power between the government and the people. There are no references to the idea that the purpose of government is to expand territory.

18. **2** A generalization best supported by the information on this map is that monsoon winds influenced trade between East Africa and India. A monsoon is a seasonal prevailing wind that lasts for several months. Monsoon winds often bring heavy rain with them. The term was originally applied to seasonal winds in the Indian Ocean and Arabian Sea. The map clearly shows that the monsoon winds blow from India and the Persian Gulf from November through March, and toward India and the Persian Gulf from April through October. The map also illustrates that the routes of both the Arab dhows (boats) and the coastal traders mirror those of the monsoon winds, and that trade routes were influenced by the direction of the monsoon winds.

WRONG CHOICES EXPLAINED:

(1) The map does not show that no trade occurred between East Africa and the Persian Gulf region. The route maps of both the Arab dhows (boats) and the coastal traders are clearly indicated on the map.

(3) The map does not illustrate the trade states that developed, nor does it focus on the interior of East Africa.

(4) The map does not mention or illustrate any information about the spread of Islam.

19. **1** One purpose of these laws was to reduce local authority and increase central control. At first, the Spanish monarchs created the *encomienda* system, which allowed the conquistadors the right to demand labor or tribute from Native Americans in a particular area. The conquistadors used this system to force Native Americans to work under the most brutal conditions. Those who resisted were hunted down and killed. Many died from disease, starvation, and cruel treatment. Reports by missionaries, such as Bartolomé de Las Casas, forced the Spanish king, Charles V, to pass the New Laws of the Indies in 1542, forbidding the enslavement of Native Americans and abolishing the encomienda system. The New Laws consisted of many regulations on the encomienda system, including its solemn prohibition of the enslavement of the Native Americans and provisions for the gradual abolition of the encomienda system. It prohibited the sending of indigenous people to work in the mines unless it was absolutely necessary, and required that they be taxed fairly and treated well. It ordered public officials or clergy with encomienda grants to return them immediately to the Crown, and stated that encomienda grants would not be hereditarily passed on, but would be canceled at the death of the individual *encomenderos*. These steps allowed the Spanish monarchs to establish these New Laws and gave the monarchs greater control over their colonies in the Americas.

WRONG CHOICES EXPLAINED:

(2) The laws did not increase religious authority and limit secular influences. They increased the influence of the king. According to Article 38, all lawsuits had to be tried before the king. There is no reference to religious courts.

(3) and (4) Neither the issue of Native American citizenship nor economic development was addressed by the New Laws. The focus of the New Laws was to increase the power of Emperor Charles V.

20. **4** One major effect of Napoleon's rule of France was that it led to a restoration of political stability. The French people hoped Napoleon Bonaparte would provide stability for the nation. Napoleon was a popular military general because of his victories against France's enemies. In 1799, Napoleon, in a coup d'etat (a sudden takeover of government), came to power in France. The Directory, which was a five-man government, had ruled France from 1795. They lost the support of the people because they made little effort to resolve the gap between the rich and the poor. The Directory was on the verge of bankruptcy and unable to defeat the European nations of Austria and Prussia. Napoleon's new government was a military dictatorship. He restricted the government so that French officials were responsible to the central government, improved the educational system, reformed the tax code so that all citizens paid taxes, and introduced the Napoleonic Code. The Code included many Enlightenment ideas, such as the legal equality of citizens and religious toleration. In 1804 he took the title of Emperor Napoleon I. The French people were willing to accept this absolute government because of their desire for political stability.

WRONG CHOICES EXPLAINED:

(1) The Roman Catholic Church lost power during Napoleon's rule. He restored friendly relations with the Catholic Church. However, in the Concordat of 1801, he promised that the state would pay the salaries of the French clergy but insisted that the Church surrender claims to land confiscated during the Revolution. He later was excommunicated because he annexed the papal states.

(2) There was no mass emigration to the Americas during Napoleon's rule. Napoleon did send a large army to put down a revolt in Haiti in 1802, but it did not lead to a mass exodus of French people to the Americas.

(3) Napoleon's rule did not lead to trade agreements with Great Britain. Napoleon established the Continental system, which forbade European countries to trade with England.

21. **4** The idea of free trade is most closely associated with laissez-faire economics. The economic theory of laissez-faire proposes that governments should not interfere with businesses. Laissez-faire stemmed from the economic philosophers of the 18th century Enlightenment. They argued that government regulation only interfered with the production of wealth. The economy would prosper without government regulation. The economic ideas of laissez-faire were skillfully presented by Adam Smith in his book *Wealth of Nations*. Smith argued that the free market—the natural forces of supply and demand—should be allowed to operate and regulate business. The free market would produce more goods at lower prices, making them affordable for

everyone. A growing economy would also encourage capitalists to reinvest new profits in new ventures. Smith and other capitalists argued that the marketplace was better off without any government regulation. Smith argued for free trade in which the trade of goods and services between or within countries flows unhindered by government-imposed restrictions. Smith believed that government intervention generally increases costs of goods and services to both consumers and producers. Smith is considered the founder of the free trade and market economy. Adam Smith's idea of laissez-faire would gain increasing influence as the Industrial Revolution spread across Europe.

WRONG CHOICES EXPLAINED:

(1) Communes are communities in which property is held in common. Living quarters are shared, and physical needs are provided for and exchanged for work at assigned jobs.

(2) Trade unionism is an organization of workers who have banded together to achieve common goals in key areas such as wages, hours, and working conditions.

(3) Subsistence agriculture is a type of farming in which the farmer and his family can barely make a living.

22. **3** In the 19th century, a major reason for Irish migration to North America was to flee widespread famine. The main cause of the mass starvation or famine in Ireland during the 19th century was the failure of the potato crop. In the 1840s, Ireland experienced one of the worst famines of modern history. The potato, introduced from the Americas, was the main source of food for most of the Irish. In 1845, a blight, or disease, destroyed the potato crop. Other crops, such as wheat and oats, were not affected. The British, who ruled Ireland, continued to require the Irish to ship these crops out of Ireland, leaving little for the Irish except the blighted potato. The result was the "Great Hunger." Out of a population of 8 million, about 1 million people died from starvation and disease over the next few years. Millions more emigrated to the United States and Canada. It is estimated that 18 percent of the Irish population was forced to migrate because of the potato famine.

WRONG CHOICES EXPLAINED:

(1) The Irish did not migrate to North America in the 19th century for universal suffrage. The struggle for universal suffrage, or the right to vote, would become a political issue in the late 19th and 20th centuries.

(2) There were no malaria outbreaks in Ireland during the 19th century.

(4) The Irish did not migrate to North America to escape a civil war. Although the Irish resented British rule, the British had established control over Ireland and formally joined the country to Britain in 1801.

23. **1** A major goal of both the Sepoy Mutiny in India and the Boxer Rebellion in China was to rid their countries of foreigners. The Sepoy Mutiny in India and the Boxer Rebellion in China were responses to European impe-

rialism. The Sepoys were Indian soldiers serving under British command. These soldiers were protesting the policies of the British East India Company. The British cartridges used by the Sepoys had to be bitten to remove the seal before inserting them into their guns. The coverings were said to be greased with pork and beef fat. In 1857, the Sepoy soldiers refused to accept these cartridges. Both Hindus, who considered the cow sacred, and Muslims, who did not eat pork, were angry. The Sepoy Mutiny (Rebellion) lasted more than a year. The British government sent troops to help the British East India Company. This was a turning point in Indian history. After 1858, the British government took direct control of India. Eventually, the British began educating and training Indians for roles in their own Indian government.

The Boxers were a secret society formed in 1899. Their goal was to drive out the foreigners who were destroying China with their Western technology. In 1900, the Boxers attacked foreign communities in China as well as foreign embassies in Beijing. In response, Western owners and Japan formed a multinational force of 25,000 troops. They crushed the Boxers and rescued the foreigners besieged in Beijing. Both of these rebellions were attacks against Western imperialism.

WRONG CHOICES EXPLAINED:

(2) Neither the Sepoy Mutiny nor the Boxer Rebellion was directed at expanding their respective territories. The Sepoy soldiers and the Boxers wanted to reestablish control over their own nation and did not seek to expand their control over neighboring countries.

(3) The Sepoys and the Boxers did expect to receive international military support. The Western nations did not send military aid to the Sepoys, because India was a British colony and other countries were fearful of British power. Western powers and Japan provided military aid to end the Boxer Rebellion rather than support their goals.

(4) The goal of the Sepoy Mutiny and the Boxer Rebellion was not to restore an absolute monarch to the throne. Both of these movements wanted to end Western imperialism or foreign domination of their country.

24. **4** Early exploration of Africa by Europeans was hindered by the many different physical features. Most of Africa is a vast plateau. Toward the edge of the continent are mountain ranges, such as the Atlas Mountains in the northwest and the Frankenberg Mountains in the southeast. The plateaus of Africa lie at different elevations, thus making travel difficult. Africans, however, migrated across the plateaus. Traders followed well-traveled routes through parts of the continent. However, the land discouraged early Europeans from exploring the continent. When they tried to sail up rivers, they found the way blocked by large waterfalls and rapids. Deserts covered more than 40 percent of Africa. These deserts included the Sahara in the north and the Kalahari and Nami deserts in the south. The Sahara has been a major land barrier to the movement of African people as well as exploration by Europeans. Tropical grasslands, rain forests, and jungles made it difficult

for Europeans to explore Africa. Although Europeans had established trading posts along Africa's Mediterranean and Atlantic coasts by the 15th century until the 19th century, its inhospitable interior of mountains, plateaus, and jungles discouraged exploration, and it remained unknown to the outside world. Africa was referred to as the Dark Continent because Europeans knew so little about it.

WRONG CHOICES EXPLAINED:

(1) European exploration was not hindered by the lack of natural resources. Africa possessed a great wealth of natural resources, such as diamonds, gold, and oil. The abundance of natural resources sparked European interest in Africa in the late 19th century.

(2) Alliances between African kingdoms did not hinder early European exploration of Africa. Europeans used the technique of dividing and conquering different African kingdoms to gain control of particular areas.

(3) European monarchs did not follow an isolationist policy toward Africa. Isolationism is a policy of avoiding conflicts or involvement with other nations. European monarchs in the 15th and 16th centuries wanted to establish their influence on the African continent to promote their countries' power.

25. **1** The action taken by the Meiji government encouraging industrialization in the 19th century was the building of a modern transportation system. During the Meiji Period, the Japanese adapted Western models of industrialization. In the Meiji Period from 1862 to 1912, Japan ended feudalism and began to modernize by selectively borrowing from the West. These reformers rallied around the emperor and unseated the shoguns, whom they claimed had weakened the power of Japan. The goal of the Meiji (enlightened rule) leader was "a rich country, a strong military." The new leaders sent Japanese students abroad to learn about Western government, economies, technology, and customs. The emperor also energetically supported the Western path of industrialization. The country built its first railroad line in 1872. The tracks connected Tokyo, the nation's capital, with the port of Yokohama, 20 miles to the south. By 1914, Japan had more than 7,000 miles of rails. Coal production, needed for the modern transportation system, grew from a half-million tons to more than 21 million tons in 1913. In addition, large state-supported companies built thousands of factories that were able to transport goods throughout the nation. Developing modern industries with an efficient transportation system enabled the Japanese economy to become as modern as any other in the world and to become competitive with the West.

WRONG CHOICES EXPLAINED:

(2) During the Meiji era, the Japanese did not limit the number of ports open to foreign trade. The government increased foreign trade with the West and other countries to help improve the Japanese economy.

(3) The Meiji government did not force families to settle on collective farms. For the first time, in 1873, the Meiji government established the right of private land ownership in Japan.

(4) The Meiji government did not establish a system of trade guilds in the 19th century. The Meiji government promoted modernization and rejected trade guilds that were associated with a medieval economy limiting their industrial growth.

26. **1** One goal of the League of Nations was to promote peaceful relations worldwide. The Treaty of Versailles, which ended World War I, created the League of Nations. The League of Nations was an international peace organization that consisted of more than 40 countries that hoped to settle problems through negotiations, not war. The countries that joined the League promised to take cooperative economic and military actions against any aggressor state. Although the League had been one of President Woodrow Wilson's Fourteen Points, the United States never joined. Lacking the support of the United States and other world powers, the League of Nations' ability to promote peace was weakened. In the 1930s, the ability to promote worldwide peace declined as the League of Nations was unable to prevent aggression or take effective actions against Japan, Italy, or Germany.

WRONG CHOICES EXPLAINED:

(2) The goal of the League of Nations was not to stimulate the economy of Europe. The League was formed to promote peace and security.

(3) The League of Nations was created in 1920. World War I had ended in 1918.

(4) The League of Nations was designed to end the strong alliance system, not encourage it. President Wilson believed that an international organization like the League of Nations could settle disputes better than the alliance system among groups of nations.

27. **2** Joseph Stalin is associated with all these policies. Joseph Stalin's economic program for the Soviet Union was known as the Five Year Plan. When taking power in 1928, Stalin proposed the first of several Five Year Plans aimed at building heavy industry (steel and iron), improving transportation, and increasing farm output. The purpose of these plans was to modernize the economy of the Soviet Union. Stalin brought all economic activity under government control to achieve this growth. Stalin appealed to the nationalism of the people by promising that his Five Year Plan would enable Russia to catch up with Western countries. Under Joseph Stalin, peasants in the Soviet Union were forced to join collective farms. In 1928, there were more than 25 million small farms in Russia. In that year, Stalin announced that these privately owned farms would be abolished and would be replaced by collective farms, which were large farms owned and operated by peasants as a group. Peasants would be allowed to keep their houses and personal belongings, but all farm animals and tools were to be turned over to the collectives. The state set all prices and controlled access to farm supplies. The government planned to provide all the necessary equipment (tractors and fertilizers) and teach farmers modern methods to increase the output of grain.

Surplus grain would be sold abroad to earn money to invest in industrial growth. The peasants resisted Stalin's policy of collectivization. Many peasants destroyed their crops and livestock in protest. Stalin showed no mercy and ordered the peasants to be shot on sight. Between 5 and 10 million peasants died. By 1935, 95 percent of Russian farms had become collectives. From 1934 to 1938, Stalin also directed a series of purge trials, consisting of trumped-up or false accusations, mock trials, and then suicides or executions. Stalin's Great Purge resulted in the deaths of those who were important in the founding of the revolution, or high military officers, and anyone who was not loyal to him. Stalin spread terror within the state, and it is estimated that he ordered the death of more than 15 million people. By 1938, Stalin's cruel and brutal methods had enabled him to establish complete control over Russia and transformed Russia into an industrial giant.

WRONG CHOICES EXPLAINED:

(1) Adolf Hitler was the Nazi dictator of Germany from 1933 to 1945.

(3) Deng Xiaoping was the Chinese Communist political leader from 1976 to 1997.

(4) Jawaharlal Nehru was the first prime minister of independent India in 1947 and served in this position until his death in 1964.

28. **1** Japan's invasion of Manchuria, Italy's attack on Ethiopia, and Germany's blitzkrieg in Poland are examples of military aggression. Military aggression is the use of armed forces or forceful actions to secure territorial gains. Throughout the 1930s, Japan, Italy, and Germany took these aggressive actions to pursue their goal of forming an empire. They scorned peace and glorified war. In 1931, Japanese military leaders seized Manchuria in pursuit of their goal for an empire. In 1935, Italy invaded the African country of Ethiopia. In both of these cases, the League of Nations did not take any concrete steps to stop these acts of aggression. On September 1, 1939, Hitler's Germany formed a blitzkrieg, which meant using armed tanks and airplanes to invade Poland. This led to the beginning of World War II.

WRONG CHOICES EXPLAINED:

(2) Appeasement is the policy of giving in to the demands of aggression to avoid war. England and France used appeasement to satisfy Hitler's demand for land during the 1930s.

(3) Containment was the policy of the United States toward the Soviet Union to prevent the spread of communism in the world after World War II.

(4) The domino theory was introduced by United States President Dwight Eisenhower in 1954. The domino theory stated that if one country in a region came under the influence of communism, the surrounding areas would fall under the influence of communism. President Eisenhower was concerned about the spread of communism in Southeast Asia.

29. **3** "The economic upheaval of the Depression had major political effects" is a fact rather than an opinion about the worldwide Depression of

the 1930s. A depression is a severe economic downturn in which large numbers of businesses fail and many workers are unemployed over an extended period of time. At the height of the Depression, as many as 50 million people were unemployed in the United States, Germany, Japan, and other industrialized countries. In the United States, Franklin D. Roosevelt, a Democrat, was elected president in 1932. His election ended 12 years of Republican domination of the presidency and led to Democratic control of the Executive branch for 20 years. In the 1930s, the Great Depression spread from the United States to Germany. More than one-third of the German forces lost their jobs. The Weimar government, a new democratic government created to run Germany after World War I, was very weak and could not cope with this catastrophe. In the early 1920s, Adolf Hitler gained control of the National Socialist, or Nazi Party. Hitler stated that the Germans were the superior race who were destined to build a new empire. The popularity of his party grew, and as the Great Depression hit Germany, support for the Nazi Party increased rapidly. In elections, unemployed workers and members of the middle class turned to Hitler's Nazi Party as a way out of the economic chaos. In 1933, Germany's president appointed Hitler as chancellor. To combat the Depression, Hitler launched a large public works program. Tens of thousands of people were put to work building highways and housing, or replanting forests. Hitler also began a crash program to rearm Germany, in violation of the Treaty of Versailles. Demand for military hardware stimulated business and helped to eliminate unemployment and raise the standard of living in Germany. Hitler established total control of the country, but few people objected to their loss of freedom because economic prosperity had been returned to Germany. Although Japan had moved toward democracy during the 1920s, there were underlying problems in Japan such as poverty among the peasants and unemployment. The Depression made these problems more apparent. In the rice-growing areas of the northeast, crop failures in 1931 led to famine. City workers suffered as the value of exports fell by half between 1929 and 1931. As many as 3 million workers lost their jobs, forcing many to go to their rural villages. These problems enabled militarists and extreme nationalists to gain power. These militarists argued that the Japanese had to expand their empire as a way of solving some of the problems created by the Depression. This approach would lead to renewed expansion and efforts to gain control of China by military aggression.

WRONG CHOICES EXPLAINED:

(1), (2), and (4) None of these statements can be supported by specific facts. It is difficult to show whether political leaders could have avoided the Depression, if Germany was hurt more by the Treaty of Versailles than by the Depression, or if World War I was the only reason for the Depression.

30. **3** The Japanese are accused of violating human rights in the city of Nanjing during World War II. Human rights are the basic rights and freedoms that are guaranteed to all people belonging to any society. In 1937, Japan

invaded the mainland of China. On December 13, after a lengthy siege, Japanese troops marched into the city of Nanjing and established a puppet government in the former Chinese Nationalist capital. After the city's surrender, one of the worst massacres in modern times took place between December 1937 and March 1938. The Japanese embarked on a campaign of murder, rape, and looting. Based on estimates made by historians and charity organizations in the city at the time, between 250,000 and 300,000 people were killed, many of them women and children. Westerners who were there estimated that the number of women raped was 20,000, and there were widespread accounts of civilians being hacked to death. The cruelty and the destruction of the city was so brutal that it became known as the "Rape of Nanjing."

WRONG CHOICES EXPLAINED:

(1) and (4) Neither of these countries invaded the Chinese mainland and the city of Nanjing.

(2) The Chinese were victims of the Japanese invasion and their human rights were violated.

31. **1** One way in which the Hitler Youth of Germany and the Red Guard of China are similar is that both organizations required unquestioning loyalty to the leader. The Hitler Youth was a paramilitary organization that existed from 1922 to 1945. Schoolchildren were required to join; the boys had to join the Hitler Youth and the girls joined the League of German Girls. One aim of the Youth movement was to instill the motivation to become loyal soldiers willing to fight for their government. Hitler's Youth movement put more emphasis on physical and military training than on academic study. On hikes and in camps, the Hitler Youths pledged absolute loyalty to Germany, promoting its greatness.

In 1962, Mao Zedong, the Communist leader of China, was concerned about the loss of enthusiasm and announced a "Cultural Revolution." Mao closed China's schools and invited students to gather in Beijing as Red Guards. They became a major force in the Cultural Revolution. The goal of the revolution was to establish a society of peasants and workers in which all were equal. The new hero was the peasant who worked with his hands. The intellectuals and artists were useless and dangerous. To help stamp out this threat, the Red Guards traveled throughout China shutting down colleges and schools. The Red Guards attacked writers, scientists, doctors, and professionals for abandoning Communist ideals. Waving copies of the "Little Red Book," Mao's sayings, Red Guards targeted anyone who resisted the regime. Exiled intellectuals or professionals were sent to work as laborers in the field. By 1969, China had become so disrupted that Mao called out the army to control the Red Guards and brought the Cultural Revolution to a close.

WRONG CHOICES EXPLAINED:

(2) Neither of these organizations helped to increase religious tolerance. Both of these organizations stressed complete loyalty to the state over religious

freedom. Hitler's Youth recognized Nazism, and the Red Guard pledged allegiance to Mao over respect to any religion.

(3) Hitler's Youth of Germany did not hinder imperialist goals of Nazism. Their goal was to become strong soldiers to help the German empire expand. The Red Guard believed in promoting the ideals of Mao's Communism, which promoted the expansion of Chinese power in foreign affairs.

(4) Neither of these groups were pro-democracy movements. These organizations stressed obedience over freedom.

32. **1** These ideas are most closely associated with the causes of the conflict in Vietnam. During the 1800s, the French carved out an empire that became known as French Indochina. It included what is today Vietnam, Cambodia, and Laos. During World War I, Asian Nationalist Ho Chi Minh emerged as the leader of the independence movement in Vietnam. During World War II, Ho formed the Viet Minh and used guerrilla warfare against the Japanese and defeated them. Ho Chi Minh believed that independence would follow. However, the French intended to regain its former colony. Vietnamese Nationalists and Communists joined the fight against the French armies. Although the French held most of the major cities, they remained powerless in the countryside. Viet Minh had widespread peasant support. For eight years, French forces battled the Vietnamese. By this time, the struggle had become part of the Cold War. The Soviet Union and China supported Ho's Communist forces. Although the United States opposed colonialism, it supported the French. U.S. President Dwight Eisenhower believed in the domino theory. According to this theory, if one nation fell to Communist forces, neighboring nations would also become Communist, like a row of falling dominoes. By 1954, the United States was paying for 80 percent of France's efforts, which was $3 million per day in 1952. In 1954, the French forces were defeated at Dienbienphu and France was forced to withdraw. A 1954 conference in Geneva led to the division of Vietnam into a Communist north and non-Communist south. Elections in 1956 would then unite Vietnam. However, the American-supported South Vietnamese government of Ngo Dinh Diem did not hold elections because Diem believed that the Communists would win. The United States supported Diem because they wanted to prevent Communism from taking over Vietnam. Ho Chi Minh, who by then was the leader of Communist North Vietnam, supported the Viet Cong, a group of Communist rebels trying to overthrow Diem. The United States sent troops to support Diem's government. The Vietnam War lasted from 1959 to 1975. By 1969, more than 500,000 Americans were serving in Vietnam. However, even with this help, the South Vietnamese could not defeat the Communists. Growing anti-war sentiment in the United States forced the country to withdraw American forces. In 1975, Communist forces captured Saigon, the capital of South Vietnam. Vietnam became reunited in 1975.

WRONG CHOICES EXPLAINED:

(2) The reasons for the Nationalist settlement of Taiwan are associated with the Communist victory in China, not Indochina.

(3) The factors that led to the Korean War are associated with the invasion of North and South Korea.

(4) The results of the Marshall Plan were directed at helping the European economy after World War II.

33. **2** South Africa is the country most closely associated with the terms *pass laws*, *homelands*, and *white minority rule*. Although South Africa won its independence from Britain in 1919, its white minority citizens alone held political power. In 1948, the Nationalist Party came to power in South Africa. This party promoted and instituted a policy of apartheid, a complete separation of the races. The government banned social contacts between whites and blacks. Apartheid established segregated schools, hospitals, and neighborhoods. Under apartheid, the government assigned black ethnic groups, such as the Zulus and Xhosas, to live in a number of Bantustans, or homelands. Supporters of apartheid claimed that the separation allowed each group to develop its own culture. The homelands, however, were in dry, infertile areas. Since South Africa needed black workers, they allowed some blacks to live outside of the homelands. To control their movement, the government enacted pass laws, requiring all black South Africans living in a town or city to carry a passbook. The passbook included a record of where they could travel or work, their tax payments, and any criminal convictions. It had to be carried at all times and produced upon demand. These laws enforced a system of inequality in South Africa.

WRONG CHOICES EXPLAINED:

(1), (3), and (4) None of these countries are associated with these terms. El Salvador is in the Americas. Iran and Israel are countries in the Middle East.

34. **1** During the Indian independence movement, the activity shown in this photograph inspired the Indian people to stop buying British goods. Gandhi, who came from a middle-class Hindu family and was educated in England, resented British colonial rule in India. During the 1920s and 1930s, he became the leader of the Indian Nationalist Movement and led a series of nonviolent actions against British rule. One effective form of protest was the boycott, in which Indians refused to buy British cloth and other manufactured goods. Gandhi urged Indians to begin spinning their own cloth and used the spinning wheel as the symbol of his nationalist movement. He rejected Western civilization because it undermined native Indian culture.

WRONG CHOICES EXPLAINED:

(2), (3), and (4) None of these activities are shown in this photograph. The photograph does not deal with rejection of Muslim rule, joining the Indian army, or expanding British textile manufacturing.

35. **4** In this passage, Mao Zedong is suggesting that China join with the Soviet Union as a partner in Communism. The Soviet Union and China were firmly committed to Communism, and to cement their ties, Mao and Stalin signed a 30-year treaty of friendship in 1950. Stalin sent economic aid and technical experts to help China modernize. However, he and Mao disagreed on many issues. Mao adapted Marxism to Chinese conditions. Marx's revolution relied on peasants rather than on factory workers. Stalin rejected Mao's view. The Soviets also assumed that the Chinese would follow Soviet leadership in world affairs. As the Chinese grew more confident, they came to resent being Moscow's junior partner. They began to compete for influence in developing nations. In addition, border disputes triggered tensions between the two countries. By 1960, border clashes and disputes over ideology led the Soviets to withdraw all aid and advisers from China.

WRONG CHOICES EXPLAINED:

(1), (2), and (3) None of these ideas are suggested in the passage.

36. **3** In this passage, Mao Zedong is using the ideas of Karl Marx. In 1948, Karl Marx collaborated with Frederich Engel to write the *Communist Manifesto*, in which he called for a worldwide revolution to end the abuses of capitalism. Marx predicted that hostility between the classes would lead to a violent revolution by workers to overthrow the capitalists. Marx believed that the revolution would come to industrial nations and that the proletariat, or factory workers, would lead the revolution creating the classless society. In China, Mao Zedong claimed to be an heir to Marx, but argued that peasants and not just workers could play leading roles in a Communist revolution, even in third world countries marked by peasant feudalism in the absence of industrial workers. Mao termed this the New Democratic Revolution. It was a departure from Marx, who had stated that the revolutionary transformation of society could take place only in countries that had achieved a capitalist stage of development with a proletarian majority. Marxism-Leninism, as espoused by Mao, came to be internationally known as Maoism.

WRONG CHOICES EXPLAINED:

(1) Thomas Malthus (1776–1834) was an English economist who wrote *The Essay on the Principle of Population* in 1798. He argued that poverty and famine were unavoidable because population growth was increasing faster than food supply.

(2) Adam Smith (1723–1790) was a Scottish economist who wrote *The Wealth of Nations* in 1776. He promoted the belief that government should not interfere in the economy and that the "invisible hand of supply and demand" will promote the best interests of society.

(4) Jiang Jieshi (Chiang Kai-Shek) (1888–1975) was the military leader of the Chinese Nationalist Party after the death of Sun Yat-sen in 1925. He was exiled to Taiwan after being defeated by the Communists in 1949.

37. **3** The conclusion that can be drawn from this time line is that long-lasting peace in the Middle East has been difficult to achieve. The historic claim of the Israelis and Arabs to the same land has been a key issue in making the peace process difficult. Israel, once called Palestine, was the home of the Jews until Rome destroyed the country in 70 A.D. Lacking a homeland, most of the Jews in Palestine scattered throughout the world. After the expansion of Islam in the 7th century, the area of Palestine fell under the control of the Arabs, and later the Ottoman Turks. In 1917, the British promised the Jews a homeland in Palestine, but not at the expense of the Arabs who were still living in the area. In 1947, the United Nations drew up a plan to divide Palestine, which was under British rule, into an Arab and a Jewish state. In 1948, Israel proclaimed its independence, but the Arabs refused to recognize the partition and invaded Israel. Israel won the war. More than half a million Arabs became refugees. These Arabs still wanted an Arab Palestinian state. Arab nations went to war with Israel in 1956, 1967, and 1973. In October 1973, Egyptian President Anwar Sadat planned a joint Arab attack on Yom Kippur, the holiest of Jewish holidays. The Israelis were caught by surprise. Arab forces inflicted heavy casualties and recaptured some of the territories lost in the 1967 war. The Israelis, under Prime Minister Golda Meir, launched a counterattack and regained most of the lost territory. After several weeks of fighting, they agreed to an uneasy truce to end the October war. In 1979, Egypt and Israel signed the Camp David Accords, an agreement to end the state of war between the two countries. Egypt recognized Israel as a legitimate state. In exchange, Israel agreed to return the Sinai Peninsula to Egypt. Because he signed the treaty, Anwar Sadat was assassinated in 1981 by Muslim extremists. Palestinians living in Israel resented Israeli rule. As their anger mounted, they turned to the Palestine Liberation Organization, or PLO, led by Yasir Arafat. During the 1970s and 1980s, the military wing of the PLO conducted a campaign of armed struggle against Israel. In 1982, the Israeli army invaded Lebanon in response to the assassination attempt against Israel's ambassador to the United Kingdom. After attacking the PLO as well as Syrian and Muslim Lebanese forces, Israel occupied southern Lebanon. Lebanon's civil forces made Israel withdraw. The invasion was a limited success in that it forced the removal of the PLO from southern Lebanon. In 1987, Palestinians, who had grown up under Israeli control in the West Bank and Gaza Strip, began a widespread campaign of civil disobedience, called the *Intifada* or uprising. The Intifada took the form of boycotts, demonstrations, attacks on Israeli soldiers, and rock throwing by unarmed teenagers. The Intifada continued into the 1990s, with little progress toward a solution. However, the civil disobedience affected world opinion, which in turn put pressure on Israel. Finally, in October 1991, Israel and Palestinian delegates met for the first time in a series of peace talks. In 1993, Israeli Prime Minister Yitzhak Rabin entered into secret negotiations held in Oslo, Norway, with PLO leader Yasir Arafat. In the document called the Declaration of Principle, Israel agreed to grant

Palestinians self-rule in the Gaza Strip and the West Bank, beginning with the town of Jericho. The difficulty of making an agreement was demonstrated by the assassination of Rabin in 1995. He was assassinated by the Jews who opposed concessions to the Palestinians. In 2004, several Qassam rocket attacks on the Israeli towns of Sederot and Negev by Palestinians from the West Bank led to air strikes and land incursions by Israel to destroy these pockets of attacks. The Israelis sought to search and destroy smuggling tunnels used by militant Palestinians to obtain weapons and ammunition. Efforts at cease-fires have fallen apart over Israeli raids on the West Bank and the inability of the Palestinian leaders to contain the small groups. In June 2008, a temporary cease-fire was negotiated, but there is doubt that the agreement will survive for a long time.

WRONG CHOICES EXPLAINED:

(1), (2), and (4) None of these conclusions can be drawn from this time line. There is no information to indicate that Israel withdrew from the Camp David Accords, that the Palestinian army is superior to the Israeli army, or that neighboring countries have not been involved in the Arab-Israeli conflict.

38. **1** The destruction of the Berlin Wall and the breakup of the Soviet Union signify the end of the Cold War. The Cold War was a period of tension and hostility between the United States and the Soviet Union beginning after World War II in 1945 and ending with the collapse of the Soviet government in 1991. In 1985, Mikhail Gorbachev came to power in the Soviet Union and wanted to end Cold War tensions. He introduced a political policy of *glasnost*, or openness. This policy ended censorship and encouraged people to openly discuss the problems of the Soviet Union. He also supported a policy of *perestroika*, which referred to restructuring the Soviet economy. Even before the collapse of the Soviet Union in 1991, Gorbachev's reforms had sparked demands for national independence in the countries under Russia's control. In October 1989, demonstrations broke out across East Germany, and when the police failed to break up the demonstrations, the East German leader was forced to resign. On November 9, 1989, the new East German leader allowed people to leave East Germany, and thousands of East Germans poured into West Germany. Within days, more than 2 million Germans crossed the border. The crowds were so huge that the government bulldozed new openings in the Berlin Wall. The Berlin Wall was torn down by joyous Germans.

As the spirit of freedom swept across Eastern Europe through Czechoslovakia, Romania, Poland, Bulgaria, and Hungary, various nationalists in the Soviet Union began to call for their own freedom. Gorbachev's policy of glasnost had unleashed the forces of ethnic nationalism and social discontent. The Soviet Union consisted of 15 separate republics made up of both Russians and non-Russians. In March 1990, the Baltic nations of Lithuania, Estonia, and Latvia declared their independence. In January 1991, Soviet troops attacked Lithuania, but the bloody assault and the lack of economic progress in the Soviet Union damaged Gorbachev's popularity. In June 1991, Boris Yelstin, who criticized the crackdown in Lithuania and the slow pace of reform, was elected president of Russia, the largest and most powerful of the Soviet republics. On August 18, 1991, Communist hard-liners overthrew Gorbachev, but their coup failed. The coup played a role in the breakup of the Soviet Union. Gorbachev recognized the independence of Lithuania and the other Baltic states, and by December, all 15 republics had declared their independence. Yelstin met with the leaders of other republics and they agreed to form the Commonwealth of Independent States (CIS), a loose federation of former Soviet territories. Only the Baltic republics and Georgia refused to join. The former Soviet Union had collapsed on December 25, 1991. Gorbachev resigned as president of the Soviet Union. By the end of 1991, Communism had ceased to exist in Russia and the Cold War ended.

WRONG CHOICES EXPLAINED:

(2) The collapse of the Taliban in Afghanistan in 2002 occurred after the Cold War had ended in 1991.

(3) The Warsaw Pact was formed in 1955 as a defensive alliance against Western Europe. The Pact included the Soviet Union and its satellite nations in Eastern Europe. The end of the Cold War and the collapse of Communism in 1991 made this pact outdated.

(4) The fall of the Berlin Wall and the breakup of the Soviet Union did not signify the power of the European Union. The European Union was an economic union formed to expand free trade and promote economic growth.

39. **2** In the 20th century, urbanization affected the developing nations of Africa, Asia, and Latin America by weakening traditional values. In many developing countries, many people have moved to the cities to find jobs and escape the poverty of rural areas. By 2025, about 54 percent of Africans will live in an urban environment. Urbanization weakens traditional culture. In cities, people tend to live in nuclear families, rather than in extended families, and traditional bonds of lineage become less important. Urban dwellers find it hard to understand the customs and traditions of village life. Marriage customs are changing since the young prefer to choose their own mates rather than accept arranged marriages. Education also provides men and women with opportunities that were not possible in traditional African societies.

The industrialization of India's economy has contributed to the growth of large cities or urban areas. In 1900, Bombay (Mumbai) had a population of 1.5 million. By the end of the 20th century, the population had grown to more than 10 million. It is the third-largest city in the world. New Delhi, the capital of India, has a population of more than 7.5 million. Urbanization weakens rigid class distinctions. In rural areas, individuals were separated from each other by the caste system, which laid down specific guidelines for each class of people. Since one group did only one kind of work, it gave its members a chance to live more or less apart from each other. City dwellers do not always know the backgrounds of their neighbors. In the city, Indians from the lower castes are free to move up in society. In offices and factories, caste or class rules are hard to maintain. Workers come from many different backgrounds. They all have to live and work together, and gradually social distinctions become less important.

In Latin America, where about 70 percent of the people live in cities, many of the newcomers find jobs in factories, offices, or stores. Many more survive by working odd jobs, such as doing laundry or mending shoes. Others roam the city looking for food in the garbage. Urbanization has brought social upheavals to many areas, including Latin America. City life has weakened the extended family of rural villages. In cities, newcomers often find that they are completely on their own without the support of parents or uncles living close by in rural villages. The struggle to make a living has caused some families to fall apart. In large cities, thousands of abandoned or runaway children roam the streets. Many are caught up in crime and violence. In the cities, many women have jobs outside the home. The increase in job opportunities and schooling among women has led to the weakening of women's role as caretaker. As people move to the cities, their ties to the Catholic Church have weakened. Many of the newcomers have been attracted to evangelical Protestant groups. Urbanization has changed the lives of people living in Africa, Asia, and Latin America.

WRONG CHOICES EXPLAINED:

(1) Literacy rates have increased, not decreased, at a higher rate than those in rural areas.

(3) Urbanization has weakened the caste system in India as well as the social structure of different countries in Africa and Latin America.

(4) Urbanization has decreased, not increased, the isolation of women. Educated women in these nations began to play a greater role in society. Some of them work in civil service or professional positions. In Latin America, women such as Mireye Moscoso, the first woman elected president of Panama, and Michelle Bachelet of Chile, who became president in 2006, have increased the role of women in society.

40. **1** The most accurate statement about the impact of the AIDS epidemic in both Africa and Southeast Asia is that life expectancy in both regions is declining. Africa has 13 percent of the world's population and 60 percent of the AIDS cases. It is estimated that by 2010, the AIDS epidemic will take the lives of more than 12,000 people each day. In some African countries such as Zimbabwe and Botswana, life expectancy could drop to only 30 years of age. According to the World Health report, only 9 of the 53 countries for which the organization has data have life expectancies over 53 years old.

Southeast Asia now accounts for 20 percent of the world's HIV infections. In this area, 95 percent of all AIDS cases are concentrated in India, Thailand, and Myanmar. It is possible that within a few years Asia will be home to more people living with HIV than any other region in the world. As in Africa, the AIDS epidemic is affecting life expectancy. It is projected that by 2025, India's life expectancy could fall by 3–13 years, depending on how quickly the disease spreads.

WRONG CHOICES EXPLAINED:

(2) Africa and Southeast Asia have not been able to use low-cost drugs to cure those infected. Unfortunately, most of the drugs are too expensive for these poor nations to afford.

(3) It has been very difficult to introduce awareness program about AIDS to eliminate the disease. Political and social conditions have prevented effective programs from developing in these countries. The recent data of different health organizations indicate that the AIDS epidemic is still spreading.

(4) Newborn babies and young children have been affected by the disease. In Africa and Southeast Asia, life expectancy for babies and children has declined.

41. **4** In August 1990, Iraq invaded Kuwait. The United Nations' response led to the Persian Gulf War of 1991. This response is an example of collective security. Collective security is a system in which groups of nations, such as the League of Nations formed in 1920 or the United Nations started in 1945, act as one to preserve the peace of all nations. In July 1990, Iraqi president Saddam Hussein blamed Kuwait for falling oil prices. He claimed Kuwait was a creation of Great Britain and belonged to Iraq. On August 2, 1990, Hussein sent Iraqi forces to invade Kuwait. Hussein wanted to seize control of Kuwait's oil resources, which would double Iraq's share of the world oil reserves and also give Iraq access to the Persian Gulf. Other nations in the Middle East, especially Saudi Arabia and the United Arab Emirates, feared that they would fall victim to Iraq. The United States saw the invasion as a threat to its ally Saudi Arabia, and to the oil flow from the Persian Gulf. If Iraq seized control of Saudi Arabia and the Emirates, it would control more than one-half of the world's oil supplies. President George H. W. Bush organized Operation Desert Storm. This was a coalition of Arab, European, and American forces whose goal was to drive Iraqi forces out of Kuwait. In Desert Storm, also known as the Gulf War, American missiles and bombers destroyed targets in Iraq. Then, under the U.N. banner, coalition forces pushed across to liberate Kuwait in four days (February 23–27). The independence of Kuwait was restored.

WRONG CHOICES EXPLAINED:

(1) *Détente* describes the relaxation of tension between the United States and the Soviet Union during the 1970s.

(2) *Empire building* refers to the efforts of powerful nations to extend their control over weaker nations.

(3) *Totalitarianism* is a system of government in which one person or group controls all aspects of the political, economic, social, and religious life of a nation.

42. **4** One similarity between the Roman Empire and the Ottoman Empire is that both declined because of corruption in government. At one time, Romans cared deeply for their republic and willingly sacrificed their lives for it. In the later centuries of the empire, although not actively disloyal, the citizens were indifferent. Romans had once considered holding political office an honor. By 200 A.D., local officials usually lost money because they were required to pay for the costly public circuses and baths out of their own pockets. Few people chose to serve the government under these conditions. Growing numbers of corrupt officials undermined the loyalty of good government. Rival armies battled to have their commanders chosen as emperor. In the 50-year period from 218 to 268, the provincial armies and the Praetorian Guard proclaimed 50 generals as emperors of Rome. Of these, 27 men briefly won the approval of the Roman Senate. Seventeen of these men were murdered. Two others were forced to commit suicide. The lack of effective government leadership contributed to the decline of the Roman Empire in the 5th century A.D.

Although the Ottoman Empire survived into the 20th century, it began to decline much earlier than that. By the beginning of the 17th century, corruption was eating away at the government. As each sultan or ruler of the Ottoman Empire grew older, his possible heirs began jockeying for power. It became customary for each new sultan to have his brothers strangled with the silk string of a bow. The sultan would then keep his sons prisoners in the harem, cutting them off from education or contact with the world. This practice produced a long line of weak and uneducated sultans who brought ruin to the empire.

WRONG CHOICES EXPLAINED:

(1) The Roman Empire reached the height of its power during the 200s and the Ottoman Empire during the late 1400s and 1500s.

(2) Neither of these empires developed parliamentary government. The Roman emperors and the Ottoman sultans ruled with absolute power.

(3) Neither of these empires ensured equality for women.

43. **3** "Lack of natural resources led to a policy of imperialism" is the most accurate statement regarding the impact of geography on Japan. Japanese foreign policy was guided by the need for raw materials. As a small island nation, Japan lacked many basic resources necessary to ensure its growth as an industrial nation. Japan's late-19th-century industrialization created the need for raw materials, especially cotton, iron ore, coal, and oil. It wanted to gain markets for its manufactured goods. Japanese nationalists also wanted to replace European imperialism with Asian imperialism. In 1895, Japan defeated China in a war and forced the Chinese to give up their claims to Korea. They also gained Taiwan and won special trading privileges. In 1910, Japan annexed Korea and forced its people to build railroads and roads for Japan's benefit. The Japanese took half of Korea's yearly rice crop to support Japanese expansion. In the 1920s and 1930s, the Japanese leaders developed the East Asia Co-Prosperity Sphere. Its aim was to conquer East Asia by taking

raw materials. In 1931, Japan invaded Manchuria, a northern province of China, which was rich in coal, iron, and fertile soil. The Japanese argued that they had won Manchuria in the same way the Western nations had gained their colonies. By 1932, they gained control of the area, began to build hydroelectric plants, and created a sizable iron and steel industry, thereby increasing Japan's economy and military power. In 1940, the Japanese invaded French Indochina as well as the former Dutch East Indies (Indonesia). These areas provided the Japanese military with the important natural resources of rubber and oil. Japanese foreign policy led to conflict with Great Britain and the United States, and eventually to the attack on Pearl Harbor on December 7, 1941. This attack led to the United States entry into World War II.

WRONG CHOICES EXPLAINED:

(1) Large plains did not serve as invasion routes for conquerors. Although mountains cover much of Japan, the seas surrounding Japan isolated and protected it from invaders.

(2) Mountain ranges do cover more than four-fifths of Japan, but there are no arid deserts in Japan causing isolation from Asia.

(4) Japan is not in close proximity to Africa. Japan is an island nation in East Asia. The country never promoted trade with Egypt.

44. **2** The Neolithic Revolution led to the development of these civilizations. About 10,000 years ago, Neolithic man began to grow food and domesticate animals. These developments led to the Neolithic or Agricultural Revolution, which meant that people no longer had to search for food, there would be an abundance of food, and permanent settlements were established. As these settlements or villages grew, people needed to work together. Skilled occupations developed and there was a need for a government to establish order. These developments created more complex societies and paved the way for civilizations to emerge. Cities grew as farmers cultivated land along river valleys and produced surplus food, which in turn led to increased population. Government had to make sure that enough food was produced and that the city was protected. Rulers also ordered that public works, such as bridges and defensive walls, be built. Thus, the first civilization developed along the river valley of the Tigris and Euphrates Rivers in Egypt. Early civilizations also developed along the Indus Valley in India and the Yellow River in China. The Neolithic Revolution allowed these civilizations to emerge.

WRONG CHOICES EXPLAINED:

(1) The Industrial Revolution, which began in England in the late 1700s, resulted in the use of machines to mass-produce goods for markets.

(3) The Green Revolution refers to the 20th-century technological advances in agriculture leading to increased food production on a limited parcel of land.

(4) The Commercial Revolution describes the changes in the economies of Europe in the late Middle Ages in which there was a growth of towns and

the beginning of a banking system. These economic changes also opened as Europe adopted a global economy based on worldwide trade.

45. **1** The Age of Exploration led directly to the establishment of European colonies. The Age of Exploration was a period in European history beginning in the 1400s and lasting until the 1600s. European nations sent explorers to Asia, Africa, and the Americas in search of trade routes, resources, and colonies. In the 15th, 16th, and 17th centuries, several nations built up large overseas empires as a result of these great explorations. The Spanish Empire at its height included practically all of South and Central America as well as a large part of what is now the United States and Mexico. Portugal established a colony in Brazil. Holland became the chief colonial power in Europe after Spain was defeated by England in 1588. Her empire included New Netherlands, the East Indies, and South Africa. France built up a vast empire in America and India. England entered the competition for colonies and by 1763, had become the top colonial power. Its territories included 13 permanent colonies in North America, as well as Canada and India.

WRONG CHOICES EXPLAINED:

(2) The Puritan Revolution began in 1642 and lasted until 1660. The Puritans revolted against the absolute rule of the Stuart kings of England.

(3) The Age of Exploration did not directly lead to the invention of the magnetic compass. The magnetic compasses contributed to the Age of Exploration because they helped make voyages less dangerous.

(4) The Congress of Vienna met in 1815 to address the issue of how to redraw the map of Europe after Napoleon's defeat.

46. **3** The French Revolution was caused by the factors shown in this partial outline. The French Revolution of 1789 refers to the events that changed the political, economic, and social conditions in France. The abuses of the Old Regime described conditions that existed in 18th-century France before the revolution. France was divided into Three Estates. The First consisted of the clergy; the Second, the nobility; the Third, the peasants and bourgeoisie (merchants, bankers, and professionals). The Third Estate made up 97 percent of the population and comprised the underprivileged. Members of the Third Estate resented their lack of economic and political rights. Under the Old Regime in France, the First Estate (clergy) owned 10 percent of the land and paid 2 percent of its income to the government. The Second Estate (nobles) made up 2 percent of the population and owned 20 percent of the land, and paid almost no taxes. The Third Estate, which made up 97 percent of the population, bore almost the entire tax burden. The peasants paid the following taxes to the government: the taille (land tax); corvée (forced labor on roads and bridges); and the gabelle (a tax on compulsory salt purchases). They paid a tithe to the Church and feudal dues to the lords. The bourgeoisie, the most influential group in the Third Estate, were as wealthy as the nobles and paid high taxes, but lacked privileges. Many thought their

wealth entitled them to a greater degree of political power. The heavily taxed and discontent Third Estate was eager for change. The immediate cause of the French Revolution was financial. Louis XIV had left France deeply in debt. Wars, like the Seven Years War and the American Revolution, strained the treasury. The French debt stood at 4 billion livres and could not be carried because revenues fell short of expenditures. The government had to borrow more and more money. By 1789, half of its tax income went just to pay the interest on this enormous debt. The treasury was bankrupt because the wealthy and the clergy resisted any attempt to end their exemption from taxes. Other economic troubles added to the financial crisis. In the late 1780s, bad harvests sent food prices rising. This inflation brought hunger to poor peasants and city dwellers. Stories about the grand lifestyles of the clergy and nobles and the inability of the government to raise any additional money to pay off the debt added to the unrest. The French Parliament (Estates General) had not met for more than 175 years. When Louis XVI called it into session to raise additional taxes, he began the revolution. The unwillingness of the king and nobles to deal with the abuses of the Old Regime led to the French Revolution.

WRONG CHOICES EXPLAINED:

(1) The Russian Revolution was caused by conditions created by World War I.

(2) The Mexican Revolution occurred because of the economic and political inequities of the late 18th and early 19th centuries created by Porfiro Diaz.

(4) The Cuban Revolution is associated with the rise of Fidel Castro and the overthrow of the dictator Fulgencio Batista in 1959.

47. **2** One way in which José de San Martin, Camillo Cavour, and Jomo Kenyatta are similar is that each leader led nationalist movements. José de San Martin was a nationalist leader in Latin America, an Argentinian Creole (an American-born descendant of Spanish settlers) whose parents sent him to Spain to serve as an officer in the Spanish Army. In 1812, San Martin returned to Argentina to fight for freedom. By 1816, Argentina had won independence. San Martin then attempted to liberate Chile. With the help of Chilean patriot Bernardo O'Higgins, San Martin helped Chile to gain independence in 1818. Then San Martin headed north to help end Spanish rule in Ecuador and Peru.

In 1852, Count Camillo di Cavour became prime minister of Piedmont (also known as the Kingdom of Sardinia). He strengthened the country by promoting industry, enlarging the army, and improving agriculture. He was also successful in getting diplomatic assistance to free Italy from Austrian domination. In 1859, he secured support from Napoleon III of France if Austria attacked Sardinia. Cavour maneuvered Austria into war and with the help of France was successful in driving Austria out of northern Italy. Farther to the south, Giuseppe Garibaldi and his volunteer army of 1,000 Red Shirts gained control of Naples and the Two Sicilies. Cavour joined Naples to enlarge the kingdom of Piedmont. By 1860, Italy had become a united nation. Cavour died in 1861 and is considered the "brains of Italian unification." Venice, and later Rome, joined Italy in 1866 and 1870, respectively.

Jomo Kenyatta was the nationalist leader of Kenya. After World War II, Kenyatta, who had been educated and living in England, became a spokesperson for Kenya's independence. In 1947, Kenyatta was chosen as the leader of the Kenyan African Union, a political movement for independence. Other Africans formed a group that the Europeans called the Mau Mau. This secret group was made up of Kikuyu farmers who were forced out of the highlands by the British, who had passed laws to ensure their domination. The goal of the Mau Mau was to force the British off the land. They began to carry out attacks against European settlers, such as burning farms and destroying livestock. Kenyatta, who was Kikuyu, had no connection to the Mau Mau but refused to condemn these actions. The British took military action against the movement and jailed Kenyatta, whom they accused of leading the movement. More than 10,000 black Kenyans and some white Kenyans were killed during the struggle for independence. In 1963, Britain granted Kenya its independence. Kenyatta was elected the first prime minister and held office until his death in 1978. He worked hard to unite all the different ethnic and language groups in the country.

WRONG CHOICES EXPLAINED:

(1) These leaders were revolutionary leaders who were concerned with uniting and gaining independence for their nations. None of them made any significant scientific discoveries.

(3) Jomo Kenyatta was the only one of these three men who fought British imperialism.

(4) These leaders were not communist revolutionary leaders. They were nationalist leaders who supported freedom for their countries. San Martin and Cavour fostered parliamentary democracy, and Kenyatta pursued a pro-Western anti-communist foreign policy.

48. **1** One way in which Vladimir Lenin's New Economic Policy and Mikhail Gorbachev's policy of *perestroika* are similar is that both allowed elements of capitalism within a Communist economic system. Lenin is considered the Father of Russian Communism. In 1917, Lenin and his Bolshevik, or Communist, Party seized control of the government and established the first Communist nation in Europe. At first, Lenin ended private ownership of land and distributed land to the peasants. Workers gained control of the factories and mines. However, a civil war lasting three years resulted in economic disaster. In 1921, Lenin was forced to adapt the New Economic Policy (NEP). Under this plan, peasants were allowed to sell surplus crops on the open market and private owners were allowed to operate retail stores for profit. The government, however, still retained control of the banking system and major industries. The New Economic Policy was a temporary retreat from Communism. Lenin died in 1924, but the change in policy revived the economy and enabled

the Communist Party to survive in Russia. In 1985, Mikhail Gorbachev introduced the idea of perestroika. Gorbachev wanted to restructure the failing state-run command economy. In 1986, he made changes to revive the Soviet economy. His goal was to stimulate growth and make the economic system more efficient. Local managers gained greater authority over their farms and factories, and people were allowed to open small private businesses. Gorbachev backed free-market reforms. Perestroika had some negative effects. Inflation increased, and there were shortages of food and medicine.

WRONG CHOICES EXPLAINED:

(2) and (3) Neither of these policies were designed to strengthen their country's military defenses or support censorship of news and of personal correspondence. Both the New Economic Policy and perestroika were developed to improve the economy of Communist Russia.

(4) Lenin died in 1924, which was 23 years before the Cold War emerged between the United States and Russia. Gorbachev's policies of economic and political reform aimed at reducing, not increasing, tension during the Cold War. Western leaders believed that Gorbachev wanted to improve relationships with Europe and the United States.

49. **3** The correct chronological order of these 19th- and 20th-century events in Chinese history is the Opium Wars (1839–1842), the Long March (1934), the Great Leap Forward (1958), and Four Modernizations (1978).

WRONG CHOICES EXPLAINED:

(1), (2), and (4) The Opium Wars must be first in any correct chronological sequence of events.

50. **4** A study of Spain during the late 1400s, the Balkan States during the early 1900s, Rwanda during the 1990s, and Central Asia today shows that ethnic conflicts have been a recurring issue in history. In Spain, Muslims, called Moors, had controlled most of the country, and many Jews had achieved high positions in finance, government, and medicine. The Reconquistor represented a centuries-long attempt to unite Spain and expel Arabs and Jews. In 1469, Ferdinand of Aragon was married to Isabella of Castille, thus uniting the Christian kingdom of Spain. In 1492, the combined armies of these kingdoms drove the Moors from Granada and from Europe. To further consolidate their power and kingdom, Ferdinand and Isabella made use of the Inquisition, a religious court controlled by the monarchy. They monitored and persecuted people for heresy, especially Jews and Muslims. A person suspected of heresy might be questioned for weeks and even tortured. Eventually by 1492, the Spanish had expelled all practicing Jews and Muslims from Spain in Europe.

The most complex national conflicts arose in the Balkan Peninsula in the 1900s. Each group longed to extend their borders. Serbia, for example, had a large Slavic population. Serbia hoped to absorb all the Slavs on the Balkan Peninsula. Other ethnic groups, such as the Bosnians, Croatians, Albanians, Bulgarians, and Romanians, all hoped to build their own countries. Many of these groups spoke Slavic but maintained their separate identities. Between 1900 and 1914, repeated uprisings and crises in the Balkans threatened both Austria-Hungary and the Ottoman Empire and made that area Europe's powder keg, ready to explode.

In Africa, ethnic conflict led to genocide in Rwanda. Before the killings in 1994, Rwanda had a population of about 7 million: 85 percent Hutu and 14 percent Tutsi. In April 1994, the president of Rwanda died in a suspicious plane crash. The president was a member of the Hutu tribe. In 1994, Hutu extremists, supported by government officials, slaughtered about 1 million Tutsis. The genocide ended when a Tutsi-led rebel army seized control of the government.

Ethnic conflicts have plagued the nations that once made up the Soviet states of Central Asia. These former Soviet Republics consist of Kazakhstan, Tajikistan, Turkmenistan, Uzbekistan, and Kyrgyzstan. These five countries contain more than 130 ethnic groups. Territorial disputes among Central Asian countries have resulted from the Soviet Union changing the border at will. When the Soviet Union was drawing up the borders of its republics, it gave very little consideration to ethnic and political realities. Border disputes existed between Uzbekistan and Kyrgyzstan, with 130 border sectors unsettled today. Uzbekistan threatened to cut off energy supplies to Kyrgyzstan, which has created a rift in relations between the two countries. The resurgence of Islamic fundamentalists in some of these republics has also contributed to conflicts in the area. After its independence from the Soviet Union in 1991, a civil war broke out in Tajikistan between government authorities advocating a secular republic, with separation from political and religious groups such as the Islamic Renaissance Party that insisted on establishing an Islamic state. In 1997, a resolution was signed between the two groups under the mediation of the U.N., Russia, and Iran. Islamic organizations obtained legitimate status and were accepted into the government. There are reports that Tajik Islamic organizations are promoting their activities in other secular governments in Central Asia.

WRONG CHOICES EXPLAINED:

(1) Civil disobedience was effective in bringing about change in India, but it had no influence in reducing violence or bringing about change in any of these areas.

(2) People were not encouraged to question tradition in Spain, the Balkan States, Rwanda, or Central Asia. People in these areas were forced to accept the dominant authority or government in power.

(3) A study would show that colonial rule had a lasting influence on Rwanda and some republics in Central Asia but not in Spain and the Balkans. In Rwanda, the former colonial rulers gave power to the minority Tutsis at the expense of the Hutus. In Central Asian republics, the dominant influence of the Russians created problems. However, in Spain the struggle was over the dominance of the Catholic Church, and in the Balkans the spirit of nationalism led to conflicts.

THEMATIC ESSAY: GENERIC SCORING RUBRIC

Score of 5:
- Shows a thorough understanding of the theme or problem
- Addresses all aspects of the task
- Shows an ability to analyze, evaluate, compare and/or contrast issues and events
- Richly supports the theme or problem with relevant facts, examples, and details
- Is a well-developed essay, consistently demonstrating a logical and clear plan of organization
- Introduces the theme or problem by establishing a framework that is beyond a simple restatement of the task and concludes with a summation of the theme or problem

Score of 4:
- Shows a good understanding of the theme or problem
- Addresses all aspects of the task
- Shows an ability to analyze, evaluate, compare and/or contrast issues and events
- Includes relevant facts, examples, and details, but may not support all aspects of the theme or problem evenly
- Is a well-developed essay, demonstrating a logical and clear plan of organization
- Introduces the theme or problem by establishing a framework that is beyond a simple restatement of the task and concludes with a summation of the theme or problem

Score of 3:
- Shows a satisfactory understanding of the theme or problem
- Addresses most aspects of the task or addresses all aspects in a limited way
- Shows an ability to analyze or evaluate issues and events, but not in any depth
- Includes some facts, examples, and details
- Is a satisfactorily developed essay, demonstrating a general plan of organization
- Introduces the theme or problem by repeating the task and concludes by repeating the theme or problem

Score of 2:
- Shows limited understanding of the theme or problem
- Attempts to address the task
- Develops a faulty analysis or evaluation of issues and events
- Includes few facts, examples, and details, and may include information that contains inaccuracies
- Is a poorly organized essay, lacking focus
- Fails to introduce or summarize the theme or problem

Score of 1:
- Shows very limited understanding of the theme or problem
- Lacks an analysis of evaluation of the issues and events
- Includes little or no accurate or relevant facts, examples, or details
- Attempts to complete the task, but demonstrates a major weakness in organization
- Fails to introduce or summarize the theme or problem

Score of 0: Fails to address the task, is illegible, or is a blank paper

PART II: THEMATIC ESSAY QUESTION

Throughout history, different belief systems have influenced the lives of their followers and how they interact in society. Hinduism and Islam are two belief systems that have shaped the lives of millions of followers with a sense of belonging and stability. They have played a significant role in our society.

Hinduism is the religion of 80 percent of the people in India. Unlike most religions, Hinduism has no founder or formal church. Hinduism developed and changed over 3,500 years, growing out of the diverse people who settled India. These groups included the original inhabitants of the Indus Valley as well as the nomadic Aryans who entered India in about 1500 B.C.

Although Hinduism is polytheistic, with countless gods and goddesses, many of their followers are united under the powerful force of one spirit known as Brahman. Hindus believe that only a few people can truly understand Brahman which is nameless, formless, and unlimited. Many small villages in India may have their own unique gods but are ultimately united through Brahman. The most important Hindu gods are Brahma the Creator, Vishnu the Preserver, and Shiva the Destroyer.

Each represents aspects of Brahman. Each of these gods can take many forms, human or animal, and each also has his own family. For example, some Hindus worship Shakti, the powerful wife of Shiva. She is both kind and cruel, a creator and destroyer. In the end, Hindus are all connected through Brahman. This connection provides order and direction to Indian society.

Reincarnation and the caste system are important parts of Hinduism. According to Hinduism, people suffer from pain and sorrow because they pursue false goals such as material riches. Hindus believe that the true goal of life is Moksha, freeing of the soul from the body so that the soul can unite with Brahman. Moksha cannot be achieved in one's lifetime; thus Hindus believe in reincarnation, or rebirth of the soul in various forms. Reincarnation allows people to continue working toward Moksha through several lifetimes.

In each lifetime, a person can come closer to union with Brahman by obeying the law of Karma. Karma refers to all the actions of a person's life that affect his or her fate in the next life. People who live virtuously earn good Karma and are reborn at a higher level. Those who do evil acquire bad Karma and are reborn into suffering. In Indian art, this endless cycle of death and rebirth is symbolized by the image of the wheel. To escape this wheel of fate, Hinduism stresses the importance of Dharma, the religious and moral duties that are expected of an individual.

The concept of Karma and Dharma helped ensure the social order by supporting the caste system. Many believe that the caste system developed in ancient times when light-skinned Aryans conquered dark-skinned non-Aryan people. Others stress that the caste system was based on occupation. The caste system assigns all people to hereditary groupings that determine their social standing, occupation, religious rituals, and marriage partners.

The caste system has four basic castes, ranking from highest to lowest, of priests, warriors and kings, merchants, and laborers. Castes are also divided into hundreds of sub-castes. Each Hindu is born into a caste and may advance to a different caste only by death and reincarnation. Hindus accept the limits imposed by the caste because they believe their actions (Karma) and their obedience to the rule of their caste (Dharma) determine whether they will be reincarnated into a better life.

An effect of the caste system was the creation of social and political stability because it is unacceptable to seek change to one's status. The caste system also hindered India's economic development for many centuries because traditional people were unwilling to take employment in factories or move to where new industries were developed. The caste system also created an outcast group called the untouchables (Harijan), who are required to do society's dirtiest and most unwanted work and are shunned by all other castes.

The principles of Hinduism and the caste system dominated every aspect of a person's life. These beliefs determined what one could eat, how one ate it, and what people one could associate with in daily life. Today, even in the most ordinary activities of daily life, Hindus turn to their religion for guidance.

In 622 A.D., the religion of Islam emerged in the Arabian Peninsula. Islam became the dominant religion in the Middle East and ranks second among the world's religions in terms of the number of followers.

An Arab, Muhammad, was the founder of Islam. He was born in Mecca in 570 A.D. Muhammad was a caravan merchant who was married and had children. He was troubled by the idol worship of the Arabs. According to Muslim tradition, the Angel Gabriel commanded Muhammad to spread the message of Islam. At first, Muhammad won few converts. The Arabs of Mecca rejected his idea that there was only one god. Muhammad's message also angered the town merchants and innkeepers. They were afraid that if they gave up all of their traditional gods, the profitable pilgrim traffic to Mecca would end.

In 622, Muhammad was forced to leave Mecca. The migration of Muhammad and his followers from Mecca to Medina is known as the Hejira. The Hejira is the turning point in Islam because it marks the beginning of the expansion of Islam. After Muhammad's death, his followers chose the year of the Hejira (622) as the first year of the Muslim calendar.

By 630, Muhammad had returned to Mecca and captured the city. Muhammad smashed the images of false gods in the city and dedicated the Black Stone to God. Before his death in 632, Muhammad had spread Islam across most of the Arabian Peninsula and established order and stability under his new religion.

The basic message of Islam is summed up in the belief that there is no god but Allah. Each Muslim is expected to follow the Five Pillars of Islam, which include a belief in only one god, Allah, and that Muhammad is his prophet. Islam, like Judaism and Christianity, promotes monotheism. Muslims were also expected to pray five times a day, give aid to the poor, and if possible make a pilgrimage to Mecca. The sacred text of Islam is the Koran (Quran). Muslims believe that the Koran contains the exact words of God as revealed to Muhammad.

For a long time, Muslims were forbidden to translate the Koran from Arabic because they believed the words were directly from God. This shared language also helped unite Muslims from many regions. Islam is both a religion and a way of life. Its teaching has helped shape the lives of Muslims around the world. Islamic law based on the Koran governs many aspects of daily life. Like Judaism and Christianity, Islamic tradition determines ethical and moral behavior.

Over time, Muslim scholars developed an immense body of law interpreting the Koran and applying it to its teaching of daily life. This Islamic system of laws, called the Sharia, regulates moral conduct, family life, business practices, and other aspects of the community. Like the Koran, the Sharia unites the many people who have converted to Islam.

One of the teachings of the Koran that strongly influenced social life in the Middle East is that women have an inferior status. Though women have legal rights and may own and inherit property, men are taught by the Koran to provide them with direction and protection. In fundamentalist areas, women are kept in seclusion in the home. They are expected to wear veils (hijab) when outside the home and are severely restricted in their contacts with men other than their husbands. The restrictions influence economic development because women, half the population, are prevented from reaching their full potential as workers and contributors to the economy.

Muslims united the nomadic Arab tribes in the 7th century and then spread their faith through the Middle East and North Africa by conquest. Trade, which was an honorable occupation for Muslims, helped them build a vast trading empire from the Silk Road to the Trans-Sahara area. Muslim merchants established trading networks with Africa, China, and India. In India, Muslim traders were an important means of spreading Islam. At the other end of the Eurasian landmass, Islam spread from North Africa to Spain. The spread of Islam changed the lives of many people because Arabic became the spoken language as well as the cultural, political, structural, and ethnic makeup of a large part of the Middle East and North Africa.

Although the belief systems of Hinduism and Islam are very different, both these religions provided a sense of unity and order for its followers. Each of these religions also had a significant role in the development of their society. They continue to influence the lives of people throughout the world today.

PART III: DOCUMENT-BASED QUESTIONS

Part A: Short Answers

Document 1

According to Raphael Lemkin, one way the world community can address the problem of genocide is for the United Nations to declare genocide an international crime or pass laws so that the crime of genocide can be prosecuted through international cooperation.

Note: This response receives full credit because it correctly states how the world community can address the problem of genocide.

Document 2a

According to Irina Lagunina, one criticism of the international community's response to genocide was that despite atrocities and mass killings in Cambodia, East Timor, and elsewhere, it took four decades before the international community finally came together and prosecuted the crime of genocide again.

Note: This response receives full credit because it cites specific criticism from the document about the lack of international response to genocide.

Document 2b

Based on this 1999 cartoon, two specific groups that have been victims of genocide are the Armenians and the Jews.

Note: This response receives full credit because it correctly identifies the groups that have been victims of genocide.

Document 3

Based on this document, one attempt made to address the problem of genocide is that various governments have moved to support international human rights and made their bilateral and multilateral influence an established force in international relations.

Note: This response receives full credit because it specifically states one attempt made to address the problem of genocide.

Document 4

According to Norman J. Vig, two environmental problems that pose a threat to the world are as follows:

1) Many of the world's largest cities are increasingly choked by pollution.

2) Moderate to high shortages of fresh water could double by 2025.

Note: This response receives full credit because it correctly cites two environmental problems posing a threat to the world.

Document 5a

Based on this document one problem desertification poses in China is that pastures, farmland, and railroads and other means of transportation will be buried under sand.

Note: This response receives full credit because it notes how desertification is creating a problem in China.

Document 5b

Based on this document one attempt that Chinese officials have made to address the problem of desertification is to build green buffers and the hope to reclaim desertified land in 75 counties of Beijing.

Note: This response receives full credit because it specifically cites how China is trying to address the problem of desertification.

Document 6

Based on this document, two ways the international community has attempted to address environmental problems are as follows:

1) A United Nations Conference on Human Environment was called in 1972 to begin to organize international efforts to safeguard the environment.

2) The World Conservation Union published a revised Red List of endangered and threatened species, creating a world standard for gauging threats to biodiversity.

Note: This response receives full credit because it identifies two ways the international community has attempted to address environmental problems.

Document 7a

According to the time line, one way a weapon of mass destruction was used was in the dropping of the atomic bomb on Hiroshima and Nagasaki in 1945.

Note: This response receives full credit because it specifically notes one way in which a weapon of mass destruction was used.

Document 7b

According to this time line, one attempt made to address a problem related to weapons of mass destruction was that the U.S., U.S.S.R., and more than 100 other nations signed the Biological Weapons Convention in 1972.

Note: This response receives full credit because it identifies one attempt to address a problem related to weapons of mass destruction.

Document 8

Based on this cartoon, one reason nuclear weapons pose a threat to the world community is that they would wipe out the entire world.

Note: This response receives full credit because it states one reason nuclear weapons pose a threat to the world community.

Document 9

Based on this article by Glase and von Hippel, an attempt being made by the United States and its allies to improve the security of highly enriched uranium (HEU) is that they have established programs to bolster security measures.

Note: This response receives full credit because it states an attempt being made by the United States and its allies to improve the security of highly enriched uranium.

DOCUMENT-BASED QUESTION: GENERIC SCORING RUBRIC

Score of 5:
- Thoroughly addresses all aspects of the *Task* by accurately analyzing and interpreting at least **four** documents
- Incorporates information from the documents in the body of the essay
- Incorporates relevant outside information
- Richly supports the theme or problem with relevant facts, examples, and details
- Is a well-developed essay, consistently demonstrating a logical and clear plan of organization
- Introduces the theme or problem by establishing a framework that is beyond a simple restatement of the *Task* or *Historical Context* and concludes with a summation of the theme or problem

Score of 4:
- Addresses all aspects of the *Task* by accurately analyzing and interpreting at least **four** documents
- Incorporates information from the documents in the body of the essay
- Incorporates relevant outside information
- Includes relevant facts, examples, and details, but discussion may be more descriptive than analytical
- Is a well-developed essay, demonstrating a logical and clear plan of organization
- Introduces the theme or problem by establishing a framework that is beyond a simple restatement of the *Task* or *Historical Context* and concludes with a summation of the theme or problem

Score of 3:
- Addresses most aspects of the *Task* or addresses all aspects of the *Task* in a limited way, using some of the documents
- Incorporates some information from the documents in the body of the essay
- Incorporates limited or no relevant outside information
- Includes some facts, examples, and details, but discussion is more descriptive than analytical
- Is a satisfactorily developed essay, demonstrating a general plan of organization
- Introduces the theme or problem by repeating the *Task* or *Historical Context* and concludes by simply repeating the theme or problem

Score of 2:
- Attempts to address some aspects of the *Task*, making limited use of the documents
- Presents no relevant outside information
- Includes few facts, examples, and details; discussion restates contents of the documents

- Is a poorly organized essay, lacking focus
- Fails to introduce or summarize the theme or problem

Score of 1:
- Shows limited understanding of the *Task* with vague, unclear references to the documents
- Presents no relevant outside information
- Includes little or no accurate or relevant facts, details, or examples
- Attempts to complete the *Task*, but demonstrates a major weakness in organization
- Fails to introduce or summarize the theme or problem

Score of 0: Fails to address the *Task*, is illegible, or is a blank paper

Part B: Essay

Throughout the 20th century, the international community has tried to address problems that affect all members of society in the world. Two of these major problems have been genocide and threats to the environment.

Genocide is a systematic effort to destroy an entire ethnic or religious group. In the 20th century, groups such as the Armenians, Jews, Bosnians, Muslims, and Tutsis in Rwanda have been victims of genocide or mass killings (Doc. 2b).

From the 16th century until World War I, a major portion of Armenia was controlled by the Ottoman Turks under whom the Armenians experienced discrimination, religious persecution, and heavy taxation. By the 1880s, the roughly 2 million Christian Armenians in the Ottoman Empire began to demand their freedom. Throughout the 1890s, Turkish troops killed tens of thousands of Armenians in response to their nationalist stirrings. When World War I erupted in 1914, the Armenians pledged their support to the Turks' enemies. In April 1915, the Turks ordered the deportation of the nearly 2 million Armenians to the deserts of Syria and Mesopotamia. Along the way, more than 600,000 died of starvation or were killed by Turkish soldiers. Many women and children were seized by Turkish officials and sold into slavery.

The Holocaust was a systematic destruction of more than two-thirds of the pre-war Jewish population of Europe. Hitler began this policy of genocide by limiting the rights of the Jewish people. In 1935, the Nuremberg laws in Germany placed several restrictions on the Jewish people. They were prohibited from marrying non-Jews or holding teaching or government jobs. Violence against Jews was encouraged. On November 9, 1938, Kristallnacht (Night of Broken Glass) spread across Germany. Nazi-led mobs attacked Jewish communities, smashed windows, looted shops, and burned synagogues. Hitler finally set up concentration camps, detention centers where the Jewish people were starved, shot, or gassed to death. It is estimated that 6 million Jews died in the Holocaust.

The breakup of Yugoslavia in 1991 and 1992 sparked ethnic violence. In Bosnia, fighting erupted among Serbs and Muslims. The Serbs, who dominated Yugoslavia, began a policy of ethnic cleansing that was designed to destroy and drive out all Muslims from the parts of the country that the Serbs claimed. In 1997, Slobodan Milosevic, the Yugoslav president, who was Serbian, sent troops to fight ethnic Albanians who were self-ruled in Kosovo. As the conflict raged, Serbs also mounted a brutal campaign of ethnic cleansing against Muslim Kosovans.

In Rwanda, ethnic conflicts between the Hutus and Tutsis led to mass violence and human rights violations. In April 1994, after the crash of the plane that was carrying the presidents of Rwanda and Burundi, both of whom were killed, ethnic violence erupted. The Hutus, who make up 85 percent of the population, launched an attack on the Tutsis. They killed more than half a million Tutsis. In response, Tutsi rebels swept across the country, and in a 14-week civil war they defeated the Hutu government. In the immediate aftermath, an estimated 1.7 million Hutus fled across the borders into the neighboring Congo, Burundi, and Tanzania.

During World War II, the Allies agreed that war crimes and criminals were to be brought to trial. The discovery of Hitler's death camps at the end of World War II led the Allies to put 22 surviving Nazi leaders on trial for "crimes against humanity." In 1946, an International Military Tribunal, representing 23 nations, put Nazi war criminals on trial in Nuremberg. Twelve Nazis were sentenced to death, seven received long sentences, and three were acquitted. These trials showed that political and military leaders could be held accountable for actions in wartime.

Although the Nuremberg trials exposed the evils of Nazism, some members of the international community wanted to take further steps to ensure that these atrocities would not reoccur. In 1946, representatives of Cuba, India, and Pakistan introduced a resolution to the United Nations declaring genocide an international crime. These nations wanted to establish ways to promote international cooperation for the prevention and punishment of these crimes (Doc. 1). Another arm of this resolution was the recommendation that genocide be dealt with in the same way as other international crimes (Doc. 1). In 1946, the United Nations General Assembly adopted an International Convention on the Punishment and Prevention of Crimes of Genocide and specifically defined the meaning of *genocide* (Doc. 2a). In 1948, U.N. members approved the Universal Declaration of Human Rights. According to this document, all people were entitled to basic rights and freedoms without distinction of any kind such as race, color, sex, language, birth, or other status. Human rights included a person's right to life, liberty, and security.

Despite these documents, human rights violations continued in the latter half of the 20th century. It took four decades, with the creation of the International Criminal Tribunal for the former Yugoslavia in 1994, before the international community finally came together to prosecute crimes of genocide (Doc. 2a). However, the international community failed to respond promptly to genocide in Rwanda and Bosnia (Doc. 3). It was not until July 1997 that Jean Kambanda, the prime minister of Rwanda since the outbreak of the conflict, was arrested. He is the first and only head of government to plead guilty to genocide. In September 1998, he was sentenced to life in prison for his crimes of genocide.

In Bosnia, the U.N. efforts at maintaining a cease-fire failed. In 1999, President Milosevic was forced to retreat from Kosovo, only after NATO, with the support of the U.N. Security Council, began a bombing campaign lasting for 72 days (Doc. 3). In 2001, Milosevic was handed over to the Hague Tribunal, and in 2002 he was brought to trial and indicted for genocide and crimes against humanity. The trial ended without a verdict because he died of a heart attack during the proceedings.

Efforts have been made through organizations and schools in different societies to raise awareness about human rights. Amnesty International, an international nonprofit agency, works to track and publicize human rights violations. Educational institutions within the United States and other countries have mandated the teaching of the importance of respecting human rights in society. By educating people about the horrors of genocide through school programs, as well as movies such as *Hotel Rwanda*, books, and museums, people are being made aware of the evil of genocide and society's obligation to prevent it from happening again.

Another international problem is the poor state of the environment. Modernization and industrialization have contributed to the problem. Excessive population growth is a problem facing many nations around the world today. It is estimated that the world population will increase to 9 billion by 2050 (Doc. 4). The population has increased because of improvements in medicine and living conditions, and has thus increased the need for food and water. The United Nations has estimated that by 2025, one-third of the world will live in countries with a shortage of fresh water (Doc. 4).

Industrialization and the growth of cities have contributed to pollution (Doc. 4). Pollution is the contamination of the environment, including air, water, and soil (Doc. 4). Industrialization has contributed to global warming. The burning of fossil fuels, such as gasoline and coal, releases large amounts of carbon dioxide into the atmosphere. This excess carbon dioxide traps more heat near the earth, a process that creates the greenhouse effect. The greenhouse effect has raised the global temperature. Overall warming can adversely affect agriculture and upset the delicate ecological balance in nature (Doc. 4). Some scientists predict that a quarter of all species could be extinct by 2050 (Doc. 4).

Desertification is a major environmental problem. Nearly one-quarter of the earth's land is threatened by this problem. Desertification is the changeover from arable land that can be farmed to desert. Desertification is a major concern in Sub-Saharan Africa and in China. In China, between 1994 and 1999, desertified land grew by 20,280 square miles (Doc. 5). The shifting land threatens farmers as well as railroads and other means of transportation that will be buried under the sand. In March of 2002, the city of Beijing experienced the worst sandstorm in a decade, and a seasonal storm known as the Yellow Dragon dumped 30,000 tons of sand on the city (Doc. 5). China is especially concerned about the problem of desertification because it will host the Olympic Games in 2008. The officials have tried to stop the sand by building green buffers (Doc. 5). They also reclaimed desertified land in 75 counties to protect Beijing (Doc. 5). The United Nations General Assembly called 2006 the "International Year of Deserts," which has led to the United Nations Convention to Combat Desertification.

The United Nations has joined together with other countries to protect global and regional resources. In 1987, 46 nations signed the Montreal Protocol. These nations urged the world to significantly reduce the use of chemicals that were damaging the earth's ozone layer. In 1992, the U.N. sponsored a conference called the Earth Summit in Rio de Janeiro, Brazil, that 178 nations attended. The United States and 34 other industrial nations issued the Rio Pact that called for nations and industries to plan economic growth to meet the present global need, without sacrificing the environmental needs of future generations (Doc. 6). However, world leaders often wonder how to achieve these goals. Are people in rich countries willing to sacrifice and do with less to preserve the environment? How can emerging nations afford costly safeguards?

In 1997, delegates from 150 nations attended the U.N.'s Third Conference of the Parties in Kyoto, Japan. They met to draw up the first international treaty for reducing CO_2 emissions in the atmosphere. The Kyoto Protocol set limits on the amount of greenhouse gases allowed for industrialized nations and allowed developing nations to set their own limits (Doc. 6). The United States has argued that cutting the use of carbon fuels to the required extent will damage its economy, and has refused to sign it.

Greenpeace, which was founded in 1971 to protest U.S. nuclear testing at Amchitka Island in Alaska, has developed into an organization to prevent environmental abuses and to heighten environmental awareness through direct nonviolent confrontations with polluting corporations and government authorities. One of Greenpeace's major concerns is the protection of the ozone layer. Members of Greenpeace believe that the major cause of ozone depletion is the release of chlorofluorocarbons (CFCs), a carbon-based combination of chlorine and fluorine used in aerosol spray cans, inhalers, and other coolants. In 1992, Greenpeace introduced Greenfreeze, an ozone- and climate-safe refrigeration technology. Greenfreeze uses a mixture of propane and isobutane to decrease the release of CO_2 into the atmosphere. In 1994, Germany banned CFC production, and the United States and Canada agreed to phase out CFC by 1996. At an environmental meeting in Montreal, Canada, in September 1997, Greenpeace indicated that countries such as Cuba, Argentina, Turkey, and Russia have adopted this new technology. Progress also has been made in the medical field. In Sweden and the Netherlands more than 60 percent of the people who suffer from asthma have switched to dry-powder inhalers.

Corporations also have made efforts to deal with air pollution. British Petroleum, under the leadership of John Browne, announced in 1998 that the oil company would increase its efforts to invest in solar energy. Toyota, the Japanese automobile giant, announced that the company would begin to manufacture the first hybrid electric car. This automobile would have twice the fuel economy and would reduce the emission of CO_2 for existing cars by one-half.

Global concern over the environment has also been heightened by the media and organizations designed to lessen the threat to our ecological balance. Organizations like the World Wildlife Federation work with the government to increase protection for endangered animals. The World Conservation Union has also published a list of endangered plants and animals called the Red List. The Red List focused on animals and plants that face extinction.

In 2006, the movie *An Inconvenient Truth* showed how the world's people are damaging the environment. People who watched the movie became more conscious of ways to cut down on their use of products that are destroying our ecosystem. Al Gore's selection as the Nobel Peace Prize winner for 2007 dramatized the importance of preserving the world's environment.

The international problems of genocide and threats to the environment have been challenges for our world. However, the efforts of the United Nations and other organizations are ensuring that we become aware of these problems and take steps to prevent them from happening. It is a continual struggle but one where awareness and cooperation can prevent and limit future damages.

Topic	Question Numbers	Total Number of Questions	Number Wrong	*Reason for Wrong Answer
U.S. AND N.Y. HISTORY				
WORLD HISTORY	1, 5, 6, 7, 8, 10, 12, 14, 15, 20, 23, 26, 27, 30, 31, 32, 34, 36, 37, 39, 41, 46, 47, 49, 50	25		
GEOGRAPHY	2, 4, 11, 13, 18, 22, 24, 28, 33, 38, 40, 43, 44, 45	14		
ECONOMICS	9, 16, 21, 25, 29, 48	6		
CIVICS, CITIZENSHIP, AND GOVERNMENT	3, 17, 19, 35, 42	5		

*Your reason for answering the question incorrectly might be (a) lack of knowledge, (b) misunderstanding the question, or (c) careless error.

Actual Items by Standard and Unit

	1 U.S. and N.Y. History	2 World History	3 Geography	4 Economics	5 Civics, Citizenship, and Gov't	Number
Methodology of Global History and Geography		1	2		3	3
UNIT ONE Ancient World		5, 8	4			3
UNIT TWO Expanding Zones of Exchange		6, 7				2
UNIT THREE Global Interactions		10, 12	11, 13	9		5
UNIT FOUR First Global Age		14, 15	18, 45	16	17, 19	7
UNIT FIVE Age of Revolution		20, 23, 46	22, 24, 43	21, 25		8
UNIT SIX Crisis and Achievement (1900–1945)		26, 27, 30	28	29		5
UNIT SEVEN 20th Century Since 1945		32, 34, 36, 37, 41	33, 38		35	8
UNIT EIGHT Global Connections and Interactions		39	40			2
Cross topical		31, 47, 49, 50	44	48	42	7
Total # of Questions		25	14	6	5	50
% of Items by Standard		50%	28%	12%	10%	100%

Examination August 2008

Global History and Geography

PART I: MULTIPLE CHOICE

Directions (1–50): For each statement or question, write in the space provided the *number* of the word or expression that, of those given, best completes the statement or answers the question.

1 Ethnocentrism is best defined as

1 the belief that one's culture is superior to all others
2 military preparation for a civil war
3 love and devotion to one's country
4 a belief in one god 1____

2 • The east is bordered by the Yellow Sea.
• The population is concentrated along the coast and in the river valleys.
• Mountains, plateaus, and deserts dominate the western region.

To which country do all of these geographic statements apply?

1 England
2 China
3 Nicaragua
4 Philippines 2____

3 Which social scientist primarily studies how people change resources into goods and services?

1 archaeologist
2 sociologist
3 economist
4 psychologist

3____

4 The Neolithic Revolution is considered a turning point in history because it

1 influenced climatic changes
2 included the domestication of plants and animals
3 encouraged a nomadic lifestyle
4 caused a decline in population

4____

5 The primary reason the Bantu-speaking people of West Africa migrated southward and eastward between 500 B.C. and A.D. 1500 was to

1 flee warfare
2 seek religious freedom
3 establish a colonial empire
4 find land for farming and grazing

5____

6 Which action is most closely associated with polytheism?

1 praying in a synagogue
2 accepting the Eightfold Path
3 worshipping many gods
4 reading the Koran

6____

Base your answer to question 7 on the graphic organizer below and on your knowledge of social studies.

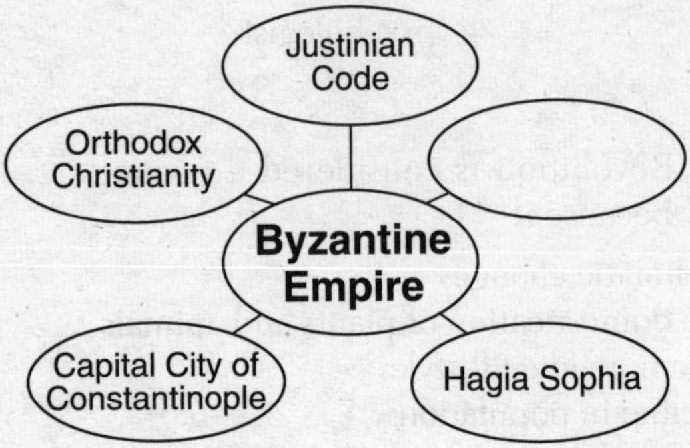

7 Which item best completes this graphic organizer?

1 Development of the Wheel
2 Preservation of Greek and Roman Culture
3 Creation of the Compass
4 Utilization of Cuneiform 7____

---

8 In western Europe, feudalism developed after the

1 Roman Empire collapsed
2 Renaissance began
3 city of Constantinople fell
4 Mongols invaded 8____

9 Letting some farmland remain unplanted as a means of increasing food production is most closely associated with

1 modern irrigation methods
2 the three-field system
3 the enclosure movement
4 slash-and-burn agriculture 9____

Base your answer to question 10 on the statements below and on your knowledge of social studies.

> . . . For many in the contemporary Arab world, the Crusades are viewed as having begun nearly a millennium of conflict with what would become the West. The Crusades are seen as representing the constant threat of Western encroachment [trespassing]. But many scholars say that is a more recent and inaccurate view of the Crusades. . . .
>
> — Mike Shuster, reporter, NPR

> The Medieval Crusades were taken and then turned into something that they never really were in the first place. They were turned into a kind of a proto-imperialism, an attempt to bring the fruits of European civilization to the Middle East, when, in fact, during the Middle Ages the great sophisticated and wealthy power was the Muslim world. Europe was the Third World. . . .
>
> — Thomas Madden, St. Louis University, History of relations between the West and Middle East, NPR, *All Things Considered*, August 17, 2004

10 These statements indicate that the history of the Crusades

1 has been neglected by experts
2 was of little importance
3 is the subject of debate and interpretation
4 illustrates the importance of tolerance and understanding

10____

Base your answer to question 11 on the Japanese print below and on your knowledge of social studies.

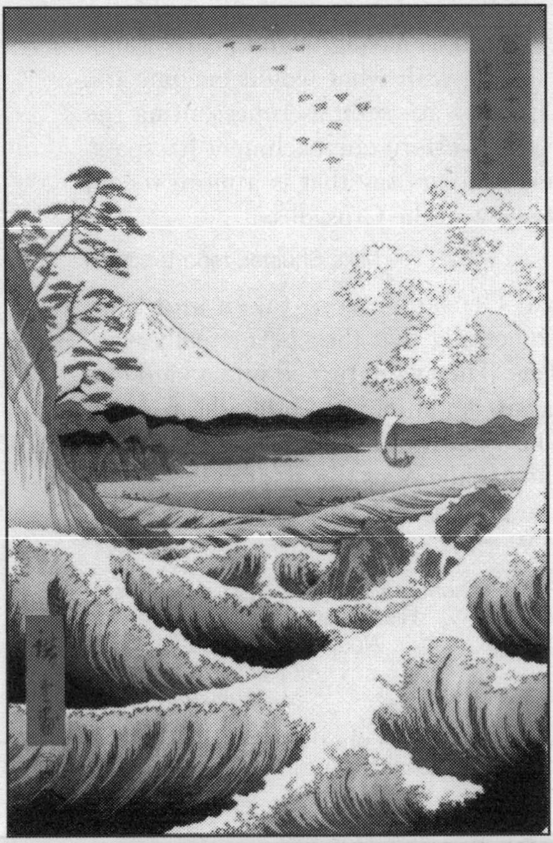

Source: *Hiroshige*, Prestel Postcard Book, 1997

11 Based on this print, which statement reflects an important theme in Japanese art and culture?

1 Nature is a powerful force.
2 Beauty is found in technological innovations.
3 Realistic portrayals create a harmonious effect.
4 Traditional activities should be expressed in simple forms.

11 ____

12 What was an impact of Korea's geographic location on the history of East Asia?

1 isolating Russia from Japan
2 protecting China from Mongol invaders
3 preventing Europeans from colonizing East Asia
4 serving as a cultural bridge between China and Japan

12____

13 Which situation was a result of Pax Mongolia?

1 Trade increased between Europe and Asia.
2 China became isolated from its neighbors.
3 Warfare between Japan and Vietnam escalated.
4 Europeans conquered the Aztecs and Incas.

13____

14 • Sir Francis Drake circumnavigated the globe.
• England defeated the Spanish Armada.
• William Shakespeare wrote his play *Richard III*.

These events occurred during the reign of

1 Charlemagne
2 Elizabeth I
3 Peter the Great
4 Suleiman the Magnificent

14____

15 Which geographic feature of Spain and Portugal most enhanced their ability to engage in exploration?

1 peninsular location
2 mountainous region
3 extensive river system
4 fertile plain

15____

16 The journeys of Vasco da Gama, Bartholomeu Dias, and Christopher Columbus became possible in the late 1400s because of the

1 support of exploration by the English government
2 trade connections established by Ibn Battuta
3 effects of the Atlantic slave trade
4 development of new navigational instruments and technology 16____

17 Which statement demonstrates a major characteristic of mercantilism in colonial Latin America?

1 Colonies developed local industries to compete with Spain.
2 Spanish colonies traded freely with English colonies.
3 Spain instituted democratic governments in its colonies.
4 Colonies were a source of raw materials for Spain. 17____

18 The encomienda system in colonial Latin America led to the

1 use of forced labor
2 establishment of trade unions
3 increase in landownership by Native Americans
4 weakening of the power of peninsulares 18____

19 Which heading best completes the partial outline below?

I. ____________________

A. Writings of Thomas Hobbes
B. Divine right theory
C. Centralization of political power
D. Reign of Louis XIV

1 Beginning of Global Trade
2 Growth of Democracy in Europe
3 Rise of Absolutism
4 Age of Exploration 19____

20 One way in which Montesquieu, Voltaire, and Rousseau are similar is that they were

1 philosophers during the Age of Enlightenment
2 chief ministers during the French Revolution
3 leaders of the Italian unification movement
4 supporters of the Counter Reformation 20____

21 Increased agricultural production in England in the late 1700s contributed directly to

1 the development of a worldwide communications network
2 the introduction of manorialism
3 a decrease in the power of the monarch
4 an increase in life expectancy 21____

22 Which statement about railroad systems in the 19th and early 20th centuries is accurate?

1 Imperialists rejected the use of railroads in their colonies.
2 European governments opposed the development of railroads.
3 Railroads helped promote the factory system and urbanization.
4 Railroads made transportation of goods less efficient. 22____

Base your answer to question 23 on the passage below and on your knowledge of social studies.

> . . . The need of a constantly expanding market for its products chases the bourgeoisie over the whole surface of the globe. It must nestle everywhere, settle everywhere, establish connections everywhere. . . .
>
> — Karl Marx and Friedrich Engels

23 Which historical event do Marx and Engels believe created the situation described in this passage?

1 Cold War
2 World War I
3 Russian Revolution
4 Industrial Revolution 23____

---

24 What was the main reason for the extensive Irish emigration to North America in the 1840s?

1 mass starvation
2 military draft
3 civil war
4 smallpox outbreak 24____

25 What was a principal reason for the success of European colonialism in Asia in the late 1800s?

1 Asians respected Europeans as representatives of an advanced civilization.
2 Europe was able to dominate military and commercial relations with Asia.
3 Europeans respected Asian laws and customs.
4 Many Asians adopted European religious practices. 25____

26 Which action in Japanese history occurred during the Meiji Restoration?

1 Japan modernized its economy.
2 Mongols invaded the islands of Japan.
3 The Japanese government adopted an isolationist policy.
4 Buddhism became the official religion of Japan. 26____

27 The annexation of Korea and Japan's invasion of Manchuria were attempts by Japan to

1 spread Shinto beliefs
2 protect human rights
3 acquire natural resources
4 establish theocratic governments 27____

Base your answers to questions 28 and 29 on the telegram below and on your knowledge of social studies.

> Nicholas II
> *Telegram to Wilhelm II*
> *July 29, 1914, 1:00 A.M.*
>
> Am glad you are back. In this most serious moment, I appeal to you to help me. An ignoble [despised] war has been declared upon a weak country [Serbia]. The indignation [resentment] in Russia, shared fully by me, is enormous. I foresee that very soon I shall be overwhelmed by the pressure upon me, and be forced to take extreme measures which will lead to war. To try and avoid such a calamity [disaster] as a European war, I beg you in the name of our old friendship to do what you can to stop your allies from going too far.
>
> — Nicky

28 Which conclusion is best supported by this telegram?

1 Russia started to mobilize for war against Serbia.
2 Nicholas II condemned the efforts of Wilhelm II.
3 Russia supported the use of extreme measures.
4 Nicholas II hoped diplomacy would prevent war. 28 ____

29 Which war is most closely associated with the telegram Nicholas II sent to Wilhelm II?

1 the Franco-Prussian War
2 the Russo-Japanese War
3 World War I
4 World War II 29 ____

Base your answers to questions 30 and 31 on the cartoon below and on your knowledge of social studies.

"THIS WILL MAKE YOU FORGET THE PEACE TERMS."

Source: Rollin Kirby, *The New York World,* March 28, 1919 (adapted)

30 This cartoonist is referring to the way Germany was affected in 1919 by

1 the Congress of Vienna
2 its defeat of Napoleon
3 the Treaty of Versailles
4 its defeat in World War II

30 ____

31 This 1919 cartoon suggests that Germany may come under the influence of

1 moderates
2 conservatives
3 radicals
4 isolationists

31 ____

32 Mohandas Gandhi's protests in India were a response to Great Britain's

1 support of Zionism
2 practice of humanitarianism
3 introduction of socialism
4 policy of colonialism

32____

Base your answers to questions 33 and 34 on the table below and on your knowledge of social studies.

Collective Farms of the USSR (Soviet Union) 1929–1940

Year	No. of collective farms in 1,000s
1929	57.0
1930	85.9
1931	211.1
1932	211.1
1933	224.6
1934	233.3
1935	245.4
1936	242.2
1937	243.7
1938	242.4
1939	241.1
1940	236.3

— Paul Halsall, *Internet Modern History Sourcebook*, (adapted)

33 Between which two years did the number of collective farms increase the most?

1 1929 and 1930
2 1930 and 1931
3 1934 and 1935
4 1939 and 1940

33____

34 Which Soviet policy is most closely associated with the information in this table?

1 Lenin's New Economic Policy
2 Stalin's five-year plans
3 Brezhnev's policy of détente
4 Gorbachev's policy of glasnost

34____

35 One similarity between Adolf Hitler and Benito Mussolini is that both

1 led fascist states
2 supported communism
3 rejected militarism
4 remained in power after World War II 35____

Base your answer to question 36 on the cartoon below and on your knowledge of social studies.

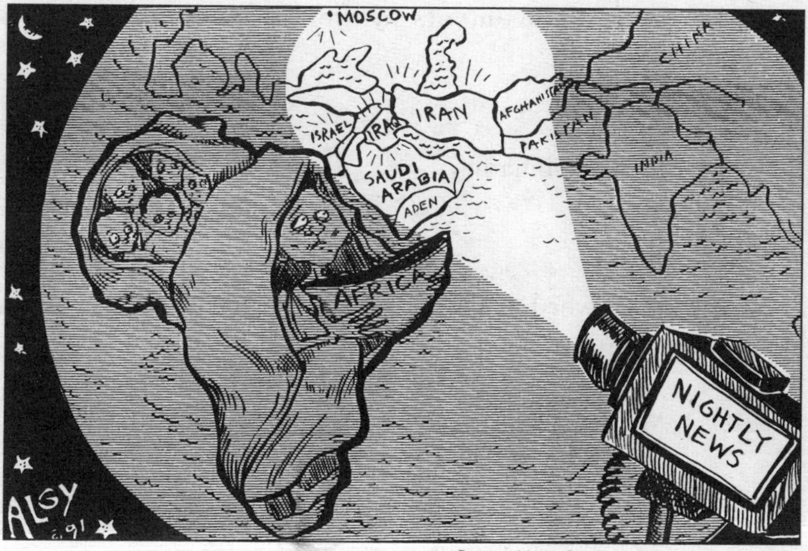

Source: Linda Godfrey, *Walworth County Week*

36 What does this cartoon suggest about news coverage of world events?

1 Social concerns are often overemphasized.
2 Africa's issues are often overshadowed by events in other regions.
3 Too much time is devoted to European affairs.
4 Africa's problems can be solved if global powers cooperate. 36____

37 What has the end of communism in the Soviet Union caused many countries in Eastern Europe to do?

1 shift to a command economy
2 maintain a communist form of government
3 pursue free-market economic policies
4 join the Warsaw Pact

37____

38 Which type of warfare did Mao Zedong, Fidel Castro, and Ho Chi Minh all engage in as leaders of revolutionary movements in their respective nations?

1 guerilla
2 trench
3 unrestricted submarine
4 biological

38____

Base your answer to question 39 on the speakers' statements below and on your knowledge of social studies.

Speaker A: Medical facilities and public transportation are readily available in New Delhi.

Speaker B: Homelessness and crime continue to increase in New Delhi.

Speaker C: New Delhi offers many employment opportunities.

39 One way in which these speakers are similar is that all are expressing their opinions about

1 rural poverty
2 interdependence
3 urban issues
4 nationalism

39____

Base your answer to question 40 on the chart below and on your knowledge of social studies.

United States Trade with Mexico and Canada
($ value in millions)

	$ Value of United States Exports to		$ Value of United States Imports from	
Year	**Mexico**	**Canada**	**Mexico**	**Canada**
1994	50,844	114,439	49,494	128,406
1998	78,773	156,603	94,629	173,256
2002	97,470	160,923	134,616	209,088

Source: *The World Almanac and Book of Facts,* World Almanac Books, 2004 (adapted)

40 The economic trend represented in this chart is most likely an effect of the creation of the

1 Organization of American States (OAS)
2 North Atlantic Treaty Organization (NATO)
3 North American Free Trade Agreement (NAFTA)
4 Organization of Petroleum Exporting Countries (OPEC) 40____

41 Which statement about the Balkan Peninsula since 1995 is most accurate?

1 Bosnia-Herzegovina and Croatia are now both controlled by Yugoslavia.
2 Ethnic tensions and conflict continue to be a problem in much of the region.
3 Slobodan Milosevic of Serbia became the first democratically elected leader of the region.
4 The Balkan Peninsula has become one of the most prosperous regions in Europe. 41____

42 Which revolution led to the concept of banking, the creation of guilds, and the development of capitalism in Europe?

1 Commercial
2 Agricultural
3 Scientific
4 Industrial

42____

43 The introduction of Buddhism into Japan and of Christianity into Africa are examples of

1 modernization
2 ethnic conflict
3 cultural diffusion
4 isolation

43____

44 A goal of both the Boxer Rebellion in China and the Mau Mau movement in Kenya was to

1 promote laissez-faire capitalism
2 end foreign control
3 develop modern industries
4 create a totalitarian state

44____

Base your answers to questions 45 and 46 on the statement below and on your knowledge of social studies.

"Therefore those preachers of indulgences are in error, who say that by the pope's indulgences a man is freed from every penalty, and saved;"

45 Which period in European history is most closely associated with this statement?

1 Roman Empire
2 Crusades
3 Protestant Reformation
4 Enlightenment

45____

46 This statement reflects a controversy over the proper

1 roles of women
2 forms of prayer
3 types of education
4 means of salvation

46____

47 Simón Bolívar, José de San Martin, and Toussaint l'Ouverture are best known as

1 scientists who supported the heliocentric theory
2 leaders of Latin American independence movements
3 early Spanish explorers of the New World
4 communist leaders of the 19th century 47____

Base your answer to question 48 on the cartoon below and on your knowledge of social studies.

Source: Mike Thompson, *Detroit Free Press* for *USA Today*, May 28, 2002

48 What is the main idea of this 2002 cartoon?

1 The technology of the Cold War now threatens peace in Asia.
2 The risk of nuclear conflict has been eliminated.
3 Nuclear power presents a possible solution to energy shortages in southern Asia.
4 Mediation has lessened tensions between India and Pakistan. 48____

49 A. Kemal Atäturk rises to power in Turkey.
B. Pericles rules during the Golden Age of Athens.
C. Ayatollah Khomeini seizes power in Iran.
D. Robespierre comes to power during the French Revolution.

What is the correct sequence of these events?

1 $C \rightarrow B \rightarrow A \rightarrow D$
2 $B \rightarrow C \rightarrow D \rightarrow A$
3 $A \rightarrow C \rightarrow B \rightarrow D$
4 $B \rightarrow D \rightarrow A \rightarrow C$

49____

50 The Communist Revolution in China differed from the 19th-century Marxist ideals because this revolution was primarily supported by the

1 warlords
2 peasants
3 factory owners
4 gentry

50____

In developing your answer to Part II, be sure to keep these general definitions in mind:

(a) explain means "to make plain or understandable; to give reasons for or causes of; to show the logical development or relationship of"

(b) discuss means "to make observations about something using facts, reasoning, and argument; to present in some detail"

PART II: THEMATIC ESSAY QUESTION

Directions: Write a well-organized essay that includes an introduction, several paragraphs addressing the task below, and a conclusion.

Theme: Geography
(How Humans Change Their Environment)

Throughout global history, human societies in various nations and regions have changed their physical environments to meet their needs. Societies have built structures, removed vegetation and resources, and modified the land to meet their needs. These changes have often had different results.

Task:

Select ***two*** different nations/regions and for ***each***

- Explain why the society modified their environment
- Explain how the people of that specific nation/region modified their physical environment
- Discuss the effect this modification had on that nation/region

You may use any nation or region from your study of global history. Some suggestions you might wish to consider include Middle East (modified the land), Africa (modified the land), Japan (modified the land), Great Britain (removed resources), South Africa (removed resources), Brazil (removed vegetation), China (built a structure), and East Germany (built structures).

You are *not* limited to these suggestions.

Do *not* select the United States or a region of the United States as an example in your answer.

Guidelines:

In your essay, be sure to:

- Develop all aspects of the task
- Support the theme with relevant facts, examples, and details
- Use a logical and clear plan of organization, including an introduction and a conclusion that are beyond a restatement of the theme

In developing your answers to Part III, be sure to keep these general definitions in mind:

(a) describe means "to illustrate something in words or tell about it"

(b) discuss means "to make observations about something using facts, reasoning, and argument; to present in some detail"

PART III: DOCUMENT-BASED QUESTION

This question is based on the accompanying documents. The question is designed to test your ability to work with historical documents. Some of these documents have been edited for the purposes of this question. As you analyze the documents, take into account the source of each document and any point of view that may be presented in the document.

Historical Context:

Throughout history, migrations of people have affected countries and regions. These migrations have been both voluntary and involuntary and include ***Africans to the Americas***, ***Jews to Palestine and Israel***, and ***Hindus/Muslims between India and Pakistan.***

Task:

Using the information from the documents and your knowledge of global history, answer the questions that follow each document in Part A. Your answers to the questions will help you write the Part B essay in which you will be asked to

Select ***two*** migrations mentioned in the historical context and for ***each***

- Describe the historical circumstances surrounding the voluntary or involuntary migration

- Discuss an impact the migration had on the country or region from which the group left *and/or* an impact the migration had on the new destination

You may *not* use the migration of Hindus and Muslims between India and Pakistan as two separate migrations.

Part A: Short-Answer Questions

Directions: Analyze the documents and answer the short-answer questions that follow each document in the space provided.

Document 1

The Big Business of Slave Trading

. . . When in 1517 Bishop Bartolomeo de Las Casas advocated [supported] the encouragement of immigration to the New World by permitting Spaniards to import African slaves, the trading of humans in the New World formally began. Las Casas was so determined to relieve Indians of the onerous [difficult] burden of slavery that he recommended the enslavement of Africans. (Later, he so deeply regretted having taken this position that he vigorously renounced it.) The ban against the use of Africans was removed, and Charles II issued licenses to several Flemish traders to take Africans to the Spanish colonies. Monopoly of the trade went to the highest bidders. Sometimes it was held by Dutch traders, at other times by Portuguese, French, or English. As West Indian plantations grew in size and importance, the slave trade became a huge, profitable undertaking employing thousands of persons and involving a capital outlay of millions of dollars. By 1540 the annual importation of African slaves into the West Indies was estimated at 10,000. . . .

Source: Franklin and Moss, *From Slavery to Freedom: A History of African Americans*, Alfred A. Knopf

1 According to Franklin and Moss, what was ***one*** reason enslaved Africans were imported to the "New World" by Europeans? [1]

____

____

Document 2

> . . . Large-scale sugar plantations, established first in Brazil and, after 1645, in the Caribbean islands, were enormously profitable. Plantations in Cuba gave more than a 30 percent return on capital investment; those in Barbados returned 40 to 50 percent. These islands became societies whose economies relied heavily on the labor of African captives. In 1789, one-third of the population of Cuba was comprised of Africans. Between 1730 and 1834, up to 90 percent of the populations of Jamaica, Antigua, and Grenada were Africans. In Brazil in 1800, half the population was African. . . .

Source: Willie F. Page, *Encyclopedia of African History and Culture*, Volume III, Facts on File

2 According to Willie F. Page, what was ***one*** impact of the arrival of Africans on Brazil and on the Caribbean Islands? [1]

____

____

Document 3

. . . **Long-Term Effects.** The trade in African slaves brought about the largest forced movement of people in history. It established the basis for black populations in the Caribbean and in North and South America. At the same time, it disrupted social and political life in Africa and opened the door for European colonization of the continent. . . .

The shift in European demand from gold, foodstuffs, and such products to slaves changed the relations among African groups and states. The prices Africans received for slaves made it more profitable for them to take captives from their neighbors than to establish networks for producing and selling other goods. In this way the slave trade encouraged strong states to raid weaker states for slaves. As a result, many African societies were torn by organized slave wars and general banditry. Successful slave-raiding and trading societies formed new states that were dominated by military groups and constantly at war with their neighbors. . . .

Source: John Middleton, ed., *Africa: An Encyclopedia for Students*, Volume 4, Thomson Learning

3 Based on this excerpt from *Africa: An Encyclopedia for Students*, state ***two*** effects of the slave trade on Africa. [2]

(1)____

____

(2)____

____

Document 4a

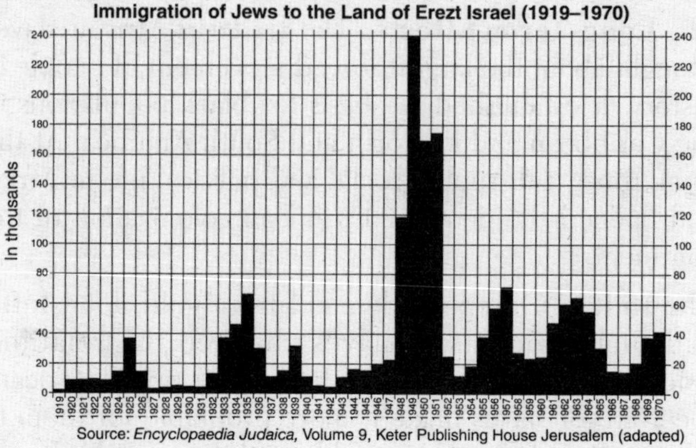
Immigration of Jews to the Land of Erezt Israel (1919–1970)
In thousands
Source: *Encyclopaedia Judaica*, Volume 9, Keter Publishing House Jerusalem (adapted)

Document 4b

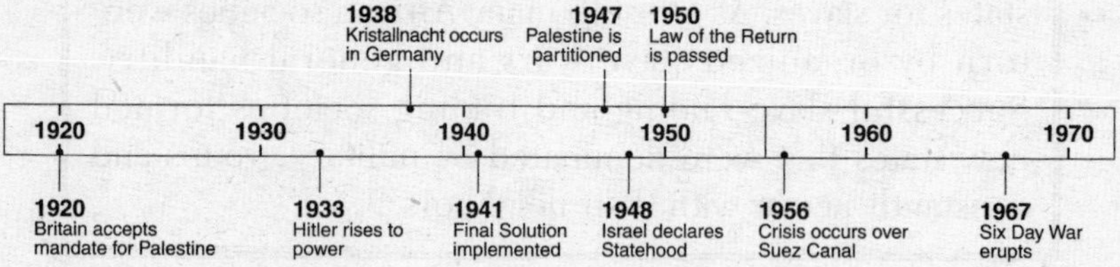
1938
Kristallnacht occurs in Germany
1947
Palestine is partitioned
1950
Law of the Return is passed
1920
1930
1940
1950
1960
1970
1920
Britain accepts mandate for Palestine
1933
Hitler rises to power
1941
Final Solution implemented
1948
Israel declares Statehood
1956
Crisis occurs over Suez Canal
1967
Six Day War erupts

4 Based on these documents, identify ***two*** specific reasons large numbers of Jewish immigrants moved to the Palestinian/Israeli region between 1920 and 1970. [2]

(1) ____

____

(2) ____

____

Document 5a

Arab Palestinians began to leave their homes in cities in December 1947. The number of Arab Palestinians leaving their homes increased to hundreds of thousands by May 1948. During the last week of April in 1948, as the fighting came closer to their home, the Palestinian family in this passage left Jaffa for Ramallah. On May 14, 1948, Israel was established. This new country included the city of Jaffa. Ramallah was in the West Bank that became part of Jordan.

> . . . I grew up hearing the description of my father's last visit to Jaffa, and it has left an indelible [permanent] impression on me. My father's entire holdings were in and around Jaffa, the products of his own hard work. His father had left him nothing. How difficult it must have been to bid all this farewell. The image of my father, his every step echoing in the empty streets of the deserted city, still haunts me. . . .
>
> He moved on to the marketplace, empty except for a few shops that had somehow remained open. He walked passed Hinn's, his barbershop, and found it closed. The courthouse was closed, as were the clinics, the nurseries, the cafés, the cinema. The place was deserted, prepared to be captured. What have we done, he wondered. How could we have all left? . . .

Source: Raja Shehadeh, *Strangers in the House: Coming of Age in Occupied Palestine*, Penguin Books

5*a* Based on this account by Raja Shehadeh, what was ***one*** impact on the city of Jaffa when the Palestinians left? [1]

____

____

Document 5b

This excerpt describes the early days of the State of Israel in 1949 when many people, including the Jews from displaced camps in Europe, were migrating into and out of the region.

> . . . At any rate, the return of the Arabs to their homes became increasingly difficult with the rise of another cataclysmic event—the mass influx of the Jews from all over the world. They had been coming, even in the midst of hostilities, at the rate of a thousand a day, in larger numbers than had been expected, and in much larger numbers than the country was ready to accommodate. The squeamishness of the Custodians of Abandoned (Arab) Property had to give way to the onrush of this deluge [flood of people] and the early comers and some of the old-timers helped themselves to whatever was left of the former Arab houses. . . .

Source: M. Z. Frank, Introduction to "From the Four Corners of the Earth," *Sound the Great Trumpet*, Whittier Books

5*b* According to M. Z. Frank, what was ***one*** effect of the Jewish migration on Israel? [1]

____

____

Document 6

Richard Willstätter, a German Jewish chemist, won a Nobel Prize in 1915. In 1938, during Nazi rule, he managed to flee Germany. Many others fled before 1938 and some fled after.

> . . . Willstätter's story demonstrates that the exodus of German Jews was one of the most astonishing migrations in history. It included not only Nobel Prize winners but thousands of other scientists, artists, academics, engineers, and professional men and women in every category. And since this was an entire population and not the usual young person in search of a fortune, it was made up of whole families, middle-aged couples, and even the elderly, like Betty Scholem, who settled in a small town in Australia, tending a sweetshop with one of her sons. Driven out of their country, they took their talent and skills and culture with them and made the rest of the world richer for it. . . .

Source: Ruth Gay, *The Jews of Germany*, Yale University Press

6 According to Ruth Gay, what was ***one*** way Germany was hurt by the migration of German Jews? [1]

____

____

Document 7

Partition

. . . Gandhi's beliefs were based, in part, on ancient Hindu ideals. This may have added to the hatred and suspicion that had always existed between Hindus and Muslims. The Muslims were afraid that they would have no power in the new India. Although the Hindu leaders, including Gandhi, tried to reassure the Muslims, no agreement could be reached. The country was finally divided into two parts—the independent Muslim state of Pakistan and a predominately Hindu state—the Democratic Republic of India. . . .

Source: Jean Bothwell, *The First Book of India*, Franklin Watts

7 According to Jean Bothwell, what was ***one*** cause of the migration of Muslims and Hindus? [1]

____

____

Document 8

History's Greatest Migration

4,000,000 People Cross the Punjab to Seek New Homes

The mass migration and exchange of populations in the Punjab—Moslems moving west into Pakistan and Hindus and Sikhs trekking east into India—have now reached a scale unprecedented in history. Accurate statistics are impossible to obtain, but it is reasonable to estimate that no fewer than four million people are now on the move both ways.

What this means in terms of human misery and hardship can be neither imagined nor described. Within the past few weeks the conditions over a wide area of Northern India, including the whole of the Indus Valley and part of the Gangetic Plain, have deteriorated steadily. It is no exaggeration to say that throughout the North-west Frontier Provinces, in the West Punjab, the East Punjab, and the Western part of the United Provinces the minority communities live in a state of insecurity often amounting to panic.

Farther afield in the eastern parts of the United Provinces and to a less extent in Bihar and Bengal, much tension and friction prevail but there has hitherto been little movement of population. . . .

Source: *Guardian*, Thursday, September 25, 1947

8 Based on this article in the *Guardian*, state ***two*** ways the region of South Asia was affected by the mass migration of people in 1947. [2]

(1) ______________________________

____

(2) ______________________________

____

Document 9

> . . . And there were many [examples where untouchables were invisible during the partition]. In January 1948, two social workers, Sushila Nayyar and Anis Kidwai, went to visit Tihar village on the outskirts of Delhi. They had heard that a rich Hindu from Pakistan had left behind huge properties when he had moved, and had therefore, like many people, effected an exchange of property with a rich Muslim in Tihar to whom the land belonged. Each took the other's property. But neither was obliged to carry on with the other's business. The Hindu, therefore, threw out all previously employed workers from his newly acquired piece of property. Most of these were Muslims, but about a third were Harijans [untouchables]. The Muslims made their way to one or the other of the two Muslim camps that had been set up in the city. But for the Harijans, displaced in a war that was basically centred around Hindu and Muslim identities, there was nowhere to go. No camps to help them tide over the difficult time. No recourse to government—all too preoccupied at the moment with looking after the interests of Muslims and Hindus, no help from political leaders whose priorities were different at the time. . . .

Source: Urvashi Butalia, *The Other Side of Silence*, Duke University Press, 2000

9 According to Urvashi Butalia, what was ***one*** impact the migration of Muslims and Hindus had on South Asia? [1]

____

____

Part B: Essay

Directions: Write a well-organized essay that includes an introduction, several paragraphs, and a conclusion. Use evidence from *at least* ***four*** documents in your essay. Support your response with relevant facts, examples, and details. Include additional outside information.

Historical Context:

Throughout history, migrations of people have affected countries and regions. These migrations have been both voluntary and involuntary and include ***Africans to the Americas***, ***Jews to Palestine and Israel***, and ***Hindus/Muslims between India and Pakistan.***

Task:

Using the information from the documents and your knowledge of global history, write an essay in which you

Select ***two*** migrations mentioned in the historical context and for ***each***

- Describe the historical circumstances surrounding the voluntary or involuntary migration
- Discuss an impact the migration had on the country or region from which the group left *and/or* an impact the migration had on the new destination

You may *not* use the migration of Hindus and Muslims between India and Pakistan as two separate migrations.

Guidelines:

In your essay, be sure to:

- Develop all aspects of the task
- Incorporate information from *at least* ***four*** documents
- Incorporate relevant outside information
- Support the theme with relevant facts, examples, and details
- Use a logical and clear plan of organization, including an introduction and a conclusion that are beyond a restatement of the theme

Answers August 2008

Global History and Geography

Answer Key

PART I (1–50)

1. 1	**14.** 2	**27.** 3	**40.** 3
2. 2	**15.** 1	**28.** 4	**41.** 2
3. 3	**16.** 4	**29.** 3	**42.** 1
4. 2	**17.** 4	**30.** 3	**43.** 3
5. 4	**18.** 1	**31.** 3	**44.** 2
6. 3	**19.** 3	**32.** 4	**45.** 3
7. 2	**20.** 1	**33.** 2	**46.** 4
8. 1	**21.** 4	**34.** 2	**47.** 2
9. 2	**22.** 3	**35.** 1	**48.** 1
10. 3	**23.** 4	**36.** 2	**49.** 4
11. 1	**24.** 1	**37.** 3	**50.** 2
12. 4	**25.** 2	**38.** 1	
13. 1	**26.** 1	**39.** 3	

PART II: Thematic Essay See Answers Explained section.

PART III: Document-Based Essay See Answers Explained section.

Answers Explained

PART I

1. **1** Ethnocentrism is best defined as the belief that one's culture is superior to all others. The word *ethnocentrism* derives from the Greek word *ethnos*, meaning "nation or people," and the English word *center*. Ethnocentrism is the belief that one's own race or ethnic group is the most important and that some or all aspects of its culture are superior to those of other groups. It is also the belief that one's own group is at the center of everything against which all other groups are judged. Ethnocentrism can lead to making false assumptions about cultural differences as well as to racism, which can be very destructive to society.

WRONG CHOICES EXPLAINED:

(2) *Militarism* is the term used to define military preparation for civil war.

(3) *Nationalism* or *patriotism* is defined as love and devotion to one's country.

(4) *Monotheism* is a belief in one god.

2. **2** All of these geographic statements apply to China. The Chinese heartlands lay along the east coast and the valley of the Yellow River, or Huang He, and the Yangtze. In ancient times, these fertile farming regions supported the largest population. Then, as now, the rivers provided water for irrigation and served as transportation routes. About 90 percent of the land that is suitable for farming lies within the comparatively small plain between the Yellow River (Huang He) and the Yangtze in eastern China. To the west and southwest of China, high mountain ranges of the Tien Shan and the Himalayas, as well as the Taklimaken Desert and the 14,000 plateaus of Tibet, proved natural barriers that helped to isolate China from all other civilizations.

WRONG CHOICES EXPLAINED:

(1), (3), and (4) None of these countries is bordered by the Yellow Sea. The populations of England, Nicaragua, and the Philippines are not concentrated along river valleys. Mountains, plateaus, and deserts do not dominate their western region.

3. **3** An economist is a social scientist who primarily studies how people change resources into goods and services. The fundamental economic problem facing all societies is that of scarcity, or limited resources. An economist studies how people use their limited resources to satisfy their wants and

needs to produce goods and services for their society. Scarcities arise because a society does not have enough resources to produce all the goods and services that people would like to have. An economist studies and analyzes how the barter system, feudalism, capitalism, or socialism enables societies to exchange resources for the goods and services they need.

WRONG CHOICES EXPLAINED:

(1) An archaeologist is a social scientist who studies the objects left by other people. Archaeologists use these objects to determine the type of civilization and government that a society developed during a particular period.

(2) A sociologist examines the social institutions of a society such as family, structure, and social relationships.

(4) A psychologist examines the development of self-image and the causes of mental illness.

4. **2** The Neolithic Revolution is considered a turning point in history because it included the domestication of plants and animals. During the Neolithic period, which lasted from 8000 B.C. to 4000 B.C., people came out of caves and settled near lakes, rivers, and seas. People settled in small communities and secured food by farming. They learned to plow the soil, domesticate animals, and use the wheel and axle for transportation. These developments led to the Neolithic Revolution, or Agricultural Revolution, which meant that people no longer had to search for food. An abundance of food and permanent settlements were now established. The Neolithic Revolution led to organized community life, as people needed to work together to meet their basic needs.

WRONG CHOICES EXPLAINED:

(1) The Neolithic Revolution did not influence climatic changes. It influenced how a society grew food and where they lived.

(3) The Neolithic Revolution discouraged a nomadic lifestyle. The domestication of plants and animals meant that members of a society did not have to travel from place to place to find food.

(4) The Neolithic Revolution did not cause a decline in population. After the Neolithic Revolution, the more abundant food supply helped the population to increase, not decline.

5. **4** The primary reason the Bantu-speaking people of West Africa migrated southward and eastward between 500 B.C. and A.D. 1500 was to find land for farming and grazing. The Bantu-speaking people lived in the savanna south of the Sahara in the area that is now southeastern Nigeria. These skilled farmers and herders migrated south and east in search of new land as the Sahara regions began to dry out. The Bantus adopted their farming methods to suit their environment. Some of their farming methods quickly exhausted the land. The search for new fertile land kept the Bantus on the move. Anthropologists suggest that as soon as the Bantus developed agricul-

ture, they were able to produce more food than they could acquire by hunting and gathering. They required more food as the population grew. The Bantus planted more land, but soon there was not enough to produce all the food needed. They could not go north in search of land because the area was densely populated and the Sahara was slowly advancing toward them. Within only 1,500 years, the Bantu-speaking people had populated much of the southern half of Africa. This constant movement in search of food caused the Bantus to displace many groups in central and southern Africa.

WRONG CHOICES EXPLAINED:

(1) The Bantu-speaking people were not fleeing warfare. Territorial warfare often broke out as the Bantus spread south, but the fighting occurred over the efforts by the Bantus to seize more land for agriculture.

(2) The Bantu-speaking people were not seeking religious freedom. They practiced animism, and none of the African groups sought to impose any religion in the area.

(3) The Bantu-speaking people were farmers and hunters and were not involved in establishing a colonial empire. The Bantus intermarried and helped to create new cultures and customs among the different areas where they migrated.

6. **3** Worshipping many gods is the action most closely associated with polytheism. Most ancient people believed in many gods. People appealed to the sun gods, river goddesses, and other spirits that they believed controlled natural forces. Other gods were thought to control human activities, such as birth, trade, or war. The Egyptians, Greeks, and Roman civilizations were polytheistic.

WRONG CHOICES EXPLAINED:

(1) Praying in the synagogue is most associated with the belief system of Judaism. Judaism is monotheistic, which is a belief in one god.

(2) The Eightfold Path is part of the basic teachings of Buddhism.

(4) Reading the Koran is part of the belief system of Islam.

7. **2** The item that best completes this graphic organizer is the Preservation of Greek and Roman Culture. Constantinople was the capital city of the Byzantine Empire. It was founded in 330 A.D. at ancient Byzantium as the new capital of the Roman Empire by Constantine I, for whom it was named. At the center of the city, Byzantine emperors and empresses lived in glittering splendor. The Byzantine Empire made its most important contributions to later civilizations by preserving much of the Greco-Roman heritage. After the fall of Rome in 476, the Byzantine Empire was regarded as the heir to Roman power and traditions and remained a political and cultural force for nearly 1,000 years after the fall of Rome. To Europe, it was a symbol of the power and glory of Rome long after the Roman Empire had faded. Emperor Justinian (527–565) preserved Roman law. He set up a team of scholars to

gather and organize the ancient laws of Rome, a collection of laws that became known as the Justinian Code. The code served as the basis of law for the Catholic and medieval rulers. Byzantine architecture combined the features of Greco-Roman and Persian architecture by devising a rectangular building topped by a round dome. Hagia Sophia, the famous church erected in Constantinople in the 6th century by Emperor Justinian, is an example of Byzantine architecture. Byzantine artists made great contributions to religious art. They produced icons, images of Jesus, the Virgin Mary, or saints of the Byzantine Church, and created mosaics, pictures or designs formed by inlaid pieces of stones, that often showed biblical scenes. Beautiful mosaics and icons adorn the interior of Hagia Sophia. The art and architecture of Constantinople reflected the importance of the Orthodox Church in the Byzantine Empire. By the time of Justinian, a division had grown between the church in Rome and the Byzantine Church. Since early Christian times, differences had emerged over church leadership. Although Justinian was not a priest, he controlled church affairs and appointed the highest officials or patriarchs in Constantinople. Byzantine Christians rejected the pope's claim to authority over all Christians. The Orthodox Christian Church, also called the Eastern Orthodox Church, was the Christian church of the Byzantine Empire. Byzantine culture represented a continuation of classical knowledge, especially its Greek and Hellenistic aspects. The Byzantine Empire preserved Greek science, philosophy, and literature. When the empire declined in the 1400s, some of the ancient texts of Greece were carried to the West and helped to stimulate the revival of learning during the later Middle Ages and the Renaissance.

WRONG CHOICES EXPLAINED:

(1) The wheel was invented by unknown people, but the Sumerians made the first wheeled vehicles.

(3) The Chinese civilization is associated with the creation of the compass.

(4) The Sumerian civilization used cuneiform, a form of writing, around 3000 B.C.

8\. **1** In western Europe, feudalism developed after the Roman Empire collapsed. The fall of Rome in 476 A.D. resulted in a period of disorder in western Europe. Roman roads deteriorated, leading to a decline of trade. As cities diminished, the cities lost population. There was no central government since each Germanic tribe exerted control over its particular area. During the early Middle Ages, the central government could not protect its subjects from local warfare or foreign invasion. Thus, small farmers surrendered their lands to powerful local nobles in exchange for their protection. This system became known as *feudalism*. Feudalism helped people survive the breakdown of central government and order. Feudalism provided stability, order, and a strict social structure based on the control of land and military power. There was a rigid class distinction in which the king was at the top and the peasant or serf was at the bottom. Everyone had a well-defined position in medieval European society. Feudal society was sharply divided into the landholding nobles, the upper class, and the great mass of peasants or serfs. People were born as serfs, knights, or lords and could not change their social position. Local nobles or lords were given lands by their rulers or kings in exchange for military service. These lords had small armies of their own made up of knights, armed warriors on horseback. During the Middle Ages, most people lived on the manor, which was the noble's estate, and the serfs gave their lords part of the harvest in return for the use of the land. In return, the lords protected the serfs from outside attackers.

WRONG CHOICES EXPLAINED:

(2) The Renaissance was a period in European history lasting from 1300 to 1600 during which there was a renewed interest in the classical civilizations of Greece and Rome.

(3) The city of Constantinople fell to the Turkish Empire in 1453. The fall of Constantinople occurred almost a thousand years after the fall of the Roman Empire in the West.

(4) The Mongol invasion took place during the 12th century. Their rule stretched throughout central Asia and China, into Russia and Europe, and into part of southwest Asia and India.

9. **2** Letting some farmland remain unplanted as a means of increasing food production is most closely associated with the three-field system. This was a system of farming that developed in medieval Europe in which farmland was divided into three fields of equal size and each of these was successively planted. With the same 600 acres, farmers used 200 acres for a winter crop of wheat or rye. In spring, they planted another 200 acres with oats, barley, or beans. The remaining 200 acres lay fallow. Under this new three-field system, farmers could grow crops on two-thirds of their land each year, not just on half of it. As a result, food production increased.

WRONG CHOICES EXPLAINED:

(1) Modern irrigation methods are used to bring water to crops by means of canals and ditches.

(3) The enclosure movement was developed in England in the 1700s. It was the method created by wealthy British landowners of taking over and fencing off public lands that were formerly used by village farmers.

(4) Slash-and-burn agriculture involves farmers clearing the land by burning existing vegetation and planting crops in the ashes.

10. **3** These statements indicate that the history of the Crusades is the subject of debate and interpretation. A major goal of the Crusades, which lasted from 1096 to 1291, was to capture the Holy Land from Islamic rulers. In 1096, Pope Urban II called for a Crusade or Holy War against the Muslims, claiming that God was on the side of the Crusaders. In 1187, the Muslim leader, Saladin, claimed that God was on his side when he recaptured

Jerusalem. Both Christians and Muslims believed that God was on their side. The lasting legacy of the Crusades is how it continues to be a source of debate and interpretation. Contemporary Arabs view the Crusades as the beginning of the conflict that has existed between the Christian and Muslim worlds for more than a thousand years. Others claim that Europeans should realize that their society benefited by their contact with the Muslim world. The Muslim world was a highly developed civilization, and a direct result of the Crusades was that Europe brought back new ideas, products, and the culture of Greece and Rome to their society. Europe also became aware of the advances in Arab civilizations in art, science, and literature. The conflicting view of the Crusades indicates that it is still a highly debated topic in the history of the relations between the Middle East and the West.

WRONG CHOICES EXPLAINED:

(1), (2), and (4) None of these choices is addressed in the reading passage.

11. **1** Based on this print, the statement that reflects an important theme in Japanese art and culture is that nature is a powerful force. This image clearly shows that nature has the power to take the shape of mountain ranges, volcanoes, trees, and bodies of water. The power of nature knows no bounds and has great power.

WRONG CHOICES EXPLAINED:

(2) There is nothing in this print that shows technological innovations or how they do or do not reflect beauty. The print shows only natural beauty, and does not indicate anything about technology.

(3) This print is not concerned with realistic portrayals, as it shows a variety of natural phenomena, all in existence with each other. The print does not realistically portray the ways in which mountains, forests, and bodies of water exist with each other and instead shows all of these things in one area, which is not a realistic portrayal of nature.

(4) There is no indication or demonstration of traditional activities in this print. The print is concerned only with nature.

12. **4** An impact of Korea's geographic location on the history of East Asia is that it served as a cultural bridge between China and Japan. Korea is a peninsula attached to the eastern mainland of Asia between China and Japan. From about 100 A.D. to 600 A.D. Korea absorbed many ideas and customs from China, including Buddhism, Confucianism, and Chinese written script. Chinese culture spread to Korea in several ways. At times, China ruled parts of North Korea. During periods of turmoil at home, Chinese refugees fled to Korea, bringing their customs with them. Many Koreans went to study in China, where they learned the Chinese language and read Confucian texts. Koreans adapted Chinese traditions as their own beliefs. An example is the belief that spirits resided in natural objects, such as rocks and trees. Among the most revered spirits were the mountain gods. In Korea, Buddhism

absorbed this belief and Korean Buddhist temples included a shrine to the mountain gods. Koreans transformed Chinese traditions and passed them on to Japan. During the 6th century, many Koreans migrated to Japan, bringing the Chinese influence with them. Korean missionaries introduced Buddhism to Japan, and by the mid-700s, the Japanese imperial court officially accepted Buddhism in Japan. The Koreans also brought the Chinese system of writing, which became Japan's first written language. These early exposures to China's advanced civilization through the Koreans impressed the Japanese. In 607, Prince Shotoku of the Japanese imperial family sent a group of Japanese nobles to China. After many years, they returned home eager to share their knowledge. Chinese influence reached all levels of Japanese life.

WRONG CHOICES EXPLAINED:

(1) Korea's geography did not isolate Russia from Japan. During the Age of Imperialism, Japan, Russia, and China competed for control of Korea. By 1905, the Japanese had defeated their rivals and won control of Korea.

(2) Korea's geography did not protect China from Mongol invaders. Mongols gained control of China as well as Korea in the 13th century.

(3) Europeans were not prevented from colonizing East Asia because of Korea's geographic location. Europeans gained control in such areas as Indonesia and Indochina.

13. **1** A situation that was a result of Pax Mongolia was that trade increased between Europe and Asia. From the mid-1200s to the mid-1300s, the Mongols imposed stability and order across much of Eurasia. This period is sometimes called the Pax Mongolia (Mongol Peace), which allowed for the exchange of goods and ideas between the East and the West. The Mongol Peace made the caravan trade route along the Silk Road safe for travel and trade. Through the Silk Road, traders transported Chinese silk and porcelain, which continued to be desired in Europe and western Asia. Other Chinese products and inventions that went west were the printing press, gunpowder, the compass, and playing cards. During the rule of Kublai Khan, foreign merchants were invited to visit China. Most of them were Muslims from India, central Asia, and Persia. The most famous European to visit China was Marco Polo, the Venetian trader. With his father and uncle, he traveled by caravan on the Silk Road and arrived at the court of Kublai Khan in 1275. Before returning home, he spent 17 years in China, where he marveled at the technological superiority of the Chinese, such as the use of gunpowder and coal, which was little known in Europe. His writings about that country's fabulous cities and the wealth of China aroused Western interest in trading with them.

WRONG CHOICES EXPLAINED:

(2) During the Mongol Peace, China was not isolated from its neighbors. European and Muslim traders visited China.

(3) There was no warfare between Vietnam and Japan during the Pax Mongolia. During this period, Japan was in a constant state of war over which feudal shogun or lord commanded complete loyalty.

(4) The European conquest of Aztecs and Incas took place in the 16th century, which was 200 years after the end of the Pax Mongolia.

14. **2** These events occurred during the reign of Elizabeth I. Elizabeth I was born in 1533 and ruled England from 1558 to 1603. Elizabeth I was the third of Henry VIII's children to rule England. In the Caribbean and elsewhere, English captains who raided Spanish treasure ships were known as *sea dogs*. The greatest of the sea dogs was Francis Drake. On his most daring expedition (1577–1580), Drake raided Spanish ships in the Caribbean and along the eastern coast of South America. Then he sailed through the Strait of Magellan around the tip of South America and captured Spanish treasures along the coast of Chile and Peru. From there, Drake sailed as far north as San Francisco Bay, crossed the Pacific Ocean, and returned home with stolen prizes valued at 600,000 pounds. Drake had become the first person since Magellan's crew to sail around the world. Instead of apologizing to Spain for his piracies, Queen Elizabeth knighted him.

In 1588, Philip II planned to attack England. Philip II claimed that Elizabeth had supported Protestant subjects who rebelled against his Catholic rule. In 1588, he assembled a fleet of 130 ships, 8,000 sailors, and 19,000 soldiers. This force, known as the Spanish Armada, reached the southwest coast of England on July 29. However, bad weather and the English fleet defeated the Spanish completely.

The Renaissance in England is also called the Elizabethan Age for Queen Elizabeth I. She patronized artists and writers. William Shakespeare wrote in Renaissance England. His plays include *Romeo and Juliet, Macbeth, Hamlet,* and *King Lear.*

WRONG CHOICES EXPLAINED:

(1) Charlemagne (742–814) was king of the Franks and emperor of the Holy Roman Empire from 800 to 814 A.D.

(3) Peter the Great was the Russian czar from 1682 to 1725. He wanted to westernize Russia.

(4) Suleiman the Magnificent was an Ottoman sultan who ruled from 1520 to 1566.

15. **1** The geographic feature of Spain and Portugal that most enhanced their ability to engage in exploration was their peninsular location. Spain is in southwestern Europe and makes up about 84 percent of the Iberian Peninsula. Portugal makes up the rest of the peninsula. These two nations were eager to break the monopoly that the Italian cities, notably Venice and Genoa, held on trade with Asia during the 15th century. Located on the Atlantic Ocean at the southwest corner of Europe, Portugal established trading outposts along the west coast of Africa. Eventually, Portuguese explorers

pushed farther east into the Indian Ocean. As the Portuguese established trading posts along the west coast of Africa, Spain also desired a direct route to the treasures of Asia. Portugal and Spain financed expeditions seeking an all-water route to Asia because their location enabled them to sail around Africa directly to Asia. Portuguese explorers, such as Bartholomeu Dias and Vasco da Gama, made Portugal an early leader in the Age of Exploration. In Spain, Christopher Columbus believed he could find a direct route to Asia by sailing westward across the Atlantic Ocean. Columbus's voyage would open the way for European colonization of the American continents, which forever changed the world. Spain and Portugal's location on the Iberian Peninsula contributed to its ability to explore other lands.

WRONG CHOICES EXPLAINED:

(2) The mountainous region would serve as an obstacle to exploration. Mountain ranges, such as the Pyrenees in Spain, would prevent the country from seeking a direct trading route.

(3) The extensive river system of both of these countries promoted travel within the country but would not provide an outlet for exploration. The Douro River in Portugal provided transportation within the country but did not serve as a basis for overseas expeditions.

(4) The fertile plains of these countries provided for agricultural growth but did not contribute to the rise of exploration in Portugal and Spain.

16. **4** The journeys of Vasco da Gama, Bartholomeu Dias, and Christopher Columbus became possible in the late 1400s because of the development of new navigational instruments and technology. Technological development during the 14th and 15th centuries contributed to exploration. Notable improvements in mapmaking and shipbuilding gave rise to the caravel, a ship with both square and triangular sails. This enabled it to sail more effectively against the wind than the square-rigged ships, and allowed Europeans to sail farther than ever before. The caravel also had an improved rudder, enabling it to achieve easier turns than earlier ships, plus a larger cargo area that enabled the caravel to carry the amount of supplies needed for longer voyages. Europeans also improved their navigational techniques. Explorers were also able to more accurately track their direction by using the magnetic compass invented by the Chinese. Sailors used the astrolabe, which had been perfected by the Muslims, to determine their location on the sea. Later, the sextant replaced the astrolabe in measuring the height of stars above the horizon. This procedure enabled sea captains to tell their distance north or south of the equator. All of these improvements made ocean voyages less dangerous.

WRONG CHOICES EXPLAINED:

(1) Vasco da Gama, Bartholomeu Dias, and Christopher Columbus were not English explorers. The Portuguese and Spanish kings supported their voyages.

(2) These voyages did not help to develop trade connections by Ibn Battuta. Ibn Battuta was a historian who visited most of the Islamic world during the 14th century. None of these European explorers had any contact with Ibn Battuta.

(3) These voyages took place before the Atlantic slave trade, which began in the 16th century. These explorations gave rise to the slave trade as Spanish and Portuguese colonies in the Americas needed slave labor to run their plantations.

17. **4** A statement that demonstrates a major characteristic of mercantilism in colonial Latin America is that colonies were a source of raw materials for Spain. Under the policy of mercantilism, Spain and other colonial powers considered their colonies to be possessions to benefit the imperial power. Mercantilism was an economic policy that Spain adapted in the 15th and 16th centuries in its quest for trade and colonies. To make the empire profitable, Spain closely controlled its economic activities, especially trade. Colonies had to export raw materials only for the mother country and could buy only Spanish-manufactured goods. Laws forbade colonists from trading with other European nations or even with other Spanish colonies. Spanish colonies in the Americas kept the wealth flowing back into the home country because colonies ensured a favorable balance of trade. This favorable balance of trade increased the wealth of the nation that was measured by the supply of gold and silver. The most valuable resources or raw materials shipped from Spanish America to Spain were gold and silver.

WRONG CHOICES EXPLAINED:

(1) Under mercantilism, colonies were not allowed to develop local industries to compete with Spain. Colonies could not set their own industries to manufacture goods. Strict laws were passed to enforce these regulations.

(2) Spanish colonies were not allowed to trade freely with English colonies. Spain passed strict navigation laws to ensure that colonies traded only with the mother country.

(3) Spain never instituted democratic government in its colonies. Spain was ruled by an absolute monarch who maintained strict control of the colonies through viceroys who ruled in his name.

18. **1** The *encomienda* system in colonial Latin America led to the use of forced labor. The purpose of the encomienda system in Latin America was to obtain labor and taxes from the native peoples in the Spanish colonies. To make the Spanish colonies profitable, Spain closely controlled their economic activities. The Spanish set up large plantations to grow cash crops, such as sugarcane and coffee, that they could ship to Spain. Finding the large number of workers needed to make the plantations profitable was a problem. During the early 1500s, the Spanish king created the encomienda system. The Spanish granted the conquistadors the right to demand taxes or labor from the people living on the land. In return, the Spanish were to pay the

Native Americans for their work, look after their health, and teach them about Christianity. The Spanish used the system to enslave Native Americans. Bartolomeo de Las Casas, a Dominican priest, spoke out against the horrors of the encomienda system, and in 1542 Spain passed a law forbidding the enslavement of Native Americans. However, Spain was too far away to enforce them. Many Native Americans were forced to become peons, workers forced to labor for landlords to pay off their debts.

WRONG CHOICES EXPLAINED:

(2) The encomienda system did not lead to the establishment of trade unions. The workers under the encomienda system were denied any basic rights to organize and worked under brutal conditions. The conquistadors brutally killed or hunted down anyone who resisted their rule.

(3) The encomienda system did not lead to an increase in land ownership by Native Americans. The Spanish did not allow Native Americans to own their land. They forced them to work on plantations.

(4) The encomienda system did not weaken the power of *peninsulares*. The peninsulares were people born in Spain who filled the highest positions in both colonial governments and the Catholic Church.

19. **3** The heading that best completes the partial outline is the Rise of Absolutism. During the Age of Absolutism (1600s and 1700s), Europeans tried to centralize political power within their nations. *Absolutism* refers to a political system in which the monarch (king or queen) has supreme power and controls without limits over the lives of the people in his or her country. The divine right theory was used to justify unlimited power by indicating that the king or queen ruled by God's authority as his earthly representative. Obedience to the king or queen was obedience to God. The ruler was responsible only to God for his actions. Thomas Hobbes was a 17th-century English philosopher who defended royal absolutism. Hobbes expressed his views in a book titled *Leviathan* (1651). The horrors of the English Civil War convinced him that all humans are basically selfish and wicked. Hobbes believed that humans were miserable in the state of nature. To escape a bleak life, people give up their freedom to a strong ruler. In exchange for law and order, people enter into a social contract by which the ruler gains absolute power. Since people act in their own self-interests, Hobbes claimed that a ruler needs total power to keep citizens under control. The best government has to be like a leviathan (the all-powerful sea monster named in the Bible). In Hobbes's view, only an absolute monarchy would impose order and demand obedience. Louis XIV of France represented the height of absolutism. He ruled France from 1643 to 1715 and claimed to rule by the Divine Right of Kings. To illustrate this attitude, it is claimed that he said, *"L'état, c'est moi,"* which means "I am the State." Louis XIV is often referred to as the Sun King. He ruled without the Estates General, which is the French Parliament, and crushed all opposition to his government. During his 72-year reign, France became the center of culture and Louis built the Versailles

Palace, which became the perfect symbol of the Sun King's wealth and power.

WRONG CHOICES EXPLAINED:

(1), (2), and (4) None of these choices refers to basic ideas of this outline, which refers to the rise of political power in Europe during the 1600s. There is no reference to trading, democracy, or exploration.

20. **1** One way in which Montesquieu, Voltaire, and Rousseau are similar is that they were philosophers during the Age of Enlightenment. These French philosophers were the thinkers of this period who were committed to bringing new ideas and thoughts to all of Europe. These men were part of an intellectual movement called the Enlightenment. The writers of the Enlightenment believed that people possessed natural rights and that society could be improved. These writers also claimed that science and reason could explain the laws of human society. They challenged traditional authority and Church authority.

Montesquieu (1689–1755) wrote *The Spirit of the Law.* To prevent despotism, he urged that those powers of the government should be separated into three branches—executive, legislative, and judicial. Each branch would check the other instead of permitting power to be concentrated in one person, the king. Montesquieu's ideas of separation of power were adapted into the United States Constitution.

Voltaire (1694–1778) was educated by the Jesuits, but challenged the authority of the Catholic Church. Although he believed in God, Voltaire hated religious intolerance, urged religious freedom, and thought that religion crushed the religious spirit. In his book *Candide,* he wrote against the evils of organized religion. After living in Great Britain for a while, Voltaire wrote *Letters on the English.* Voltaire praised Britain's limited monarchy and civil liberties and denounced the French government's censorship, injustices, and despotism.

Rousseau (1712–1778) criticized the abuses of society and put forth his ideas in his book *The Social Contract.* Rousseau maintained that people in the state of nature were happy and possessed natural rights but were corrupted by the evils of society, such as the inequalities of distribution of property. People entered into a social contract to form a government, agreeing to surrender all their rights for the common good. Rousseau believed in the will of the majority, which he called the general will. If the government failed in its purpose, the people have the right to replace it.

The ideas of these Enlightenment writers had a great impact throughout Europe in the 1700s, especially France.

WRONG CHOICES EXPLAINED:

(2) and (3) None of these men were chief ministers during the French Revolution of 1789 nor leaders of the Italian unification movement in 1860. These men were not alive when these historical events occurred.

(4) These men were born in the 17th century, many years after the Counter-Reformation of the 16th century.

21. **4** Increased agricultural production in England in the late 1700s contributed directly to an increase in life expectancy. The Agricultural Revolution contributed to a rapid growth of population that continues today. Britain's population soared from 5 million in the 1700s to almost 9 million in the 1800s. The population of Europe as a whole grew from roughly 120 million to about 190 million during the same period. The population boom of the 1700s was caused by declining death rates rather than by rising birth rates. The Agricultural Revolution reduced the risk of famine. Because people ate better, women were healthier and had stronger babies. Increased food production, along with improved medical care, further slowed deaths from disease.

WRONG CHOICES EXPLAINED:

(1) The development of a worldwide communications network was connected to the growth of industrial technology, not to increased agricultural production.

(2) Manorialism was an economic system associated with the Middle Ages. By the 18th century, manorialism did not exist in Europe.

(3) The rise of democracy in the late 1700s contributed to a decrease in the power of the monarch.

22. **3** A statement about railroad systems in the 19th and early 20th centuries that is accurate is that railroads helped promote the factory system and urbanization. Entrepreneurs could now build factories in many more locations. Factories no longer needed to be close to supplies of raw materials, and the railroads did not have to follow the course of a river. This meant that tracks could go places where rivers did not run, allowing factory owners and merchants to ship goods over land. By offering quick and reasonable transportation, the railroads encouraged country people to take city jobs. The growth of the factory system, in which goods were manufactured in a central location, brought waves of job seekers to cities and towns. Between 1800 and 1850, the number of European cities boasting more than 100,000 inhabitants rose from 22 to 47. Most of Europe's urban area doubled in population. The railroads helped the growth of the factory system and brought about rapid urbanization, or the movement of people to the cities. Some cities, such as Manchester, England, grew from a market town of 45,000 in 1760 to about 300,000 in 1850.

WRONG CHOICES EXPLAINED:

(1) Imperialism did not reject the use of railroads in their colonies. European imperialistic countries in Asia and Africa used the railroads to ship their goods to markets, providing greater contact throughout their colonies. For example, India became economically valuable after the British estab-

lished a railroad network. Railroads transported raw products from the interior to the ports and then sent back manufactured goods.

(2) European governments did not oppose the development of the railroads. The British government supported economic growth and promoted the Liverpool–Manchester railroad that connected the port of Liverpool with the city of Manchester. Other European countries, such as Germany and France, promoted railroad building to spur industrial growth.

(4) Railroads made the transportation of goods more, not less, efficient. The importance of ensuring that goods were transported to factories and to markets required railroads to develop schedules for the arrival and shipping of goods to a specific destination. Different time zones were instituted throughout many countries to make the shipping of goods more efficient.

23. **4** The Industrial Revolution is the historical event that Marx and Engels believe created the situation described in this passage. The Industrial Revolution began in the English textile industry in the 18th century, and resulted in the shift from manufacturing goods by hand to the use of machinery. It also brought economic, political, and social changes. The Industrial Revolution was marked by the rise of the factory system and the production of goods, resulting in the increased wealth of a nation. However, to remain prosperous, nations needed a readily available supply of raw materials, and had to look for new markets for the products that their industries turned out. In addition, businesspeople sought places where they could invest their profits and make even more money. All of these factors led to the search for areas where Europeans could guarantee a reserved area for their manufactured goods. With the Industrial Revolution, people began working in factories. Men, women, and children worked 12 to 16 hours a day in unsafe conditions. Marx and Engels asserted that industrialization benefited the wealthy and exploited the poor. They also believed that industrialization created prosperity for a few and poverty for many. In 1848, Marx and Engels wrote *The Communist Manifesto.* Marx argued that economics was the driving force in history. The class that possessed economic power, whether through ownership of land, banks, or factories, controlled the government and social institutions. In an industrialized society based on private ownership, the capitalists ruled. Marx argued that the entire course of history was a class struggle between the "haves" and the "have-nots." In ancient Rome, plebeians battled patricians; in feudal society, serfs opposed lords; in industrialized Europe, the proletariat (have-nots) clashed with the capitalists (haves). Marx believed that the class struggle was international, because workers in each nation faced the same problems and the same capitalist oppressors. Marx predicted that the proletariat eventually would rise up and overthrow the capitalists and create their own society. The proletariats would take control of the means of production and establish a classless community society in which wealth and power would be equally shared. The motto of the communist society would be organized "from each according to his abilities; to each according to his needs."

WRONG CHOICES EXPLAINED:

(1) The Cold War refers to the period of tension and hostility between the United States and Russia because of their different political and economic systems. The Cold War began in 1945 and ended in 1991.

(2) World War I describes the military struggle among the Allied powers of England, France, the United States, and Italy against the Central powers of Germany and Austro-Hungary. World War I began in 1914 and ended in 1918.

(3) The Russian Revolution led to the establishment of the first Communist government in Europe in 1918 and the overthrow of Czar Nicholas II.

24. **1** Mass starvation was the main reason for the extensive Irish emigration to North America in the 1840s. In the 1840s, Ireland experienced one of the worst famines of modern history. The potato, introduced from the Americas, was the main source of food for most of the Irish. In 1845, a blight, or disease, destroyed the potato crop. The British, who ruled Ireland, continued to require the Irish to ship these crops outside Ireland. The result was the "Great Famine." Out of a population of 8 million, about 1 million people died from starvation and disease over the next few years. More than 1 million people emigrated to the United States and Canada.

WRONG CHOICES EXPLAINED:

(2) and (3) Neither of these choices was the main reason for Irish emigration. Britain controlled Ireland in the 19th century and there was no military draft for the Irish, nor did a civil war break out in the country.

(4) Diseases, such as smallpox, did kill millions of people but did not result in extensive Irish migration. It was the lack of food that contributed to Irish migration.

25. **2** A principal reason for the success of European colonialism in Asia in the late 1800s was that Europe was able to dominate military and commercial relations with Asia. Superior technology helped to foster imperialism. The combination of the steamboat and the telegraph enabled European powers to increase their mobility and to quickly respond to any situations that threatened their dominance. The rapid-fire machine gun also gave them a military advantage and was helpful in persuading Asians to accept Western control. After the British crushed the Sepoy Mutiny in 1859, they sent in more troops and put India directly under their control. The British saw India as a source of raw materials and as a market for their factory-made goods across the subcontinent. After the Suez Canal opened in 1869, British trade with India soared, but it remained an unequaled partnership favoring the British. The British flooded India with inexpensive machine-made textiles, ruining India's once prosperous weaving industry. In 1839, Chinese warships clashed with British merchants over the importation of opium. This triggered the Opium War, where gunships equipped with the latest in firepower bombarded Chinese

coastal and river ports. With outdated weapons and fighting methods, the Chinese were easily defeated. In 1842, Britain made China accept the Treaty of Nanking. China had to open up five ports to foreign trade and the British gained control of Hong Kong, which they controlled until the end of the 20th century. The treaty was the first of a series of treaties that forced China to make trading concessions to Western powers. The military might of the West forced China to accept these unequal economic treaties.

WRONG CHOICES EXPLAINED:

(1) Asian countries like China did not respect Europeans as representatives of an advanced civilization. The Chinese considered Westerners barbarians and wanted to restrict trade with the West. However, the Chinese were too weak to prevent the West from gaining more trading rights.

(3) Europeans did not respect Asian laws and customs. Europeans were convinced that they had superior cultures and forced people to accept modern or Western ways. Thomas Macaulay, a British historian, claimed that the whole native literature of India was not worth one shelf of books in any European library.

(4) Many Asian nations did not adopt European religious practices. Despite efforts by European missionaries to spread Christianity, Buddhism, Hinduism, and Confucianism are still the dominant religions in Asia.

26. **1** The action in Japanese history that occurred during the Meiji Restoration is that Japan modernized its economy. The Japanese focused on modernizing Japan's economy to compete with Western nations. In the Meiji Period from 1862 to 1912, Japan reversed its policy of isolation, ended feudalism, and began to modernize by borrowing from Western powers. The goal of the Meiji leader, or enlightened ruler, was to make Japan a strong military and industrial power. The Meiji emperor realized that the nation had to modernize to avoid becoming a victim of imperialism. Japanese leaders sent students abroad to Western countries to learn about their forms of government, economies, technology, and customs. The government also brought foreign experts to Japan to improve industry. The Japanese adopted a constitution based on the model of Prussia with the emperor as the head. The new government was not intended to bring democracy, but to unite Japan and make it equal to Western powers. The Meiji government established a banking system and modern shipyards, as well as factories for producing cement, glass, and textiles. The leaders also built up a modern army based on a draft and constructed a fleet of steam-powered iron ships. By imitating the West, Japan remained independent, but also became an imperial power.

WRONG CHOICES EXPLAINED:

(2) The Mongols invaded the island of Japan in 1274, close to 400 years before the Meiji Restoration.

(3) The Japanese government rejected an isolationist policy during the Meiji Restoration. The government wanted to open up relations with the

West to help them improve their economy. The Japanese introduced Western business methods.

(4) Buddhism is not the official religion of Japan but is one of their dominant belief systems. Buddhism was introduced into Japan during the 6th century.

27. **3** The annexation of Korea and Japan's invasion of Manchuria were attempts by Japan to acquire natural resources. As a small island nation, Japan lacked many basic resources necessary to ensure its growth as an industrial nation. Japan's late-19th-century industrialization created the need for raw materials, especially cotton, iron ore, coal, and oil. It wanted to gain markets for its manufactured goods. Japanese nationalists also wanted to replace European imperialism with Asian imperialism. In 1895, Japan defeated China in a war and forced the Chinese to give up their claims to Korea. They also gained Taiwan and won special trading privileges. In 1910, Japan annexed Korea and forced its people to build railroads and roads for Japan's benefit. The Japanese took half of Korea's yearly rice crop to support Japanese expansion. In the 1920s and 1930s, the Japanese leaders developed the East Asia Co-Prosperity Sphere. Its aim was to conquer East Asia by taking China, which was rich in coal, iron, and fertile soil. The Japanese argued that they had won Manchuria in the same way the Western nations had gained their colonies. By 1932, they had gained control of the area, begun to build hydroelectric plants, and created a sizable iron and steel industry, thereby increasing Japan's economy and military power.

WRONG CHOICES EXPLAINED:

(1) Japan was not attempting to spread Shinto beliefs when they annexed Korea or invaded Manchuria. The Japanese invaded these areas for economic, not religious, reasons. They never sought to impose any of their religious ideas on the countries they conquered.

(2) The Japanese did not protect human rights when they invaded Korea or Manchuria. In Korea, the Japanese imposed a harsh rule on the colony and set out to destroy the Korean language and identity. When the Japanese invaded the city of Nanking in China in 1937, their methods were so brutal that the invasion has become known as the "Rape of Nanking."

(4) The Japanese did not establish theocratic governments in these areas. A theocracy is a nation ruled by religious leaders. These areas were controlled by puppet governments that were ruled by the Japanese military.

28. **4** A conclusion best supported by this telegram is that Nicholas II hoped diplomacy would prevent war. Nicholas II was the czar of Russia and Wilhelm II was the kaiser of Germany. On June 28, 1914, Archduke Francis Ferdinand and his wife were traveling through Sarajevo, the capital of Bosnia. Gavrilo Princip, a member of a radical Slavic nationalist group opposing Austrian rule, shot and killed the archduke and his wife, setting off a chain reaction that led to World War I. Archduke Ferdinand was the heir to

the throne of the Austro-Hungarian Empire. Austria blamed Serbia for the murder of the archduke and his wife. Austria decided to deal firmly with Serbia and made harsh demands. Serbia refused to comply with any of the demands, such as permitting Austria to investigate the assassination plot within Serbia. The Austro-Hungarian Empire declared war on Serbia on July 28. Russia, a Slavic nation and friend of Serbia, mobilized its forces in preparation for war. This telegram was sent on July 29, the day after Austro-Hungary had declared war on Serbia. Nicholas II was not completely aware that the German kaiser had given a blank check of support to Austro-Hungary in dealing with Serbia. Austro-Hungary and Germany were members of the Triple Alliance by which they promised to support each other during a military conflict. Unfortunately, Nicholas II hoped that diplomacy would avert war. Germany declared war on Russia on August 1, after Russia refused Germany's request to mobilize. On August 3, Germany declared war on France. On August 4, Great Britain joined France and declared war on Germany. On August 6, Austria declared war on Russia. Nicholas II's pleas to avoid a major European conflict failed.

WRONG CHOICES EXPLAINED:

(1), (2), and (3) None of these conclusions is supported by the telegram. There is no mention of Russian mobilization, Nicholas does not condemn the efforts of Wilhelm II, nor does he support the use of extreme measures. The telegram focuses on Nicholas II's reluctance to get involved in going to war.

29. **3** World War I is most closely associated with the telegram Nicholas II sent to Wilhelm II. World War I lasted from 1914 to 1918. Nicholas II was the last czar of Russia, who ruled from 1894 until he was forced to abdicate in March 1917. He proved unable to manage the country and command the Russian army during World War I. His government ended with the first Russian Revolution of 1917. The Communists, who had taken over the government in November 1917, executed Nicholas II and his family on July 17, 1918. Wilhelm II was the emperor of the German Empire. He ruled the German Empire from 1888 to the end of World War I in November 1918. He lived in exile from 1919 until his death on June 4, 1941.

WRONG CHOICES EXPLAINED:

(1), (2), and (4) None of these choices is correct. The Franco-Prussian War lasted from 1870 to 1887. The Russo-Japanese War was in 1905, and World War II began in 1939 and ended in 1945.

30. **3** This cartoonist is referring to the way Germany was affected in 1919 by the Treaty of Versailles. The Treaty of Versailles contained many harsh provisions. Many Germans blamed the Treaty of Versailles for the country's troubles. According to Article 231, the Germans had to accept full responsibility for the war by signing the war-guilt clause. As a result, Germany had to pay reparation payments of more than $32 million. Many

Germans believed that these reparations contributed to the nation's economic decline. To pay for the heavy reparations payments to the Allies, Germany had to print more money. As a result, the value of the German currency, the mark, fell rapidly. Severe inflation set in. The Germans needed more money to buy even basic goods. It was reported that in 1923, a loaf of bread cost 200 billion marks. People took wheelbarrows full of money to buy food. Eventually, the mark became worthless. Despite a brief recovery in the mid-1920s, the Great Depression destroyed any hope of recovery. In the 1930s, Adolf Hitler and the Nazi party gained support by claiming that Hitler would tear up the Versailles Treaty and denounce the war-guilt clause.

WRONG CHOICES EXPLAINED:

(1), (2), and (4) None of these events is depicted in the cartoon. The Congress of Vienna and Napoleon's defeat occurred in the 19th century. The Allied nations defeated Germany in 1945. This cartoon refers to conditions in Germany in 1919.

31. **3** This 1919 cartoon suggests that Germany may come under the influence of radicals. The radicals in this cartoon are the Bolshevists or Communists. In 1917, the Communists had come to power in Russia and there was fear among Germans that Communism would overrun their country. A core belief of Communism was that Communism was a worldwide movement that was destined to spread to all industrial countries. The poor economic conditions in Germany during the 1920s were made worse by the Great Depression. Nearly 6 million people, or about 30 percent of the workforce, was unemployed in 1932. Civil unrest broke out in the country. Many conservative Germans were fearful that the Communists, as in Russia, were strong enough to overthrow the weak Weimar government. Thus, many conservative leaders turned to Adolf Hitler and the Nazi party. They believed that he could stand up to the Communist party but that they could still control him. In January 1933, Hitler was appointed chancellor of Germany and called for a new election. Six days before the election, a fire destroyed the German Reichstag building where Parliament met. By stirring up the fear of Communism, Hitler and his allies won by a slim majority. Within a year, Hitler was master of Germany. He destroyed the Communists and the fear that the people had about their gaining power in Germany. In the process, he established dictatorial control over the entire country.

WRONG CHOICES EXPLAINED:

(1), (2), and (4) There is no reference to moderates, conservatives, or isolationists. Moderates and conservatives want limited change. Isolationists are those groups that seek to limit or avoid involvement in the affairs or conflicts of other nations.

32. **4** Mohandas Gandhi's protests in India were a response to Great Britain's policy of colonialism. Colonialism is a policy of dominating or

extending control over another country. In the 1920s and 1930s, Mohandas Gandhi became the leader of the Indian nationalist movement that wanted independence from Great Britain. Gandhi was a pacifist who believed in the principle of *satyagraha*, which in English is called *passive resistance* or *civil disobedience*. Gandhi believed that one perfect civil resister was enough to win the battle of right and wrong. Gandhi launched his campaign of nonviolent civil disobedience to weaken the British government and its economic power in India. One effective method of protest was the boycott in which Indians refused to buy British cloth and other manufactured goods. Gandhi urged Indians to begin spinning their own cloth and used the spinning wheel as a symbol of his rejection of Western civilization. He also called on the people to refuse to attend government schools, pay taxes, and vote in elections. Gandhi used these nonviolent methods to show the British the futility of denying India its freedom. India would not achieve its independence until 1947, one year before Gandhi's assassination on January 30, 1948.

WRONG CHOICES EXPLAINED:

(1) Gandhi's protests were not designed to support Zionism. Zionism was a worldwide organization to build or gain support for a Jewish homeland in Palestine.

(2) Gandhi would not have protested if Great Britain had followed a humanitarian policy toward India. This would have guaranteed Indians the freedom that Gandhi wanted for his country.

(3) Gandhi's protests were to promote freedom for India, not socialism. Socialism deals with economics, not political freedom.

33. **2** The number of collective farms increased the most between 1930 and 1931. In 1930 there were 85.9 thousand collective farms, and by 1931 there were 211.1 thousand farms. By 1931 there were an additional 125.2 thousand collective farms in Russia, the highest increase of any year.

WRONG CHOICES EXPLAINED:

(1) Between 1929 and 1930 the number of collective farms increased by only 28.9 thousand farms.

(3) Between 1934 and 1935 the increase was only 12.1 thousand farms.

(4) Between 1939 and 1940 the number of collective farms decreased rather than increasing.

34. **2** A Soviet policy that is most closely associated with the information in this table is Stalin's five-year plans. In 1928, Stalin launched the first of a series of five-year plans to build industry and increase farm output. Under Joseph Stalin, peasants in the Soviet Union were forced to join collective farms. In 1928, there were more than 25 million small farms in Russia. In that year, Stalin announced that these privately owned farms would be abolished and would be replaced by collective farms. Collectives were large farms owned and operated by peasants as a group. Peasants would be allowed to

keep their houses and personal belongings, but all farm animals and tools were to be turned over to the collectives. The state set all prices and controlled access to farm supplies. The government planned to provide all the necessary equipment (tractors and fertilizers) and teach farmers modern methods to increase the output of grain. Surplus grain would be sold abroad to earn money to invest in industrial growth. The peasants resisted Stalin's policy of collectivization. Many of them destroyed their crops and livestock in protest. Stalin showed no mercy and ordered that the peasants be shot on sight. Between 5 and 10 million peasants died. By 1935, 95 percent of Russian farms had become collectives.

WRONG CHOICES EXPLAINED:

(1) Lenin's New Economic Policy was introduced in 1921 in the Soviet Union. The policy provided for some restoration of private property to ease the economic crisis created by the civil war in Russia during 1918 to 1921.

(3) Brezhnev's policy of détente refers to the relaxation of tension between the United States and Russia during the 1970s.

(4) Gorbachev's policy of glasnost were the efforts he made to introduce political reforms in the Soviet Union during the 1980s.

35. **1** One similarity between Adolf Hitler and Benito Mussolini is that both led fascist states. A fascist or totalitarian state is one in which the government controls every aspect of a citizen's life through a one-party dictatorship. Adolf Hitler, the leader of the Nationalist Socialist Party, or Nazis, who controlled Germany from 1933 to 1945, built a one-party government that became known as the Third Reich. He had unlimited power. He used his secret police, the Gestapo, to suppress all opposition and had little regard for the civil rights of the people. Schoolchildren were taught Nazi ideas and had to join the Hitler Youth organization to learn to be good Nazis. Newspapers, radio, and films praised the virtues of Nazism. The Third Reich became one of the most brutal dictatorships in the world, and was responsible for the deaths of millions of people throughout Europe.

Benito Mussolini was the leader of the Fascist Party that ruled Italy from 1922 to 1943. As head of the fascist state, Mussolini (Il Duce) made Italy into a dictatorship. Mussolini allowed the existence of one political party, the Fascist Party, and limited legislative elections to yes/no votes on a single list of fascist-chosen candidates. The Black Shirts (Mussolini's secret police) crushed all opposition. Unions were abolished, strikes were outlawed, and the press was censored. Mussolini exhorted the people to "believe, fight, and obey."

WRONG CHOICES EXPLAINED:

(2) Both of these leaders were opposed to Communism. Hitler and Mussolini came to power because many people believed that they were the only groups that could control the Communists.

(3) Hitler and Mussolini did not reject militarism. They promoted a strong military to restore the country's pride and greatness.

(4) Neither of these men remained in power after World War II. Mussolini was shot by Italian partisans in 1945 and Hitler committed suicide in 1945.

36. **2** This cartoon suggests about news coverage of world events that Africa's issues are often overshadowed by events in other regions. The cartoon shows that the nightly news focuses and shines its light on events that are happening in the Middle East, especially Saudi Arabia, Iraq, and Israel. The news also highlights the issues in Afghanistan, as well as Pakistan and Russia. Unfortunately, the news, as the cartoon indicates, spends little time on the AIDS epidemic, famine, and overpopulation, which are shown in the background. The cartoon shows that these problems are not given much attention because there is no light shining on the continent of Africa, whereas the light burns brightly on the Middle East and areas close to it.

WRONG CHOICES EXPLAINED:

(1), (3), and (4) The cartoon supports none of these choices. There is no reference to social concerns, European affairs, and whether Africa's problems can be solved if global powers cooperate.

37. **3** The end of Communism in the Soviet Union has caused many countries in Eastern Europe to pursue free-market economic policies. A free-market system is one in which the individual businesses have the freedom to operate for profits with little or no government interference. After the fall of Communism in 1991, countries in Eastern Europe adopted a policy of economic liberalization. The state withdrew from economic control, and various small and large industrial firms were assigned the task of forming new enterprises by strengthening the private sector. Poland is now one of the premier economies among the nations that make up Eastern Europe. Because of its economic growth through private enterprise, Europe invited Poland to be a member of the European Union in 2004. It is estimated that Poland has one of the strongest economies among the various East European countries. Hungary, like Poland, made a transition from a state-run economy to a market economy. Through privatization and tax reduction of Hungarian businesses, the country experienced economic growth. By the beginning of the 21st century, 90 percent of the businesses in Hungary had been privatized. The other countries in Eastern Europe have primarily adopted the market economy since the fall of Communism.

WRONG CHOICES EXPLAINED:

(1) Eastern European countries have rejected a command economy, in which government dictates what is to be produced. They have accepted the free enterprise system.

(2) No countries in Eastern Europe have maintained a Communist form of government.

(4) The Warsaw Pact ended in 1991 with the collapse of Communism.

38. **1** Mao Zedong, Fidel Castro, and Ho Chi Minh all engaged in guerrilla warfare as leaders of revolutionary movements in their respective nations. Mao Zedong (1893–1976), the son of a well-to-do peasant from the Hunan province, founded the Communist Party in 1921. During the late 1920s and 1930s, Mao emerged as leader of the Chinese Communists. Mao believed that the Communists would succeed in China only by winning the support of the peasants. He insisted that the Communist forces treat the peasants fairly. Unlike the other Chinese armies, the Communists paid the peasants for the food their forces required. With the support of the peasants, Mao's army grew in numbers. The civil war between the nationalists and Communists was halted during World War II as the forces joined to fight the Japanese. After World War II ended, the civil war resumed. In 1949, Mao's Communists were victorious and he established the People's Republic of China.

Fidel Castro, who was born in 1927, was the son of a wealthy Spanish Cuban farmer. He became involved in politics while studying law at the University of Havana. He strongly criticized the government of dictator Fulgencio Batista. On July 26, 1953, Fidel Castro launched an attack on army barracks in Moncada. The attack failed and most involved were killed or captured. Castro was captured and sentenced to 15 years in jail, but was pardoned after just two years. He then went into exile in Mexico, where he trained and assembled the 26th of July Movement. With the support of Che Guevara, Castro invaded Cuba in 1956. Returning to Cuba, the revolutionaries hid in the Sierra Maestra mountains, gaining support among the peasants. In 1959, Castro overthrew the dictatorship of Batista and seized power in Cuba.

Ho Chi Minh (1890–1969) was a nationalist and Communist leader who sought independence for Vietnam. He fought against French colonialism in Vietnam. Ho Chi Minh (which means "He Who Enlightens") turned to the Communists for help in his struggle. During the 1930s, Ho's Indo-Chinese Communist Party led revolts and strikes against the French, who jailed Vietnamese protesters and sentenced Ho, the party leader, to death. Ho fled his death sentence and continued to lead the nationalist movement from exile. He returned to Vietnam in 1941, a year after the Japanese seized control of the country. He and other nationalists founded the Vietminh (Independence League). The Japanese left in 1945, but the French wanted to regain their former colony. However, in 1945, Ho announced Vietnam's independence from the French. He joined with Vietnamese nationalists and Communists to fight the French. After the French were defeated in 1954, he continued his struggle against the United States, which wanted to prevent the Communists from taking over South Vietnam. In 1975, the Communist forces took over Saigon, the capital of South Vietnam, and renamed it Ho Chi Minh City. Vietnam was finally united.

WRONG CHOICES EXPLAINED:

(2) Trench warfare is a form of warfare used in World War I, in which opposing armies fight each other from trenches dug in the battlefield.

(3) Unrestricted submarine warfare was used by Germany to attack ships without warning, including neutral ships, and unarmed passenger lines found in enemy waters.

(4) Biological warfare is the use of bacteria, viruses, or other diseases, causing organisms or toxins found in nature to kill people.

39. **3** One way in which these speakers are similar is that all are expressing their opinions about urban issues. The industrialization of India has contributed to the growth of large cities or urban areas. New Delhi, the capital of India, has more than 15 million people. Medical facilities and public transportation, however, are readily available in New Delhi. A typical family in New Delhi now lives within walking distance of more than 70 private health care providers. In addition, the Delhi Transport Corporation is a major bus service that provides for the city and operates the world's largest fleet of environmentally friendly buses. The Delhi Metro, a mass rapid-transit system, also serves many parts of the city. One of the reasons why New Delhi has grown so rapidly is that the city offers many employment opportunities. New Delhi is the second-largest commercial center in South Asia after Mumbai (Bombay). New Delhi has attracted many multinational corporations, including those in the technology, telecommunications, and media sectors. All of these industries have improved employment opportunities. Although New Delhi is an important commercial center, crime and homelessness have created concerns for civic leaders. In 2005, New Delhi accounted for the highest percentage of crimes reported in 35 cities in India with a population of 1 million or more. The city also has the highest rate of crime in the country against women and children. The increased homelessness, like the crime rate, is a problem for New Delhi. It is estimated that there were about 1.5 million homeless people in 2007, and that number is rising because the city has not provided for low-cost housing and permanent shelter. As New Delhi continues to grow, it must address the ongoing problems of homelessness and rising crime.

WRONG CHOICES EXPLAINED:

(1), (2), and (4) None of these speakers is addressing rural poverty, interdependence, or nationalism. These statements focus on the problem of the city or urban areas of New Delhi.

40. **3** The economic trend represented in this chart is most likely an effect of the creation of the North American Free Trade Agreement (NAFTA). The principal aim of NAFTA, which was signed in 1993, was to increase economic cooperation among the United States, Mexico, and Canada. The agreement was designed to eliminate tariffs and other trade barriers among these member nations within 15 years. The treaty created one huge regional market of more than 380 million people. The chart indicates that exports and imports to and from Mexico and Canada increased between 1994 and 2002. United States' exports increased by close to \$47 million to Mexico and by about \$55 million to Canada. Imports also increased during

these years by close to $93 million from Mexico and by about $91 million from Canada. These statistics show that NAFTA has increased economic activities among these three nations.

WRONG CHOICES EXPLAINED:

(1) The Organization of American States (OAS) is a regional organization set up in 1948 to promote common defense of the Western Hemisphere.

(2) The North Atlantic Treaty Organization (NATO) is a defensive alliance formed in 1949 as a way to contain Communism.

(4) The Organization of Petroleum Exporting Countries (OPEC) was founded in 1960 to control the production and price of oil.

41. **2** A statement about the Balkan Peninsula since 1995 that is most accurate is that ethnic tensions and conflict continue to be a problem in much of the region. The breakup of Yugoslavia in 1991 and 1992 sparked ethnic violence. In Bosnia, fighting erupted between Serbs and Muslims. Serbs began a campaign of ethnic cleansing that was designed to drive Muslims out of the parts of Bosnia that Serbia claimed. Many Bosnians became refugees and were either brutalized or killed. In 1995, representatives from all warring sides met in the United States and agreed to a peace settlement. NATO troops were sent into Bosnia to enforce the peace. In 1997, violence broke out between Serbians and Albanians living in the Kosovo region of Serbia. Albanians resented Serbian control and wanted to unite with Albania. Serbians began a systematic mass murder of the Albanians living in Kosovo. In March 1999, NATO forces began air attacks on the Yugoslavian troops in Kosovo and on other Serbian cities. After 72 days, President Slobodan Milosevic of Serbia was forced to pull his troops out of Kosovo. Although NATO agreed that Kosovo would remain part of Serbia, U.N. administrators and 35,000 NATO-led peacekeeping troops (which included some 5,000 U.S. troops) entered Kosovo to maintain peace. In March 2004, serious unrest in Kosovo led to 19 deaths and the destruction of 35 Serbian Orthodox churches and monasteries. International negotiations began in 2006 to determine the final status of Kosovo. Eventually on February 17, 2008, Kosovo declared its independence. The Kosovo declaration of independence polarized the country between Kosovo Serbs and the Kosovo Albanians. Effective control of Kosovo has been organized along these lines.

WRONG CHOICES EXPLAINED:

(1) Bosnia-Herzegovina is not controlled by Yugoslavia. They became independent from Yugoslavia in 1991.

(3) Slobodan Milosevic of Serbia was not the first democratically elected leader of the region. He was a dictator who was tried for war crimes against humanity in 2002 but died of a heart attack in March 2006 before the Hague Tribunal could render a verdict.

(4) The Balkan Peninsula is one of the poorer regions in Europe. Many of the people have been forced to migrate to more prosperous countries in Western Europe.

42. **1** The Commercial Revolution led to the concept of banking, the creation of guilds, and the development of capitalism in Europe. The Commercial Revolution also refers to the economic changes that opened up Europe to a global economy based on worldwide trade during the 16th and 17th centuries. During the Commercial Revolution, Western Europe changed from the relatively static localized economy typical of the later Middle Ages to the beginning of a dynamic worldwide profit-oriented system called *capitalism*. Entrepreneurs engaged in business enterprises, taking risks and facing competition in the hope of making a profit. Banks arose in Western Europe to meet the needs of business enterprises for funds. The growth of banks was aided by the increased supply of currency resulting from the importation of New World gold and silver. As merchants gained more profits and reinvested more money in other enterprises, businesses and banks spread across Europe and permanently changed the economic life of the continent. Even the Catholic Church, which had prohibited usury—the lending of money for interest—had to relax its rule. The Church realized that capital played a vital and productive role in the developing business enterprises. These new methods of doing business were part of the Commercial Revolution that transformed the economy.

WRONG CHOICES EXPLAINED:

(2) The Agricultural Revolution refers to changes in farming methods in England during the 1600s that dramatically increased farm production.

(3) The Scientific Revolution was a major change in European thought that began in the 16th and 17th centuries. Scientists began to challenge traditional authority and use reason and observation to reach conclusions.

(4) The Industrial Revolution was a historical event that began in the textile industry in England in the 18th century. The Industrial Revolution refers to the changes resulting from the production of goods by hand to the use of machinery.

43. **3** The introduction of Buddhism into Japan and of Christianity into Africa are examples of cultural diffusion. Cultural diffusion is the spreading of ideas and customs from one people to another. Buddhism is a religion that was founded in India in the 6th century B.C. It later spread to China during the 1st century A.D. and eventually spread to Japan by 1200 A.D. By the time Buddhism reached Japan, it was divided into many sects. The samurai followed Zen Buddhism. They believed that Buddhism offered a way to develop the mental and physical control that their way of life demanded.

Christianity was a belief system that began in Palestine with the teaching of a Jewish man, Jesus, about 30 A.D. Christianity grew and spread to become the official religion of the Roman Empire by 392 A.D. Under Roman rule, Christianity spread to the cities of North Africa. Saint Augustine, one of the most influential Christian thinkers of the late Roman Empire, was born in present-day Algiers. In the 19th century, European missionaries also helped spread Christianity throughout the African continent. Christianity is currently one of Africa's most widespread religions with a following of some 51 percent of the population. In 1900, there were only 9 million Christians in Africa, but by the year 2000 there were an estimated 380 million Christians.

WRONG CHOICES EXPLAINED:

(1) *Modernization* is a change in a nation from a traditional economy or way of life to the use of new technological ideas and methods.

(2) *Ethnic conflict* is when one group of people fights another group because of cultural or historical differences.

(4) *Isolation* is following a policy of avoiding involvement with other nations.

44. **2** A goal of both the Boxer Rebellion in China and the Mau Mau movement in Kenya was to end foreign control. In 1899, groups of Chinese formed secret groups called the Society of Righteous and Harmonious Fists. Westerners called them the Boxers because they practiced a form of Chinese boxing. The goal of the Boxers was to drive out the foreigners who were destroying their land with new technology like telegraphs and machinery. The Boxers gained strength from their beliefs in Chinese rituals and traditions. One group, made up of women called the Red Lanterns, thought that their red handkerchiefs and red lanterns could be used to stop foreign bullets. In June 1900, the Boxers launched a series of attacks across China, resulting in the death of several hundred foreigners and thousands of Chinese Christians. They besieged the foreign embassies in Beijing, the capital of China. An international police force of 25,000 troops from the Imperialist powers, including the United States, crushed the rebellion within two weeks.

Jomo Kenyatta was the nationalist leader of Kenya. After World War II, Kenyatta, who had been educated and living in England, became a spokesman for Kenya's independence. In 1947, Kenyatta was chosen as the leader of the Kenyan African Union, a political movement for independence. Other Africans formed a group that the Europeans called the Mau Maus. This secret group was made up of Kikuyu farmers who were forced out of the highlands by the British, who had passed laws to ensure their domination. The goal of the Mau Maus was to force the British off the land. They began to carry out attacks against European settlers, such as burning farms and destroying livestock. Kenyatta, who was Kikuyu, had no connection to the Mau Maus but refused to condemn these actions. The British took military action against the movement and jailed Kenyatta, whom they accused of leading the movement. More than 10,000 black Kenyans and 100 white Kenyans were killed during the struggle for independence. In 1963, Britain granted Kenya its independence. Kenyatta was elected the first prime minister, and he held office until his death in 1978. He worked hard to unite all the different ethnic and language groups in the country.

WRONG CHOICES EXPLAINED:

(1) Laissez-faire capitalism is an economic policy saying that there should be a "hands-off" stance or limited government involvement with private business.

(3) and (4) Neither of these choices is correct. The goal of these movements was to establish independence for their countries. The Boxers and the Mau Maus were not interested in developing modern industries or a totalitarian state.

45. **3** The Protestant Reformation is the period in European history most closely associated with this statement. The Protestant Reformation refers to the period beginning in 1517, when the Europeans broke from the Roman Catholic Church and formed a new Christian church. On October 31, 1517, Martin Luther, a German monk, posted his *95 Theses* on a church door in Wittenberg, a university town. In these statements, he challenged the sale of indulgences and other papal practices. Luther's attack struck a chord throughout Germany. His actions led to the Protestant Reformation because its supporters protested against the Catholic Church. Martin Luther's demands for reform, which included a denial of papal authority and the belief that the Bible was the only guide for salvation, led to the establishment of many different Protestant churches throughout Europe. Powerful northern European and northern German rulers welcomed the revolt against Rome as a way of getting valuable Church property. Thus, many northern German rulers protected Luther from attack and punishment. The Protestant Reformation led to a series of religious wars in the 1520s between Catholics and Lutherans, which led to the Peace of Augsburg. This agreement, signed in 1555, allowed the rulers of a country to decide the religion of the people. Thus, most of northern Europe and northern Germany became Protestant and southern Europe remained Catholic. The Protestant Reformation ended the religious unity of Europe, which had existed for almost a thousand years.

WRONG CHOICES EXPLAINED:

(1), (2), and (4) None of these choices is reflected in this statement. There are no references to the Roman Empire, the Crusades, or the Enlightenment. The Roman Empire existed from 200 B.C. to 476 A.D. The Crusades occurred in the 11th to 13th centuries and the Enlightenment in Europe during the 17th and 18th centuries.

46. **4** This statement reflects a controversy over the proper means of salvation. The Roman Catholic Church taught that people could win salvation by faith and good works. In 1517, Martin Luther was offended by the deeds of a friar named Johann Tetzel. Tetzel was raising money to rebuild St. Peter's Cathedral in Rome by selling letters of indulgences. Indulgences were certificates issued by the Church that reduced or even canceled punishment for a person's sins. People purchased indulgences believing that the documents would ensure their admission to heaven. Tetzel also encouraged people to

buy indulgences for their dead relatives. Luther preached against the sale of indulgences, believing that people could gain salvation by faith alone. He claimed that faith in God was the only way to gain heaven and that the pope could not grant a pardon for sins. Luther also attacked the Church practices of simony, selling appointments to Church officers or appointing relatives to Church offices regardless of their ability. He also rejected five of the seven sacraments because the Bible did not mention them.

WRONG CHOICES EXPLAINED:

(1), (2), and (3) None of these choices can be supported by the passage. This passage criticizes the sale of indulgences and makes no reference to the role of women, forms of prayers, or types of education.

47. **2** Simon Bolivar, José de San Martin, and Toussaint l'Ouverture are best known as leaders of Latin American independence movements. Simon Bolivar, who was born to a wealthy Venezuelan Creole family in 1783, always envisioned an independent and united Latin America, free from Spanish domination. As a young man, he studied in Europe. His love of freedom was strengthened by the ideas of the French Revolution. Before returning from Europe, Bolivar promised that he would not rest until he broke the chain put upon the people of Latin America by the Spanish. He became known as the "Liberator" for his role in the wars for independence against Spain. In 1819, he helped free Venezuela, and by 1824 had secured the freedom of Colombia, Ecuador, Peru, and Bolivia.

Like Bolivar, José de San Martin was a Creole. He was born in Argentina, but went to Europe for military training. In 1816, he helped Argentina win freedom from Spain. He then joined the independence struggle in other areas. San Martin led an army across the Andes from Argentina to Chile. He defeated the Spanish in Chile before moving into Peru to strike further blows against colonial rule. Bolivar and San Martin tried to work together, but their views were too different. In 1822, San Martin stepped aside, letting Bolivar's forces win the final victories against Spain.

In 1791, Haitian slaves exploded in a revolt against French rule. Toussaint l'Ouverture, an ex-slave, emerged as the leader. It is said that he got the name l'Ouverture ("opening" in French) because he was so skilled at finding openings in the enemy lines. Although untrained, Toussaint was a brilliant and inspiring commander. The struggle was long, but by 1798, Toussaint and the rebels had achieved their goal. Enslaved Haitians had been freed. Although Haiti was still a French colony, Toussaint forces controlled most of the island. In January 1802, Napoleon sent 16,000 men to reconquer Haiti. In May, Toussaint agreed to halt the revolution if the French would end slavery. Despite the agreement, the French soon accused him of planning another uprising. They seized him and sent him to prison in the French Alps. In 1803, he died in a cold mountain prison. However, Haiti's struggle for independence continued, and in 1804, Haitian leaders declared independence. It was the first black colony to free itself from European control.

WRONG CHOICES EXPLAINED:

(1) These men were revolutionary leaders and not scientists who supported the heliocentric theory that the sun was the center of the universe.

(3) None of these men were Spanish explorers of the New World. These men lived during the 19th century. Spanish exploration occurred during the 16th century.

(4) These men were nationalist, not Communist, leaders. They promoted democracy.

48. **1** The main idea of this 2002 cartoon is that technology of the Cold War now threatens peace in Asia. Until the collapse of Communism in 1991, the world was fearful of a nuclear war between the United States and Russia. Since 1992, as the cartoon depicts, the torch of fear of nuclear conflict has passed to India and Pakistan. The proliferation of nuclear weapons has raised fear in the world community. In May 1998, India set off five nuclear tests, surprising the international community, which widely condemned India's pro-nuclear stance. Despite international urging for restraint, Pakistan responded by conducting several nuclear tests of its own. Both of these nations have refused to sign the Nuclear Non-Proliferation Treaty. The United States slapped sanctions on both countries. However, many people in India and Pakistan were jubilant because they believed that the possession of nuclear weapons makes them part of the elite nuclear club that is composed of the United States, England, France, Russia, and China. The international community is fearful that India and Pakistan will rely entirely on nuclear weapons to maintain their security. These sanctions were lifted after the terrorist attacks of September 11, 2001, when the United States sought allies against al-Qaeda. The United States has continually taken steps to mediate the peace between these countries and stabilize the military balance. However, in 2006, the United States and India signed a nuclear agreement, allowing these countries to share nuclear reactors. India, in return, has agreed to accept international safeguards or inspection of its nuclear facilities. This agreement still faces opposition from political parties in India as well as congressional leaders in the United States. Pakistan has also expressed fears about this agreement because it could accelerate the arms race. In a concession to Pakistan, the United States has promised to provide more than $230 million to help the country upgrade its F16 fighter jet, seen as crucial for maintaining military parity with India.

WRONG CHOICES EXPLAINED:

(2), (3), and (4) None of these ideas is contained in the cartoon.

49. **4** The correct sequence of these events is first, Pericles rules during the Golden Age of Athens (460 B.C. to 429 B.C.); second, Robespierre comes to power during the French Revolution (1793); third, Kemal Ataturk rises to power in Turkey (1923); fourth, Ayatollah Khomeini seizes power in Iran (1979).

WRONG CHOICES EXPLAINED:

(1) and (3) Pericles rules must be first in any chronological sequence of events.

(2) Ataturk's rise to power must come before Ayatollah Khomeini's seizing of power in Iran.

50. **2** The Communist Revolution in China differed from the 19th-century Marxist ideals because this revolution was primarily supported by the peasants. Karl Marx believed that Communism would inevitably come to a country that had undergone the Industrial Revolution. The working class, or the urban proletariat, was seen as the main source of the revolution. Mao Zedong, the founder of the Chinese Communist Party, believed that the peasantry would be the driving force behind the revolution. His model was the Chinese Communist Rural Protracted People's War of the 1920s and 1930s, which eventually enabled the Communists to come to power. Furthermore, unlike Marxism, which made large-scale industrial development its priority, Mao and the Communists made all-around rural development the priority. Mao thought the strategy made sense in a country in which most of the people were peasants. Mao also connected political ideology with military strategy. He claimed that political power grew out of the barrel of a gun and that the peasants could be mobilized to undertake a people's war of armed struggle involving guerrilla warfare.

WRONG CHOICES EXPLAINED:

(1) The warlords opposed the Chinese Communists. The Chinese warlords had forced the peasants to pay taxes and support their army. The Communists gained the peasants' support by promising to end these unfair practices.

(3) The factory owners also opposed the Communists. Although China was not an industrialized country, the limited number of factories did not cooperate with the Communists.

(4) The gentry, or landlords, did not support the Communists. The Communists had promised to redistribute land to the peasants.

THEMATIC ESSAY: GENERIC SCORING RUBRIC

Score of 5:

- Shows a thorough understanding of the theme or problem
- Addresses all aspects of the task
- Shows an ability to analyze, evaluate, compare and/or contrast issues and events
- Richly supports the theme or problem with relevant facts, examples, and details
- Is a well-developed essay, consistently demonstrating a logical and clear plan of organization
- Introduces the theme or problem by establishing a framework that is beyond a simple restatement of the task and concludes with a summation of the theme or problem

Score of 4:

- Shows a good understanding of the theme or problem
- Addresses all aspects of the task
- Shows an ability to analyze, evaluate, compare and/or contrast issues and events
- Includes relevant facts, examples, and details, but may not support all aspects of the theme or problem evenly
- Is a well-developed essay, demonstrating a logical and clear plan of organization
- Introduces the theme or problem by establishing a framework that is beyond a simple restatement of the task and concludes with a summation of the theme or problem

Score of 3:

- Shows a satisfactory understanding of the theme or problem
- Addresses most aspects of the task or addresses all aspects in a limited way
- Shows an ability to analyze or evaluate issues and events, but not in any depth
- Includes some facts, examples, and details
- Is a satisfactorily developed essay, demonstrating a general plan of organization
- Introduces the theme or problem by repeating the task and concludes by repeating the theme or problem

Score of 2:

- Shows limited understanding of the theme or problem
- Attempts to address the task
- Develops a faulty analysis or evaluation of issues and events
- Includes few facts, examples, and details, and may include information that contains inaccuracies
- Is a poorly organized essay, lacking focus
- Fails to introduce or summarize the theme or problem

Score of 1:

- Shows very limited understanding of the theme or problem
- Lacks an analysis of evaluation of the issues and events
- Includes little or no accurate or relevant facts, examples, or details
- Attempts to complete the task, but demonstrates a major weakness in organization
- Fails to introduce or summarize the theme or problem

Score of 0: Fails to address the task, is illegible, or is a blank paper

PART II: THEMATIC ESSAY QUESTION

Throughout history, societies have made changes to their land or surrounding environment that have been the key to their development. Environment and human activity are interconnected. People have altered their physical geography to help them meet their needs. Two important examples of these changes were the irrigation system developed in Mesopotamia and terrace farming in Japan.

In ancient Mesopotamia, which in ancient Greek means "land between the rivers" (the Tigris and Euphrates), the civilizations of Sumer and Babylon faced a number of environmental obstacles. The flooding of the rivers was unpredictable. Sometimes it came as early as April, sometimes as late as June. After the flooding stopped, the hot sun dried out the mud. Little or no rain fell, and the land became like a desert. The Sumerian farmers had no way to water their fields during the dry summer months to get crops to grow. Over a period of time, the Sumerians managed to build dikes to hold back the floodwaters and irrigation ditches to carry water to their fields. This irrigation system allowed the farmers to produce a plentiful crop.

Constructing the irrigation system required a number of people working together. Temple priests or royal officials were needed to plan the projects and supervise the digging. These projects also created a need for laws to settle disputes over how land and water would be distributed. These laws laid the foundation for organized government.

Sumerian city-states grew prosperous from the large amount of crops produced on the farms as a result of this new effective water system. These surpluses allowed Sumerians to increase long-distance trade, exchanging the extra food and other goods for items they lacked. The surplus of food contributed to the growth of different civilizations. By 2500 B.C., new cities and civilizations were springing up all over the Fertile Crescent (present-day Syria, northern Iraq, and Turkey). These civilizations included not only Sumerians and Babylonians, but Assyrians and Chaldeans. These developments had major consequences for the world. From Sumerians, the world received a written language, cuneiform, which was adopted by the Assyrians and the Babylonians. The Babylonians used their written language to write the Hammurabi Code, which was the first written code of laws. Other achievements included iron technology and *zuggurats* (pyramid-like temples). The use of irrigation systems, however, did have a negative effect on the environment. It reduced a river's flow and added salt to the land, making it slightly harder for plants to grow.

The Japanese are another society that made changes to their environment. More than four-fifths of Japan is mountainous terrain, which limits the amount of arable land to coastal planes and narrow river valleys. As a result, the Japanese developed methods of intensive farming using only available pieces of land. To create more planting land, they used terrace farming. This method of farming entailed growing crops on the side of hills or mountains by creating swamps and deltas to help make use of their limited farmland.

The farmers developed an irrigation system that flooded the rice paddies with water to ensure increased food production. Terrace farming allowed the Japanese, until recently, to produce all the food they needed to feed their population.

One of the effects of terrace farming is that it enabled the Japanese to industrialize. After Matthew Perry came to Japan in 1853, the Japanese realized that they had to open trade with the West and to industrialize. During the Meiji Restoration from 1862 to 1912, the Japanese began to selectively borrow from the West in order to build a strong industrial country.

As with the Industrial Revolution in England, urbanization followed the Meiji Restoration. Terrace farming, like the Agricultural Revolution in Europe, enabled Japan to feed its urban population. Unfortunately, a negative effect of industrialization was that it created the need for raw materials and the need to gain secure markets for its manufactured goods. These circumstances contributed to Japan's territorial growth between 1894 and 1905 and led to the rise of militarists in the 1930s who demanded renewed territorial expansion for their empire that led to World War II in 1941.

Throughout history, societies have changed their physical environments to better serve their needs. The development of the irrigation system in Mesopotamia and terrace farming in Japan are two examples of these situations. These changes have had a tremendous impact upon these societies and their surrounding areas with both positive and negative results.

PART III: DOCUMENT-BASED QUESTIONS

Part A: Short Answers

Document 1

1) According to Franklin and Moss, one reason enslaved Africans were imported to the "New World" by Europeans was because slaves were needed on the plantations and slave trade was profitable.

Note: This response receives full credit because it identifies a reason why Europeans imported slaves to the New World.

Document 2

2) According to Willie F. Page, one impact of the arrival of Africans on Brazil and on the Caribbean Islands was that island economies relied heavily on the labor of African captives.

Note: This response receives full credit because it cites one impact of the arrival of Africans on Brazil and on the Caribbean Islands.

Document 3

3) Based on his excerpt from *Africa: An Encyclopedia for Students,* two effects of the slave trade on Africa are as follows:

1) The social, political, and economic life of Africa was disrupted.

2) Slave trade encouraged strong states to raid weaker states for slaves.

Note: This response receives full credit because it states two specific effects of the slave trade on Africa.

Document 4a and 4b

4a and 4b) Based on these documents, two specific reasons large numbers of Jewish immigrants moved to the Palestinian/Israeli region between 1920 and 1970 are as follows:

1) Hitler's rise to power.

2) The Final Solution was implemented in 1941.

Note: This response receives full credit because it identifies two specific reasons why large numbers of Jewish immigrants moved to the Palestinian/Israeli region between 1920 and 1970.

Document 5

5a) Based on this account by Raja Shehadeh, one impact on the city of Jaffa when the Palestinians left was that it was deserted and only a few shops remained open in the marketplace.

Note: This response receives full credit because it cites one impact on the city of Jaffa after the Palestinians left.

5b) According to M. Z. Frank, one effect of the Jewish migration on Israel was that some of the immigrants helped themselves to abandoned Arab houses.

Note: This response receives full credit because it states one effect of the Jewish migration on Israel.

Document 6

6) According to Ruth Gay, one way Germany was hurt by the migration of German Jews was by the loss of Nobel Prize winners and thousands of other scientists, artists, academics, engineers, and professional men and women in every category.

Note: This response receives full credit because it states how Germany was hurt by the migration of German Jews.

Document 7

7) According to Jean Bothwell, one cause of the migration of Muslims and Hindus was that Muslims were afraid that they would have no power in the new India.

Note: This response receives full credit because it identifies one cause of the migration of Muslims and Hindus.

Document 8

8) Based on this article in the *Guardian,* two ways the region of South Asia was affected by the mass migration of people in 1947 are as follows:

1) Hindus and Sikhs moved from Pakistan into India.

2) There was much human misery and hardship.

Note: This response receives full credit because it gives two specific ways the region of South Asia was affected by the mass migration of people in 1947.

Document 9

9) According to Urvashi Butalia, one impact the migration of Muslims and Hindus had on South Asia was that the Harijans (untouchables) and Muslims lost their jobs.

Note: This response receives full credit because it cites specific information on the impact of the migration of Muslims and Hindus on South Asia.

DOCUMENT-BASED QUESTION: GENERIC SCORING RUBRIC

Score of 5:
- Thoroughly addresses all aspects of the *Task* by accurately analyzing and interpreting at least **four** documents
- Incorporates information from the documents in the body of the essay
- Incorporates relevant outside information
- Richly supports the theme or problem with relevant facts, examples, and details
- Is a well-developed essay, consistently demonstrating a logical and clear plan of organization
- Introduces the theme or problem by establishing a framework that is beyond a simple restatement of the *Task* or *Historical Context* and concludes with a summation of the theme or problem

Score of 4:
- Addresses all aspects of the *Task* by accurately analyzing and interpreting at least **four** documents
- Incorporates information from the documents in the body of the essay
- Incorporates relevant outside information
- Includes relevant facts, examples, and details, but discussion may be more descriptive than analytical
- Is a well-developed essay, demonstrating a logical and clear plan of organization
- Introduces the theme or problem by establishing a framework that is beyond a simple restatement of the *Task* or *Historical Context* and concludes with a summation of the theme or problem

Score of 3:
- Addresses most aspects of the *Task* or addresses all aspects of the *Task* in a limited way, using some of the documents
- Incorporates some information from the documents in the body of the essay
- Incorporates limited or no relevant outside information
- Includes some facts, examples, and details, but discussion is more descriptive than analytical
- Is a satisfactorily developed essay, demonstrating a general plan of organization
- Introduces the theme or problem by repeating the *Task* or *Historical Context* and concludes by simply repeating the theme or problem

Score of 2:
- Attempts to address some aspects of the *Task*, making limited use of the documents
- Presents no relevant outside information
- Includes few facts, examples, and details; discussion restates contents of the documents

- Is a poorly organized essay, lacking focus
- Fails to introduce or summarize the theme or problem

Score of 1:
- Shows limited understanding of the *Task* with vague, unclear references to the documents
- Presents no relevant outside information
- Includes little or no accurate or relevant facts, details, or examples
- Attempts to complete the *Task*, but demonstrates a major weakness in organization
- Fails to introduce or summarize the theme or problem

Score of 0: Fails to address the *Task*, is illegible, or is a blank paper

Part B: Essay

The migration or movement of people from one area to another has had a great impact on history. Migrations have caused social, political, and economic upheaval. The involuntary migration of Africans across the Atlantic Ocean to the Americas and the voluntary migration of Hindus/Muslims between India and Pakistan in 1947 have had a lasting influence on the surrounding regions and countries.

During the 1500s, Spain ruled an empire that extended from Mexico to Peru. To make the empire profitable, Spain closely controlled its economic activities. A major source of wealth for the king was the mining of gold and silver and agricultural production. Sugarcane was introduced into the West Indies and elsewhere and quickly became a profitable resource. Sugarcane had to be grown on plantations, large estates run by an owner or the owner's overseer. Most plantations in Central and South America also produced coffee or fruit crops, such as bananas. Finding the large number of workers needed to make the plantations profitable was a major problem.

In the 1500s, the king of Spain rewarded the conquistadors (Spanish explorers who had claimed the land for Spain in the Americas) with *encomiendas*. An encomienda gave these Spanish conquistadors the right to demand labor or tribute from the Native Americans in a particular area. They used this system to force Native Americans to work under poor and brutal conditions. Those who resisted were hunted down and killed. Disease and starvation and cruel treatment caused a catastrophic decline in population. Four out of every five Native Americans died during the first year in the mines. On the sugar plantations of Hispaniola, harsh and brutal treatment led to the destruction of the entire population of the Arawak people.

In 1517, a Dominican friar, Bartolomeo de Las Casas, in his book *General History of the Indies*, described the abuses of the encomienda system and pleaded in person with the Spanish king to stop the abuses against the Native Americans. Prodded by Las Casas, Spain passed New Laws of the Indies, banning the enslavement of Native Americans. However, by this time most

Indians in the Caribbean had died from mistreatment and diseases brought by the Europeans. To fill the labor shortage, Las Casas suggested that Spain use Africans instead to work the mines and plantations (Doc. 1). Las Casas thought that Africans were immune to tropical diseases and had skills in farming, mining, and metal working. Later, Las Casas regretted that advice because it furthered the brutal African slave trade (Doc. 1). Through his efforts, the ban against the use of African slaves was removed and King Charles II issued licenses to different European countries to take Africans to the Spanish colonies (Doc. 1).

The buying and selling of Africans for workers in the Americas became a big business (Doc. 1). As the demand for sugar products skyrocketed, the Spanish imported millions of slaves. In 1540, it was estimated that more than 10,000 African slaves per year were brought to the West Indies (Doc. 1). By 1650, nearly 300,000 African slaves labored throughout Spanish America on plantations and in gold and silver mines.

As other European nations (England, France, Holland, and Portugal) established colonies in the Americas and the demand for cheap labor grew, these nations also began to import and enslave large numbers of Africans. By the beginning of the 1600s, Portugal surpassed the Spanish in the importation of Africans to the Americas. They dominated the sugar market and these sugar plantations became enormously profitable throughout the Americas. Plantations in Cuba returned more than a 30 percent profit and Barbados returned between 40 and 50 percent profit on capital investments (Doc. 2).

The importation of African slaves in the Americas had a direct impact on many countries in the region. Many of the islands in the West Indies began to rely heavily on the labor of African slaves for their economies (Doc. 2). During the 17th century, 40 percent of all Africans brought to the Americas went to Brazil. By the 1800s, half of all the population of Brazil was African (Doc. 2). In Cuba, by 1789, one-third of the population was African and 90 percent of the population of Jamaica, Antigua, and Grenada were African between 1730 and 1894 (Doc. 2).

The long-term effects of the African migration to the Americas have had a profound impact on both Africa and the Americas. In Africa, the shift in European demand from gold, foodstuffs, and such products, to slaves changed the relations among African groups and slaves (Doc. 3). In Africa, numerous cultures lost generations of their fittest members to European traders and plantation owners. By the mid-1800s, when the overseas trade was finally stopped, an estimated 11 million enslaved Africans had reached the Americas. In West Africa, the loss of countless numbers of young women resulted in some small states disappearing forever. At the same time, there arose new African states whose way of life depended on the slave trade. The rulers of these powerful new states waged war against other Africans so they could gain control of the slave trade in their region and reap the profits (Doc. 3). The slave trade also devastated African societies by introducing guns into the continent. Guns were in demand by African rulers seeking to conquer new territories. Firearms, which African chiefs and kings traded for potential slaves, also helped spread war and conflicts throughout Africa (Doc 3). These conditions would open up Africa to European domination by the end of the 19th century (Doc. 3).

Although they were unwilling participants in the growth of the colonies in the Americas, African slaves contributed greatly to the Americas' economic and cultural development (Doc. 3). Without their backbreaking work, colonies such as Haiti and Barbados may not have survived. Enslaved Africans also brought their expertise, especially in agriculture. Africans from the upper Guinea region in West Africa brought their rice-growing techniques to South Carolina.

The influx of so many Africans to the Americas has also left its mark on the very population itself. The blending of Native American, African, and European peoples and traditions resulted in a new American culture. These people spoke Spanish, but also used Native American and African words. A social structure developed, thus placing people in a hierarchy. The Spanish-born people at the top of the class structure were known as *peninsulares*. *Creoles* was the name given to those of European descent who were born in the colonies. *Mestizos* were people of mixed Native American and European descent, and *mulattoes* was the term used to describe people of mixed African and European descent.

Africans also added to the cultural mix with their farming methods, cooking style, and crops, including okra and palm oil. African drama, dance, and song heightened Christian services. Africans forged new religions that blended African and Christian beliefs.

The formation of India and Pakistan in 1947, like the mass migration of African slaves to the Americas, had far-reaching effects on its nations and its people. In the early days of the nationalist movement, Muslims and Hindus worked together for self-rule in India. During the 1920s and 1930s, however, divisions grew between the large Hindu Congress Party and the Muslim League. They worried that a Hindu-run government would oppress Muslims. The British encouraged the conflict, hoping to weaken the nationalists. The Muslims, led by Muhammad Ali Jinnah, demanded a separate Muslim nation. Deep differences in religious beliefs and suspicions had led to clashes between Hindus and Muslims (Doc. 7). As a result, many Muslims feared that their rights would not be respected in a country dominated by Hindus (Doc. 7).

Mohandas Gandhi, whose policy of civil disobedience or passive nonresistance had helped to make the world aware of the British injustices, had become the leader of the Indian Independence Movement in 1920. He reached out to Muslims to unite all of India. Gandhi hoped that Hindus and Muslims could work together in an independent India, but no agreement could be reached between the two groups (Doc. 7).

In 1946, widespread rioting broke out between Hindus and Muslims. In August, after days of rioting in Calcutta left more than 5,000 people dead and more than 15,000 people hurt, Gandhi walked through the worst areas and began to accept the idea that the partition of India into two nations was unavoidable. It was the best way to reduce violence between Hindus and Muslims. On July 26, 1947, the British government passed the Indian

Independence Act. The Act ended British rule in India. It provided for the partition or division of the Indian subcontinent into separate and independent nations. One was the Hindu-dominated India and the other was Pakistan with a Muslim majority (Doc. 7).

During the summer of 1947 millions of Hindus and Muslims crossed the borders of India and Pakistan in both directions. It is estimated that more than 400 million people crossed the Punjab to seek new homes (Doc. 8). During the mass migration, centuries of distrust plunged northern India into savage violence (Doc. 8). Sikh and Hindu mobs slaughtered Muslims fleeing into Pakistan, and Muslims massacred Hindu and Sikh neighbors (Doc. 8). The mass migration of people also affected jobs for many Muslims. Employed Muslim workers were thrown out when the Hindus migrated to their newly acquired area (Doc. 9). In the process of their migration, the Harijans, or untouchables, were also displaced, but the government made no effort to help them (Doc. 9). Gandhi, who was horrified at the partition and violence as well as the mistreatment of the untouchables, who were considered children of God, refused to celebrate Indian Independence. On January 30, 1948, he was shot and killed by Hindu extremists who believed that Gandhi had betrayed his people because he was doing too much for the Muslims. Gandhi's death discredited the extremists and helped to end the worst violence. Still Hindu/Muslim tensions persisted.

Fear and mistrust still existed between India and Pakistan. At independence, border conflicts ignited a war over Kashmir. Its Hindu monarch decided to join India, but its Muslim majority wanted to be part of Pakistan. Since then, Pakistan and India have fought several wars over Kashmir.

The nuclear issue between Pakistan and India has also created tension between them. In 1998, Pakistan and India both tested nuclear weapons, and there is fear that these weapons could be used in future confrontations.

The conflict between Muslims and Hindus continues to exist in India itself. There are still about 100 million Muslims living in India. In 1992, Hindu fundamentalists called for the destruction of a Muslim mosque in Ayodhya. This conflict touched off rioting, and the mosque was destroyed. Recently, the report of Indian archaeologists that they found evidence of a Hindu temple under the ruins of a 16th-century mosque added to the tensions between Hindus and minority Muslims. Some believe the two bombings in Bombay in August 2003 were caused by militant Islamic groups who are critical of these findings. At least 45 people were killed in these blasts.

Both the involuntary migration of Africans to the Americas and the voluntary movement of people within India and Pakistan have created problems. Africa's economic and political development are still affected by problems created by the slave trade. The lingering effects of the mass migration of Hindus and Muslims have left continued animosity between the two groups. As we near the end of the first decade of the 21st century, the impacts of these migrations are still influencing the development of these regions and their surrounding areas.

Topic	Question Numbers	Total Number of Questions	Number Wrong	*Reason for Wrong Answer
U.S. AND N.Y. HISTORY				
WORLD HISTORY	1, 4, 6, 7, 8, 10, 14, 18, 23, 25, 26, 28, 29, 30, 32, 36, 37, 38, 41, 44, 45, 46, 47, 49	24		
GEOGRAPHY	2, 5, 9, 11, 12, 15, 16, 24, 27, 39, 43, 48	12		
ECONOMICS	3, 13, 17, 21, 22, 33, 34, 40, 42, 50	10		
CIVICS, CITIZENSHIP, AND GOVERNMENT	19, 20, 31, 35	4		

*Your reason for answering the question incorrectly might be (a) lack of knowledge, (b) misunderstanding the question, or (c) careless error.

Actual Items by Standard and Unit

	1 U.S. and N.Y. History	2 World History	3 Geography	4 Economics	5 Civics, Citizenship, and Gov't	Number
Methodology of Global History and Geography		1	2	3		3
UNIT ONE Ancient World		4, 6	5			3
UNIT TWO Expanding Zones of Exchange		7, 8	9			3
UNIT THREE Global Interactions		10, 14, 45, 46	11, 12	13, 42		8
UNIT FOUR First Global Age		18	15, 16	17	19	5
UNIT FIVE Age of Revolution		23, 25, 26, 47	24, 27	21, 22	20	9
UNIT SIX Crisis and Achievement (1900–1945)		28, 29, 30		33, 34	31, 35	7
UNIT SEVEN 20th Century Since 1945		32, 37, 38, 41		40, 50		6
UNIT EIGHT Global Connections and Interactions		36	39, 48			3
Cross Topical		44, 49	43			3
Total # of Questions	0	24	12	10	4	50
% of Items by Standard	0%	48%	24%	20%	8%	100%